FABRICATING THE *TENJUKOKU SHŪCHŌ MANDARA* AND PRINCE SHŌTOKU'S AFTERLIVES

JAPANESE VISUAL CULTURE

Volume 17

Managing Editor
John T. Carpenter

Fabricating the *Tenjukoku Shūchō Mandara* and Prince Shōtoku's Afterlives

BY

CHARI PRADEL

BRILL

Leiden – Boston
2016

Published by
BRILL
Plantijnstraat 2
2321 JC Leiden
The Netherlands
brill.com/jvc

Text Editing
Melanie B.D. Klein

Indexing
Cynthia Col

Design
Peter Yeoh, New York

Production
High Trade BV, Zwolle, The Netherlands
Printed in Slovenia

ISBN 978-90-04-18260-8

Library of Congress Cataloging-in-Publication Data
Detailed Library of Congress Cataloging-in-Publication data are available on the internet at http://catalog.loc.gov

Copyright 2016 by Koninklijke Brill NV, Leiden, The Netherlands. Koninklijke Brill NV incorporates the imprints Brill, Brill | Hes & De Graaf, Brill | Nijhoff, Brill | Rodopi and Hotei Publishing.

All rights reserved. No part of this publication may be reproduced, translated, stored in a retrieval system, or transmitted in any form or by any means, electronic, mechanical, photocopying, recording or otherwise, without prior written permission from the publisher.

Brill has made all reasonable efforts to trace all right holders to any copyrighted material used in this work. In cases where these efforts have not been successful the publisher welcomes communications from copyright holders, so that the appropriate acknowledgements can be made in future editions, and to settle other permission matters.

Authorization to photocopy items for internal or personal use is granted by Koninklijke Brill NV provided that the appropriate fees are paid directly to The Copyright Clearance Center, 222 Rosewood Drive, Suite 910, Danvers, MA 01923, USA. Fees are subject to change.

Subvention for the publication of this volume was generously supplied by The Metropolitan Center for Far Eastern Art Studies.

For Daniel and Ken

Contents

Acknowledgements ... viii
Note to the Reader ... xi

PROLOGUE ... 1

1 MATERIAL AND VISUAL EVIDENCE ... 13
Fabric Structures and Embroidery Stitches: A Short Summary ... 15
Methodology for the Visual Analysis ... 19
Analysis of the Motifs on the Shūchō Fragments ... 21
Conclusion: Visual Evidence ... 79

2 THE EMBROIDERED INSCRIPTION AND THE *IMPERIAL BIOGRAPHY* ... 83
Writing in Ancient Japan ... 84
The Inscription in the *Imperial Biography* ... 87
Prince Shōtoku and Princess Tachibana ... 90
Issues with the *Imperial Biography* Inscription ... 93
Role of Kinship Groups ... 100
The *Jōgū Shōtoku hōō teisetsu* ... 104
Conclusion ... 107

3 TENJUKOKU SHŪCHŌ IN SEVENTH-CENTURY JAPAN ... 111
Embroidery as Pictorial Medium and Status Symbol ... 112
Curtains in East Asia ... 116
Infusion of New Ideas from China ... 120
Political Nuances in the Shūchō ... 121
Afterlife Beliefs and Funerary Practices ... 124
Tenjukoku as an Afterlife Realm ... 127
Conclusion ... 130

4	**FROM SHŪCHŌ TO TENJUKOKU MANDARA**	133
	Pure Land Buddhism and the Cult of the Prince	134
	Chūgūji and the Nun Shinnyo	148
	From Shūchō to Tenjukoku Mandara	150
	Conclusion	159
5	**THE RESTORATION, FRAGMENTATION, AND SECULARIZATION OF THE TENJUKOKU MANDARA**	163
	The Tenjukoku Mandara in the Lore of the Shōtoku Cult	164
	The Edo Period: From Religious Icon to Antique	168
	Reconstructing the Tenjukoku Mandara	171
	Conclusion	194
	EPILOGUE	197

Appendix: Fabrics and Stitches	205
Endnotes	214
List of Characters	239
Bibliography	246
Illustration Credits	263
Index	264

Acknowledgements

As an undergraduate in Lima (Peru), I had the unusual opportunity to study the pre-Columbian textiles at the storage facilities of the Museo Nacional de Arqueología y Antropología in Pueblo Libre, and the Museo Amano in Miraflores. At the Museo Nacional, I spent hours sketching the colorful embroidered designs from the garments, mantles, and fragments made by members of the Paracas culture (ca. 800–100 BCE). At the Museo Amano, I explored the variety of cotton and wool fabrics with beautiful patterns created by the weavers of the Chancay culture (ca. 1000–1400). In those days, the lack of archaeological excavation reports and documentary evidence made it difficult to interpret these textiles. I began my study of the Tenjukoku Shūchō Mandara for my first seminar in the Ph.D. program at the University of California, Los Angeles. Back then, I did not suspect that this embroidered fabric of less than one square meter would become a lifelong project.

This book is the end of a long journey made possible by the support of many people. After graduation, I was fortunate to stay in Los Angeles, where I benefitted from the continuous contact that I enjoyed with my UCLA professors. First of all, I am deeply indebted to Donald McCallum, my mentor and friend, who shared his knowledge of and enthusiasm for ancient Japan. I visited his office frequently for long chats about my latest findings and his own research, always leaving with words of encouragement. Unfortunately, Professor McCallum did not get to see this project finished. William Bodiford, from the Department of Asian Languages and Cultures, spent many Fridays helping me translate a key liturgical text, which allowed me to understand how the Tenjukoku Shūchō Mandara was perceived in the thirteenth century. The translation of this document was crucial in reassessing the significance of the Tenjukoku Shūchō Mandara. Herman Ooms, from the Department of History, read some early drafts and made helpful suggestions.

In the early stages of my research, I had the opportunity to meet Ōhashi Katsuaki and Sawada Mutsuyo, both of whom shared with me their firsthand knowledge of the Tenjukoku Shūchō Mandara, for which I am grateful. Naitō Sakae of Nara National Museum surprised me when he arranged a special viewing of the work and shared his insights about the puzzling fragments.

Parts of this book have been presented in conferences and invited talks at the University of Kansas and the University of Maryland. My good friends and colleagues, Sherry Fowler and Yui Suzuki, gave me the opportunity to present my work at these respective institutions, where I received feedback and interesting comments. Sherry, Yui, and Karen Gerhart, from the University of Pittsburgh, read and commented on many drafts of the manuscript and always offered advice and words of encouragement.

A special note of gratitude goes out to all of the people and institutions that allowed me to reproduce their works. In Japan, I am particularly indebted to Chūgūji, the nunnery that owns the Tenjukoku Shūchō Mandara, and to Hōryūji, which provided permission for the publication of works at the temple, its Great Treasure Hall, and the Gallery of Hōryūji Treasures at Tokyo National Museum. Both institutions waived their permission fees; the photographs were provided by the Nara National Museum photographic archive. Special thanks are due to Narimatsu Hitomi, who kindly guided me through the process. Myōrin Aya and Furutani Takuya, from DNP Art Communications and the Shōsōin office, respectively, were also helpful. The following institutions provided digital images free of charge: Ikarugadera, the Asuka Board of Education, and Nara National Research Institute for Cultural Properties. I am especially grateful to Watari Katsuya for his kindness. Shitennōji and the Museum of the Kashihara Archaeological Research Institute gave permission to scan images from their publications. My greatest gratitude goes to Mita Kakuyuki, from the Tokyo National Museum, who generously shared his set of photographs of the Tenjukoku Shūchō Mandara. The excellent quality of the photographs allowed me to better understand the fabric structures and embroidery stitches. Dr. Mita also gave me permission to publish the images. I believe that all of the institutions from which I requested permissions kindly agreed to grant them due to Toshiko McCallum's ability to translate my direct letters into polite Japanese. She also helped me to revise the List of Characters. I am very grateful for her friendship, love, and constant encouragement.

In Korea (Republic of Korea), I wish to thank the National Museum of Korea, Gongju National Museum, and ICOMOS-Korea for providing photographs free of charge. Burglind Jungman of UCLA, Soyeong Lee of the Metropolitan Museum of Art in New York, and Lena Kim gave me advice and useful contact information. I am especially indebted to Soyeon Kim, a UCLA graduate student, who handled all communications with the Korean institutions. I would not have been able to procure images from Korea without her help. For the Chinese works, the Cultural Relics Press granted permission to scan photographs from their publications. Hui-shu Lee of UCLA and Annette Juliano of Rutgers University gave me advice about requesting the photographs. Sonya Lee of the University of Southern California kindly took care of correspondence with the press, and my student, Tong Xue, wrote the list of works in Chinese for me. I am grateful to all of them.

At California State Polytechnic University, Pomona, a special acknowledgement must be made to my friend and fellow art historian Alison Pearlman. Her enthusiasm for her research and writing is contagious, and has helped me to keep up with my research projects despite our heavy teaching commitments and workload. I would also like to thank the former chair of the Department of Art, Babette Mayor, for supporting my sabbatical leave, as well as my graphic-design colleagues, Crystal Lee, Raymond Kampf, Melissa Flicker, Sarah Meyer, and Anthony Acock, for answering my design queries. I would like to express my gratitude to Juliann Wolfgram for teaching my classes during my sabbatical, and I also thank my students. In the fall of 2015, students taking Japanese art history read my article on the Tenjukoku Shūchō Mandara. Their comments after a careful reading were useful for clarifying certain points in the manuscript. In addition, I am fortunate to have had the assistance of talented graphic design students. Cheryl Laner, Jason Lin, Summer Furzer, and Christian Gutierrez made time in their busy schedules to help me with the drawings and reconstructions. At the Printing Lab, Paulo Sandoval, Tina Cho, Ryan Colwick, and Nicolas Rios always welcomed me to the lab with a smile, and efficiently scanned the necessary photographs for me.

I am especially thankful to the two anonymous reviewers for their thorough reading of the manuscript and their insightful comments, which contributed to the improvement of this volume. Special words of gratitude go to Melanie Klein, for her expert editing and patience. I cannot thank her enough for her careful reading of the text, and for refining the style of this book. I am grateful to Cynthia Col for working on the index. Inge Klompmakers and Anna Beerens at Brill assisted me through the publication process and kindly replied to all of my queries. Anna's responses were always comforting. I thank John Carpenter, Curator of Japanese Art at the Metropolitan Museum of Art and managing editor of Brill's Japanese Visual Culture series, for supporting the publication of my manuscript.

This project would not have been possible without the financial support of many institutions. I would like to offer my thanks to the Getty Foundation for a Getty Postdoctoral Fellowship, and to Cal Poly Pomona for three mini-grants from the Faculty Center for Professional Development, as well as the President's Travel Award and a year-long sabbatical leave, which allowed me to go to Japan to conduct research, and also to complete the manuscript. I am also grateful to The Metropolitan Center for Far Eastern Art Studies for their generous support.

Sharon Takeda, Senior Curator and Department Head of Costume and Textiles at the Los Angeles County Museum of Art, always showed interest in my project and responded to my calls for help. She put me in contact with Rika Hiro of USC and Nicole LaBouff, formerly the Wallis Annenberg Curatorial Fellow at LACMA, both of whom assisted me with the appropriate English terms for fabric structures and stitches. Many individuals have helped me to complete this project, yet none of them is responsible for any of the errors in this book; they are mine alone.

Many colleagues and friends have shared information and given me words of encouragement, for which I am grateful, especially Akiko Walley, Junghee Lee, Yoko Shirai, Hollis Goodall, Julie Nelson Davis, Lori Meeks, Rachel Fretz, Guolong Lai, and the late Terry Milhaupt. Special words of thanks go out to my mother, sisters, and brothers-in-law for their unwavering support. I would also like to thank my friends in Japan for the good times spent together while doing research there, especially Nobuko Kajitani (former Conservator-in-Charge of the Department of Textile Conservation at the Metropolitan Museum of Art), Iijima Midori, Hiroshi and Susana Kobayashi, Isami and Makiko Mukai, Emiko Sato, Katsuki Reiko, and the Yoshii family.

My husband Daniel and my son Ken are mentioned last, but they are, and always will be, the most important people in my life. Daniel had to live with me and Prince Shōtoku for many years, and continuously offered his love, support, and pragmatic advice with a reassuring smile. Ken happened to be back home before the deadline for the revised manuscript and all of the required material. After his experience writing his dissertation, he perfectly understood the situation. His computer and drawing skills came in handy, and his calm demeanor made the process less frantic, and even enjoyable. Muchas gracias, papá e hijo.

Note to the Reader

NAMES OF JAPANESE and East Asian individuals are given in traditional order (surname first). Life or reign dates of historical figures are provided when known. Following established convention, Japanese rulers who reigned prior to the late seventh century are referred to as "Great King" (a translation of *ōkimi*), regardless of gender; hence, Great King Suiko, a female monarch. Foreign-language terms are assumed to be Japanese unless otherwise indicated.

In the figure captions, dimensions are given in the order height x width x depth, unless otherwise indicated. The List of Characters is comprised mainly of Japanese terms, names, places, and sources, with some Chinese included as well.

Prologue

In the second month of 1274, the nun Shinnyo (b. 1211) from the nunnery of Chūgūji shed tears when she found an embroidered mandara (S. *mandala*) in the repository of the seventh-century temple Hōryūji. During efforts to revamp the nunnery, a fellow nun had seen this mandara in a dream, where it bore an inscription that included the date of death of the nunnery's founder, Queen Consort Anahobe no Hashihito (d. 621). The nuns had been searching for it ever since. Afraid that she might make mistakes reading the long inscription on the mandara, Shinnyo took it to Kyoto, the capital, to seek help. Significantly, she learned that the embroidered artifact originally had been made in honor not only of Anahobe, but also of her son, Prince Toyotomimi, popularly known as Prince Shōtoku (574–621 or 622).[1] At the time of the discovery, Shōtoku was the focus of a devotional cult, and the nuns saw the recovery of the mandara as a miraculous event associated with the prince's benevolence. Thinking to repair the damaged mandara, Shinnyo must have led a successful fundraising campaign, because a "new mandara," renamed the Tenjukoku (Land of Heavenly Lifespan) Mandara, was consecrated in the eighth month of 1275 by the monk Jōen (act. late 13th century). Presently, the remains of this embroidered artifact belong to Chūgūji in Ikaruga, Nara Prefecture, but are held by Nara National Museum for preservation.

This book is the first comprehensive study published in any language about this puzzling assemblage of fragments known today as the Tenjukoku Shūchō Mandara (fig. 1).[2] The fragile embroidered fragments are randomly pasted on a piece of paper measuring 88.8 by 82.7 centimeters, mounted as a hanging scroll. Additional small fragments are found in the collections of the Shōsōin, an eighth-century imperial repository at the ancient Nara temple Tōdaiji (fig. 2); Hōryūji, Nara Prefecture (fig. 3); Chūgūji (fig. 4); and Tokyo National Museum (figs. 5, 6). In 1952, the assemblage was designated a National Treasure by the Japanese government for several reasons. First, extensive textual evidence provides the history and date of the fragments; second, some of the fragments are the oldest extant examples of Japanese embroidered textiles; and third, the inscription on the embroidery "conveys the Buddhism experienced by Prince Shōtoku."[3]

The composite name Tenjukoku Shūchō Mandara is derived from several textual sources. As indicated above, *Tenjukoku* can be translated as Land of Heavenly Lifespan; *shūchō* means embroidered curtains; and *mandara* is the Japanese transliteration of the Sanskrit term *mandala*, usually defined as a cosmic diagram. One section of an inscription originally embroidered on the artifact states that a pair of *shūchō* with a representation of Tenjukoku was made after the deaths of Prince Shōtoku and his mother Anahobe in the early seventh century. Yet the history of the fragments is not limited to

Moon design, Tenjukoku Shūchō Mandara, detail of fig. 11.

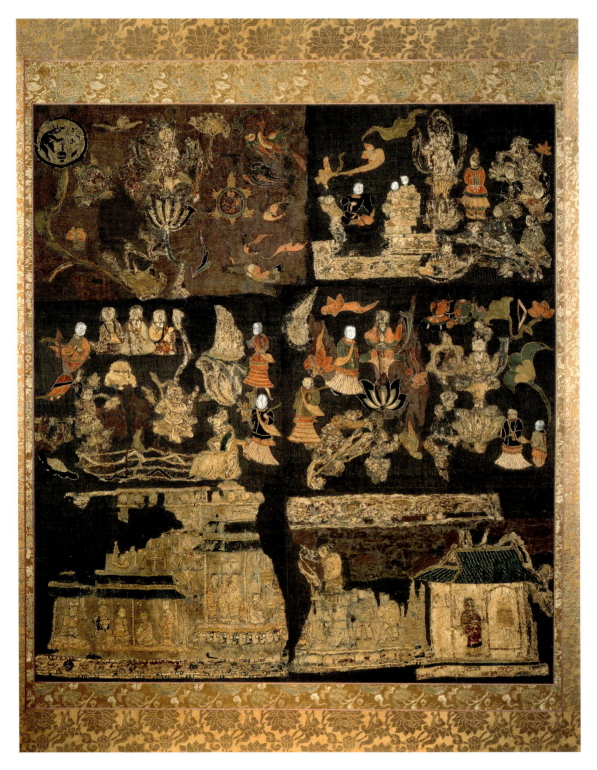

1　Tenjukoku Shūchō Mandara. 7th, 13th, and 18th centuries. Embroidered silk. 88.8 x 82.7 cm. Chūgūji, Nara Prefecture. National Treasure.

3   Fragment of the Shūchō with design of a seated figure. 7th century. Embroidered silk. 4.4 x 4.2 cm. Hōryūji, Nara Prefecture.

2   Fragments of the Shūchō, with designs of incomplete turtles, flowers, unidentified motifs (probably beasts), and characters. 7th century. Embroidered silk. Shōsōin, Nara Prefecture.

4   Fragments of the Tenjukoku Mandara with designs of seated monks and turtle (no. 99). 13th century. Embroidered silk. Monks: 7.2 x 13.5 cm; turtle: 8 x 6.8 cm. Chūgūji, Nara Prefecture.

5   Fragments of the Shūchō, with designs of incomplete turtle, lotus flower, and swirly motif. 7th century. Embroidered silk. Incomplete turtle: H. 7.2 cm. Tokyo National Museum.

6   Fragment of the Tenjukoku Mandara, border with spade-shaped motifs and circles. 13th century. Embroidered silk. Tokyo National Museum.

this time period. Documents dated from the thirteenth through the nineteenth century state that the embroidery was discovered in 1274, and was called a *mandara*. Studies by Japanese textile specialists have confirmed that some fragments were made in the seventh century and others in the thirteenth; therefore, the composite name Tenjukoku Shūchō Mandara is appropriate for the assemblage. For the sake of clarity, Shūchō is used here to refer to the seventh-century artifact; Tenjukoku Mandara for the thirteenth-century portion; and Tenjukoku Shūchō Mandara for the composite assemblage of both sets of fragments.

The assemblage and its corpus of textual material, particularly the inscription, have been studied by a number of Japanese scholars, including textile specialists, art historians, historians of ancient Japan, Buddhologists, and philologists. All of the existing studies begin by examining the inscription embroidered on the Shūchō, which is recorded in *Jōgū Shōtoku hōō teisetsu* (Imperial Biography of the Saintly Virtue Dharma King of the Upper Palace; hereafter *Imperial Biography*), a document compiled between the late eighth and eleventh century. In brief, the inscription can be divided into two parts. The first part contains a genealogy of Prince Toyotomimi (Shōtoku) and one of his wives, Princess Tachibana, beginning with Great King Kinmei (r. 539–71) and Soga no Iname (d. 570). The second part states that the prince and his mother died in 622 and 621, respectively, and that the grieving princess requested a visual representation of her prince in Tenjukoku, where she believed him to be reborn. The princess's wish was granted by her grandmother, Great King Suiko (r. 593–628), who ordered her ladies-in-waiting to make a pair of embroidered curtains.[4] The inscription ends with the names of the project's supervisor and the craftsmen who participated.

This inscription narrates the circumstances of the manufacture of the embroidery and the people involved in the project. Because most of them are key figures of the Asuka period (ca. 550–645), scholars concluded that the original artifact was made in the first quarter of the seventh century. Moreover, because this period had been seen as the time of the Buddhist transformation of Japan, when this imported religion was adopted as the religion of the court, the Shūchō was categorized as a work associated with Buddhism. As such, it reflected the impact of the newly introduced beliefs in general, and of Prince Shōtoku in particular. In many cases, textual material associated with the discovery of the artifact in the thirteenth century was used to further support the Buddhist significance of the embroidery and its inscription.

Due to the close association between Prince Shōtoku and the assemblage, a few words about him are necessary. An extensive corpus of textual material from the early eighth century onward states that he was the son of Great King Yōmei (r. 585–87) and Queen Consort Anahobe no Hashihito. These sources affirm that Shōtoku played a major role in the politics and religious life of the Asuka period. On the political side, he served as regent for his aunt, Great King Suiko, and traditionally is credited with the creation of a system of "cap ranks" for ministers and other officers, and the promulgation of a Seventeen-Article Constitution (*Kenpō jūshichijō*), a set of moral and political principles. On the religious side, he appeared to be a pious Buddhist with a deep knowledge of the sutras, someone able to lecture and write commentaries on them. Furthermore, a number of stories credit Shōtoku with the propagation of Buddhism in Japan to the extent that he was labeled "the father of Japanese Buddhism"; other sources claim that he was the incarnation of a bodhisattva. In the late nineteenth and early twentieth centuries, when the modern discipline of history was introduced in Japan, scholars questioned the historical value of the sources associated with Prince Shōtoku. Early modern Japanese historians, such as Kume Kunitake (1837–1931), Tsuda Sōkichi (1873–1961), and Fukuyama Toshio (1905–1995), pointed out certain implausibilities, as well as incongruities in the texts related to the prince. Yet, in the dominant trend of Japanese historiography, propounded especially by Sakamoto Tarō (1901–1987), the questionable narratives were accepted as historical facts, thereby making Prince Shōtoku an exceptional historical figure.[5]

This mainstream view of the prince was challenged in the late 1990s. The historian Ōyama Seiichi (b. 1944) convincingly demonstrated that a "Prince Umayado" (another of Toyotomimi's names) existed, but that the compilers of *Nihon shoki* (Chronicles of Japan; 720) enhanced and added events to his life, thus creating the extraordinary mythical figure known today as "Prince Shōtoku."[6] This prince became the focus of a devotional movement known as *Taishi shinkō* (cult of the prince), which began in the eighth century and proliferated in temples associated with him, such as Shitennōji in Osaka and Hōryūji. The movement was embraced by the various schools of Buddhism, taking many forms and spreading throughout Japan.[7] Ōyama's theory has been accepted by the scholarly community, and current scholarship focuses on understanding "Prince Shōtoku" as a cultic figure, rather than as an orthodox historical figure.[8]

The cult of the prince took a variety of forms, and different religious communities wove narratives about him into their lore.[9] Shōtoku was believed to have been reborn multiple times to spread Buddhism in Japan. Stories identify him as the reincarnation (or earlier incarnation) of important Buddhist figures, such as the Chinese monk Huisi (J. Eshi; 515–577), one of the patriarchs of the Tendai school; or Emperor Shōmu (r. 724–49), a devout Buddhist known for establishing Tōdaiji and a network of provincial temples throughout the country, among other things. In the ninth century, he began to be worshipped as an incarnation of the bodhisattva Guze Kannon (World-Saving Avalokiteśvara).[10] Furthermore, at the apex of the cult's popularity in the twelfth through sixteenth century, Shōtoku was worshipped in his own human form, as attested by a number of paintings and sculptures. The standard iconographical configurations, which are based on the hagiographical account *Shōtoku Taishi denryaku* (Hagiography of Prince Shōtoku; 10th century), are the two-year-old prince praising the Buddha; the sixteen-year-old filial prince praying for the recovery of his father; the prince riding his horse and flying over Mount Fuji; the prince as regent; and the prince lecturing on the *Lion's Roar Sutra* (S. *Śrīmālā-devī-siṃhanāda-sūtra*; J. *Shōmangyō*; see fig. 95).[11] The life of the prince also was illustrated in narrative picture scrolls, hanging scrolls, and folding screens.

Sakamoto's orthodox understanding of the prince influenced the way most scholars studied the material related to Shōtoku, including the Tenjukoku Shuchō Mandara. In most studies of the artifact, the seventh-century inscription, the assemblage of fragments, and the sources associated with the related events of the thirteenth century have been used as evidence of the advanced Buddhist beliefs present in the Asuka period, and held by the prince. The issue most widely discussed is the term Tenjukoku, which does not appear in any of the canonical Buddhist sutras. Because the inscription clearly suggests that Tenjukoku is an afterlife abode, scholars have attempted to determine which of the many pure lands that exist in Buddhist thought is represented on the Shūchō. Without a scriptural basis for the term, scholars have offered a wide variety of interpretations relying on isolated pieces of textual or contextual evidence, but seldom have addressed the visual material comprehensively.[12] For instance, Tsuji Zennosuke (1877–1955), Matsumoto Bunzaburō (1869–1944), and Shigematsu Akihisa (b. 1919) all proposed that Tenjukoku was Tosotsuten (S. Tuṣita Heaven), the abode of Miroku (S. Maitreya), the Buddha of the Future. In a 1901 article, Tsuji used textual evidence, supporting his theory on a postscript to the *Imperial Biography* that states, "Tenjukoku refers to heaven." Thus he concluded that if Tenjukoku was heaven, it must be the Tuṣita Heaven.[13] Matsumoto, on the other hand, took into account the historical context for the Shūchō in a 1912 study. He researched the cult of Miroku in India and East Asia, and argued that Tenjukoku had to be Tuṣita Heaven because of the popularity of this deity in the Asuka period.[14] Shigematsu came to the same conclusion in a 1964 book because he found the term "Tosotsu tenju" (Tuṣita Heavenly Lifespan) when researching Buddhist sutras associated with Miroku.[15]

In contrast to linking Tenjukoku to Tuṣita Heaven, other scholars—also using textual material associated with Prince Shōtoku—have attempted to demonstrate that Tenjukoku is a Buddhist pure land. In a 1911 book, Ōya Tōru (1850–1928) argued that, because Shōtoku wrote commentaries on the *Vimalakīrti Sutra* (S. *Vimalakīrti nirdeśa sūtra*; J. *Yuimakyō*), he must have desired to live in Myōkikoku (S. Abhirati), the land of the Buddha Ashuku (S. Akṣobhya), where the pious layman Yuima (S. Vimalakīrti) was reborn.[16] In the same way, Ōya Tokujō (1882–1950) used the controversial inscription on the Shaka triad of 623 housed in the Golden Hall of Hōryūji in articles published in 1928. This inscription states that the icon was made for the recovery of the prince's health, or failing that, for his rebirth in a pure land. According to Ōya Tokujō, because the bronze Buddha is Śākyamuni (J. Shaka), the Historical Buddha, the prince must have preferred this particular Buddha; and for this reason, Tenjukoku must be Vulture Peak (S. Gṛdhrakūṭa; J. Ryōzen), the mountain where he expounded many sutras.[17]

The most widely accepted theory is that Tenjukoku represents the Western Pure Land of Amida (S. Amitābha).[18] Although the evidence cited varies, most scholars refer to the corpus of documents narrating the events that followed the discovery of the mandara in 1274.[19] Certainly, the statement that Tenjukoku is Amida's Pure Land is found in these documents; the frequency of its recurrence makes the information seem positively reliable.[20] Furthermore, a postscript on a copy of the *Flower Garland Sutra* (S. *Avataṃsaka sūtra*; J. *Kegonkyō*), dated to 537, was believed to state that Tenjukoku was associated with the west, the direction in which Amida's Pure Land is found.[21] The art historian Ōhashi Katsuaki (b. 1942), who spent more than thirty years studying the Tenjukoku Shūchō Mandara, relied on these sources and further supported his theory with one of the designs on the fragments: a figure emerging from a lotus, the typical method of being transported to rebirth in Amida's Pure Land (see figs. 11, 13, 17, 62). He thus concluded that Tenjukoku is a representation of Amida's Pure Land.[22] Yet, even if the case can be made that Tenjukoku indeed was seen as Amida's Pure Land in the thirteenth century, none of the studies questioned the reasons behind this assumption, or examined the whole corpus of visual and textual materials in their respective historical context to explore the linkage between Amida's Pure Land and the embroidery.

In addition to theories explaining Tenjukoku as a Buddhist concept, other studies have proposed that the term refers to an ideal land, a heavenly realm, or even India.[23] Interestingly, based on the presence of turtle designs in the fragments, Mochizuki Shinjō (b. 1899), Fukui Kōjun (b. 1898), and Shimomise

Shizuichi (b. 1900) have postulated some association with Chinese Daoist beliefs relating to transcendents, because in this belief system, turtles are connected with longevity.[24] Although the scholars behind all of these diverse theories have examined portions of texts and a few designs in isolation, none of them has offered a comprehensive analysis of the designs or of the texts associated with the Tenjukoku Shūchō Mandara in their entirety.

While my study has benefited from previous scholarship, I take a different approach. Rather than continuing along the Buddhist line of inquiry to interpret the embroidered artifact, I place the Shūchō and its iconographical program (the extant designs and their meaning) more broadly within the context of East Asian funerary traditions and cultic worlds. In addition, instead of considering the fragments and their corpus of related documents as material for recreating Shōtoku's historical persona, following the current approach to the prince, I explore the role played by the Tenjukoku Shūchō Mandara in creating his cultic figure in the medieval period.

In fact, I follow the "biographical approach to things" proposed by Igor Kopytoff and applied by Richard Davis.[25] Kopytoff sought to recreate the cultural history of things by asking questions similar to those asked about people: "Where does the thing come from and who made it? What has been its career so far, and what do people consider to be an ideal career for such things? What are the recognized 'ages' or periods in the thing's 'life,' and what are the cultural markers for them? How does the thing's use change with its age, and what happens to it when it reaches the end of its usefulness?"[26] Kopytoff's approach was applied specifically to the commodization of objects, but Davis used this model together with the notion of interpretative communities from the reader-response literary theory.[27] He successfully applied this model in his 1997 book *Lives of Indian Images*. Tracing the history of a group of Indian images, Davis explained that most scholars are inclined "to focus on understanding the moment of creation of images," yet the biographical approach to these images revealed that "their identities were not fixed once and for all at the moment of fabrication, but they were repeatedly remade through the interaction with humans."[28] For Davis, "the subsequent 'reinterpretations' of these objects in new settings are equally worthy of disciplined inquiry."[29]

Following the biographical method, I analyze both the visual and textual materials in their respective historical contexts. First, I carefully analyze the designs on the Shūchō's fragments to determine the iconographical program likely embroidered on the curtains. Because not many contemporaneous artifacts or monuments are extant in Japan, I use pictorial examples from China and the Korean peninsula, especially those found in the funerary context. This approach is viable because, on the one hand, the inscription clearly indicates that Tenjukoku was an afterlife abode; and on the other, archaeological and textual evidence demonstrates that China, the Korean peninsula, and the Japanese islands were in close contact between the third and eighth centuries, primarily by means of migrating populations. Acknowledging the importance of migration, rather than concentrating on the royals and elites mentioned in the inscription, I investigate the role played by the designers and supervisors, who were members of immigrant kinship groups. These people contributed significantly to the culture of the Asuka and Hakuhō (645–710) periods by introducing and sustaining new continental technologies, including writing, textile and ceramic production, and—as Michael Como has demonstrated—even in shaping the cult of Shōtoku.[30] Following this pan–East Asian line of inquiry, I suggest that the Shūchō was used either in funerary rituals or in memorial services, and that the term Tenjukoku might not be Buddhist, or Daoist, but a result of the "popular Chinese religious beliefs" transmitted by immigrants.[31]

In addition, instead of using documents that narrate the events of the thirteenth century to anachronistically interpret a seventh-century artifact, I carefully analyze each of these documents in the context of its own day; the liturgical text composed by the monk Jōen for the dedication ceremony, in particular, reveals how the artifact was viewed at the time. Through painstaking research, I determine that the nun Shinnyo's quest to find the mandara was actually an effort to know the date of the death of the alleged founder of the nunnery. Once the Shūchō was discovered, due to the unusual pictorial representation for that time, the artifact was called the Tenjukoku Mandara and used to promote a form of the Shōtoku cult at Chūgūji related to the Pure Land school of Buddhism. This Pure Land form had its origins at the prince's tomb in Shinaga, Kawachi Province (present-day Osaka Prefecture), and spread particularly to Hōryūji and Chūgūji in the late thirteenth century.

In brief, this book traces the biography of the fragments of the Tenjukoku Shūchō Mandara within the context of the cult of Prince Shōtoku, beginning with the history of the making and reception of the Shūchō in the late seventh century, and then addressing the transcription of the inscription on the piece in the late tenth or early eleventh century. The study continues with the discovery of the Shūchō by the Chūgūji nuns and its new life as the Tenjukoku Mandara in the thirteenth century, the incorporation of the artifact into the lore of the cult of the prince in the fourteenth and fifteenth centuries, its fragmentation and mounting in the eighteenth century, and the new value of the inscription as an ancient document during the late Edo period (1615–1868).

ORGANIZATION OF THIS STUDY

This book is divided into five chapters; it also includes an Epilogue and Appendix. Chapter One, entitled "Material and Visual Evidence," introduces the technical features of the fragments, such as the structures of the different fabrics and stitches used to embroider the designs. In addition, the designs on the seventh-century fragments are analyzed. In this chapter, only the basic technical information that allows us to easily differentiate the seventh-century fragments from those of the thirteenth century is presented. The Appendix contains a detailed explanation of the different fabric structures and embroidery stitches, based on studies by various Japanese textile specialists. Understanding the different fabrics, threads, and stitches is crucial for differentiating the fragments and drawing conclusions about the production of the embroideries, but due to the highly technical nature of this material, this section is separated from the main body of the text.

Following this summary, the extant designs on the Shūchō fragments are analyzed in order to determine the iconographical program. The vast majority of the designs are also found in mural paintings from tombs in the kingdom of Goguryeo (37 BCE–668 CE) on the Korean peninsula, dated to the fifth through seventh century. Moreover, some of these motifs can be traced back to China from the Han dynasty (206 BCE–220 CE) to the Northern and Southern Dynasties (ca. 4th–6th century), where they were associated with the Chinese conception of heaven and other beliefs. In spite of the incomplete nature of the visual evidence, a partial reconstruction of the Shūchō's pictorial program based on the more complete examples from China and Korea is proposed.

Chapter Two, "The Embroidered Inscription and the *Imperial Biography*," presents an in-depth analysis of the inscription embroidered on top of the turtle designs. Although only one turtle and some scattered graphs survive from the original Shūchō, the text of the whole inscription is available in later documents. The aforementioned *Imperial Biography* includes the earliest version, which was added to the manuscript in the tenth or eleventh century. This chapter begins with an overview of the origins of writing in Japan, with the purpose of clarifying assumptions regarding literacy during the Asuka period and the traditional early-seventh-century date for the inscription. The major role played by immigrant kinship groups in the development of writing and literacy is also revealed. Drawing on this understanding of writing, a new translation and analysis of the inscription recorded in the *Imperial Biography* is presented.

Because the inscription includes the names of rulers, princes, and princesses, previous scholarship assumed that the Shūchō was a product of imperial patronage. Original research on the project's supervisor and craftsmen recorded in the inscription, however, shows that they were members of powerful immigrant kinship groups (some Chinese, but mostly Korean) who not only had easy access to the materials necessary to produce a textile of such quality, but were also associated with people trained in a variety of crafts, including sewing and embroidery. An examination of the available evidence about the activities of these immigrant groups leads to the conclusion that the inscription was composed, and the embroidery made, in the late seventh century by members of these groups in the Asuka region.

As this study focuses on understanding Prince Shōtoku as a cultic figure, a critical analysis of the *Imperial Biography*'s manuscript is also presented. Studies of the *Imperial Biography* reveal that, in the late tenth or early eleventh century, inscriptions from three works then housed in Hōryūji (including the Shūchō) were added to the manuscript, likely to create an evidence-based narrative that stressed the role of the prince, the imperial line, and Hōryūji in the spread of Buddhism. In this manner, the original meaning of the embroidery's inscription was transformed into a Buddhist account.

In Chapter Three, "Tenjukoku Shūchō in Seventh-Century Japan," the significance of the embroidered curtains bearing a representation of Tenjukoku in late-seventh-century Japan is explored, and a new interpretation of the term *Tenjukoku* is proposed. In the process, a number of topics are examined. First, despite the scarcity of extant embroidered fabrics, the prevalence of embroidery in seventh-century Japan and its use for the manufacture of Buddhist icons are addressed. Second, archaeological, artistic, and textual evidence from China, Korea, and Japan is analyzed to explore the role of curtains in these cultures. Due to the content of the inscription and the pictorial program, the Shūchō might have been used in memorial services to commemorate the deaths of Anahobe and Shōtoku, a practice that may have included some subtle political message. Third, because immigrant groups likely played a role in the making of the Tenjukoku Shūchō, the activities of members of these groups are also discussed, particularly those who went to China to study and returned as the bearers of new continental beliefs and practices. Fourth, beliefs about the afterlife and funerary practices in place at the time of the Shūchō's creation are examined, leading to the conclusion that the word *Tenjukoku* may not have been a Buddhist concept, but was one of many popular Chinese religious ideas that cannot be categorized as Buddhist or Daoist.[32]

Chapter Four, "From Shūchō to Tenjukoku Mandara," discusses the activities in the late thirteenth century of the nun Shinnyo from Chūgūji, and the fabrication of the Shūchō's Buddhist history. As stated above, Shinnyo, a devotee of Prince Shōtoku, wanted to restore the nunnery of Chūgūji, which at the time was believed to have been established by the prince's mother, Queen Consort Anahobe. The nun wished to have a memorial service performed to honor Chūgūji's founder, but she did not know the date of her death; the discovery of the embroidery in 1274, with its ancient inscription, answered this question. Some sources suggest that Shinnyo had a copy of the embroidery made when she brought it to the capital for repair, and these sources are analyzed to determine if this was the case.

In the dedication ceremony held in 1275 by the Tendai monk Jōen, the Shūchō acquired its new name, the Tenjukoku Mandara. Importantly, the ceremony's liturgical text equates Anahobe, Shōtoku, and Shōtoku's wife with Amida and his attendant bodhisattvas. The text also presents them as living in "Tenjukoku, which is Amida's Land of Bliss." Previous scholars used this phrase to argue that Tenjukoku was Amida's Pure Land, and extrapolated that this belief existed in Japan in the early seventh century. On the contrary, the emergence of the Pure Land form of Shōtoku's cult in the early thirteenth century likely led to the identification of the subject on the curtains, and of Tenjukoku, as the Land of Bliss. The embroidery was an ancient artifact originally made for Shōtoku and his mother, and the unfamiliar subject depicted on it was used to prove that the deified royal family lived in their own Land of Bliss called Tenjukoku. The nuns must have hoped to attract Shōtoku devotees to Chūgūji to compete with the thriving Pure Land cults.

In Chapter Five, "The Restoration, Fragmentation, and Secularization of the Tenjukoku Mandara," the biography of the fragments in the premodern period is completed, and a reconstruction of the Tenjukoku Mandara is proposed. Documents from the fourteenth through early nineteenth century that include mention of the artifact are evaluated to assess their reliability as sources for the reconstruction of the repaired embroidery. A close analysis of these texts reveals that each was compiled to serve a specific agenda. Texts from the fourteenth and fifteenth centuries show that the artifact was integrated into the lore of the Shōtoku cult, while documents of the eighteenth and nineteenth centuries demonstrate that monk-scholars and antiquarians studied the inscription and the fragments as an ancient epigraph and the remains of an antique object rather than a religious icon.

After evaluating the reliability of these documents, the size and composition of the thirteenth-century Tenjukoku Mandara are recreated. Although the physical evidence is fragmentary, a close analysis of the extant fragments and designs, the textual evidence, and the events of the late thirteenth century enable such a reconstruction. Interpreting the thirteenth-century events discussed in the previous chapter, it seems probable that the seventh-century embroidery was damaged and subsequently repaired. The well-preserved sections of the ancient artifact, which included designs unknown by Shinnyo's time, were crucial for supporting the credibility of the story that the embroidery had ancient ties to Shōtoku and his mother. In addition, replicated designs found in both the Shūchō's pieces and the Tenjukoku Mandara fragments support the theory that some of the designs were copied from the original and represented multiple times within the composition. Based on this theory of repair (rather than replacement), the unit of measurement and the width of the fabric used in the seventh century comprise key pieces of information for reconstructing the Tenjukoku Mandara's size. After determining the number of bolts of fabric that had to be sewn together to make the Shūchō, it appears that the embroidered artifact was large, about eight meters wide and two and a half meters long. To reconstruct the composition, the motifs found on the thirteenth-century fragments are analyzed to recreate the iconographical program of the renovated artifact. When this program is taken together with the designs on the Shūchō, as well as two brief descriptions available in the textual sources, the logical conclusion is that the appearance of the repaired Tenjukoku Mandara preserved most of the Shūchō's iconographical program with new scenes from Shōtoku's hagiography added.

In the Epilogue, the introduction of the Tenjukoku Shūchō Mandara into modern art historical discourse is discussed, and efforts to preserve the artifact are addressed. By recreating the biography of the embroidered fragments and studying the corpus of associated textual material, it becomes clear that medieval monks and nuns, and modern scholars alike, used the mandara and its recorded history to fabricate Prince Shōtoku's Buddhist afterlives.

I

Material and Visual Evidence

THE FRAGMENTARY CONDITION of the embroidered fabrics, and their current arrangement, make it difficult for viewers to understand the Tenjukoku Shūchō Mandara. This assemblage consists of the remnants of two different sets of embroideries made about six hundred years apart. Regrettably, no information about the reasons for the current layout of these fragments is available; it is therefore difficult to determine if this layout is associated with the original composition. Basically, the Tenjukoku Shūchō Mandara is a composition that has been created by the random placement of a few pieces of an incomplete puzzle. This circumstance certainly invites an exploration of the assemblage and its history.

This chapter focuses on an analysis of the material evidence—the fabrics and threads—and the visual evidence—the embroidered designs—of the Tenjukoku Shūchō Mandara. An examination of the material evidence allows us to separate the fragments of the seventh-century Shūchō, the original embroidered curtains, from those of the thirteenth-century Tenjukoku Mandara, while a study of the visual evidence enables a partial reconstruction of the subject embroidered on the Shūchō. Because this study follows the "biographical method," the visual analysis concentrates on the designs embroidered on the Shūchō fragments. Most scholars have considered all of the designs on the assemblage together when reconstructing the Shūchō's iconographical program, based on their assumption that the Tenjukoku Mandara was a replica that looked exactly the same as the first artifact. Here the designs on the Shūchō and Tenjukoku Mandara are analyzed separately.[1]

The first section, "Fabric Structures and Embroidery Stitches," addresses the material evidence, and continues with an in-depth analysis of the extant motifs on the Shūchō fragments. In the second section, "Methodology for the Visual Analysis," the sources and approach for the visual analysis and reconstruction of the Shūchō's iconographical program are explained. The scarcity of comparable Japanese visual material necessitates a pan–East Asian approach to identifying the motifs and evaluating their significance and placement in the composition. The third section, "Analysis of the Motifs on the Shūchō Fragments," divides the design elements into three main categories: people, the celestial realm, and Buddhist motifs. An analysis of the designs with regard to their continental precedents is essential to proposing a partial reconstruction of the subject represented on the Shūchō—Tenju-

Right side of section A, Tenjukoku Shūchō Mandara, detail of fig. 11.

7 Diagram of the Tenjukoku Shūchō Mandara indicating the three different ground fabrics. Arrows indicate the direction of the warp. Line drawings by Cheryl Laner and Summer Furzer, adapted from Mita Kakuyuki, "Gihō kara mita Tenjukoku Shūchō," 80.

koku, or the Land of Heavenly Lifespan—and exploring its meaning, as well as the artifact's date of manufacture. Due to the fragmentary condition of the Shūchō, comparison with Chinese and Korean visual evidence is necessary for theorizing the placement of the designs. Each motif requires clear analysis and explanation to elucidate its original form and significance.

FABRIC STRUCTURES AND EMBROIDERY STITCHES: A SHORT SUMMARY

Upon studying the structures of the fabrics, and the threads and types of embroidery stitches used on the Tenjukoku Shūchō Mandara, Japanese textile specialists have discovered certain distinctive characteristics.[2] The fragments in one group, identified as the remains of the Shūchō, are composed of two layers of fabric: purple gauze over a purple plain weave. All of the designs on these fragments are embroidered using stem stitch with tightly twisted silk threads, their bright colors preserved. Each design is outlined and completely filled with fine parallel lines of stem stitches, exhibiting a time-consuming technique.

Among the fragments identified as those from the Tenjukoku Mandara, two different types of ground fabric are found: purple twill and white plain weave, both lined with paper underneath. Textile specialists have explained that the designs were drawn on this lining paper, which was then placed under the ground fabric; finally both layers were embroidered together. It is likely that the double layer of fabric in the Shūchō fragments had the same function. Whereas the Shūchō's embroidered threads are tightly twisted, those on the Tenjukoku Mandara fragments are loose and faded. Moreover, a variety of stitches are used to create the designs, especially those types that allow for a speedy covering of the design surface, such as satin stitch, surface satin stitch, couching, and outline stitch.

Surprisingly, the Shūchō fragments show a complex weaving technique, embroidery threads of excellent quality with well-fixed colors, and fine craftsmanship. The embroidered designs on the later fragments look haphazard by contrast, and lack the same artistry. In short, the bright, well-preserved sections of the artifact are the remains of the Shūchō, and the faded sections with loose threads are from the mandara (fig. 7). In addition to the embroidered fragments, two different types of brown fabric are pasted around the designs. The contrast between these undecorated fabrics suggests that they might have been pasted at different times, perhaps in efforts to preserve the fragments.[3]

In addition to clarifying the technical aspects of the fabrics and embroidery stitches, studies by textile specialists also have confirmed the dates of the two sets of fragments as suggested by the corresponding textual material. The Tenjukoku Mandara fragments were compared to a number of *shūbutsu* (embroidered fabrics with Buddhist subjects) from the thirteenth century, which share similar ground fabrics and embroidery threads. Due to the scarcity of surviving embroidered textiles dated to the seventh century, however, confident dating of the Shūchō fragments to this period, as suggested by the inscription, is much more challenging. The oldest extant textiles of considerable size are found in the collections of Hōryūji and the Shōsōin.[4] These collections contain textiles dating from the late seventh through mid-eighth century, some made in Japan and others imported via the Silk Road.[5]

Besides the Shūchō fragments, the only other group of embroidered fragments of considerable size dated to the seventh century is comprised of the remains of a banner with designs of celestial beings in the collection of Hōryūji (fig. 8).[6] A total of seventeen fragments have survived, ranging from 5 to 13 centimeters in width and about 66 centimeters in length for the longest example.[7] These fragments were originally attached to an extant bronze banner used for ordination ceremonies (*kanjōban*), also from Hōryūji, but currently housed in the Gallery of Hōryūji Treasures at Tokyo National Museum (see fig. 34). The embroidered banner's ground fabric is a thin crepe (*chijimi*). Most of the fragments bear motifs of celestial beings seated cross-legged on lo-

8   Fragment of an embroidered banner with design of celestial beings. 7th century. Silk. 42.5 x 11.5 cm. The Gallery of Hōryūji Treasures, Tokyo National Museum.

tus pedestals. Some play musical instruments, and each wears a long, fluttering, multicolored scarf that rises above his or her head. Scattered lotus flowers and clouds also surround some celestial beings.

When Sawada Mutsuyo studied the banner fragments some fifteen years ago, she noticed that, as in the Shūchō fragments, two layers of fabric overlap and the embroidery threads are tightly twisted. The designs on the banner, however, are embroidered with running stitch (*tsugi harinui*) rather than stem stitch. Running stitch is the most basic stitch; the thread is carried forward in and out of the fabric to form a line of alternating stitches on each face.[8] In the banner, the stitches are very close together and worked in contiguous lines following the contours of the motifs, making a two-sided design. Although the embroidery stitches are different, both the Shūchō and the banner share a similar embroidery method using lines of stitches to fill in the designs on a double layer of fabric.[9] Due to these similarities, and based on the date suggested by the Shūchō inscription, Sawada concluded that both were made in the early seventh century.[10] In fact, the Tenjukoku Shūchō Mandara and the Hōryūji embroidered banner have been heralded as examples of Buddhist art from the Asuka period.

Textile specialists have pointed out other characteristics that differentiate these seventh-century embroideries from those of the eighth century. On the seventh-century examples, the embroidery is limited to the designs, and the ground fabric serves as background. The majority of eighth-century embroideries, especially those found in the Shōsōin, use filaments of silk that are not twisted, and the designs are embroidered with multiple variations of satin stitch (figs. 9, 9a).[11] Furthermore, following the embroidery style of China's Tang dynasty (618–907), in most cases the whole surface is covered with stitches. Two well-preserved Tang examples that show this last characteristic are both *shūbutsu*: the embroidery tableau of a *Buddha Preaching*, formerly housed at the temple Kajūji in Kyoto (figs. 10, 10a); and *Śākyamuni Preaching on Vulture Peak*, found in the Dunhuang caves in China's Gansu Province and currently held by the Brit-

MATERIAL AND VISUAL EVIDENCE

9a   Detail of fig. 9.

9   Fragment of an embroidered banner with peacock design. 8th century. Silk. 81.2 x 30 cm. Shōsōin, Nara Prefecture.

ish Museum, London. In the first example, the designs and the background are covered with chain stitches, whereas in the second case, chain stitch and satin stitch are used.[12]

Although the above conclusions regarding the dating of the Shūchō fragments seem convincing, other features call them into question. For instance, a 2012 study by Mita Kakuyuki proposed a late-seventh-century date for the embroidered banner's fragments based on the stylistic features of the designs. He compared the embroidered motifs on the banner, particularly the lotus pedestals and the bodies of the celestial beings, to motifs found in the murals in Hōryūji's Golden Hall. Based on the formal similarities, he determined that the bronze banner and its embroidered attachments must have been made as part of the temple's reconstruction after the fire of 670.[13] Mita's study dates the banner to the late seventh century, or the Hakuhō period, debunking the traditional Asuka-period dating. The same may be true for the Shūchō fragments. Due to the lack of comparable material evidence, however, the question of dating also must rely on a reconstruction of the history of the Shūchō's production based on its design scheme and specific textual sources.

10   *Buddha Preaching*. 8th century. Embroidered silk. 200 x 105 cm. Formerly at Kajūji, Kyoto. Collection of the Nara National Museum. National Treasure.

10a Chain stitch, detail of fig. 10.

METHODOLOGY FOR THE VISUAL ANALYSIS

Reconstructing the Shūchō's iconographical program is particularly challenging due to the extremely incomplete nature of the visual evidence. Furthermore, only a few pictorial works dated to the seventh and early eighth centuries exist in Japan for comparison. Therefore, early scholars attempting to reconstruct the subject matter of the Shūchō relied mostly on textual evidence, or addressed a limited number of designs. Until recently, pictorial examples dated to the seventh century were limited to the Tamamushi Shrine (see fig. 33) and the aforementioned bronze banner and its corresponding embroidered remains, both at Hōryūji. The discovery of the mural paintings dated to the late seventh or early eighth century in the Takamatsuzuka and Kitora tombs in Nara Prefecture, in 1972 and 1983, respectively, added to the visual sources in Japan

(see figs. 23, 24, 36, 37).[14] The subjects represented in both tombs, the Four Divinities (C. *sixiang*; J. *shishin*) and the constellations, are associated with Chinese cosmology. Moreover, the style of representation of the figures at Takamatsuzuka confirms the strong connection with Tang China.

In addition to the material discussed above, archaeological and historical evidence supports the idea that Chinese culture was transmitted to the Japanese islands through the Korean peninsula before the islands had direct contact with China. Immigrant kinship groups from the three Korean kingdoms of Baekje, Silla, and Goguryeo played an important role in the transmission of new continental technology.[15] For this reason, a pan–East Asian approach must be taken for identifying the motifs on the Shūchō fragments. Although some of the motifs on the fragments can be traced back to China's Han dynasty, the vast majority is depicted in funerary and Buddhist monuments and artifacts from the Northern and Southern Dynasties in China and the Three Kingdoms period (ca. 300–668) on the Korean peninsula, particularly from Baekje and Goguryeo. As well as finding and analyzing comparable designs and iconographical programs in the visual materials from these regions, the origins and evolution of some of the motifs must be considered, with particular attention paid to the changes taking place in funerary iconography due to the stimulus of Buddhism.

The mural paintings of the Goguryeo tombs are particularly important for reconstructing the Shūchō's iconographical program and understanding the meaning of Tenjukoku.[16] The Goguryeo murals may be divided chronologically into three periods. The first period corresponds to the fourth and early fifth century; the second period, from the mid- to late fifth century; and the third, the sixth and early seventh century (Table 1).[17] Tombs of the first period show strong Chinese influence, with visual programs derived from sites dated to the Eastern Han dynasty (25–220). Common subjects found in these tomb murals include door guardians; homage or banquet scenes; procession scenes; domestic scenes with an emphasis on representations of kitchens, storehouses, and stables; and entertainment scenes. Furthermore, they reveal similar representations of the heavens with regard to the arrangement of the planets and stars, the sun and moon, cloud patterns, flying celestial beings, and mythical beasts.[18] The iconographical program seen in murals from the second period includes some of the subjects mentioned above, with the notable introduction of the Four Divinities. In murals from the third period, the Four Divinities, which also are found in the Takamatsuzuka and Kitora tombs in Japan, are especially prominent.[19]

Miwa Stevenson's 1999 study demonstrated that precedents for the funerary iconography seen in the Goguryeo tombs may be found in China.[20] For this reason, no discussion of this subject is complete without reference to Wu Hung's 2010 book, *The Art of the Yellow Springs*, which offers an innovative approach to the study of funerary art in China.[21] This book analyzes the structures, funerary paintings, and paraphernalia of tombs from conceptual, contextual, and historical points of view. It offers a methodology for explaining tombs and their furnishings (including pictorial representations) in relation to history, memory, cosmology, and religious beliefs. Particularly significant for the understanding of the Shūchō's iconographical program are the mural paintings in the Chinese tombs. Although neither the paintings on the walls nor the objects buried in these tombs were meant to be seen by the living, Wu Hung explains that their complex iconographical programs nevertheless hold symbolic meaning. Notably, he categorizes the subject matter of the designs into three broad groups: those associated with earth, with heaven, and with paradise. Together they create what he calls a "tripartite universe." All three categories are not present in each tomb; murals in some tombs focus on one aspect, while others combine them into a cosmic representation.[22] Wu also demonstrates that Chinese funerary iconography is not standardized, even though tomb decoration was bound by convention and the use of common motifs. But because tombs belonged to individuals, each person made specific choices to reflect personal desires.[23]

This understanding of Chinese funerary art is applicable to the motifs on the Shūchō as well. With reference to the more complete iconographical programs found in China and the Korean peninsula, an in-depth analysis of the designs on the Shūchō fragments may be carried out.

Date/Location	Tombs in the Pyongyang and Anak areas	Tombs in the Ji'an and Huanren areas
First period 4th to early 5th century	Anak No. 3 (357) Deokhungri (Tokhungri) (408)	Gakjeochong (Tomb of the Wrestlers) Muyongchong (Tomb of the Dancers)
Second period Mid- to late 5th century	Ssangyeongchong (Twin Pillar Tomb) Susanri Anak No. 2 Deokhwari (Tokhwari) Nos. 1, 2	Samsilchong (Tomb of the Three Chambers) Jangcheon (Changchuan) No. 1
Third period 6th to early 7th century	Jinpari Nos. 1, 2 Gangseo daemyo (Kangso Great Tomb) Gangseo gungmyo (Kangso Middle Tomb)	Sasinchong (Tomb of the Four Divinities) Ohoebun No. 4 Ohoebun No. 5

Table 1   Dates and locations of frequently mentioned Goguryeo tombs

ANALYSIS OF THE MOTIFS ON THE SHŪCHŌ FRAGMENTS

In order to easily distinguish the motifs on the fragments, they may be sorted into categories and identified according to their placement in the layout of the assemblage. The layout of the Tenjukoku Shūchō Mandara may be divided into six sections, following the rectangular areas marked by the different fabrics pasted around the designs: section A is the section at upper left (figs. 11, 12); section B, at upper right (figs. 13, 14); section C, middle left (figs. 15, 16); section D, middle right (figs. 17, 18); section E, lower left (see figs. 86, 87); and section F, at lower right (see figs. 88, 89). Furthermore, in the line drawings corresponding to each section, each design is identified by the section's letter followed by an assigned number.

Most of the extant motifs on the Shūchō have survived in small pieces of fabric. Each fragment contains a single design, except for the right side of section A. This section contains the largest fragment of purple gauze, which preserves a number of contiguous designs. This large fragment is particularly important because it gives us a hint of the Shūchō's original composition and the relationship between the designs.

The primary categories of motifs for visual analysis are the representation of people, the representation of the celestial realm, and designs associated with Buddhism. By analyzing these motifs, studying a number of comparative examples, and considering the placement of each design in more complete compositions, a tentative composition for the Shūchō may be established.

People

Male and female figures are conspicuous among the extant designs on the Shūchō fragments. A close examination of these figures reveals that they wear garments similar to those found in the Goguryeo murals. Most surviving figures, depicted in three-quarter view, wear gender-specific clothing. A total of five male figures from the Shūchō is found in sections B and D. The two male figures in section B are an incomplete seated figure (B-4) and a standing figure (B-5; fig. 19). The seated figure wears a navy blue upper garment with a red neckline, and a red lower garment. The head of the standing figure is damaged, but traces of a headdress are visible. This figure wears a red jacket with green trim on the collar, the wide cuffs, and the lower hem, and a white belt around the waist; his hands are tucked into his sleeves. He also wears a pleated lower garment in yellow over long green pants with red cuffs, and pointed yellow shoes. The pleated garment is an overskirt known in Japanese as *hirami* or *hiraobi*.[24] The three headless figures seated in a group (D-6) in section D appear to be male, as they have belts around their waists like the figures in section B. This group is very similar, if not identical, to B-11 from the thirteenth-century fragments. These men, who seem to be kneeling, also have their hands tucked into their sleeves.[25]

Female figures from the Shūchō appear in sections C and D. All women wear long skirts, some with wavy lines to represent tiers of ruffled fabric (C-3, D-5), and others with vertical parallel lines suggesting pleats or a pattern of stripes (C-4, D-3, D-10, D-11).[26] They all wear a *hirami* under a long jacket with a round neckline and trim on the hem and cuffs. Each of the figures carries a bag-like item that seems to be an oblong piece of fabric that is tied at the shoulder and hangs across the chest to the opposite hip; this is known in Japan as *tasuki* (fig. 20).[27] Two of the women (C-4, D-5) hold a long stick over the left shoulder. Because some female figures represented in *haniwa* (clay tomb figurines dating from the third to sixth century) are portrayed wearing long pleated skirts, and because actual skirts of this type are found in the Shōsōin (fig. 21), it is likely that pleated skirts were worn in Japan from the fifth through eighth century.

Long skirts, however, are not found exclusively in Japan. In fact, the style of clothing seen in the fragments shows the cultural commonalities between Japan and the Korean peninsula (fig. 22). Female figures wearing comparable skirts are represented in the Goguryeo murals of the second period, such as those at Susanri (fig. 22a), Taeanri,

11　Tenjukoku Shūchō Mandara (section A), detail of fig. 1.

MATERIAL AND VISUAL EVIDENCE

12 Line drawing of Tenjukoku Shūchō Mandara (section A). Line drawing by Cheryl Laner.

Motifs from the Shūchō
- A-1   Moon
- A-2   Half-palmette
- A-3   Red bird
- A-4   Auspicious cloud
- A-5   Sprouting-bud design
- A-6   Turtle (no. 26)
- A-7   Fragments of ribbons
- A-8   Fragment of torso from a figure emerging from a lotus
- A-9   Unidentified
- A-10 Fragment of a sprouting-bud design
- A-11 Unidentified

Motifs from the Tenjukoku Mandara
- A-12 Figure emerging from a lotus with hands in prayer
- A-13 Lotus leaf
- A-14 Lotus leaf
- A-15 Unidentified
- A-16 Unidentified
- A-17 Turtle (no. 69)

FABRICATING THE *TENJUKOKU SHŪCHŌ MANDARA* AND PRINCE SHŌTOKU'S AFTERLIVES

13   Tenjukoku Shūchō Mandara (section B), detail of fig. 1.

MATERIAL AND VISUAL EVIDENCE

14 Line drawing of Tenjukoku Shūchō Mandara (section B). Line drawing by Cheryl Laner.

Motifs from the Shūchō
B-1 Floral motif
B-2 *Hengeshō* or metamorphosis phase
B-3 Unidentified
B-4 Seated male figure
B-5 Standing male figure
B-6 Small lotus flower

Motifs from the Tenjukoku Mandara
B-7   Border with spade-shaped motifs
B-8   Border with circles
B-9   Figure holding an offering
B-10 Fragment of zig-zag motif
B-11 Group of three seated male figures
B-12 Figure emerging from a lotus, holding a tray
B-13 Fragment of a celestial being with an offering
B-14 Seated figure
B-15 Seated figure holding a lotus flower
B-16 Seated figure
B-17 Seated figure
B-18 Seated figure holding a lotus flower
B-19 Lotus flower

15 Tenjukoku Shūchō Mandara (section C), detail of fig. 1.

16   Line drawing of Tenjukoku Shūchō Mandara (section C). Line drawing by Cheryl Laner.

Motifs from the Shūchō

C-1   Upper body of a celestial being
C-2   Lower body of a celestial being
C-3   Standing female figure
C-4   Standing female figure holding a stem
C-5   Fragment of a lotus flower or leaf

Motifs from the Tenjukoku Mandara

C-6   Three seated monks
C-7   Incense burner
C-8   Fragment of a seated figure holding a flower
C-9   Seated male figure holding a flower
C-10 Small lotus flower
C-11 Zig-zag design representing a pond
C-12 Fragment of a lotus pedestal with reversed petals
C-13 Seated figure with bare torso
C-14 Fragment of a lotus pedestal
C-15 Fragment of a turtle (no. 1)

17 Tenjukoku Shūchō Mandara (section D), detail of fig. 1.

18 Line drawing of Tenjukoku Shūchō Mandara (section D). Line drawing by Cheryl Laner.

Motifs from the Shūchō

D-1 Incomplete figure emerging from a lotus with hands in prayer
D-2 Half-palmette
D-3 Female figure
D-4 Fragment of a flaming flower
D-5 Female figure
D-6 Incomplete group of three seated male figures
D-7 Fragment of a leaf design
D-8 Fragment of zig-zag motif, lotus leaf, and lotus flower
D-9 Lotus leaf
D-10 Female figure
D-11 Fragment of a female figure
D-12 Fragment of a flaming motif

Motifs from the Tenjukoku Mandara

D-13 Turtle (no. 65)
D-14 Figure emerging from a lotus with hands in prayer
D-15 Male figure, probably dancing
D-16 Figure with hands in prayer
D-17 Seated figure with a small lotus flower
D-18 Unidentified
D-19 Unidentified

19 Standing male figure, Shūchō (B-5), detail of fig. 13.

20 Standing female figures, Shūchō (D-3, D-5), detail of fig. 17.

MATERIAL AND VISUAL EVIDENCE

21 Pleated wrap skirt. 8th century. Silk. 106 x 118 cm (at waist). Shōsōin, Nara Prefecture.

22 Female and male figures on the west and north walls of the main chamber, Susanri tomb. Second half of 5th century. Mural painting. Nampo Province.

22a Two women, detail of fig. 22.

and Ssangyeonchong.[28] The similarities in clothing are not limited to the representation of women. The garments worn by the male figures on the north wall of the Susanri tomb are also similar to those of the standing figure (B-5); the only difference is the V-shaped collar and the absence of *hirami* on the figures seen in this Goguryeo tomb mural. This visual evidence suggests that Goguryeo was the main source for the figures on the Shūchō fragments. Yet Chinese sources, such as the *Zhoushu* (Book of Zhou; 636) and *Beishi* (History of the North; 659), describe the clothing worn in Baekje as being similar to that of Goguryeo.[29] Furthermore, later textual evidence suggests that Baekje-style clothing might have been worn in Yamato, the region of present-day Nara Prefecture that served as the ruling base for the imperial court from the third to eighth century. *Fusō ryakki* (Concise History of Japan; compiled late 11th or 12th century) records that, in 593 (Suiko 1), when relics were placed in the pagoda of Hōkōji (another name for the temple Asukadera), about a hundred people wore Baekje-style garments, delighting the spectators.[30] Either way, the similar clothing worn in Goguryeo, Baekje, and Yamato is one of the many cultural aspects that show the close connections between these three cultural spheres.

The people represented seem to be involved in specific activities. Ōhashi has suggested that the women are aligned in a procession because some face to the right while others face left. In addition, on the assumption that the stick-like elements held by two of the women on the Shūchō fragments are flower stalks, like those held by some of the figures on the thirteenth-century fragments (B-15, C-9), he has proposed that the composition included a memorial service.[31] Processions are a common subject in the Goguryeo tomb murals (fig. 22), as well as in many funerary and Buddhist monuments from the Northern and Southern Dynasties (see fig. 64).[32] This subject is also depicted in Takamatsuzuka tomb in Asuka, Nara Prefecture. On the east and west walls of this small burial chamber, two groups of four male figures each and two groups of four female figures each, for a total of sixteen people, appear to participate in a procession or gathering (figs. 23, 24).[33] Each of the men holds an object, such as an open umbrella, an umbrella bag, or a portable chair. One of the women in the group on the west wall holds a round fan, and another, a *nyoi* (a type of scepter; fig. 24a). Similar objects also are carried in procession scenes at the entrance to the Chinese Buddhist cave temples of the Northern Wei period (386–535), such as Gongxian No. 1 (Henan Province), and also in early Tang tombs, such as the tomb of Princess Yongtai (Li Xianhui, 685–701) in Qianxian, Shaanxi Province, dated to 706 (fig. 25). Nevertheless, the style of the human figures in the Takamatsuzuka tomb murals is different from that seen in the Goguryeo tombs and the Shūchō fragments. The Takamatsuzuka figures are more naturalistic, and some are represented frontally while others appear in three-quarter view and some in profile. Furthermore, the figures overlap, giving a sense of three-dimensional space, as seen in the murals discovered in the 1960s and 70s in the tombs of Prince Zhanghuai (Li Xian, 654–684), Princess Yongtai, and Prince Yide (Li Chongrun, 682–701), all dated to the early eighth century and located in Qianxian.[34]

In addition to the visual connection with continental tomb art, information about garments from textual sources suggests that some of the figures portrayed on the Shūchō were members of the ruling elite. For instance, a sumptuary ruling from 605 (Suiko 13) recorded in *Nihon shoki* states, "princes and ministers were ordered to wear *hirami*."[35] As mentioned above, all of the female figures and the only complete male depicted on the fragments wear this garment. An entry from 682 (Tenmu 11), however, indicates that the use of this garment was later prohibited: "princes and public functionaries were forbidden to wear caps of rank, aprons, *hirami*, and pants."[36] It cannot be confirmed if both rulings were enforced, or if they are chronologically accurate. Yet, based on such evidence, we can surmise that the figures represented were members of the ruling elite.

Considering the similarities in dress and style of representation between the surviving figures depicted on the Shūchō fragments and those seen in

23 Group of females, sun, Azure Dragon, and group of males on the east wall, Takamatsuzuka tomb (replica). Late 7th–early 8th century. Mural painting. Wall: approx. 115 x 265 cm. Asuka, Nara Prefecture. Replica: Nara National Research Institute for Cultural Property.

24 Group of males, moon, White Tiger, and group of females on the west wall, Takamatsuzuka tomb (replica). Late 7th–early 8th century. Mural painting. Wall: approx. 115 x 265 cm. Asuka, Nara Prefecture. Replica: Nara National Research Institute for Cultural Property.

MATERIAL AND VISUAL EVIDENCE

24a Detail of fig. 24.

25   Procession of women from the south side of the east wall of the front chamber, tomb of Princess Yongtai. 706. Mural painting. Qianxian, Shaanxi Province.

the Goguryeo tomb murals, it is possible to propose that the standing female and male figures on the Shūchō were aligned in processions, standing on the same ground line, much as depicted in the Susanri tomb. In this tomb, the group of male figures faces east, and the group of females, west. In addition to people aligned in processions, the seated figures seen on the Shūchō (B-4, D-6, and fig. 3) imply that clusters of seated people also originally appeared, perhaps participating in assemblies. The style of the extant figures also suggests that they might have been created before the figures depicted in the Takamatsuzuka tomb murals.

The Celestial Realm

The representation of the moon with the hare (A-1) and the designs on the right side of section A (fig. 26; see also figs. 11, 12) strongly suggest that heaven, as conceived by the Chinese, was included in the Shūchō's composition. As mentioned previously,

26 Motifs on continuous fragment, Shūchō (section A), detail of fig. 11.

27 Moon design, Shūchō (A-1), detail of fig. 11.

the fragment on the right side of section A is particularly important because it is the only large piece of ground fabric from the Shūchō that preserves the original arrangement of the designs. This fragment includes a green half-palmette (A-2), a red bird (A-3), a turtle with graphs (A-6), a cloud design (A-4), a sprouting-bud motif (A-5), ribbons (A-7), and an unidentified design, perhaps foliage (A-9).[37] Similar combinations of designs are found in some continental representations of the heavenly realm; key to the identification of this portion of the composition as part of the sky is the cloud design, represented with parallel comma-shaped lines arranged horizontally and capped by a quivering form.

The Chinese concept of heaven is a complex topic that has been researched by a number of Sinologists. For the purposes of this study, Lillian Tseng's 2011 book, *Picturing Heaven in Early China*, is relevant as the only study that focuses on the pictorial representation of this concept, and that interprets heaven from a multidisciplinary point of view. Tseng's book includes comprehensive references to ideologies and beliefs about heaven found in textual material, and, most importantly, details the visual conventions established in the Han period.[38] Unfortunately, no similar comprehensive study about the representation of heaven in the Northern and Southern Dynasties period, which is chronologically closer to the fragments, is yet available. Thus arguments for pictorial representations from this period in Japan are based on Tseng's research and on scattered studies about the representation of heaven in the Northern and Southern Dynasties. These studies show that the Han visual representation of heaven was enriched with the introduction of Buddhist designs, leading to the creation of a Chinese heaven that included Buddhist pictorial elements. A number of tombs and funerary monuments, as well as Buddhist cave temples dating from the Northern and Southern Dynasties period, show this combination of Han motifs and new elements, such as the representation of floral designs and flying celestial beings derived from Indian models.[39] Similar trends are found in the representations of the celestial realm seen in the Goguryeo tombs.[40]

In addition to people participating in processions and gatherings, the Shūchō's composition likely included a celestial realm represented as per Chinese pictorial conventions for heaven, which encompassed celestial bodies, clouds, fantastic animals, and flying celestial beings.

Celestial Bodies: The Sun and the Moon
In the upper left corner of section A, the circle with a stylized hare standing on its hind legs, pounding on a jar in front of a tree (A-1), is the Chinese representation of the moon (fig. 27). In China, the moon is never represented alone; it is always complemented by the sun, shown with a bird inside its circular outline. Therefore, although only the moon has survived, the original composition of the Shūchō must have included both the sun and the moon.

The representation of the sun and moon inhabited by animals originated in Han China, and is explained in a series of textual sources. Although some variations are found, in general a bird—sometimes a three-legged crow—is depicted inside the sun disk, and a hare or toad (or both) is found inside the moon disk. In the case of the moon, the hare sometimes is portrayed pounding ingredients to make the elixir of immortality.[41] Among the widely known examples are painted silk banners found in tombs from the Western Han dynasty (206 BCE–9 CE), such as Mawangdui Tomb No. 1 in Changsha (Hunan Province), dated to 168 BCE; and Jinqueshan Tomb No. 9 in Linyi (Shandong Province), dated to the first or second century.[42] In the banner from the former, the sun is represented as a red circle enclosing a black bird in the upper right corner, and a crescent moon is depicted with a toad and a hare in the upper left corner (fig. 28). A.G. Bulling has indicated that the toad stands for the waxing moon, and the hare for the full moon.[43]

28 Banner from Mawangdui Tomb No. 1, Changsha, Hunan Province. 168 BCE. Silk with painted design. 205 x 92 cm (at top), 47.4 cm (at bottom). Hunan Provincial Museum.

In addition to these two painted banners, Western Han painted tombs dating to the first century BCE also include the sun and moon as part of the iconographical program. These motifs are seen on the ceilings of the tomb of Bo Qianqiu and Tomb 61, both located in Luoyang (Henan Province); and the Jiaoda tomb in Xi'an (Shaanxi Province).[44] The

29 Crow in the sun and hare in the moon from tomb at Jianjia, Danyang County, Jiangsu Province. Late 5th century. Rubbings of brick relief murals. Nanjing Museum, Jiangsu Province.

design on the ceiling of Tomb 61 is interpreted as a cosmological representation that includes the sun, moon, and constellations, which are depicted by dots joined by lines and cloud forms. The iconography of the painting on the ceiling of the tomb of Bo Qianqiu is more complex. In addition to the sun and moon, the scene includes figures riding mythological creatures, fantastic animals, and wavy cloud-like elements.[45]

Later archaeological remains reveal that the representation of the sun and moon continued after the Han period, spreading over a wide geographical area and a long period of time. For instance, a lacquered and painted coffin was discovered in a tomb from the Northern Wei dynasty in the city of Guyuan in the Ningxia Hui Autonomous Region; the tomb is dated to about 470–80. Although the painting is damaged, the sun, moon, and fantastic beasts are depicted on the upper portion of the coffin's lid, above two architectural structures housing the Queen Mother of the West and King Father of the East, both identified by inscriptions. A serpentine band with swirling designs in between the two structures represents the River of Heaven or the Milky Way. Luo Feng has viewed the sun and the moon on this coffin as representing heaven, and the whole composition as a visualization of the Daoist ideal of ascending to heaven.[46]

Likewise, these two celestial bodies were part of the iconographical program of the Southern Dynasties brick tombs in Danyang County, Jiangsu Province, dated to the Southern Qi period (479–502).[47] In one of these tombs, although the actual representations have not survived, inscriptions on bricks indicate that the motifs were located on the ceiling between the corridor entrance and the first stone door.[48] The only sun and moon to survive intact in these brick tombs are found in a tomb at Jianjia. In this case, a three-legged bird with wings outspread stands inside the sun, and a hare stands on its two hind feet in the moon, with its front paws pounding a pestle on a mortar, in front of a cassia tree (fig. 29).[49] This representation of the moon closely parallels the moon depicted on the Shūchō fragment.

In tombs on the Korean peninsula, following the Chinese models, the sun and moon are portrayed on the domed ceilings accompanied by stars and constellations, auspicious animals, and heavenly beings. Examples are found in the tomb at Deokhungri, from the first period; in the Ssangyeonchong tomb and Deokhwari Nos. 1 and 2 (figs. 30, 31), from the second period; and in Jinpari No. 1 and the Gangseo gung-

30 East side of the ceiling of the main chamber, Deokhwari Tomb No. 2. Late 5th–early 6th century. Mural painting. South Pyongyang Province.

31 West side of the ceiling of the main chamber, Deokhwari Tomb No. 2. Late 5th–early 6th century. Mural painting. South Pyongyang Province.

32   Sun on the east side of the ceiling of the main chamber, Gangseo gungmyo tomb. Second half of 6th–first half of 7th century. Mural painting. Nampo Province.

myo tomb (fig. 32), from the third period. The sun and moon are also found in some tombs from Baekje. This kingdom adopted the tomb style prevalent in the Southern Dynasties, particularly in the use of bricks to build barrel-vaulted structures.[50] They did not use pictorial tiles, but painted murals. Three tombs with mural paintings have been discovered in Baekje territory. One of them, Songsanri Tomb No. 6, located in the city of Gongju in Chungnam (South Chungcheong) Province, includes two disks on the southern wall that might represent the sun and moon.[51]

The sun and moon as part of the iconography of the celestial realm also reached the Japanese islands. In Takamatsuzuka tomb, the sun disk appears on the eastern wall, and the moon disk on the western wall (see figs. 23, 24). As both are damaged, it is not known if the disks included their corresponding animals. On the ceiling of this tomb, to complete the representation of the sky, twenty-eight constellations and smaller groups of stars are represented by golden dots joined by red lines. Similarly, in Kitora tomb, the sun and moon are on the ceiling, to the east and west, flanking an astronomical chart that is more complex than the example in Takamatsuzuka.[52] The depictions of celestial bodies in Kitora tomb are also damaged, but some traces of a bird with three legs may be found in the sun disk.[53]

In addition to examples painted in tombs, two aforementioned works of Buddhist art also include depictions of the sun and moon: the Tamamushi Shrine (fig. 33) and the bronze banner from Hōryūji (fig. 34). On the Tamamushi Shrine, in the scene identified as the "World of Mount Sumeru" located on the lower back panel, the two disks are depicted at the top of the composition to the left and right (fig. 33a). The red sun disk includes a three-legged

33   Tamamushi Shrine. 7th century. Wood, lacquer, and tile. H. 226.6 cm. Great Treasure Hall, Hōryūji, Nara Prefecture. National Treasure.

33a "World of Mount Sumeru." Lower back panel of Tamamushi Shrine, fig. 33.

34a Sun and moon on canopy, detail of fig. 34.

34 Bronze banner. 7th century. Gilt bronze. H. 551 cm. The Gallery of Hōryūji Treasures, Tokyo National Museum. National Treasure.

bird with wings spread, but the moon disk is damaged and unreadable.[54] On the bronze banner, the disks appear in the canopy section at top, which consists of four triangular openwork plaques, each with celestial figures playing musical instruments (fig. 34a). These four triangular plaques are joined to create a square, and the sun and moon are found on the base of each of two opposing triangles. Because only the upper halves of the disks are visible, the head of the hare, the top of a vase, and a tree can be seen in the moon disk, and a bird's head and wing in the sun disk. The style of representation of the hare is similar to that seen on the Shūchō.[55]

Although only a representation of the moon has survived on the Shūchō fragments, based on the examples discussed above, a red sun disk with a bird or a three-legged crow must have been part of the Shūchō's iconographical program. As in the continental examples, the sun disk would have been placed to the east, and the moon disk, to the west. Furthermore, the visual evidence in Japan suggests that, in the seventh century, the Chinese conventions for representations of the sun and moon were used in both funerary and Buddhist contexts. Because these two motifs are never seen in isolation, it is important to address other design elements to reach a more definite conclusion about the original iconographical scheme found on the Shūchō.

35   Red bird, Shūchō (A-3), detail of fig. 11.

Red Bird and Turtle as Heavenly Omens

In addition to the sun and moon, constellations, auspicious clouds, fantastic animals, celestial beings, and floral designs also are included in depictions of the Chinese celestial realm. On the Shūchō, two animal designs—the red bird and the turtle design with graphs—likely represent omens that were believed to appear in the sky.

The red bird with a white underside (A-3) is depicted in profile, facing left. The red and white wings are extended, with green feathers spread at their ends. Unfortunately the tail seems to be missing (fig. 35). In China, mythical red birds were known by two names: *zhu niao* (J. *shujaku*), or the Red Bird of the South; and *fenghuang* (J. *hōō*), commonly translated as phoenix.[56] Although no formal differentiation between the two birds seems to exist, a red bird is identified as *shujaku* when it is grouped with the Azure Dragon of the East, the White Tiger of the West, and the Dark Warrior of the North (a snake intertwined with a turtle) as the well-known Four Divinities. These animals were associated with the four directions, yin yang, and Five Phases (C. *wu xing*; J. *gogyō*) as follows:

The animal symbolism of the four cardinal directions became widespread during the Han dynasty, but the idea might have originated earlier, in the Warring States period (ca. 480–221 BCE) or Qin

Direction	Phase or Element	Animal symbol	Yin or Yang
East	Wood	Azure Dragon	Yang
South	Fire	Red Bird	Yang
West	Metal	White Tiger	Yin
North	Water	Dark Warrior	Yin
Center	Earth	No symbol	Neutral

dynasty (221–206 BCE).[57] The Four Divinities were believed to guide the deceased to the world of deathlessness, and as such, the group became an important subject in funerary monuments.[58] Examples of the Four Divinities in China abound.[59]

The group was also popular in Korea, where the Four Divinities became the main subject matter for Goguryeo tomb murals, beginning in the second period. At Yakusuri (Nampo City) and Deokhwari Nos. 1 and 2, representations of the Four Divinities are located in the lantern roofs. In the tombs of the third period, such as Jinpari Nos. 1 and 2, Gangseo daemyo (see fig. 42) and Gangseo gungmyo, Sasinchong, and Ohoebun Nos. 4 and 5, each of the Four Divinities occupies a whole wall corresponding to its direction. The subject is also found in some Baekje tombs, including the aforementioned Songsanri No. 6.[60]

In Japan, two tombs bearing images of the Four Divinities have been discovered thus far. In Takamatsuzuka tomb, the Red Bird has been destroyed, but the Dark Warrior appears on the north wall (fig. 36); on the west and east walls, respectively, in between the groups of men and women and below the sun and moon disks, the Azure Dragon and the White Tiger are depicted (see figs. 23, 24). In addition, in Kitora tomb, the Four Divinities—including the Red Bird (fig. 37)—appear on their respective walls, and so far, six of the twelve animals of the Chinese zodiac, portrayed with animal heads and human bodies, have also been discovered.[61] It is important to note that depictions of the Four Divinities were not exclusive to funerary iconography. Like representations of the sun and moon, in Japan they were also portrayed on certain Buddhist monuments, such as the pedestal of the sculpture of the Buddha Yakushi (S. Bhaiṣajyaguru) from Yakushiji in Nara, dated to the early eighth century.[62]

Because only a red bird is extant on the fragments, it is difficult to assert that the Four Divinities were represented on the Shūchō. Textual evidence from the thirteenth century suggests that a dragon may also have been part of the composition. The nun Shinnyo, who was involved in the discovery of the embroidery, wrote a brief description of the Tenjukoku Mandara, stating, "The turtles had the inscription and there was a detailed dragon design, all embroidered."[63] Some incomplete animal heads are among the small fragments from the Shūchō in the Shōsōin collection (see fig. 2), but it is impossible to confirm that they are the remains of a dragon figure. If the Four Divinities were depicted, we could argue that the iconographical program of the Shūchō was associated with the Five Phases. But the red bird as depicted in China was not limited to its role as a member of the Four Divinities; it was also believed to be an omen.

In China, belief in omens appearing in the sky was associated with the concept of the Mandate of Heaven established in the Western Zhou dynasty (1046–771 BCE). This belief developed out of the need to demonstrate that the ruler had approval from heaven for his reign. In the Han dynasty, Confucian scholars articulated the discourse of

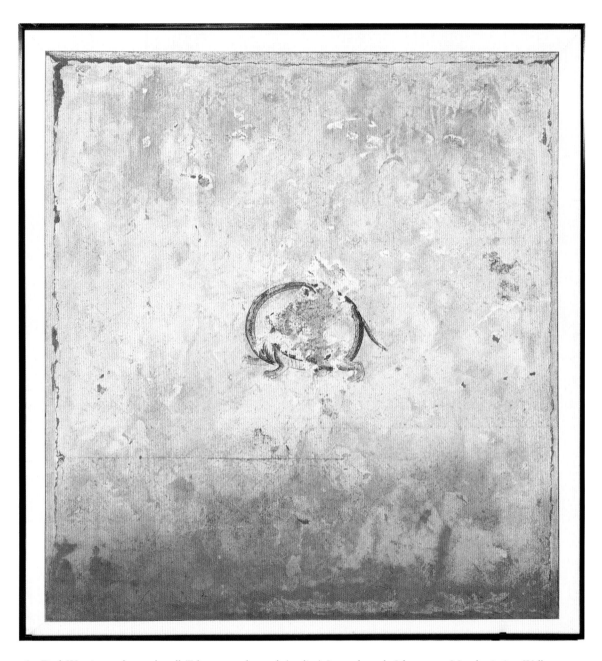

36 Dark Warrior on the north wall, Takamatsuzuka tomb (replica). Late 7th–early 8th century. Mural painting. Wall: 113.4 × 109.2 cm. Asuka, Nara Prefecture. Replica: Nara National Research Institute for Cultural Property.

37 Red Bird on the south wall of the burial chamber, Kitora tomb. Late 7th–early 8th century. Mural painting. Asuka, Nara Prefecture.

auspicious omens as well as the practice of naming reign eras after them. Textual sources indicate that omens were illustrated as early as 109 BCE, but these illustrations are no longer extant.[64] Furthermore, books describing omens were popular beginning in the Eastern Han dynasty, and indexes in multiple scrolls were made during the Northern and Southern Dynasties period. These indexes, which included both auspicious and inauspicious omens, consisted of illustrations of the figures with their corresponding explanations.[65] A ninth-century copy of an index (now at the Bibliotèque Nationale, Paris) was found at Dunhuang. In the top row of the scroll are drawings of auspicious omens, such as various types of turtles, dragons, and birds, and at the bottom, a paragraph identifying each of them and explaining its meaning.[66] Omens were powerful; because they were believed to confirm or deny the mandate of each sovereign, emperor, or founder of a dynasty, they held considerable political significance.

Omens that appeared in the sky were depicted in the tombs and memorial shrines of the Han dynasty, such as the engraved stone slabs of the Wu Liang Shrine in Shandong Province (dated to the Eastern Han), where each is identified by name in a cartouche.[67] Other types of omens are portrayed in the painted or engraved tombs of officials, suggesting that a variety of categories existed. Tseng has stated that the omens in officials' tombs symbolized the benevolent reputation of the tomb occupant.[68] Murals in Goguryeo tombs and textual evidence in Japan suggest that, while not as prominent as in China, belief in omens reached the Korean peninsula and the islands.

In Korea, figures of omens are also represented on the ceilings of Goguryeo tombs, especially those dated to the fifth century, such as Muyongchong and Deokhungri, and in the seventh-century Gangseo daemyo and Gangseo gungmyo. On these ceilings, the red bird is depicted together with other fantastic animals, the sun and moon, constellations, and transcendents or celestial beings. The Deokhungri tomb is particularly important because all of the figures are associated with cartouches containing inscriptions that identify each of the motifs on

38 Line drawing of the west side of the antechamber and main chamber of the Deokhungri tomb. 408. Nampo Province.

the ceiling (figs. 38–41).⁶⁹ Stevenson has pointed out that the scene depicted on this ceiling is a representation of Daoist immortals and the ascent of the deceased to heaven. Two of the inscriptions in the cartouches certainly make explicit references to the pursuit of the Dao. Stevenson also has noted, however, that the captions indicate that the vast majority of the designs represent omens (figs. 39a, 41a). Because celestial bodies are also portrayed in the tomb's dome, she has concluded that the dome imagery must represent the *gaitian* (heavenly canopy) cosmology of the Han dynasty and its systems of astrological divination. Stevenson has stated that the ceiling's motifs are an assemblage of astrological symbols and omens of good fortune that refer to the virtues of cosmic order and harmony. She has further argued that, because this representation of the heavens is located above the scenes of official successes and domestic bliss depicted on the walls below, the ceiling legitimizes the status and success of the deceased and his descendants, linking them to the generative cosmic pattern and presence.⁷⁰ Based on the identification of the fantastic beasts depicted in the Deokhungri tomb, it is possible that the unidentified animals on the ceilings of other tombs, such as Gangseo daemyo (fig. 42), also represent omens.⁷¹

If the red bird on the fragment is indeed an omen, it is likely that other fantastic animals—such as dragons, *kirin* (C. *qilin*; a chimerical beast), heavenly horses, and celestial deer—were part of the iconographic program of the *Shūchō*. The complete composition likely could be compared to the compositions on the ceilings of the Deokhungri and Gangseo daemyo tombs. The latter tomb has a lantern roof, with the beams of the corbelled dome creating well-defined registers. The lower registers contain symmetrically and rhythmically arranged fantastic beings (fig. 43). Each of the omen figures, particularly the red birds, is repeated multiple times on the ceiling, which may also have been the case on the *Shūchō*.

The other animal on the continuous fragment (section A) is the most puzzling of the motifs: the turtle with four characters on its shell. The only turtle from the *Shūchō* that has survived bears the characters 部間人公 (A-6; fig. 44), corresponding to the name of Prince Shōtoku's mother. Among the small pieces kept in the Shōsōin, three incomplete turtles, and also small pieces with the charac-

MATERIAL AND VISUAL EVIDENCE

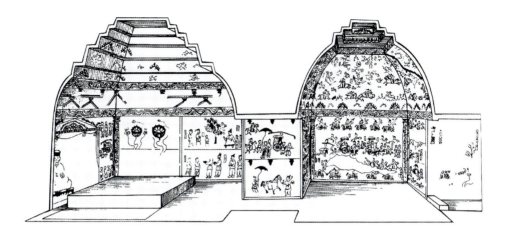

39   Line drawing of the east side of the antechamber and main chamber of the Deokhungri tomb. 408. Nampo Province.

39a   Hunting scene and omen figures on the east side of the antechamber, Deokhungri tomb.

FABRICATING THE *TENJUKOKU SHŪCHŌ MANDARA* AND PRINCE SHŌTOKU'S AFTERLIVES

40

41

40 Line drawing of the north wall of the antechamber of the Deokhungri tomb. 408. Nampo Province.

41 Line drawing of the south wall of the antechamber of the Deokhungri tomb. 408. Nampo Province.

41a Omen figures on the south wall of the antechamber, Deokhungri tomb.

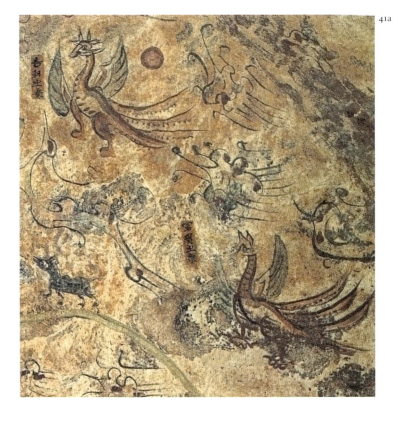

MATERIAL AND VISUAL EVIDENCE

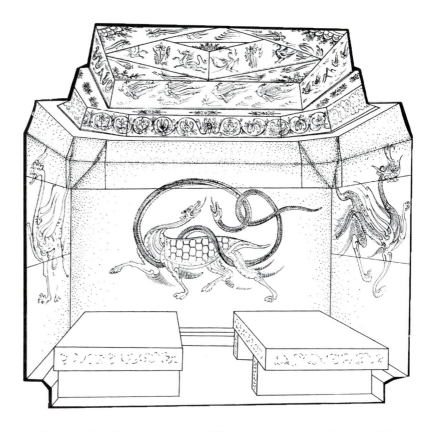

42 Line drawing of the main chamber of Gangseo daemyo tomb. Second half of 6th–first half of 7th century. Nampo Province.

43 West side of the ceiling of the main chamber, Gangseo daemyo tomb. Second half of 6th–first half of 7th century. Mural painting. Nampo Province.

44 Turtle with graphs, Shūchō (A-6), detail of fig. 11.

ters 奈, 甘, 居, 佛, and 娶, are found (see fig. 2). On the Shūchō, enough turtles must have been present to carry the whole inscription; the number suggested by thirteenth-century sources is one hundred. Turtles had multiple meanings in ancient China, and were associated with longevity and immortal lands (such as Penglai and Kunlun). For this reason, some scholars have argued that Tenjukoku was associated with immortality beliefs. Yet the turtle design on the Shūchō is distinctive because it contains four graphs. Textual evidence suggests that turtles with graphs in Japan represent omens.

The design of a turtle with graphs on its shell does not seem to be found in China or the Korean peninsula. Some objects and narratives, however, explain the association of turtles with writing. In China, a number of seals with turtle-shaped grips have been found, such as the example from Mawangdui No. 2, which bears four characters indicating rank and official titles.[72] Pedestals in the form of turtles also support Chinese steles with epigraphs, including one carved during the Liang dynasty (502–87) for the prince Xiao Hong, who died in 526. The stele is located near Nanjing in Jiangsu Province.[73]

In addition to these objects, the *Hetu* ([Yellow] River Chart) and *Luoshu* (Luo [River] Writing), ancient Chinese arrangements of the Eight Trigrams (*ba gua*) and Five Phases, were used to explain the association of turtles with writing.[74] The history and multiple layers of meaning contained within *Yellow River Chart* and *Luo River Writing* are complex and beyond the scope of this book. Popular legends, however, explain that the *Yellow River Chart* is based on a series of fifty-five dots that were seen on the back of a dragon that emerged from the Yellow River. It was believed that the mythical Chinese hero Fuxi received them and created the Eight Trigrams.[75] *Luo River Writing* is associated with the mythical sovereign Yu the Great. He learned the diagram from the pattern on the shell of a turtle that appeared from the Luo River. Because this story involves a turtle, *Luo River Writing* is also known as "Turtle Writing" in later traditions.[76] Nevertheless, "Turtle Writing" does not specifically refer to graphs on a turtle. Hence, the turtles with graphs on the Shūchō likely were not associated with the *Hetu* or *Luoshu*.

An archaeological discovery and a number of textual references in Japan are key to understanding the significance of the turtle with graphs. In January 2000, the discovery of a stone receptacle carved in the shape of a turtle made sensational news (fig. 45). For scholars, it opened new venues for interpreting the Shūchō's turtle-with-graphs motif and, more importantly, for expanding our understanding of ritual life in seventh-century Japan. The turtle-shaped receptacle was excavated in Asuka just a few meters southeast of the Buddhist temple Asu-

45   Turtle-shaped stone receptacle. 7th century. Granite. 2.4 x 2 m. Asuka, Nara Prefecture.

kadera. As soon as the receptacle was discovered, scholars pointed out its similarity to the turtle motif on the Shūchō.[77] Both turtles are stylized, with a thick border accentuating the shape of their circular carapaces. They show feet with four toes that look like flippers, and a triangular tail; the two eyes are located on the top of the head. The Shūchō turtle, however, has a pointed mouth, whereas the stone turtle has an indentation in the mouth area. This indentation connects to a cartouche-shaped container next to it. The formal characteristics of the two turtle designs suggest that they are representations of snapping turtles (*suppon*). Interestingly, a container lid in the shape of a snapping turtle is found in the Shōsōin collection, with the Big Dipper painted on its carapace (fig. 46).

Further excavations at the site revealed that the turtle- and cartouche-shaped containers were part of a complex that included a sloped plaza paved with stones (fig. 47). In addition, the containers were linked to a hydraulic system, indicating that they functioned specifically as water basins.[78] The turtle-shaped basin is carved in granite from the

46   Container with turtle-shaped lid. 8th century. Stone. 3.5 x 15 cm (from nose to tail). Shōsōin, Nara Prefecture.

Asuka area, and measures 2.4 by 2 meters; its circular border is 19 centimeters thick. The water container in the center measures 1.25 meter in diameter and is about 20 centimeters deep, and reveals a hole in the mouth and another in the tail. The mouth of the turtle connects to the spout of the cartouche-shaped basin, which measures 1.65 by 1 meter.[79] Archaeologists discovered a column surrounded by three walls constructed with sandstone ashlars. The column is hollow and has a conduit in the middle, which allows pressurized water to rise and flow from the top of the column (fig. 48). A channeled wooden ramp must have been placed to allow the water to flow down to the cartouche-shaped basin, and from its spout into the turtle's mouth, into the circular basin, and then out of the hole in the tail. Regrettably, it is not known how this site was used.[80] The materials incorporated, however, have allowed archaeologists to date the site.

Because the sandstone ashlars used to build the walls came from Tenri (in Nara Prefecture), the stone-turtle site has been associated with Great King Saimei (r. 655–61; a female ruler who had previously reigned as Kōgyoku, 642–45), based on records in *Nihon shoki*. In 656, Saimei embarked on a series of public works; one project included the digging of a canal from Mount Kagu to Mount Isonokami in Tenri to transport stone. According to *Nihon shoki*, two hundred barges were loaded with stones from Mount Isonokami and floated downstream to the mountain east of her palace, where the stones were piled up to form a wall.[81] From this information, archaeologists have concluded that the site was built in the second half of the seventh century.

The discovery of the stone turtle is important for understanding the Shūchō and seventh-century Japan. On the one hand, although the turtle-shaped receptacle and the embroidered turtle are different in terms of the materials used and their sizes, their stylistic similarities suggest that they were probably made around the same time (late seventh century) and perhaps in the same geographical area (Asuka). On the other hand, although the exact function of the stone-turtle site remains unknown, it is clear that it was not associated with Buddhist practices, despite being near Asukadera. In fact, the plaza with the stone turtle strongly suggests that Buddhism was not the only cultic practice in the region.

Other than this possible link to the stone turtle, three Japanese texts compiled in the eighth century mention turtles with graphs. All instances are related to belief in the appearance of this animal as an omen; in two cases, the finding of these turtles was considered auspicious. For example, *Nihon shoki* records that, in 670, a turtle with the character *shin* 申 (monkey) on its shell was caught in the capital.[82] The turtle was described as being yellow on top and black underneath, and about six inches in length.[83] A poem in *Man'yōshū* (Collection of Ten Thousand Leaves; compiled mid-8th century) composed by the builders of the Fujiwara palace (site of the imperial court between 694 and 710) mentions a turtle with multiple graphs. The poem refers to timber from Mount Tanakami in Ōmi (present-day Shiga Prefecture) being floated down the Uji River to the construction site of the palace of Heavenly Sovereign Jitō (r. 686–97):

> … and from Kose that draws the ungoverned lands
> towards the sun palace that we built
> a marvelous turtle (神亀) bearing the inscription
> "our land will become the everlasting realm" (我国者常
>   世尓成牟)
> announcing the new reign emerges …[84]

The third instance is found in *Shoku Nihongi* (Chronicles of Japan Continued; completed 797). This source tells us that, in 727, a turtle measuring 5 *sun* 3 *bu* in length and 4 *sun* 5 *bu* in width, with the

47 Plaza with turtle-shaped stone receptacle. 7th century. Asuka, Nara Prefecture.

48 Turtle-shaped stone receptacle, cartouche-shaped stone basin, and ashlar stone wall. 7th century. Granite and sandstone. Asuka, Nara Prefecture.

phrase 天王貴平知百年 (the peaceful rule of the emperor will last one hundred years) on its carapace, was offered to the emperor.[85] The appearance of this turtle was considered to be a "great omen," and for this reason the era name was changed from Jinki to Tenpyō (天平), using two of the graphs from the message. In addition to turtles with graphs, white turtles and turtles with the Big Dipper on their shells were also allegedly found.[86] Entries in *Shoku Nihongi* positively indicate that the compilers were familiar with Chinese omen lore, as specific Chinese omen manuals are quoted. For instance, in an entry for 768–69 (Jingo-keiun 2), the *Ruiyingtu* (Diagram of Auspicious Omens) of Sun Rouzhi (6th century) is quoted to explain the meaning of a particular auspicious turtle: "When a king is fair and impartial and the old people are honored, when usages from former times are not lost and the benefits of virtue are extended, then the numinous turtle (霊亀) appears."[87] Belief in omens was one of the many aspects of Chinese culture that were adopted in Japan.

With this evidence about turtles and graphs, we can argue that the embroidered turtle with graphs, taken together with the red bird, the cloud design, and other fantastic animals, was portrayed in the celestial realm as an omen figure. The difference between the textual references to turtles and the figure on the Shūchō is that the texts mention the finding of a single turtle with a message (sometimes in multiple graphs) on its carapace, whereas on the Shūchō, a hundred turtles with four graphs each were lined up to complete a long inscription. The hundred turtles had to be placed in a precise order to facilitate the reading of the inscription that they carried. In addition, as in the Goguryeo tomb murals, the evenly spaced turtles were intermingled with red birds and other auspicious animals such as dragons, heavenly horses, and *kirin*, which were probably repeated multiple times. An analysis of the sprouting-bud design will further support the theory that this large fragment of the Shūchō corresponded to the celestial realm.

Sprouting-Bud Motif, Celestial Beings, and Transcendents

A particularly intriguing motif consists of a leaf-shaped element on the tip of a red bud that rests on a green, crescent-shaped form with three circles, above a yellow, comma-shaped appendage with red lines, which we may call the "sprouting-bud" motif (A-5). Studies by Yoshimura Rei and Sakai Atsuko have revealed that, in China, this sprouting-bud design and its variations usually are associated with Buddhist celestial beings (C. *tianren*; J. *tennin*), as seen at Gongxian Cave No. 3 (fig. 49); transcendents or immortals (C. *xian*; J. *sen*); or heavenly animals that glide through the sky surrounded by clouds. Although a complete representation of a celestial being or transcendent is not available among the surviving designs on the Shūchō, using some of the fragments, the figure of a transcendent that was likely associated with the sprouting-bud design on the curtains may be reconstructed.

Before delving into this process, two terms require some clarification: Buddhist heavenly beings and transcendents.[88] The term "Buddhist heavenly beings" is used here to refer to the flying figures that are derived from Indian models. These flying figures are usually bare-chested, and wear a dhoti or Indian skirt and a long scarf. (The Sanskrit word *apsara* refers specifically to heavenly maidens, and so it is not employed here.) The term "transcendents" is used to refer to flying beings represented with feather-like garments or clothing covering the whole body; the garments sometimes are portrayed with sharp, angular edges. These figures, who may ride dragons or other animals, represent *xian*, generally identified in English as "immortals" or "wizards." Robert Campany instead advocates for the term "transcendents," arguing that the practices associated with *xian* did not aim toward immortality or eternal stasis, but "to transcend"—to reach a higher status than what the best human beings could achieve.[89]

Regarding the sprouting-bud design, Yoshimura Rei has stated that this design was part of a process of "birth by transformation" (*keshō*), a three- or four-phase system that resulted in the production of a Buddhist celestial being or transcendent. He

49   Buddhist celestial being and sprouting-bud motif on the south side of the stupa-pillar, Gongxian Cave No. 3. Early 6th century. Relief carving. Henan Province.

dedicated much of his academic career to the study of representations of this process and its spread in East Asia, focusing on Buddhist cave temples and funerary monuments of the Northern and Southern Dynasties in China, funerary arts of the Three Kingdoms period in Korea, and also on works dated to the Asuka period in Japan.[90]

The sprouting-bud motif is specifically associated with what Yoshimura has called the "Southern-type birth by transformation."[91] An example of this process is found in the Guyang Cave at Longmen, in China's Henan Province, dated to the early sixth century.[92] The four phases are portrayed above the mandorla of a Buddha image on the northern wall (fig. 50). Accordingly, the first phase is a heavenly lotus (J. *ten renge*), followed by the sprouting-bud motif with a twisted, comma-shaped appendage, which Yoshimura termed "metamorphosis" (*hengeshō*). (Many variations in the forms of this second step are found.) The third phase is the "birth by transformation," which consists of the upper body of a being sprouting out of an enlarged comma-shaped element. The figure usually is bare-chested and wears a scarf.[93] The last and final phase depicted in this relief is a transcendent, represented twice, who appears to fly swiftly, propelled by a cloud, the action emphasized by the long, flowing scarf and robe with wide sleeves. In other representations, however, some of the phases are omitted, to the point that only the celestial being is portrayed right next to a sprouting-bud motif (see fig. 49) or a celestial lotus; such scenes appear on the ceiling of the Lotus Cave in Longmen and in Cave Nos. 2 and 3 of Tianlongshan in Shanxi Province.[94] The design is also found on sarcophagi, where it is associated with fantastic creatures.[95]

Because this process seems to have originated in South China, Yoshimura designated it as the "Southern type." The oldest known depiction of the sprouting-bud motif is found in the Huqiao tomb (Danyang, Jiangsu Province), dated to about 493, which is believed to be the resting place of the official Xiao Daosheng and his consort. This tomb from the Southern Qi period is built with pictorial tiles, creating a composition that covers the whole wall on each side. The western wall contains a scene of a transcendent teasing a tiger, and the eastern wall, a scene with a dragon. Above the tiger's body, three celestial beings (one of them damaged) roam the skies, as suggested by the dynamically represented cloud scrolls, floral motifs, and flowers with comma-shaped appendages. According to Yoshimura, here the process consists of three phases (fig. 51), beginning with a heavenly lotus with half-palmette motifs arranged in various patterns (I1); this phase is followed by the metamorphosis, represented by a blooming lotus flower with a comma-shaped appendage, or a similar motif with a palmette emerging from the bud (II1, II2). The final product is a transcendent, identified by the feathery garment on top of his upper garment and pants (III).[96]

Because Yoshimura first found depictions of the "birth by transformation" process in Buddhist cave temples, he assumed that it reflected Buddhist belief. Indeed, he based the name of the process on the last form of birth as enumerated in the Buddhist idea of four forms: 1) birth from the womb (*taishō*), as with human beings and animals; 2) birth from an egg (*ranshō*), as with birds; 3) birth from moisture (*shisshō*), as with larvae and insects; and 4) birth from transformation (*keshō*), existence created by the force of one's own past karma, as in the case of celestials and bodhisattvas. Audrey Spiro, however, has disagreed with Yoshimura. She has stated that the representation of these flying beings was not related to Buddhist ideas, but was based on indigenous Chinese beliefs; and that the elegant forms seen in the Southern Qi depiction were related to aristocratic culture.[97]

Transformation and metamorphosis are key concepts in yin-yang and Five Phases thought (and later in Daoism) as ways of achieving transcendence. Isabelle Robinet, referring to the writings of the minor official and prolific author Ge Hong (283–343), has noted that, among the diverse practices proposed by him, certain methods of metamorphosis "allowed the adept to sublimate and purify his body, even to change into a winged immortal." In addition, Robinet has observed that Daoist texts that convey the concept of transformation include images such as "the precious stone removed from the matrix" or "the insect emerging from the chrysalis." The latter seems to be portrayed in the process of "birth by transformation."[98] In another study, Robinet has discussed a Daoist text that describes the different appearances assumed by divinities when manifesting in different forms; this text would also help Daoist adepts in their own metamorphoses, which would take place during meditation. While meditating, the adept could cause colored breaths to appear, and sometimes these breaths would be transformed into divinities. "Born" of the void "by transformation" (C. *huasheng*) within the heavenly sphere, in contrast to terrestrial beings who are "born of an embryo" (C. *taisheng*), these divinities manifest themselves in front of the adept.[99]

Whereas Yoshimura has argued that the sprouting-bud motif was represented as part of a process

50 Southern-type birth by transformation, detail from niche on the northern wall, Guyang Cave. 6th century. Relief carving. Longmen grottoes, Henan Province.

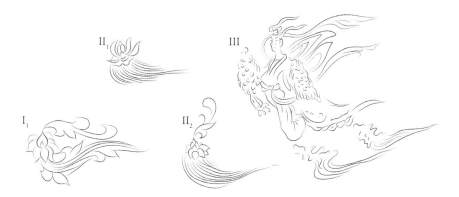

51 Process of birth by transformation as depicted in motifs from the Huqiao tomb. Ca. 493. Danyang, Jiangsu Province. Line drawing by Christian Gutierrez, adapted from Yoshimura Rei, "Nanchō tennin zuzō no Hokuchō oyobi shūhen shokoku e no denba," 12.

52　Stone sarcophagus of Yuan Mi from Lijia'ao, Henan Province. 523. Black limestone. Minneapolis Institute of Art.

of transformation associated with Buddhist beliefs, Sakai Atsuko has found evidence to contradict this association.[100] She has determined that the sprouting-bud motif was a mélange of the "clouds of energy" (C. *yunqi*; J. *unki*) design seen during the Han dynasty and the floral motifs (especially the lotus and palmette) introduced in South China during the fifth century.[101] Sakai arrived at this conclusion when she noticed that variations on the bud motif combined with palmettes, particularly in the tombs at Dengxian (Henan Province) and the Huqiao tomb, follow the same contours as the "clouds of energy" motif used in the Han dynasty.[102] For this reason, in Sakai's view, when the floral motifs were introduced in the fifth century, these must have been added to the basic "clouds of energy" form.[103] After studying a number of scenes in which the sprouting-bud motif appears, Sakai concluded that the design held multiple meanings; it could be a signifier for flow and movement, and also part of a process, as suggested by Yoshimura. In short, the sprouting-bud design stood for movement and life in the heavens, and was only used for a brief period of time, from the late fifth to the mid-sixth century.[104] The decorative scheme on a stone sarcophagus in the Minneapolis Institute of Art recovered from the Northern Wei tomb of Yuan Mi (or Prince Zhenjing, d. 523), located in Lijia'ao, southwest of Luoyang in Henan Province, is an example of Sakai's theory (fig. 52). The sprouting-bud motif, located between designs of a bird and square window on the side of the sarcophagus toward the right, is part of this dynamic representation of the celestial realm.

While Sakai has based her argument for the origins of the sprouting-bud design on formal ele-

ments, Inoue Tadashi has addressed the significance of the combination of lotus flowers and *qi* (J. *ki*; energy).¹⁰⁵ As he explains, these two items represent sources of life in their respective cultures of origin. In India, the lotus flower was associated with birth and creation. For example, in the Hindu myth of Vishnu Anantaśayana (Vishnu sleeping on the serpent Ananta), Vishnu, in his cosmic sleep, creates Brahma, who appears in a lotus flower that grows from Vishnu's navel. In China, the *Huainanzi*, a Han-period compendium of thought, explains that *qi* is the creative force, an invisible source of life and energy. The Chinese cosmogonic myth states that the primordial *qi* created heaven and earth, yin and yang, the four seasons, the sun and moon, the stars and planets, fire and water, and all things.¹⁰⁶ The ancient Chinese made the invisible *qi* visible in the form of "clouds of energy," usually represented by swirling lines shaped as Cs and commas. According to Inoue, when Buddhism arrived in China, the idea of "birth by transformation" was reinterpreted as birth by transformation by *qi*, to render the concept understandable to the Chinese.¹⁰⁷ Therefore, he has argued that the combination of these two elements reveals the syncretic view of a Buddhist "birth by transformation" that combines the Indian view of the lotus as a source of divine life and the Chinese view of *qi* as the source of life.

The dynamic representation of the sprouting-bud motif and other floral motifs in certain compositions from China and Korea certainly sustains the interpretations offered by Sakai and Inoue. Either as a phase in a process of transformation, or as a syncretic symbol of *qi*, the sprouting-bud motif does appear to contain a special generative energy in the scenes in which it is portrayed. The studies carried out by Sakai and Inoue show that Buddhism not only brought new ideas, but also a new visual repertoire. Indian Buddhism was adapted to Chinese beliefs and concepts, and the Indian and Chinese symbols of life—the lotus and *qi*, respectively—were combined to represent the idea of the source of life, especially life in the celestial realm.

The idea of an association between the sprouting-bud motif and a celestial being or transcendent was transmitted from South China to Baekje, and then to Goguryeo. Such an association is depicted in the Gangseo daemyo tomb murals from Goguryeo and on the wooden pillow found in the tomb of King Muryeong (d. 523) from Baekje. On the ceiling of the Gangseo daemyo tomb, below the two registers containing heavenly animals, groups of symmetrically arranged transcendents and Buddhist-type celestial beings appear to fly through the sky.¹⁰⁸ Many of these beings are preceded by sprouting-bud designs, and surrounded by clouds. This tomb is particularly interesting because each of the walls contains depictions of a different type of flying being: transcendents riding animals appear in the northwestern and southeastern corners (see fig. 43); self-propelled transcendents (distinguished by their clothing with sharp and pointed shapes) are found on the south side and in the southwestern corner;

53 Buddhist-type celestial beings on the bottom register of the north side of the ceiling, Gangseo daemyo tomb. Second half of 6th–first half of 7th century. Mural painting. Nampo Province.

and Buddhist-type celestial beings are depicted on the north side (fig. 53). In this case, the sprouting-bud design does not represent part of a process of transformation, but appears as a symbol that suggests the transformational origin of these beings or the idea that they are flying in the heavens.

The wooden pillow from King Muryeong's tomb, the Korean example from Baekje, is shaped roughly like a trapezoid, and its surface is divided into hexagons (figs. 54, 55). In the lowest register of hexagons, four flowers alternate with three sprouting-bud motifs. Because of the number of bud motifs, Yoshimura has described the design as a detailed phase-by-phase transformation process, and concluded that the presence of this process attests to the existence in Baekje of belief in rebirth in a pure land.[109] Yet each flower and bud motif is associated with a corresponding motif in the row above; from right to left, these motifs represent a fish-like form, a bird, and the metamorphosis of a celestial being, interspersed with hexagons containing sprays of flowers and half-palmettes. This design instead seems to be associated with the Chinese idea of heaven.

Based on all of the evidence discussed above, on the Shūchō, the sprouting-bud motif appears to represent part of a transformation process, which results in a transcendent. Many of these motifs likely were portrayed on the composition.[110] For example, in section B, a flower with a comma-shaped appendage (B-2) matches the metamorphosis, or second phase, proposed by Yoshimura. Note that B-2 is not actually attached to the floral motif that appears to its left (B-1), which may not have been part of the original design. The metamorphosis imagery would have been somewhere near A-5, (the sprouting-bud design) and would have led to a celestial being (fig. 56). Although a complete figure that corresponds to this being is not found among the extant designs, two fragments with depictions of garments with sharp, angular lines suggest that the figure might have been a transcendent. Fragment C-1 shows an incomplete figure wearing a red garment with green accents, tied around the waist with a yellow sash. The upper garment has a long right sleeve and a green ribbon that appears to be blown by the wind. The lower body is incomplete. Fragment C-2 represents the lower body of a similar figure, showing the lower section of a red jacket with a black hem and wide pants that are also being blown to the figure's right. These two fragments have been pasted together, and do not comprise a single design. When these pieces are combined, however, the resulting composite figure is a flying celestial, perhaps a transcendent (fig. 57). Although the reconstructed figure is not as elegant as the figure from the Huqiao tomb, the combined image

MATERIAL AND VISUAL EVIDENCE

54 Wooden pillow from the tomb of King Muryeong, Gongju, South Chungcheong Province. Early 6th century. Painted wood and gold foil. 23.7 x 44.2 cm. Gongju National Museum. Treasure No. 164.

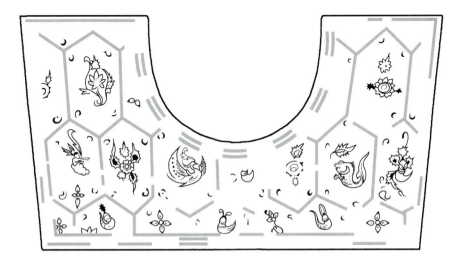

55 Line drawing of the pillow from Muryeong's tomb, fig. 54. Line drawing by Cheryl Laner, adapted from Yoshimura Rei, "Kudara Mutei ōhi ki makura ni egakareta tennin tanjō zu," 124.

56　Reconstruction of the process of birth by transformation, Tenjukoku Shūchō Mandara (A-5, B-2, reversed C-1). Based on the process as depicted at the Huqiao tomb, fig. 51. Line drawing and reconstruction by Christian Gutierrez.

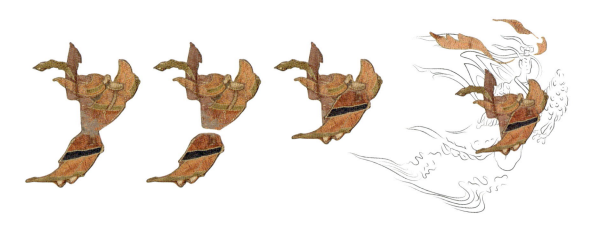

57　Reconstructed transcendent, Shūchō (C-1, C-2, A-7). Reconstruction by Christian Gutierrez.

definitely represents a Southern-style transcendent, wearing a jacket with a sash or belt tied around the waist, long pants, and a flowing scarf, and perhaps also red ribbons on the head (A-7).[111] Furthermore, based on the presence of an incomplete bud motif (A-10) on the assemblage and two damaged examples among the Shōsōin fragments, the sprouting-bud design, the metamorphosis design, and the transcendents likely were repeated multiple times in the depiction of the celestial realm.

Half-Palmette

The last design for discussion on the large fragment is the green half-palmette (A-2) located near the beak of the red bird. In addition to this example of the motif on the large fragment, two others appear in section D (see fig. 17): a red half-palmette by itself (D-2), and another included as a component of a figure emerging from a lotus (D-1). The palmette design was used widely in China from the late fifth through the seventh century, and is found in Buddhist art as well as funerary monuments and artifacts. In some cases, palmettes appear with other designs in decorative borders, and in others, swirling half- and full palmettes, along with clouds, emphasize the sense of movement of the heavens when surrounding a fantastic animal, celestial being, or monster figure.

Theories regarding the origins of this design in China are conflicting. For one view, Jessica Rawson has argued for the Western origins of the design and its arrival with Buddhism.[112] For another, Susan Bush has contended that the palmette and other floral motifs replaced the cloud scroll prevalent in the Han dynasty, and that the proliferation of these new motifs was related to the tastes of the Southern dynasties.[113] Rather than regarding these theories as opposing viewpoints, these two studies may be seen to complement each other and reveal the versatility of the palmette design as well as the dissemination of the motif through East Asia.

Rawson has asserted that the half-palmette design is derived from the Mediterranean palmette motif, which consists of elongated leaves arranged in a fan shape that resembles a palm leaf; the source of this foliage design, however, is actually the acanthus.[114] In China, the half-palmette was combined in a variety of patterns and used as an ornamental design for all types of objects and media. Rawson has stressed that, in the early eighth century, the addition of naturalistic features transformed the stylized half-palmette into floral designs such as the peony scroll.[115] The half-palmette motif was used in northern China as a decorative element in Buddhist architecture and sculpture, and also appears on a variety of utilitarian artifacts. The earliest Chinese representation of the half-palmette is found in Yungang Cave No. 9 (Datong, Shanxi Province), dated to the late fifth century. On the walls of this cave, in decorative borders, the half-palmette is used in a variety of combinations, appearing in continuous wavy scrolls or arranged symmetrically within elliptical forms.[116] By the early sixth century, the half-palmette design is also included in the halos of some Buddhist images from caves of the Northern Wei period, such as the Lotus Cave at Longmen. These round halos feature an open lotus flower in the center, framed by a half-palmette scroll.[117]

The half-palmette is also depicted on artifacts found in tombs in northern China, such as the aforementioned lacquered coffin from Guyuan and a stone pole base found in the tomb of the Northern Wei official Sima Jinlong (d. 484), also in Datong (fig. 58). In the painting on the coffin's lid, below the Queen Mother of the West and the King Father of the East, a pattern of joined diamond shapes with rounded sides covers the surface. Each diamond contains two symmetrically arranged half-palmettes and a fantastic beast. On the sides of the coffin, a different pattern consisting of half-palmettes arranged in an undulating line within a border frames the scenes.[118] The half-palmette design is represented on the sides of the stone pole base from Sima Jinlong's tomb. In this case, too, two half-palmettes are arranged symmetrically, but within ovals rather than rounded diamonds. These ovals are also inhabited by seated figures that look Indian, depicted with naked torsos, short dhotis or skirts, and long, fluttering scarves, and seated in various relaxed poses.[119]

Although Rawson's evidence for the use of the design in northern China is convincing, the leading role of the north in artistic matters during the Northern and Southern Dynasties period has been questioned by some scholars. For instance, Alexander Soper asserted that the Chinese-style Buddha image did not originate in the Northern Wei Buddhist caves, but in the south.[120] Following Soper's theory, Susan Bush has argued that floral scrolls, including the palmette design, were first represented in monuments and artifacts from the Southern dynasties, and then spread to northern China. Palmettes and half-palmettes are prominent on the pictorial tiles from the Dengxian tombs in Henan Province, dated to the late fifth century.[121] Each of these tiles, which measure 38 by 19 by 6 centimeters, bears a frame with palmette-derived designs and floral motifs. These frames enclose individual fantastic beasts surrounded by clouds and sprouting-bud motifs, scenes of filial piety, processions of soldiers and horsemen, and other subjects. Pal-

58　Figures framed by half-palmette designs on a stone pole base from the tomb of Sima Jinlong. Mid-5th century. W. 32 cm. Datong, Shanxi Province. Rubbings from Shanxi sheng Datong shi bowuguan and Shanxi sheng wenwu gongzuo weiyuanhui, "Shanxi Datong shijiazhai Beiwei Sima Jinlong mu," 25.

mette motifs are also depicted on two funerary monuments from the Liang dynasty, located near Nanjing in Jiangsu Province: the pillar of the prince Xiao Jing, who died in 523; and the aforementioned stele of Xiao Hong.[122] The sides of the stele include framed squares, each inhabited by a monster or fantastic animal surrounded by floral, palmette, and bud motifs. On the front of the stele, the main motif is a monster squatting on a reverse lotus pedestal flanked by symmetrically placed dragons, with half-palmette designs sprouting from their mouths; this feature also is seen on the engraved sarcophagus from Minneapolis (see fig. 52). A very dynamic composition of floral sprays and palmette motifs fills the space. The palmettes from the south differ from those of the north in the fluid and dynamic treatment of the design. Bush has argued further that the influence of the dynamic Southern style of

59 Headdress ornaments from the tomb of King Muryeong, Gongju, South Chungcheong Province. Early 6th century. Gold. H. 30.7 cm. Gongju National Museum. Treasure No. 154.

floral motifs is particularly evident in the paintings on the northern and eastern sides of the ceiling of Cave No. 285 at Dunhuang, dated to 538, and also in the Gongxian caves in Henan Province.[123] In short, Chinese artists seem to have taken full advantage of the versatility and decorative quality of the half-palmette design, and integrated this motif into the decorative programs of Buddhist and funerary monuments and artifacts.

The half-palmette design made its way to the Korean peninsula during the Three Kingdoms period, especially to Baekje and Goguryeo.[124] In Baekje, the flame-shaped gold plaques attached to silk headdresses from the tomb of King Muryeong and his wife are composed of repeated half-palmette motifs (fig. 59). As with the sprouting-bud design, the use of the half-palmette on Baekje pieces from the sixth century suggests a nearly direct transmission from southern China. In Goguryeo, the full and half-palmette are prominent elements in the decorative borders of tombs of the sixth and early seventh century located in the Pyongyang area, such as Jinpari No. 1, Gangseo daemyo, and Gangseo gungmyo (see fig. 32). In Jinpari No. 1, palmettes and half-palmettes swirl in the sky mingling with lotus flowers and cloud motifs as a background for

60 Leaf-shaped horse trapping from the Fujinoki tomb, Ikaruga, Nara Prefecture. 6th century. Gilt bronze. Agency for Cultural Affairs Collection. Museum of the Kashihara Archaeological Research Institute, Nara Prefecture.

the Four Divinities, whereas in Gangseo daemyo and gungmyo, half-palmette scrolls decorate the lintels of the lantern roofs.

In Japan, horse trappings decorated with the half-palmette design are found in funerary mounds dated to the late sixth century, such as the leaf-shaped ornaments in gilt bronze and saddle from the Fujinoki tomb in Ikaruga, Nara Prefecture (fig. 60). In addition, half-palmette scrolls similar to those seen on the Northern Wei Buddhist images from Longmen are engraved on the halos of the Shaka triad and the Yumedono Kannon at Hōryūji, housed in the temple's Golden Hall and Yumedono (Hall of Dreams), respectively, and dated to the seventh century. Furthermore, the half-palmette is arranged in a variety of patterns on bronze openwork; examples include the aforementioned bronze banner in the Gallery of Hōryūji Treasures and the decorative bronze borders on the Tamamushi Shrine, which also features painted palmettes.[125]

In conclusion, it seems that the half-palmette arrived in China in the late fifth century among the designs introduced through Buddhist art. Determining whether the motif was used first in the north or in the south is beyond the scope of this study; what is clear is that the half-palmette soon gained wide use in a variety of contexts in the Northern and Southern Dynasties period. The design was transmitted almost immediately from southern China to Baekje in the sixth century, as it appears on the stele of Xiao Jing and the golden plaques of King Muryeong's headdress. The design seems to have reached the Japanese islands by the mid-sixth century. Based on the Chinese and Korean examples discussed above, it is likely that the green half-palmette on the Shūchō (A-2) sprouted from the beak of the red bird, as seen with the Red Bird of the Four Divinities in Gangseo daemyo tomb (fig. 61).[126] The use of the half-palmette in the Shūchō's iconographical program confirms the existence of a common visual vocabulary in East Asia that was used in Buddhist and funerary monuments. Much like the sprouting-bud motif, the role of this design appears to have been purely decorative in some cases, while in others, the dynamic composition suggests that these motifs symbolized energy.

Through this analysis of the motifs found on the right side of section A, the only large fragment of the Shūchō that preserves part of the original composition, it is possible to conclude that the Shūchō included a representation of the celestial realm with the sun and moon, a large number of fantastic animals, multicolored clouds, and heavenly beings accompanied by the sprouting-bud design and metamorphosis imagery. Except for the sun and moon, these motifs were repeated multiple times (and because the inscription was encoded on the backs of multiple turtles, these designs must have been placed in an orderly manner). The composition might have looked like the ceiling of the Gangseo daemyo tomb (see fig. 43). In this tomb, the lintels of the lantern ceiling create four distinct registers. The bottom register contains floral designs; the one

61　Red Bird on the southwest wall of the main chamber, Gangseo daemyo tomb. Second half of 6th–first half of 7th century. Mural painting. Nampo Province.

above this shows the sprouting- and blooming-bud motifs and clouds intermingling rhythmically with different flying beings; and the two upper registers contain a variety of heavenly animals, mostly mythical birds.[127]

Designs Associated with Buddhism

In addition to the half-palmette design, two other motifs arrived in China with Buddhism: the figure emerging from a lotus (D-1), and lotus flowers and leaves (B-2, B-6, C-5, D-4, D-8, D-9, D-12).

Figure Emerging from a Lotus

In previous studies, the figure emerging from a lotus was used to support the theory that Tenjukoku was a representation of a Buddhist pure land. The idea of birth from a lotus is certainly associated with Buddhism, yet this design is also found in funerary monuments from China and the Korean peninsula, suggesting that it was integrated into Chinese funerary iconography and then transmitted to Korea and Japan. Although only one isolated motif of this type from the Shūchō has survived (D-1), three more appear in the fragments of the Tenjukoku Mandara.

The second largest of the Shūchō fragments includes the figure emerging from a lotus (fig. 62). The design has a floating sense of upward movement, and consists of a figure with hands in prayer rising from a flower with five petals, which appears to be a lotus. The figure wears an upper garment that flares upwards at the sides, and a lower garment shaped like a trumpet. To the right of the figure, the end of a scarf floats upward, and a stem ending in a half-palmette rises from the lotus flower. An incomplete design with a flame (D-12) appears below this half-palmette. Other than this large fragment, a small fragment of a torso has survived (A-8), indicating that this design, like many others in the composition, was repeated.[128]

Yoshimura Rei, who has called this motif "birth by transformation in a lotus flower" (*renge keshō*), found the design in the Buddhist cave temples of the Northern Wei dynasty at Yungang, Longmen, and Gongxian, as well as on the Shūchō fragments.[129] He has contended that the motif was based on the Indian idea of birth from a lotus.[130] After studying many examples, Yoshimura concluded that this design also represented the final product of a process of transformation portrayed in three or four phases, with some variations. In the first phase, a head emerges from the lotus flower, which acts like a womb. The second phase portrays the head and torso of the figure, who appears with a flowing scarf and hands in prayer (similar to the example on the Shūchō); and the final phase is the figure of a bodhisattva standing on a lotus pedestal, or a Buddhist celestial being flying through the sky.[131]

Yoshimura studied Buddhist sutras and inscriptions on Buddhist sculptures to determine the meaning of this design. His name for the motif came from an idea stated in two sutras, the *Lotus Sutra* (S. *Saddharmapuṇḍarīka Sūtra*; J. *Hokkekyō*) and the *Buddha of Measureless Life Sutra* (S. *Sukhāvatīvyūha Sūtra*; J. *Muryōjukyō*). The first sutra states,

> The Buddha declared to the *bhikṣus*: In the ages yet to come, if there is a good man or a good woman who, hearing the Devadatta Chapter of the Scripture of the Blossom of the Fine Dharma [*Lotus Sutra*], with a pure heart believes and reveres it, evincing no doubts or uncertainties, he shall not fall to the level of hell, hungry ghosts, or beasts, but shall be reborn in the presence of the Buddhas of all directions, constantly hearing his scripture where ever he may be reborn. *If he is in the presence of the Buddha, he shall be reborn in a lotus blossom.*[132]

According to the second sutra, in the chapter about the types of believers, when people of superior faith die, they are reborn in Sukhāvatī, the Pure Land of Ultimate Bliss, where "they are reborn naturally and miraculously in the center of a lotus made of the seven precious substances, and they dwell in the state from which there is no falling back."[133] Based on these two sutras, Yoshimura concluded that the "birth by transformation in a lotus" design was a visual representation of the aspiration to be reborn in a pure land, a belief that spread during the Northern Wei period.[134]

MATERIAL AND VISUAL EVIDENCE

62   Figure emerging from a lotus, Shūchō (D-1), detail of fig. 17.

63   Line drawing of the ceiling of Gongxian Cave No. 4. Early 6th century. Henan Province.

Stylistically, the figure emerging from the lotus on the Shūchō fragment is similar to those found in the Gongxian caves.[135] Five caves, dated to around the early sixth century, include the design in their iconographical programs. The figures are found in three specific areas. First, the design is repeated on the ceilings of Cave Nos. 1, 3, and 4. The flat ceilings of these three caves are divided into squares, each of which contains different figures. Motifs of a figure emerging from a lotus alternate rhythmically with three different designs of lotus flowers combined with palmettes and half-palmettes (figs. 63, 63a). Second, the figure emerging from a lotus is also repeated on the uppermost section of the walls, alternating with an arch motif or a flower in a horizontal register (fig. 64).[136] The

63a Figure emerging from a lotus on the ceiling of Gongxian Cave No. 4.

64   Line drawing of the south wall of Gongxian Cave No. 4. Early 6th century. Henan Province.

third location of the design is in the spandrels between the niches containing Buddha images, where the figure emerging from the lotus is flanked by two flying celestial beings on clouds and accompanied by the sprouting-bud motif. Because all of these designs show a symmetrical composition, it is likely that the motif on the Shūchō fragment is incomplete. A scarf, half-palmette, and perhaps also a flame design must have been present to the left of the figure as well (fig. 65).

Although Yoshimura's arguments for naming the motif "birth by transformation in a lotus" are compelling, the term "figure emerging from a lotus" may be more appropriate due to evidence from tombs in China and Goguryeo. A pictorial tile with the design has been found in the Dengxian tombs (fig. 66); in addition, on the Korean peninsula, Yoshimura has located the motif of a head appearing to emerge from a flower in the Goguryeo tomb of Samsilchong (Tomb of the Three Chambers), dated to the fifth century. The style of this figure is similar to those seen at Yungang, as both show a lotus with a head sprouting from it.[137] Other examples of figures emerging from lotuses

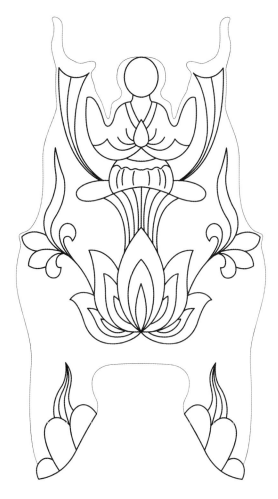

65 Reconstructed figure emerging from a lotus, Shūchō (D-1, D-12). Line drawing by Summer Furzer.

66 Line drawing of a figure emerging from a lotus on a pictorial tile from the Dengxian tombs. 5th–6th century. Henan Province. Line drawing by Summer Furzer, adapted from Henan Sheng wen hua ju wen wu gong zuo dui, *Deng Xian cai se hua xiang zhuan mu*, 36.

are found in the Ji'an region, such as in Jangcheon Tomb No. 1, dated to the mid-fifth century; and Ohoebun Tomb No. 4, dated to the sixth century. These two tombs merit some exploration because, in both cases, the figures emerging from lotus blossoms alternate with a flaming design, which also appears to have been the case on the Shūchō. In addition to the incomplete flaming design (D-12) next to the figure emerging from a lotus, a flaming flower has also survived (D-4); another small piece with the same motif is found among the fragments preserved in the Shōsōin.

In Jangcheon Tomb No. 1, flaming flowers alternate with the motif of a head sprouting from a flower. Interestingly, this is the only tomb with a confirmed Buddhist iconographical program that includes representations of a Buddha, bodhisattvas, and celestial beings on the ceiling. The first level of the lantern roof contains depictions of celestial animals; on the second level, the east wall features a Buddha and worshippers, and the north and south walls, bodhisattvas; and on the third and fourth levels, celestial beings are portrayed. In the corners of the second level, flowers with two

67 Line drawings of the east and north walls of Jangcheon Tomb No. 1. Mid-5th century. Ji'an City, Jilin Province.

sprouting heads are painted. This same design alternates with flaming flowers above the door lintel (fig. 67).[138] Because the iconographical program of this tomb is definitely Buddhist, we could surmise that the figures emerging from the flowers represent the idea of birth in a Buddhist land.

The same argument cannot be made for Ohoebun Tomb No. 4. The iconographical program of this tomb is Daoist; included are figures of transcendents riding on fantastic animals, as well as the mythical Chinese culture heroes Fuxi and Nuwa. Each of the Four Divinities is located on the wall corresponding to its cardinal direction. These figures are painted over a complex background that consists of three rows of rhomboidal shapes arranged as a net. Every other rhombus serves as a frame for a palmette flanked on each side by flames that look similar to D-12. In the alternating rhombuses, a figure dressed as a Chinese scholar stands on an open lotus above two symmetrically placed half-palmettes, while sprouting buds and lotus flowers fill in the blank space (fig. 68). Although the styles of representation of the figures emerging from lotuses at Jangcheon and Ohoebun differ, they both seem to portray the same idea in the Buddhist and Daoist contexts. These two different examples support Wu Hung's aforementioned notion that the decorative programs employed in tombs were personal choices. All inhabitants of Goguryeo did not hold the same beliefs, and different cultural repertoires coexisted.

Based on the examples discussed above, the motif of a figure emerging from a lotus likely was repeated multiple times on the embroidered curtains, alternating with flaming flowers (D-4), as at Jangcheon. It is plausible that, as seen in the Jangcheon and Gongxian murals, these motifs appeared just below the representation of the celestial realm.

Lotus Flowers and Leaves

As seen in monuments and artifacts from China and Korea, the lotus flower, as well as the palmette design, enhanced many compositions. On the assemblage of embroidered fragments, besides the motifs of the figure emerging from a lotus and the flaming flower, other floral designs have survived, such as an isolated smaller flower (B-6), lotus leaves (C-5, D-9), and another flower and leaf attached to a triangular design (D-8). In addition, many other small fragments bearing images of flowers and leaves are kept in the Shōsōin collection.

Because Yoshimura has associated the figure emerging from a lotus with the Buddhist belief in birth from a lotus, he has proposed that, on the Shūchō, this birth took place in the pond. Using the thirteenth-century remains of a pond (C-11), he has argued that the first phase of the rebirth was represented by a lotus flower (D-8), followed by the flaming flower (D-4), and then by the figure emerging from a lotus (D-1).[139] Ōhashi has accepted Yoshimura's proposal because it supports his hypothesis that Tenjukoku was Amida's Pure Land.[140]

Judging from the compositions of the Goguryeo tomb murals, it is likely that a pond with lotus flowers and leaves was also part of the Shūchō's composition. The pond, however, was not associated with birth in paradise, but rather was included as a component of an ideal landscape. Two examples from Goguryeo support this theory. At the Deokhungri tomb, dated to the fifth century, the east wall of the rear chamber is divided into four cells; the upper left cell contains two large, stylized, blooming lotus flowers with stems, accompanied by additional smaller flowers (see fig. 39). At the sixth-century Jinpari Tomb No. 4, a landscape with a lotus pond is depicted in the corridor of the tomb. The pond is situated between mountains covered with trees, and the lotus leaves and flowers are symmetrically arranged and surrounded by palmettes and sprouting-bud designs in the sky. Based on this surviving water design and the extant lotus flowers, leaves, half-palmettes, and sprouting-bud motifs, a similar landscape for the Shūchō can be reconstructed from the fragments (fig. 69).[141]

68 East wall of Ohoebun Tomb No. 4. Late 6th–early 7th century. Mural painting. Dawangcun, Ji'an City, Jilin Province.

CONCLUSION: VISUAL EVIDENCE

The vast majority of the designs on the Shūchō fragments, except for the turtle motif with graphs, have precedents in the funerary and Buddhist monuments of China and the Korean peninsula.[142] Based on the foregoing analysis of the surviving representations of the moon (A-1) and, importantly, the designs on the largest extant fragment (with a half-palmette, red bird, cloud design, turtle with graphs, and sprouting-bud motif), it is clear that the celestial realm as visualized by the Chinese in the Northern and Southern Dynasties period was part of the iconographical program of the Shūchō. Some designs, such as the representation of the moon, the red bird, and the cloud, had been included in funerary iconography since the Han dynasty. Other designs, such as the lotus flower, the sprouting-bud motif and its associated celestial being, and the figure emerging from a lotus, arrived with Buddhism and were employed profusely in cave temples from the Northern and Southern Dynasties dated to the late fifth and sixth centuries.

The new pictorialization of the celestial realm combining Han designs and Buddhist elements was established in China during this time, and was then transmitted to the Korean peninsula. In some cases (notably in Baekje), only isolated designs, such as

FABRICATING THE *TENJUKOKU SHŪCHŌ MANDARA* AND PRINCE SHŌTOKU'S AFTERLIVES

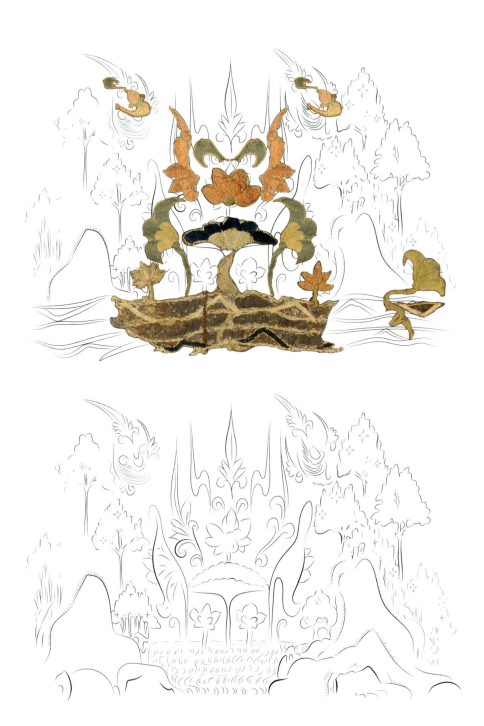

69 Reconstruction of a lotus pond, Tenjukoku Shūchō Mandara (A-5, B-6, C-5, C-10, C-11, D-2, D-7, D-8, D-9), by Christian Gutierrez. Based on lotus pond at Jinpari Tomb No. 4. 6th century. Pyongyang. Line drawing by Christian Gutierrez, adapted from Yoshimura Rei, "Nanchō tennin zuzō no Hokuchō oyobi shūhen shokoku e no denba," 24.

the sprouting-bud motif, were introduced by the early sixth century. In other instances, most of the Chinese designs were adopted, as seen especially in the Goguryeo tombs dated to the fifth through seventh centuries. Although some of the designs on the Shūchō fragments can be traced back to China, the direct source for most was the Korean peninsula, especially Goguryeo and Baekje. This is particularly evident in the surviving fragments representing people, both men and women, who wear garments similar to those portrayed in the Goguryeo tomb murals.

The partial reconstruction of the composition of the Shūchō proposed here is based on the more complete Chinese and Korean examples. It is likely that the lower section of the composition included scenes of this world, and the upper section, the heavenly realm. The former included processions of men and women, like the procession depicted in the Susanri tomb, with females to the east and males to the west. Gatherings also were portrayed, as suggested by the seated male figure wearing a black jacket, and the three headless seated figures. In addition, somewhere the composition contained a pond with lotuses, or perhaps more than one, as portrayed in Jinpari Tomb No. 4.

In the representation of the celestial realm, the turtle designs with graphs must have dominated the composition, because a large number of them were required to carry the inscription. The turtles must have been placed in an ordered and regularly spaced fashion to facilitate the reading of the inscription. As Ōhashi has pointed out, these motifs mingled with the other designs, as indicated by the only large surviving fragment.[143] Thus, the turtles were interspersed with the representation of the sun and moon (the former to the east and the latter to the west), dynamic clouds, a variety of heavenly animals and celestial beings, and sprouting-bud designs to animate the scene. This heavenly realm probably looked like the ceiling of the Gangseo daemyo tomb (see figs. 42, 43), where all of these designs (except for the turtles) are portrayed in a very organized manner. Fantastic animals appear in the top two registers; below them, celestial beings alternate with sprouting-bud motifs and clouds; and the lowest register features a floral design. On the Shūchō, it seems probable that an alternating pattern of figures emerging from lotuses and flaming flowers (as seen at Jangcheon Tomb No. 1; see fig. 67) marked the border between the heavenly realm and the scenes of this world.

It is evident that, in designing the Shūchō, the artists involved used the pan–East Asian visual vocabulary and conventions found in funerary and Buddhist art of the fifth through seventh centuries in China and Korea. As in China, while conventions were followed in the design, individual choices also were made. The individual choice most prominently displayed on the Shūchō seems to have been the use of turtles with graphs to carry the inscription.

Due to the few surviving designs on the fragments and the scarcity of comparative visual material, it is difficult to use stylistic criteria as a precise dating tool. Yet the style of representation of the male and female figures on the fragments is closer to that of the Goguryeo figures of the fifth and sixth centuries, particularly in terms of body proportions and the three-quarter view, than to the more naturalistic figures seen in the Takamatsuzuka tomb, dated to the late seventh or early eighth century. Based solely on the material and visual evidence (fabrics, embroidery stitches, and designs), the Shūchō could have been created at any time after the death of Prince Shōtoku in 622. For a more definitive conclusion, it is crucial to analyze the inscription, as this was an intrinsic part of the composition, and also consider the historical and cultural context of the Shūchō's creation.

2

The Embroidered Inscription and the *Imperial Biography*

The fragments of the Shūchō, the oldest extant examples of embroidered textiles in Japan, also include remnants of an inscription. In an unusual touch, this inscription is recorded on the backs of turtle motifs, each turtle carrying four graphs. A total of nine graphs have survived from the Shūchō: four graphs, 部間人公, appear on a turtle on the assemblage (see facing page); and five small pieces with the graphs 奈, 甘, 居, 佛, and 娶 are held in the Shōsōin collection (see fig. 2). The Shūchō and its inscription were intertwined from the creation of the embroidered curtains, but the inscription took on a life of its own when it was recorded in the aforementioned *Jōgū Shōtoku hōō teisetsu*, or *Imperial Biography*, one of the many documents associated with the cult of Prince Shōtoku.[1]

Scholars generally have accepted that the inscription recorded in the *Imperial Biography* is that found on the Shūchō, because a postscript mentions the unusual feature of it being recorded on turtles. Furthermore, the nine embroidered graphs listed above are definitely found in the manuscript. Such a small number of characters might not be enough evidence to support that this transcription is legitimate. Two documents from the late thirteenth century also include the text of the embroidered inscription, as do later writings.[2] In the 1960s, the scholar Iida Mizuho studied the different transcriptions, and concluded that the original inscription was copied directly from the embroidery to the *Imperial Biography* in the late tenth or early eleventh century, and also to the other documents in the late thirteenth century. In addition, he noted that the various versions contain a few differences, including omitted or different graphs, or a changed sequence, but that these changes do not substantially alter the content of the inscription.[3]

The first half of the inscription recorded in the *Imperial Biography* contains a genealogy; the second half narrates the circumstances of the embroidery's manufacture, and the people involved in the process. People mentioned include rulers, princes and princesses, ministers, and craftsmen of the Asuka period. The inscription bears dates suggesting that the embroidered panels (and the embroidered inscription) may have been produced in the first quarter of the seventh century; therefore, the inscription has been considered an important historical text of the Asuka period. The corpus of Japanese-language scholarship about the inscription is vast. This text has been the focus of study for historians, epigraphers, linguists, paleographers, art historians, architectural historians, and scholars of literature and

Turtle with graphs, Shūchō, detail of fig. 11.

Buddhism. Many eminent scholars of ancient Japan have written about the inscription, but no consensus on its date of compilation has yet been reached. At present only a small number of scholars accept the early-seventh-century date, while the vast majority agree on a late-seventh-century date, and some propose dates ranging from the eighth to the eleventh century.

To explore the inscription in multiple contexts, this chapter begins with the section "Writing in Ancient Japan," which presents a brief overview of the origins of writing in the country with the purpose of clarifying assumptions regarding the spread of writing in the court during the Asuka period. The second section, "The Inscription in the *Imperial Biography*," includes a translation of the inscription; and the third, "Prince Shōtoku and Princess Tachibana," explores the lives of two of the royals mentioned in the text. The fourth section, "Issues with the *Imperial Biography* Inscription," addresses selected past and current interpretations of, and positions on, problematic issues pertaining to the inscription. Clarifying these controversies is helpful for proposing a more precise dating of the text.

The fifth section, "Role of Kinship Groups," is devoted to an examination of the kinship groups associated with the project's supervisor and designers. A closer look at these groups reveals that they might have played an active role in the creation of the embroidery. Finally, the last section, "The *Jōgu Shōtoku hōō teisetsu*," is a short discussion of the *Imperial Biography* and its contents. Studies on this document have shown that inscriptions from two bronze sculptures in Hōryūji's Golden Hall, along with the *Shūchō's* inscription, were added to the manuscript in the late tenth or early eleventh century. The addition of these texts created an evidence-based narrative about the role of Shōtoku in the establishment of Buddhism in Japan, and changed the original meaning of the inscription on the Shūchō.

WRITING IN ANCIENT JAPAN

Until recently, and despite a lack of evidence, the Asuka period was believed to be a time when literacy flourished in Japan. Prince Shōtoku was marshaled as a paragon of literacy, as stated in many of the textual sources associated with him.[4] For instance, in *Nihon shoki*, the prince is credited with writing the Seventeen-Article Constitution, lecturing on the *Lion's Roar Sutra* and the *Lotus Sutra*, and also compiling, with Soga no Umako (ca. 551–626), the *Record of the Heavenly Sovereigns* (*Tennō ki*), the *Record of the Country* (*Kokki*), and others.[5] In addition, commentaries on the *Lotus*, *Vimalakīrti*, and *Lion's Roar Sutra* said to have been written by the prince are among the treasures held by Hōryūji.[6] In the same way, *Gangōji garan engi narabi ni ruki shizaichō* (Account of the Establishment of the Monastery Gangōji and List of Accumulated Treasures, 747; hereafter, *Gangōji engi*) states that, "by imperial command, [Prince Umayado Toyotomimi] made a record of the origins of Gangōji [another name for Asukadera], the vow of the Empress Toyomike [Suiko], and various ministers."[7] Current scholarship recognizes that the content of these sources is hagiographic rather than historical.

In addition to these references to the writing abilities of the prince, evidence of literacy in the prince's day is provided by a group of texts (including inscriptions and genealogies) that is believed to date to the late sixth and early seventh centuries. Because of this date, Ōya Tōru has classified them as "Suiko chō ibun" (Remnant Texts of the Suiko Court); they are listed in Table 2. Except for the three texts inscribed on extant bronze monuments (nos. 3, 5, and 7), the rest are known only through versions recorded in later sources.

Ōya has dated these texts to the time of Great King Suiko because their content suggests that they were written sometime in the late sixth or early seventh century; furthermore, some of them were written in *man'yōgana*, classical Chinese graphs used as phonograms (rather than ideograms) to transcribe the sounds of native words. Ōya's study focused on tracing the origins of the sounds of cer-

Inscription locations/alleged dates	Recorded in/date
1. Stele from Dōgo Springs in Iyo (Ehime)/596	*Shaku Nihongi*, quoted from *Iyo fudoki*/Kamakura period
2. Finial of the pagoda of Gangōji (Asukadera)/596	*Gangōji engi*/747
3. Halo of Yakushi image in Hōryūji Golden Hall/607	*Imperial Biography*/10th–11th century
4. Mandorla of Buddha from Gangōji/609	*Gangōji engi*
5. Mandorla of Shaka triad in Hōryūji Golden Hall/623	*Imperial Biography*
6. Tenjukoku Shūchō/622	*Imperial Biography*
7. Mandorla of Shaka triad from Hōryūji collection/628	
8. Quote from *Jōgūki*	*Shaku Nihongi*, also in *Shōtoku Taishi Heishi den zakkanmon*/Kamakura period
9. Genealogy of *Jōgū Taishi*	*Shōtoku Taishi Heishi den zakkanmon*

Table 2 Remnant Texts of the Suiko Court

tain *man'yōgana*, and he concluded that these were derived from the sounds assigned to the graphs in China's Zhou dynasty (1046–256 BCE).[8]

Recent studies, however, reveal that the use of *man'yōgana*, and writing in general, was introduced to Japan from the Korean peninsula in the fifth century, specifically from the kingdom of Baekje.[9] But to understand the process of the transmission of writing, it is necessary to address China. Chinese graphs were invented to represent native Chinese words, but the Chinese also developed a transcription system to write foreign words using Chinese graphs.[10] To transliterate foreign words, a graph with a similar reading (sound) as the word or syllable in question was used, so graphs representing specific Chinese words could also function as phonograms. On the Korean peninsula, the kingdom of Goguryeo was the first to adopt the Chinese writing system. It is likely that the Chinese taught Goguryeo's scribes the phonogram transcription system, as the Chinese writing system was being adopted and adapted to the language of Goguryeo. It is not clear how this system was introduced to Baekje, but after analyzing epigraphs and texts from Goguryeo, Baekje, Silla, and Japan's Yamato region containing phonograms, John Bentley has concluded that the evidence suggests that scribes from Baekje taught Yamato's scribes classical Chinese as well as the use of phonograms.[11]

Because evidence of the development of writing and literacy in the Yamato court in the late sixth and early seventh centuries is not substantial, the early dates of most of these Remnant Texts have been questioned, and form the subject of heated debate (particularly those recorded in *Gangōji engi* and the *Imperial Biography*, including the inscriptions on the bronze sculptures).[12] Interestingly, most of these texts are related to Shōtoku; therefore, some scholars have suggested that they must be reassessed as documents of the cult of the prince, rather than as historical documents.[13]

David Lurie has addressed the complexities of the adoption and adaptation of the Chinese writing system brought to Japan by way of the three kingdoms of Korea. Contrary to previous theories, he contends that writing and literacy only spread in ancient Japan in the late seventh century.[14] As he explains, the evidence suggests that inscribed objects arrived in the Japanese archipelago as early as the first century CE, when the Wa (inhabitants of the Japanese islands) were included in the Chinese tributary system. In addition, excavated artifacts dated to the fifth century, such as bronze swords and mirrors with inscriptions written by scribes from the Korean peninsula, constitute evidence of diplomatic relations between these two geographic areas. Lurie has argued, however, that these objects functioned simply as symbols of political authority or spiritual power, rather than as carriers of messages. In his view, such inscribed objects were used in a society that was largely illiterate until the seventh century.[15]

The assumption also has been made that when Buddhism was introduced to the Japanese islands in the mid-sixth century, it brought with it a corpus of sutras, and consequently literacy. Lurie, however, has stated that the texts narrating the introduction of the new religion—*Nihon shoki*, *Gangōji engi*, and the *Imperial Biography*—do not make any reference to the Buddhist practices of copying or reading sutras, or their ceremonial use. *Nihon shoki* mentions sutras as one of the items sent by King Seongmyeong (r. 523–54) of Baekje in 552 during the reign of Great King Kinmei, and also sent in 577 during the reign of Great King Bidatsu (r. 572–85). Moreover, specific sutra titles are only mentioned in records of lectures given by the prince during Suiko's reign. As most scholars now agree that these lectures merely comprise one more element in the construction of the Shōtoku myth, concrete evidence of literacy in the first quarter of the seventh century is absent.[16]

Particularly important to our understanding of writing in the Yamato court is the discovery of *mokkan* (wooden tablets used as surfaces for writing), which have been found in archaeological excavations all over Japan. These items have helped to demonstrate the technical innovations in writing that allowed for the growth of literacy from the mid-seventh century. For instance, *mokkan* dated to the late seventh century exhibit writings that use Chinese graphs, but the texts are not in Chinese. The graphs only serve as logographs (characters representing words or phrases) associated with Japanese words, and in most cases these logographs are arranged in accordance with Japanese rather than Chinese syntax. In addition to their role as logographs, Chinese graphs were also used as phonograms to spell out syllables (regardless of the graphs' meaning).[17] *Mokkan* also have revealed connections with the few inscribed artifacts from the Korean peninsula that have been found in Japan, confirming the statements in historical sources that scribes from the three kingdoms played a key role in the transmission of writing to Japan.[18]

Although extant evidence suggests that writing as a system of communication in the Yamato court was adopted from the three kingdoms of the Korean peninsula, especially Baekje, scant written material has survived in Korea to allow us to retrace the expansion of writing in the Three Kingdoms period itself.[19] Members of immigrant kinship groups served as scribes and readers for the powerful Yamato chiefdoms after bringing writing technology in the fifth century, but not much is known about their activities due to a gap in the evidence of writing in the sixth century.[20] What is clear is that the spread of writing through the Japanese archipelago in the late seventh century went hand in hand with political events on the peninsula, particularly the defeat of Baekje in 663, which led to the unification of the peninsula by Silla. As a consequence of these events, a massive migration to the Japanese archipelago took place in the last quarter of the seventh century. This new wave of migration and the unification of Silla also led to the building of a bureaucratic, centralized state in Japan, which culminated in the compilation of *Kojiki* (Records of Ancient Matters) in 712 and *Nihon shoki* in 720 by the Yamato court.

THE INSCRIPTION IN THE *IMPERIAL BIOGRAPHY*

As mentioned above, only nine embroidered graphs from the Shūchō have survived. Four other turtles are extant (exhibiting a total of sixteen graphs), but these were made in the thirteenth century and did not exist when the inscription was transcribed into the *Imperial Biography*. Because the use of graphs on turtles comprises an unusual way of recording an inscription, this motif is mentioned in all of the sources that include the inscription, facilitating its identification. A postscript to the *Imperial Biography* states that the inscription was carried on turtles' shells, but does not mention their number.[21] The first document to mention the figure of one hundred turtles is *Chūgūji engi: Chūgūji mandara ama Shinnyo kishō tō no koto* (The Chūgūji Account: About the Prayer of the Nun Shinnyo and the Mandara of Chūgūji) of 1274.

Some special considerations must be taken into account with the inscription as recorded in the *Imperial Biography*. It seems risky to assert that the *Imperial Biography*'s version is an exact copy of the original embroidered inscription, as fabric is a fragile material and the state of preservation of the Shūchō when the inscription was transcribed is unknown. In addition, the oldest extant manuscript of the *Imperial Biography*, currently at the temple Chion'in in Kyoto, is dated to the mid-eleventh century.[22] To further complicate matters, some discrepancies exist between the Chion'in manuscript's version of the inscription and later examples. The former contains 398 graphs, whereas all of the later versions include 400 characters.

Yet Iida Mizuho has demonstrated that the omissions and discrepancies do not substantially alter the content of the inscription. For this reason, his reconstructed version, with four hundred graphs, has become the authoritative text used by most scholars. (The four-hundred figure is based on the thirteenth-century sources, which emphasize that the inscription was carried by one hundred turtles with four graphs each.) In his study, Iida has listed seventeen differences between the *Imperial Biography*'s inscription and later versions, the main issues being the order of the graphs, omissions, and some different graphs.[23] Iida has explained that the main reason for the discrepancies might be that some of the scribes were confused by the order of the graphs in the uncommon text embroidered on the turtles. The graphs were meant to be read in the following order: top, right, left, and bottom. Certain versions of the inscription reveal that some scribes did not follow this order, or perhaps, because the fabric was damaged and they could not read some of the graphs, they came up with their own (possibly altering the order as well).

The possibility that the thirteenth-century versions could be redrafts of the *Imperial Biography* inscription has been considered by Iida. He has confirmed, however, that the thirteenth-century renderings are not copies of the *Imperial Biography* version, but were copied directly from the artifact. Proof of his hypothesis is the turtle with the graphs 皇前日啓 (turtle no. 69) from the thirteenth-century mandara. These four graphs appear in the thirteenth-century documents, but are missing from the Chion'in version. Thus, it is likely that the four graphs must have been on the Shūchō, but were missed by the *Imperial Biography*'s scribe. Iida has concluded that the inscription was copied directly from the embroidered artifact twice: in the middle of the Heian period (794–1185) by the scribe of the *Imperial Biography*, and in the thirteenth century, when the Shūchō was rediscovered.[24] Not all scholars agree with Iida. For instance, Okimori Takuya has suggested that it is impossible to confirm that the *Imperial Biography*'s version is a faithful rendition of the original inscription, and that perhaps some of the troubling issues could be the result of the scribe's choices.[25]

Because Iida's arguments are convincing, his reconstructed version is used in this study. The four hundred graphs in one hundred groups of four are reproduced in figure 70, and the inscription is translated into English below.[26] Most of the manuscripts studied by Iida do not divide the graphs into groups of four, or into columns with graphs in multiples of four, except for the remains of a calligraphy

70 Shūchō inscription recorded in the *Imperial Biography*, as reconstructed by Iida Mizuho, "Tenjukoku Shūchō mei no fukugen ni tsuite," 33. Diagram of distribution of characters on turtles by Jason Lin, with numbering by Summer Furzer.

piece, dated to the Kamakura period (1185–1333), containing twelve characters of the inscription per column.[27] In fact, the first document that shows the graphs divided into one hundred sets of four is dated to the nineteenth century.[28]

The Shūchō inscription recorded in the *Imperial Biography* reads as follows:

> The Heavenly Sovereign (*sumera no mikoto* or *tennō*) Amekuni oshihiraki hironiha no mikoto [Kinmei], who ruled the *tenka* from the palace of Shikishima, took the daughter of Senior Minister (*ōomi*) Soga named Iname no Sukune as a wife.[29] Her name was Kitashi hime no mikoto and he gave her the title of Senior Queen Consort (*ōkisaki*).[30] She gave birth to Tachibana toyohi no mikoto [Yōmei], and to his younger sister Toyomi kekashikiya hime no mikoto [Suiko]. He also took a younger sister of the Senior Queen Consort named Oane no mikoto as a wife, and made her his Queen Consort (*kisaki*). She gave birth to Anahobe Hashihito no hime miko. A son of the Shikishima palace sovereign named Nunakura no Futotama shiki no mikoto [Bidatsu] took his younger half-sister Toyomi kekashikiya hime no mikoto as a wife, and gave her the title of Senior Queen Consort. She ruled the *tenka* from the Osada palace and gave birth to a prince named Owari. Tachibana toyohi no mikoto took his half-sister princess Anahobe Hashihito as a wife, and gave her the title of Senior Queen Consort. She lived in the Ikebe palace and gave birth to Toyotomimi no mikoto. He took the daughter of Prince (*ōkimi*) Owari named Tachibana no Oiratsume as a wife, and made her his Queen Consort.[31] In the evening of the twenty-first day *mizunoto-tori* of the twelfth month of the year *kanoto-mi* (Suiko 29, or 621), the queen mother (*haha no miko*) Anahobe Hashihito passed away. The following year, in the middle of the night of the twenty-second day *kinoe-inu* of the second month, the prince passed away. The devastated Princess Tachibana went to see the Heavenly Sovereign [Suiko, her grandmother] and said, "I grieve the loss of my prince (*ōkimi*) and the queen mother. My prince said, 'This world is empty; the only truth is the Buddha' (*seken wa munashi, tada hotoke nomi kore makoto nari*).[32] He appreciated this *minori*.[33] As a reward, my prince must have been born in 'The Land of Heavenly Lifespan' (Tenjukoku). But, I cannot visualize that land. Please, somehow create an illustration of the place to which my prince was transported (or where he resides)." The Heavenly Sovereign was deeply moved and said, "I cannot see my grandchild suffering." She commanded a group of lady attendants of the court (*uneme*) to make two panels of embroidered curtains (*shūchō nichō*). The design was drawn by Yamato no Aya no Makken, Koma no Kasei, and Aya no Nukakori, and the manufacture was supervised by Kurahitobe Hata no Kuma.

A postscript probably written when the inscription was transcribed states that "the two panels of embroidered curtains were in a repository at Hōryūji, and the graphs were embroidered on turtles." In addition, commentaries explain the readings of some of the graphs, and also state that "Tenjukoku is a synonym for heaven."[34]

In the above translation, the sentences of the inscription appear clear and straightforward, presenting the genealogy of a couple, Prince Toyotomimi and Princess Tachibana (fig. 71), followed by the dates of the deaths of Princess Tachibana's mother-

THE EMBROIDERED INSCRIPTION AND THE *IMPERIAL BIOGRAPHY*

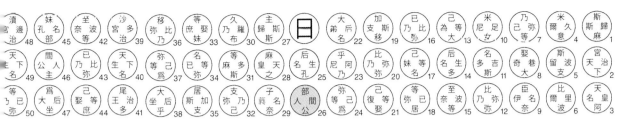

in-law and husband, in 621 and 622, respectively. After the deaths of these two beloved figures in her life, Tachibana asked her grandmother, Suiko, to have a visual representation made of her husband's afterlife abode, which she called Tenjukoku. Seeing her granddaughter's grief, Suiko granted Tachibana her wish by ordering the lady attendants of the court to manufacture two panels of embroidered curtains. The last sentence in the inscription lists the names of the draftsmen and supervisor.

Tōno Haruyuki has explained that this inscription is an account of the people involved in, and the circumstances of, the creation of the Shūchō, rather than a record of the manufacture and dedication of an artifact, as is usually the case with inscribed objects. The date of manufacture is not recorded in this epigraph.[35] Yet, because the inscription suggests that the artifact was made after the deaths of Anahobe and Shōtoku, and because of the apparent involvement of Suiko, it has been assumed that the Shūchō was made between 622 and 628 (after the death of the prince and before Suiko's death), and thus may be dated to the Asuka period. Nevertheless, issues and controversies surrounding this inscription do not allow for such a straightforward conclusion.

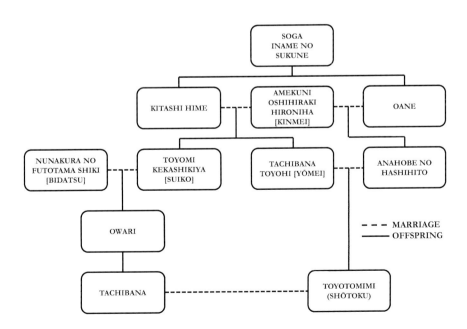

71   Genealogy of Prince Toyotomimi and Princess Tachibana from the Shūchō inscription as recorded in the *Imperial Biography*. Chart by Ken C. Pradel.

89

PRINCE SHŌTOKU AND PRINCESS TACHIBANA

Among the many names used to refer to Shōtoku in the early historical sources, the choice of Toyotomimi in the Shūchō inscription bears examination. Typically, ancient historical sources include a variety of names for the same person, especially rulers. Wada Atsumu has noted that, in the entries from around the second half of the seventh century in *Kojiki* and *Nihon shoki*, and in some inscriptions, several names are used for each ruler. For one example, as Wada explains, the given name (*jitsumei*) of Great King Tenji (r. 661–72) was Prince Kazuraki; his popular name (*tsūshō*) was Naka no Ōe; his Japanese-style posthumous name was Ame mikoto hirakasu wake; and after his death, as a sign of respect, he was referred to by his palace name, the ruler of the Ōmi Ōtsu palace. In the same way, the given name of Heavenly Sovereign Tenmu (r. 673–86) was Prince Ōama; his Japanese-style posthumous name was Ama no nunahara oki no mahito; and after his death, he was referred to as the ruler of the Asuka Kiyomihara palace.[36] The names for these rulers used in modern historical writing (i.e., Tenji and Tenmu) are their Chinese-style posthumous names. Between 762 and 764 (Tenpyō hōji 6–8), such names were assigned to past rulers from the mythical Jinmu (r. 660–585 BCE, in traditional reckoning) to Jitō, and also to Monmu (r. 697–707), Genmei (r. 707–15), and Genshō (r. 715–24).

In the case of Prince Shōtoku, although this name is widely used in modern historiography, it is not commonly found in ancient or medieval Japanese sources. In ancient documents, the prince is known by a variety of names, yet most of the time, he is simply called Taishi (prince). When multiple names are used, the literal translations of these names might reveal how the prince was perceived. For instance, in *Kojiki*, Shōtoku is the only prince or princess recorded by not only a palace name, but two additional names as well: Ue no miya (or Kamitsumiya) Umayado Toyotomimi (literally, "Upper Palace, Stable Door, Gifted with the Power of Discernment"). Ōyama Seiichi has suggested that the recording of multiple names for the prince demonstrates that his deification began before the compilation of *Kojiki*.[37]

Slightly later sources include the names Umayado Toyotomimi, and hints of his deification as King of the Buddhist Dharma are indicated by the addition of the term *minori*, or Buddhist Law. For example, *Nihon shoki* states that his name was Umayado no mikoto (Prince Stable Door), also known as Toyomimito Shōtoku (Gifted with the Power of Discernment, Saintly Virtue) or Toyotomimi Minori no Ōkimi (Gifted with the Power of Discernment, Great King of the Dharma), or Minori no nushi no mikoto (King Master of the Dharma).[38] Similarly, in *Hōryūji garan engi narabi ni ruki shizaichō* (Account of the Establishment of Hōryūji and List of Accumulated Treasures, 747; hereafter, *Hōryūji engi*), he is called Tōgū Jōgū Shōtoku Hōō (Eastern Palace, Upper Palace, Saintly Virtue, Dharma King).[39] In the *Imperial Biography*, although the title of the manuscript includes "Dharma King" (*hōō*), the section dedicated to the names of the prince does not mention this term, and gives another, slightly different name. This text states that the prince could listen to eight people at the same time and discern their individual points; he could hear one thing and understand eight. For this reason, he was called Umayado Toyoto yamimi (Stable Door, Gifted with the Power of Discernment, Eight Ears). This entry also mentions that he was known as Shōtoku no miko (Prince of Saintly Virtue), and because he lived in the south upper palace, he was also known as Kamitsumiya no miko (Prince of the Upper Palace).[40] Ōyama has stated that the name Shōtoku (Saintly Virtue) was particularly important in the deification of the prince, because it fits the idea of a saint or virtuous person in Buddhism, Confucianism, and Daoism, which is the image that the compilers of *Nihon shoki* were trying to create.[41]

As noted above, in the Shūchō inscription as recorded in the *Imperial Biography*, the prince is called Toyotomimi. Because the inscription is written in *man'yōgana*, the meaning of this name is difficult to interpret. Shinkawa Tokio has explained that the term *toyo* generally is used to embellish a name; therefore, the prince's name must have been Tomimi, which can be translated as "Ten Ears." Shinkawa contends that perhaps this name is the source for the episode in *Nihon shoki* that states that the prince could attend to the cases of ten people at once, and decide on all of them without error.[42] The Chinese graphs used for Tomimi or Mimito in later hagiographic sources, however, suggest that the meaning of the name was related to his powers of discernment and ability to explain things. Thus Shinkawa has proposed that Toyotomimi was one of the names used during the prince's lifetime.[43] Applying the pattern of names that Wada has observed to Shōtoku, it is likely that Umayado was his given name, and Toyotomimi was his popular name. Then, Shōtoku would be his Chinese-style posthumous name, and Kamitsumiya or Jōgū (Upper Palace) would signify the respectful way to refer to the prince after his death.[44] Compared to the hagiographic sources discussed above, the embroidered inscription, which refers to the prince only as Toyotomimi, would appear to have been composed before his image as King of the Dharma was created, or by people with a different agenda.

In the *Imperial Biography*'s inscription, Princess Tachibana seems to be a woman closely related to the prince. Yet little information appears about her, or about the other women allegedly involved with Shōtoku. According to *Nihon shoki*, the eldest of the five daughters of Suiko and Bidatsu, Uji no Kaidako, married "Shōtoku, the heir to the throne."[45] The *Imperial Biography* does not mention Uji no Kaidako, but lists three other wives of the prince and their respective children. The first wife listed is Hokikimi no Iratsume, daughter of Kashiwade no Katabuko no Omi, who bore eight children. The second is Tojiko no Iratsume, daughter of Soga no Umako, who had four children; and Princess Tachibana is third. Tachibana was the daughter of Prince Owari, the fifth of the seven children born to Suiko and Bidatsu; she had two children with Shōtoku (figs. 72, 73).[46] The information presented regarding these women is limited to their names, the names of their fathers, and the number of children that they bore. In order to understand the roles of these women in the life of Prince Shōtoku (or in the construction of his persona), scholars have speculated about the reasons behind these unions.

Ōyama has suggested that the record of the marriage of Uji no Kaidako and Prince Shōtoku is fictitious, another construction of the compilers of *Nihon shoki*. He argues that the compilers must have realized that the relationship between Great King Suiko and the prince—aunt and nephew—

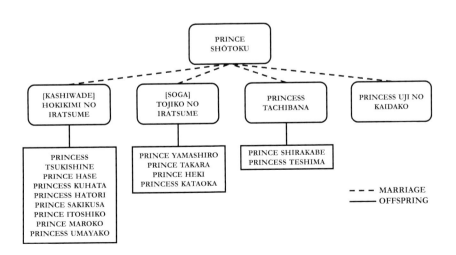

72 Prince Shōtoku's wives and children. Chart by Ken C. Pradel.

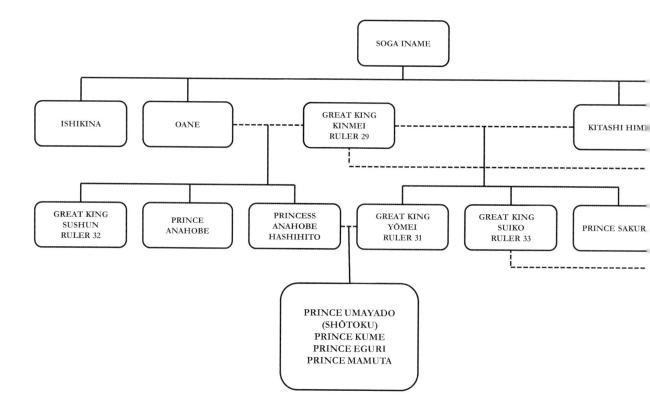

was not strong enough to justify Shōtoku's position as the next in line to rule, and therefore they included the marriage to Suiko's daughter as part of their construction of the prince.[47] Conversely, Takioto Yoshiyuki has indicated that the reason that Uji no Kaidako was not included in the *Imperial Biography* was because she did not bear any children.[48]

The first wife listed in the genealogy included in the *Imperial Biography* is Princess Kashiwade, who appears as the daughter of Katabuko from the Kashiwade kinship group, one of the families of *tomo no miyatsuko* (service functionaries) who were closely involved with the Yamato court as providers of ceremonial food.[49] The Kashiwade also seem to have played a role in diplomatic relations with the Korean peninsula and internal military affairs. If *Nihon shoki*'s information is accurate, in 570, Katabuko was assigned to entertain the Goguryeo envoy in Koshi Province (in the present-day Hokuriku region), and in 587, a Katafu (perhaps Katabuko) Kashiwade is listed among the supporters of the Soga in the Soga–Mononobe conflict.[50] Shōtoku's marriage to Princess Kashiwade could have formed the reason behind the establishment of the prince's palace in Ikaruga. This area was a Kashiwade stronghold, as evidenced by the association between Hōrinji (also known as Miidera; the temple located to the north of Hōryūji) and a certain Takahashi Ason, who was in charge of the temple's affairs; Takahashi was the surname given to the descendants of the Kashiwade kinship group.[51] Tamura Enchō has suggested that this kinship group played a major role in the spread of Buddhism in the area of Ikaruga, and that perhaps both Ikarugadera (as the original iteration of Hōryūji was known) and the current Hōryūji were built by the Kashiwade as a center for the prince's cult.[52]

Furthermore, it is believed that Princess Kashiwade was the consort who died a day before the prince, as stated in the inscription on the mandorla of the Shaka triad in Hōryūji's Golden Hall. This inscription indicates that one of the prince's consorts

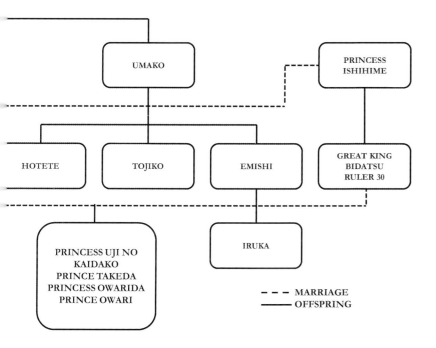

73 Genealogy of the Kinmei–Soga line. Chart by Ken C. Pradel.

had been sick, and died on the twenty-second day of the second month. This consort has been identified as Princess Kashiwade, perhaps due to the prominence of her kinship group in the area. The graphs used in the inscription are not those typically employed to render the name Kashiwade, but most scholars have assumed that they were read as such.[53] In any case, the evidence that this deceased consort was Princess Kashiwade is not conclusive.[54]

Takioto has suggested that Shōtoku was married to Princess Tojiko in order to ensure support from the Soga kinship group, and that he married Princess Tachibana in order to strengthen his relationship with Great King Suiko.[55] In the *Imperial Biography*'s inscription, the latter wife is referred to simply as Tachibana, but in the other genealogies, she appears as Inabe Tachibana. The Inabe were a group of specialized workers in construction technology, who seem to have come from Baekje.[56] If the *Imperial Biography*'s version of the Shūchō's inscription is reliable, it offers an unusual glimpse into the role of women in ancient Japan, and the opportunity to hear their voices. Princess Tachibana is not only the person recorded as the wife who requested the making of a pictorial representation of the prince in Tenjukoku, but she is also the bearer of the words allegedly uttered by Shōtoku: "This world is empty; the only truth is the Buddha."

ISSUES WITH THE *IMPERIAL BIOGRAPHY* INSCRIPTION

As mentioned previously, in early modern historiography the inscription was accepted as a product of the first quarter of the seventh century, but some of its features raised questions about this early dating. Some of these issues are still the subject of ongoing debate, whereas others have been resolved by archaeological discoveries and new scholarship. In general, these issues relate to several aspects of the transmission of continental culture to the Japanese islands in the Asuka and Hakuhō periods. Questions include the employment of the term *tennō* (Heavenly Sovereign) and its political implications, the use of Japanese-style posthumous names for rulers, the use of *man'yōgana* in relation to the adoption of the Chinese writing system, and discrepancies in the dates recorded in relation to the calendric systems used in ancient Japan. A discussion of all of these controversial points will allow us to understand some of the key elements related to the transformation of the Yamato state into a centralized government.

Tennō

The appearance of the term *tennō* on the Shūchō and in the inscription on the halo of the Yakushi image (607) in Hōryūji's Golden Hall has been considered evidence of the use of the term in the Asuka period. Both inscriptions have been the subject of heated debate, because the political changes associated with the term do not match the political circumstances of this period. Moreover, a puzzling aspect of the use of the term in the *Imperial Biography*'s version of the Shūchō inscription is that, although the text includes four historical rulers (Kinmei, Bidatsu, Yōmei, and Suiko), the title of *tennō* is not used for all of them. This term is only used for Kinmei, the *tennō* of the Shikishima Palace, and to refer to Suiko in the second part of the inscription.[57]

Tennō is an ideologically charged term associated with the unification of regional chiefdoms into a centralized bureaucracy led by the Yamato court. One aspect of this new ideology was a shift in the designation of the ruler from Great King (*ōkimi*) to Heavenly Sovereign (*tennō*), and a radical change in the form of government.[58] A brief summary of the views surrounding this term will aid in determining the probable date of the Shūchō's inscription.

Senda Minoru has summarized the scholarship regarding the use of the term *tennō* in ancient Japan, noting that scholars are divided into two conflicting groups. One group argues that the term *tennō* was used during Suiko's reign, and the other advocates for the use of the term only after the so-called Taika Reform of 645. This bipartite argument is rooted in the debate started by Tsuda Sōkichi and Fukuyama Toshio; later scholarship appears to have followed these positions and taken sides. Archaeological discoveries in the 1990s, however, suggest that the term came into use much later, during the reign of Tenmu (r. 673–86).[59]

Scholars who support the idea that *tennō* was used during Suiko's time follow the theory propounded by Tsuda Sōkichi in the 1920s.[60] Tsuda based his argument on the fact that the term appears in the aforementioned inscription on the halo of the Yakushi image in Hōryūji's Golden Hall, and in the *Imperial Biography*'s inscription. He also stated that no evidence could be found that *tennō* was used before Suiko's time. In contrast, in the 1930s, Fukuyama Toshio argued that, while the date recorded on the halo of the Yakushi sculpture indeed corresponds to 607, the inscription was written at a later date as an account of the origins of the image. According to Fukuyama, the term *tennō* as seen in "the *tennō* of the Ikebe Palace" and "the *ōkimi tennō* of the Owari Palace," referring to Yōmei and Suiko, respectively, in the Yakushi inscription, was used anachronistically to designate rulers of the past, and not the regnant Suiko. In his view, the scribe probably invented the combined term *ōkimi tennō* to refer to Suiko, as *tennō* was used to designate the ruler at the time when the inscription was composed, while Suiko must have been called *ōkimi* in older sources.[61] Further evidence for this argument is the fact that the cult of Yakushi began during Tenmu's reign with the beginning of the construction of Yakushiji in 680.[62] Therefore, Fukuyama concluded that the inscription on the Yakushi image and the term *tennō* are both products of Tenmu's reign. In addition, stylistic analysis demonstrates that the Yakushi image was made intentionally in the archaic style of the early seventh century, but was produced at a later time.[63]

Recent archaeological excavations support Fukuyama's conclusions. In 1991, a *mokkan* inscribed with the term *tennō* was excavated at the Asuka pond (Asukaike) site. Although it is not inscribed with a date, this *mokkan* is associated with two others that bear dates corresponding to 670 (Tenji 9), 676 (Tenmu 5), and 677 (Tenmu 6). On the basis of this finding, most scholars now agree that the term *tennō* was first used during the reigns of Tenmu and Jitō.[64] To further investigate this issue, Tōno Haruyuki has analyzed the entries in *Nihon shoki* that include the term *tennō* during the reigns of these monarchs, and has noticed that, in the Jitō chronicles, the term *tennō* alone is used in some instances as a synonym for Tenmu. Tōno thus has concluded that Tenmu was the first ruler in Japan to be called *tennō* as part of the political changes brought about by the compiling, initiated in 681, of the Asuka Kiyomihara Code, possibly the first collection of *ritsuryō* (a system of legal and administrative codes) in Japan.[65]

Although scholars such as Ōhashi Katsuaki still assert that the appearance of the term *tennō* in the *Imperial Biography*'s inscription is evidence of its use in the early seventh century, the materials currently available strongly support the theory that the term was used in the late seventh century as the Yamato court moved towards a centralized, bureaucratic form of government. Therefore, it is probable that the Shūchō's inscription was composed around that time.

Japanese Posthumous Names

The use of Japanese posthumous names (such as Toyomi kekashikiya for Suiko) in the inscription is another controversial point. Hayashi Mikiya has noted that, in the *Imperial Biography*'s version of the Shūchō inscription, rulers are listed by their Japanese-style posthumous names (*wafū shigō* or *wafū okurina*); this practice also is followed in *Kojiki* and *Nihon shoki*. In the other Remnant Texts mentioned above, however, rulers are identified by their palace names. For this reason, Hayashi contends that the Japanese-style posthumous names began to be used during Tenmu's time, when the two historical accounts were compiled. Furthermore, because the convention of associating rulers with their palaces (also seen in the inscription) developed after the Taika Reform, the original embroidered inscription must be dated after 645.[66]

Iida, who proposes an early-seventh-century date for the inscription, has recognized that the appearance of posthumous names is problematic. Yet he points out that, because it is not known exactly when those names began to be used, it might be possible that the embroidered inscription presents the first extant instance of the use of such names.[67] A more convincing theory that includes contextual analysis has been proposed by Wada. He argues that the custom of giving rulers posthumous names is related to the introduction of *mogari* funeral rites from China and the Korean peninsula. *Mogari* is the funerary ritual that begins when a temporary burial place, known as *moya* or *mogari no miya*, is built as the locus of memorial rites until the permanent inhumation of the corpse.[68] Wada has indicated that, in the entries related to the *mogari* of Jitō and Monmu in *Shoku Nihongi*, the deceased rulers were assigned their Japanese-style posthumous names during the last presentation of eulogies (*shinobigoto*), right before the interment. Similarly, in the records of Jomei (r. 629–41) and Tenmu in *Nihon shoki*, their Japanese-style posthumous names are listed right after the last presentation of eulogies. Because the first record of an imperial *mogari* is that of Great King Kinmei, Wada has concluded that the practice of giving Japanese-style posthumous names to rulers might have begun in the late sixth century.[69] If Wada's theory is correct, then the use of such names poses no problem for the early dating of the Shūchō's inscription. It is likely, however, that the inscription was composed after Suiko's death, because her Japanese-style posthumous name is included rather than her given name, Princess Nukatabe.[70]

Man'yōgana

As mentioned above, a particular feature of the *Imperial Biography*'s inscription, and some of the other Remnant Texts, is the use of *man'yōgana*, classical Chinese graphs employed as phonograms rather than ideograms. In the inscription, the names of most of the people mentioned are written in *man'yōgana* that differ from those used in *Nihon shoki*, *Kojiki*, or *Man'yōshū*. For example, as the linguist Okimori Takuya explains, the name "Soga" appears multiple times in the *Imperial Biography*, written in a variety of ways. The way that it is rendered in the Shūchō inscription is unusual, but not unique, as the same phonograms are used in two other inscriptions: the inscription on the Gangōji pagoda finial, and the inscription on the mandorla of the sixteen-foot Buddha from Gangōji, both recorded in *Gangōji engi*.[71] The similarities between these texts are not limited to the way in which "Soga" is written, but also include the phonograms for names of rulers and palaces.[72] When Fukuyama Toshio studied these two inscriptions, he dated the section of the finial inscription that contains the same phonograms as the Shūchō inscription, and the Shūchō inscription itself, to the mid-seventh century, but the mandorla inscription to the years 690 through 710.[73]

After Ōyama Seiichi put forward his theory about the construction of Prince Shōtoku, scholars began to revisit some of the Remnant Texts. Sema Masayuki has pointed out that some phonograms reveal the old Korean pronunciations (*kokan'on*), which is understandable as the Chinese writing system arrived in Japan by way of the Korean peninsula.[74] This is particularly evident in the three inscriptions mentioned above. Sema focuses his study on five phonograms that appear in these three inscriptions, comparing them to their occurrences in the earliest Japanese written sources.

As Sema explains, three of the five phonograms (奇 *ga*, 宜 *ga*, and 移 *ya*) are used in documents from the Korean peninsula, in entries in Japanese sources derived from reports from the peninsula, and in some records from the eighth century. Sema cites the work of Inukai Takashi, who also has studied phonograms on *mokkan* from the Asuka pond and North Ōtsu sites (Shiga Prefecture). According to Inukai, some of the phonograms on the *mokkan* from these sites are related to the inscription on the Inariyama sword, an iron artifact with Baekje origins excavated from a burial mound in Saitama Prefecture and believed to date from 471 or 531. Furthermore, these phonograms are also found in the entries in *Nihon shoki* from *Kudara hongi* (Annals of Baekje, K. *Baekje bongi*), the entry about the vow to produce the sixteen-foot Buddha in Kinmei's records, and the Shūchō inscription. The other two phonograms (至 *chi* and 支 *ki*) used in the three inscriptions are found in *Samguk sagi* (Historical Record of the Three Kingdoms; 1145), particularly in the names of places, and in the proper names of Baekje-derived records in *Nihon shoki*. From this evidence, Sema has concluded that the phonograms used in the inscriptions recorded in *Gangōji engi* and in the Shūchō inscription differ from those found in *Nihon shoki*, *Kojiki*, and *Man'yōshū* because they were written by scribes from Baekje. In his view, these inscriptions cannot be dated to the late sixth or early seventh century; a date between the late seventh and early eighth century is more appropriate.[75]

Yoshida Kazuhiko has focused on the graphs used for the names recorded in the genealogy portion of the *Imperial Biography*'s inscription. Although it generally had been acknowledged that all eleven names were written with phonograms, Yoshida noticed that only nine names appear solely in this form. The names of Prince Owari and Anahobe are written by combining phonograms and logographs. Anahobe, for example, is written using the logograph 孔 (*ana*), despite the fact that the phonograms 阿 (*a*) and 奈 (*na*) are used many times elsewhere in the inscription.[76] In addition, Yoshida notes that certain logographs in the text were not used in the seventh century, such as 巷 (*so*) and 弥 (*mi*).[77] As these two logographs were first used in the ninth century, Yoshida has concluded that the inscription must have been written at a later date, employing phonograms to make the inscription look like a text from the seventh or early eighth century. According to Yoshida, both the Shūchō's inscription and the Shūchō itself should be dated to the mid-eleventh century.[78] It is probable that Yoshida is correct in dating the inscription as late as the eleventh century, as this is the actual date of the Chion'in manuscript, the earliest extant version of the *Imperial Biography*. The scribe likely included some graphs in use at the time when he transcribed the inscription, especially if the embroidery was damaged. But Yoshida's dating of the Shūchō's remains to the eleventh century is difficult to accept, as the visual evidence strongly suggests a seventh-century date.

As the work of these scholars has shown, the use of the *man'yōgana* seen in the inscription is not problematic if the inscription was the product of scribes from Baekje rather than the official scribes of *Nihon shoki*, *Kojiki*, and *Man'yōshū* (who also probably hailed from immigrant kinship groups). It is widely acknowledged that writing technology was brought to Japan by immigrants from Baekje, and that a branch of the Yamato no Aya kinship group, the Fumibe, took care of the writing needs of the Yamato court.[79] The fact that the same logographs were used in the Shūchō inscription and in the two Gangōji inscriptions suggests that these three inscriptions were written by the same group of scribes, or perhaps commissioned by the Soga, who built the temple. The Yamato no Aya must have been involved, not only because they had strong connections with the court's scribes, but also because the name of their kinship group appears in two of the three inscriptions. In short, the specific use of certain *man'yōgana* in the Shūchō inscription certainly suggests that it was composed by people associated with the Soga clan, which had firm ties to Baekje in the late seventh century.[80]

Dates and Calendrical Systems

Scholars have debated two issues regarding the dates recorded in the Shūchō inscription. First, the date of the prince's death does not correspond to the dates recorded in other sources. Second, research on ancient calendrical systems suggests that the death dates of Anahobe and Shōtoku are not rendered according to the same calendar.

In *Nihon shoki*, the date of the prince's death is recorded as the second day of the fifth month of Suiko 29 (621).[81] In the Shūchō inscription, the inscription on the mandorla of the Hōryūji Shaka triad, and elsewhere in the *Imperial Biography*, it is the twenty-second day of the second month of Suiko 30 (622). Ōyama, for whom everything about the prince is a later construction, has argued that the latter date is derived from the *Lotus Sutra* ceremony sponsored by Empress Kōmyō (701–760) and the monk Dōji, held in 736 in the Tōin (Eastern Compound) of Hōryūji. This ceremony is considered to be an early manifestation of the Shōtoku cult.[82] Perhaps the existence of two different dates suggests that, in addition to the Yamato court's narrative as presented in *Nihon shoki*, another group (or groups), promoting the veneration of the prince in various cultic centers, created different narratives with different dates.

The date of Anahobe's death is not recorded in *Nihon shoki*, and the inscription on the Shaka triad only states that she passed in the twelfth month. In the Shūchō inscription, the date given is the twenty-first day *mizunoto-tori* of the twelfth month of *kano-to-mi* (Suiko 29, or 621). According to Miyata Toshihiko, the problem with this date is the concordance of the day (the twenty-first) and the date in the sexagenary cycle, the ancient system used to designate years, months, and days that combines ten "stems" (*kan*) and twelve "branches" (*shi*). If the calendrical system used during Suiko's reign was the Genka (C. Yuanjia) calendar, the twenty-first day is not *mizunoto-tori*, but a day later, *kinoe-inu*; or if the date was *mizunoto-tori*, the correct day of the month would be the twentieth. Miyata has concluded that this discrepancy shows that the inscription was written at a later time, when the Genka system was no longer used. The scribe who wrote the inscription must not have been familiar with this calendrical system, and thus made the mistake.[83] Miyata has suggested that, while the embroidered artifact was made during Suiko's reign, the inscription was written after 643 (Kōgyoku 2) and before the demise of the prince's family.[84] Because the Shūchō and the inscription are intertwined, however, this conclusion does not make sense. Iida, who proposes an early-seventh-century date, has dismissed Miyata's claim as irrelevant, and argued that the system used during Suiko's reign was the Boinreki (C. Wuyinli) of the Tang dynasty, which was developed in 618.[85] Yet no reference to this calendar appears in any Japanese source.

Information about the calendrical systems used in ancient Japan is scant. The only reference to specific calendars in *Nihon shoki* in an imperial order that instructed the use of the Genka and Gihō (C. Yifeng) calendars in 690.[86] Based on this premise, Kanazawa Hideyuki has reviewed the calculations for the sexagenary cycles in the Genka and Gihō calendars, and concluded that the dates of the deaths of Prince Shōtoku and Anahobe recorded in the inscription are both rendered correctly, if the Gihō system was used.[87] Therefore, Kanazawa has proposed that the inscription was written by the end of the seventh century.[88] More research on the calendrical systems used in ancient Japan is necessary in order to reach a conclusion about this issue.

The Prince's Statement and Tenjukoku

The devastated Princess Tachibana went to see the Heavenly Sovereign [Suiko, her grandmother] and said, "I grieve the loss of my prince (ōkimi) and the queen mother. My prince said, 'This world is empty; the only truth is the Buddha.' He appreciated this *minori*. As a reward, my prince must have been born in 'The Land of Heavenly Lifespan' (Tenjukoku). But, I cannot visualize that land. Please, somehow create an illustration of the place to which my prince was transported (or where he resides)."

This segment of the inscription has been considered particularly valuable as evidence of the beliefs and practices of Prince Shōtoku, and also as proof that belief in birth in a pure land existed during the Asuka period. As mentioned previously, Tenjukoku generally has been accepted to represent the pure land where the prince was reborn, despite the fact that this term does not appear in any of the canonical Buddhist sutras. Some scholars, however, have argued that the presence of this term reflects the beliefs of Princess Tachibana.[89] The translation and interpretation of this portion of the inscription are crucial to understanding the meaning and intent of the Shūchō.

To reconstruct the four hundred graphs of the inscription, Iida has studied the extant later versions, and has compared the Chion'in manuscript to ten others from the thirteenth century onward.[90] According to Iida, the discrepancies between the versions do not alter the meaning of the inscription. A change in one particular graph, however, may influence the interpretation of the text. The last phrase, which has been translated as "the place to which my prince was transported (or where he resides)," is transcribed in slightly different forms. In the Chion'in manuscript, the four graphs that comprise the phrase are 往生之状 (*ōjō no yosu*), and in the later versions, they are 住生之状 (*sumitamafu no yosu*). The radical (in this case, the left-hand portion) of the first character is different. *Ōjō* can mean "going to rebirth" or "being born in a Buddhist pure land." *Sumitamafu sama* means "to reside" or "to live." Iida has chosen the latter option, thinking that the graph 住 must have been present in the original embroidery. Because both graphs are similar, however, he also has contemplated the possibility that scribes from the thirteenth century and later might have meant to write 往.[91]

The choice of graphs in this case is problematic, as the two options can completely change the content of the inscription. If *ōjō no yosu* is accepted as the correct phrase (as a number of scholars have suggested), and translated as "the Buddhist pure land where my prince was born," and *minori* is translated as "Buddhist Dharma," then this portion of the text reads as follows:

> My prince said, 'This world is empty; the only truth is the Buddha.' He appreciated the Buddhist Dharma. As a reward, my prince must have been born in 'The Land of Heavenly Lifespan' (Tenjukoku). But, I cannot visualize that land. Please, somehow create an illustration of the Buddhist pure land where my prince was born.

Because it is impossible to know the original graphs embroidered on the Shūchō, the four-graph phrase has been translated here as "the place to which my prince was transported (or where he resides)." In this way, the interpretation of these sentences is not restricted to a Buddhist context. This is especially relevant in light of the fact that the visual analysis does not support a reading of the subject as Buddhist. Moreover, *minori* is not exclusively a Buddhist term; it also may mean the system of state law and imperial bureaucracy, and was used in a Daoist context to refer to divine law.[92] A more definite conclusion about this portion of the inscription must be left to a consideration of the historical context for the creation of the Shūchō.[93]

Genealogy

The genealogy included in the inscription shows the family relations of Prince Toyotomimi and his wife, Princess Tachibana. Both of their ancestries are traced back to Great King Kinmei and the minister Soga no Iname (ca. 506–570), two key figures in the politics of late-sixth-century Japan. Yoshie Akiko has analyzed the content and form of the genealogy in order to clarify its purpose, and also to shed light on its date.[94] As she explains, the format of this genealogy is "A takes B as a wife, and C is born." Kinmei took Kitashi hime as a wife, and Yōmei and Suiko were born; Kinmei also took Oane as a wife, and Anahobe was born. Bidatsu took Suiko as a wife, and Owari was born; Yōmei took Anahobe as a wife, and Toyotomimi was born (see fig. 71).[95] Yoshie has pointed out that the Shūchō genealogy is selective. Eleven people are mentioned, and the relationships recorded are selected marriages and selected offspring of those unions. Therefore, in Yoshie's view, the main purpose of this genealogy was to record the marriage of Prince Toyotomimi and Princess Tachibana, emphasizing their close family ties for three or four generations as descendants of Great King Kinmei and Soga no Iname.[96] (For a more complete genealogy of the Kinmei–Soga line, see fig. 73.) Furthermore, only descendants that have a clear connection to both lines are included. For instance, Bidatsu's mother is not included because, although she was Kinmei's sister, she did not have a Soga mother. Similarly, Princess Tachibana's mother is omitted, perhaps because she was not related to either of the two lines.

Yoshie has advocated an early-seventh-century date for the creation of this genealogy, due to her belief that the statements made in the text only would have been possible when the Soga kinship group was still in power. She has deemed it impossible that such a genealogy could have been created during the time of Tenmu and Jitō, because all of the rulers after Suiko up to Jitō were descendants of Prince Oshisaka no Hikohito (b. ca. 556), son of Great King Bidatsu and Hirohime, a daughter of the Okinaga kinship group.[97] As these people might not have had any interest in highlighting the Kinmei–Soga line, Yoshie has concluded that the only person with such an interest, as a descendant of this line, was Princess Tachibana herself. Thus, according to Yoshie, the inscription and the embroidered artifact must have been created while Princess Tachibana was alive, as she was the only person with a stake in clarifying her relationship to the prince, stressing her position as a descendant of the ruling elites of the Asuka period.[98]

Some scholars, such as Ōhashi, support Yoshie's dating, while others contend that her arguments are not convincing.[99] Among those who do not support her interpretations is Ōyama. Because everyone mentioned in the inscription, except for Princess Tachibana, appears in *Nihon shoki*, Ōyama has stated that this genealogy was made up based on the information provided there; and because neither the princess nor her mother are mentioned in *Nihon shoki*, Ōyama has concluded that Tachibana must be a fictitious individual created by the writer of the inscription, who was likely someone associated with Hōryūji.[100]

Yoshie has made a convincing argument regarding the purpose of the genealogy in the inscription. The selective quality of the text certainly indicates that the reason behind this genealogy was to emphasize that Shōtoku and Princess Tachibana were descendants of the Yamato court and the Soga kinship group; the only person interested in making such a statement would have been Tachibana. In addition, the fact that Iname's daughter, Kitashi hime, appears in the inscription as Kinmei's Senior Queen Consort, whereas in *Nihon shoki*, she and Oane are listed simply as consorts, reveals a Soga bias. Could it thus be possible that Tachibana lived long enough to be involved in the making of the Shūchō and its inscription?

It is assumed that all members of Prince Shōtoku's family died in 643, when Soga no Iruka (d. 645) forced Prince Yamashiro, Shōtoku's eldest son, and his family to commit suicide in Ikaruga. This incident is recorded in various sources. As *Nihon shoki* states, "Finally he [Prince Yamashiro] and the younger members of his family, with his consorts, strangled themselves at the same time, and died together."[101] Later hagiographies, such as *Jōgū Shōtoku Taishi den hoketsuki* (Supplemental Record of the Biography of Prince Shōtoku from the Upper Palace; ca. 9th century) and *Shōtoku Taishi denryaku*, list the names of the twenty-three deceased princes and twenty-five deceased princesses. All were Shōtoku's siblings, children, and grandchildren.[102] Their deaths were indeed the end of his line, yet it is likely that his wives might not have been there.

In the Nara period (710–94) and earlier, married couples usually lived separately, in a system known as *tsuma doikon* (duolocal or visiting marriage). Marital relationships were not stable unions continuing over time, but temporary arrangements.[103] Consorts did not live in the ruler's palace, and the households of the two were managed independently. In fact, even with regard to Shōtoku's other wives, Tojiko lived in the Palace of Okamoto, and Princess Kashiwade resided in the Palace of Akunami.[104] Therefore, as Shōtoku's alleged wives are not mentioned by name in accounts of the mass suicide, and due to the period's marital arrangements, it is possible that Tachibana was not in Ikaruga in 643. As Prince Owari's daughter and Suiko's granddaughter, she might have been in the Asuka area, and may have lived long enough to request the making of the Shūchō. She (or the person who composed the genealogy or the entire inscription) might have included Suiko's name in order to increase the object's importance.

Yoshie has pointed out that once Jomei, Suiko's successor, became Great King, it would have been impossible for Tachibana to compose the inscription or have the Shūchō made, as she would no longer have held any connection to the court. Yet Princess Tachibana and Jomei were related; both were Bidatsu's grandchildren. Furthermore, certain members of the Soga kinship group remained active at court. If *Nihon shoki* is to be believed, the main Soga line disappeared from the political life of the Yamato court in 645 when Soga no Iruka and his father, Soga no Emishi (587–645), both died, yet other Soga lineages maintained their position.[105] Umako's grandchildren, Soga no Kurayamada no Ishikawamaro (d. 649) and Soga no Akae, continued to hold the position of *ōomi* (senior minister) and married their daughters into the Yamato court.[106] Kurayamada's daughter, Chi no Iratsume, was a junior consort of Great King Kōtoku (r. 645–54).[107] Importantly, two of his other daughters became concubines of Great King Tenji and mothers of future rulers. Ochi no Iratsume gave birth to Princess Uno, the future Heavenly Sovereign Jitō; and her younger sister, Mei no Iratsume, gave birth to Princess Abe, the future Heavenly Sovereign Genmei. Akae's daughters fared similarly: Hitachi no Iratsume was one of Tenji's concubines, and Ohonu no Iratsume was one of Tenmu's consorts.[108]

By continuing to marry their daughters into the royal house, members of the Soga kinship group likely managed to maintain their high status as part of the ruling elite until the early eighth century.[109] If this was the case, Tachibana could have found supporters among the Soga's female descendants at court. Unfortunately, it is not possible to reach a definite conclusion about the authorship of the inscription because we do not known how old Princess Tachibana was when Shōtoku died, or how long she lived. If Tachibana had died before the Shūchō was produced, the other possibility is that people associated with the Kinmei–Soga line, such as the immigrant kinship groups that provided services to the court and elite, used their skills and resources to honor Prince Shōtoku and his mother. The activities of these groups and their association with the Soga family bear further examination.

ROLE OF KINSHIP GROUPS

The last part of the inscription lists the draftsmen of the Shūchō's design, Yamato no Aya no Makken, Koma no Kasei, and Aya no Nukakori; and the overseer, Kurahitobe Hata no Kuma. Most scholars have stated only that these men were members of the immigrant groups from Korea that served the Yamato court, and have not offered any insights into their activities. Although the textual sources do not provide specifics about these individuals, their names indicate that they were members of powerful immigrant groups of the Asuka and Hakuhō periods: the Aya and the Hata. Research into these immigrant kinship groups suggests that their role might have been beyond that ascribed to them in the inscription. They may have been involved at all levels of the production of the Shūchō, including the formulation of the inscription.

It is generally acknowledged that continuous waves of migration to the Japanese islands took place between the fourth and seventh century. The process peaked three times: first, between the late fourth and early fifth century; second, in the late fifth century; and third, in the late seventh century.[110] Some immigrants came from China, but mainly they came from the Korean peninsula, from the kingdoms of Kaya, Baekje, Goguryeo, and Silla, with political turmoil being the main reason for these massive migrations.[111] Even though immigrants appear in *Nihon shoki* as having arrived as prisoners, tribute, or gifts from one king to another, these people were products of a culture far more advanced than that present in the Japanese islands, and as such, they played a major role in the cultural, economic, technological, religious, and political development of the Yamato court.

It is known that the Aya and the Hata, for example, arrived as specialized workers. The history of these two groups can be recreated, but not much is known about the activities of the Koma. Kasei was probably an immigrant, or the descendant of an immigrant, from the kingdom of Goguryeo. Many monks from Goguryeo are mentioned in *Nihon shoki*, among them Shōtoku's putative teacher, Hyeja (J. Eji), and also a painter named Koma no Ekaki no Komaro, who was apparently a painter of Buddhist figures.[112] Information about the Aya and the Hata is relatively abundant, and is not limited to the entries in *Nihon shoki*. Because they collaborated with Heavenly Sovereign Tenmu in the 672 Jinshin Disturbance (*Jinshin no ran*), a succession dispute that followed Tenjin's death, they not only managed to keep their positions, but continued to play important roles in the political and religious arenas during the Nara and Heian periods.[113] Details about their activities are also found in *Shinsen shōjiroku* (Record of Titles and Surnames Newly Selected), a ninth-century genealogical compendium. In this document, the Aya trace their ancestry to Emperor Gaozu (r. 202–195 BCE) of the Western Han dynasty and Emperor Ling (r. 168–189 CE) of the Eastern Han; and the Hata trace theirs to Qin Shi Huang Di (r. 220–210 BCE), who unified China and became first emperor of the Qin dynasty (221–206 BCE).[114] Because of these ancestral claims, the Aya and the Hata used the Chinese graphs for the Han and Qin, respectively, to write their names. Such claims about the choice of these graphs are mythical. Rather, it is likely that these groups began to immigrate in the fifth century; the Aya probably came from Kaya or Baekje, and the Hata, from Silla.[115]

The Hata traditionally have been associated with silk production and weaving. Information about them, and their activities, cannot be found in *Nihon shoki*; only three Hata are mentioned. Among them is Hata no Kawakatsu, known for his activities in support of Buddhism.[116] The heritage of the Hata appears to be a later construction recorded in *Shinsen shōjiroku* and *Kogoshūi* (Gleanings from Ancient Stories), a mytho-historical text written by Imbe no Hironari in 807 in order to reassert and reclaim his lineage's prerogatives at court. In the latter, the Hata claim descent from the Korean Prince Yuzuki, who is mentioned in *Nihon shoki* but not associated there with the Hata.[117] *Nihon shoki* tells us that Yuzuki arrived in 283 from Baekje, offering to bring one hundred and twenty districts of people from his own land in an alliance with the Japanese throne, but that their travel was prevented by men from Silla. For this reason, Yuzuki's men stayed in Kaya until Katsuraki no Sotsuhiko was sent to bring them to Japan.[118] The Hata probably made the connection with Yuzuki because a branch of this group had settled in Katsuragi (in present-day Nara Prefecture).[119]

The other controversial point is the association of the Hata with silk production and weaving. In *Nihon shoki*, a vague narrative somehow relates the Hata with silk. In 471, the Hata were dispersed, and the *omi* and *muraji* (two of the many *kabane*, ancient hereditary titles denoting rank and political standing) did not allow the Hata *miyatsuko* to control the dispersed members.[120] Hata no Sake presented his grievance to the Great King, who commanded that the Hata house should be assembled and given to Sake, who then led 180 kinds of *suguri* (another *kabane*) service groups and presented an abundance of fine silks as tribute. For this reason, Hata no Sake was given the title of Uzumasa ("piled up higher," referring to piles of fabric).[121] In *Kogoshūi*, the *Nihon shoki* account is expanded, and although little detail is given, the Hata are proclaimed as weavers.[122]

> The silk and fine silk felt good against the skin, and that is why the reading for this kinship group's name is Hada (skin). The silk presented by the Hada kinship group was used to wrap around the hilts of swords used in ceremonies worshiping the deities. It is still thus in the present. This is the origin of the weavers of Hada.[123]

An interesting point has been made by Katō Kenkichi, who argues that the main occupation of the Hata was not the production of silk fibers or loom-woven fabrics; instead, they were in charge of the administration of storehouses (*kura*) for tribute goods such as silk fibers and fabrics, salt, copper, and other items. In fact, the member of the Hata mentioned in the inscription is designated a Kurahitobe. *Kurahito* refers to the person in charge of the administration of storehouses, and *be* denotes a group of specialized workers.[124] According to Tsude Hiroshi, most *kurahito*—an occupation that may have existed since the fifth century—were of immigrant origin, and were trained in a variety of skills associated with storehouses, including their construction, the systematic storage of goods, and record-keeping (which necessitated literacy).[125] Katō has placed the origin of *kurahito* a bit later, explaining that the graph 椋 used for *kura* in the inscription was used in the Baekje administrative system established in the sixth century, yet he acknowledges the possibility that the position already existed in the fifth century at the Yamato court.[126]

The assumption that *kurahito* existed in the fifth century might relate to an account in *Kogoshūi* that narrates the establishment of the Kurahitobe. In this account, the ancestors of the Hata, the Aya, the Kawachi no Fumibe (a branch of the Yamato no Aya who served as scribes), and the Soga are all involved in the administration of storehouses. According to the narrative, during the reign of Great King Richū (r. 400–405), the three Han of Korea brought an enormous amount of tribute.[127] To house all of these goods, the court ordered the construction of the Internal Storehouse (Uchikura) next to the Imi Storehouse used to keep official property. Achi no Omi and a scholar from Baekje, Wani (ancestors of the Aya and Fumi, respectively), received the command to keep the storage records, and the position of Kurahitobe was born. As the tribute from the provinces increased, Soga no Machi no Sukune (ancestor of the Soga) was authorized to inspect the Imi, Internal, and Large Storehouses. The Hata placed the items in the storehouses, and the Kawachi no Fumibe and Yamato no Fumibe recorded the inventory of the storehouses in record books. Later, the Aya received the surnames of Uchikura and Ōkura (Large Storehouse), the Aya and Hata were put in charge of the keys to the Internal and Large Storehouses, and the Kurahitobe was assigned to manage the storehouses.[128]

If the information from *Kogoshūi* is accurate, the Hata were in charge of the administration of storehouses rather than the production of silk and woven goods. They worked hand in hand with the Yamato no Aya and Kawachi no Fumi, the scribes who took care of record-keeping. Thus, Kurahitobe Hata no Kuma was probably someone from the Hata kinship group who was in charge of storehouses, and his duties might have included the storage of goods given as tribute as well as imported goods from the Korean peninsula or China.

Regarding the Aya, *Nihon shoki* contains information about their arrival and settlement in the Japanese islands. The Aya might have arrived in the fifth century from the Korean peninsula. One of the activities of the Yamato no Aya seems to have been the supervision of specialized workers, particularly those coming from Baekje. According to *Nihon shoki*, in 463, Yamato no Aya no Tsuka was instructed to accommodate the recently arrived Aya (Imaki no Aya) in Momohara, Lower Momohara, and Makami no Hara (all in the Asuka region). The newly arrived members included a potter, a saddle maker, a painter, a brocade weaver, and an interpreter.[129] Moreover, in 472, the leader of the Aya was ordered to bring the specialized workers of the kinship group together, and their manager (*tomo no miyatsuko*) was granted the title of *atai* (one of the lowest *kabane*).[130] One cohort settled in the Asuka area and became known as the Yamato no Aya; another settled in Kawachi Province (in present-day Osaka Prefecture) and became known as the Kawachi no Aya.

Further evidence of the role of the Yamato no Aya as supervisors of specialized workers is found in narratives of the *kinunuibe*, people who specialized in dressmaking. The narratives suggest that dressmaking or tailoring was a woman's skill brought from Baekje, and that various groups of *kinunui* settled in different locations in the islands. *Nihon shoki* states that a female *kinunui* (dressmaker), who was sent by the ruler of Baekje as tribute, became the progenitor of the female *kinunui* of Kume (in present-day Nara Prefecture).[131] In addition, the ancestors of the Yamato no Aya, Achi no Omi and Tsuka no Omi, who allegedly arrived in 289, are portrayed as key figures in the migration of other *kinunui*.[132] In 306, they were sent to Wu (J. Kure) in south China (the region surrounding present-day Suzhou) to procure female *kinunui*. They first went to Goguryeo, but could not find their way to Wu, so the king of Goguryeo provided them with two guides. When they successfully reached the land of Wu, the king of Wu gave them four craftswomen: Ehime, Otohime, Kurehatori (Kure weaver), and Anahatori or Ayahatori (Aya weaver). In 310, the envoy returned from Wu; Ehime was offered to the Munakata Shrine in Tsukushi (Kyushu), and the other three to the deity Ōsazaki no mikoto. According to the text in *Nihon shoki*, the descendants of these women were the *kinunui* of Kure and Kaya (probably in present-day Nara Prefecture).[133] The same four women are mentioned in a similar story involving two men who were also members of the Aya kinship group: Musa no Suguri no Ao from the scribes' specialized group (Fumibe); and Hinokuma no Hakatoko, who was an employer of people (Tamitsukai). These men were sent to the land of Wu in 464, and returned in 466; they were then sent again in 468, returning in 470. According to this version of the story, Ehime was presented to the Ōmiwa Shrine in Nara, and Otohime was appointed as the *kinunui* of Aya (probably in present-day Nara Prefecture). Kurehatori and Anahatori became the founders of the *kinunui* of Asuka and Ise (in present-day Mie Prefecture).[134]

These narratives suggest that the Aya might have been associated with the introduction of weaving and sewing technology from the continent, perhaps from south China (Wu) or Baekje. As Gina Barnes has pointed out, the fact that the sources indicate the existence of people who were in charge of bringing specialized workers to Japan suggests that migration was controlled, and that immigrants could not establish their livelihoods in the crafts without an association with a known group.[135] Additionally, the narratives stress the religious significance of weaving, and the places where the *kinunui* settled seem to be associated with shrines, such as Ise, Miwa, and Munakata.

In addition to being involved with the immigration of specialized craftspeople, members of the Yamato no Aya and the Aya were among those sent to study in China during Suiko's time.[136] Also, although not portrayed in a positive light, the Yamato no Aya and the Aya were very close to the Soga kinship group. Yamato no Aya no Koma assassinated Great King Sushun (r. 588–93) upon the command of Soga no Umako, and had a clandestine relationship with Umako's daughter, Kawakami no Iratsume. Koma was killed in turn by Umako after the latter found out about the affair.[137] The Aya were involved with Soga no Emishi and Iruka; members of the Aya seem to have served as security guards at the widely criticized palace-like houses built by Emishi and Iruka on Amakashi Hill in Asuka, where these Soga men proclaimed themselves *ōomi* and *omi*.[138] Later, in 645, the Aya also organized a defense force to protect Emishi after Naka no Ōe (the future Great King Tenji) and his followers killed Iruka. Knowing that it was a lost battle, however, the Aya deserted.[139] The Yamato no Aya must have been important in ancient Japan due to their connections to the Soga, or perhaps they were powerful in their own right: *Nihon shoki* tells us that Heavenly Sovereign Tenmu granted clemency to this kinship group in spite of all of the problems that they had caused from the reigns of Suiko through Tenji.[140]

From all of the above, it seems that the individuals listed as the overseer and draftsmen of the Shūchō were members of kinship groups that might have played a role beyond those ascribed in the inscription. If the Hata were indeed in charge of storehouses, Kurahitobe Hata no Kuma must have had easy access to the materials needed to produce the embroidered curtains. Yamato no Aya no Makken and Aya no Nukakori must have coordinated with the Fumibe branch of their kinship group to compose the inscription, and also could have provided the labor force necessary for the execution of the project due to their ties to specialized workers, namely *kinunui*. Although the noun *kinunui* means "dressmaking," perhaps that was not the only task handled by these workers. The graph 縫 (*nui*) denotes sewing as well as embroidering. Both crafts use the same tools and materials: needles, scissors, thread, and fabric. As discussed previously, stem stitch and running stitch, the stitches used to embroider the Shūchō fragments and the Hōryūji embroidered banner, are the most basic of the stitches. These two stitch types can be used for decorative purposes, but are also employed in basic sewing. People trained in the use of needles and thread for sewing garments also must have been able to embroider and quilt. The existence of women who specialized in such work casts doubt on the statement in the inscription that Suiko "commanded a group of lady attendants of the court (*uneme*) to make two panels of embroidered curtains." The fact that nothing is known about the activities of the *uneme* renders this claim especially suspicious. A 646 entry in *Nihon shoki* states only that "they were sisters or daughters of district officials, who were good-looking and had to have one male and two female servants [each]."[141]

If one of the objectives of the inscription was to highlight the Soga kinship group's connections with the Yamato court since the time of Kinmei and Iname, and the marriage of Princess Tachibana to Prince Toyotomimi, then the Aya (especially) and the Hata may have been interested in emphasizing such connections due to their strong ties with the Soga. If this is the case, then it is no coincidence that two members of the Yamato no Aya are listed as patrons of the pagoda finial at Gangōji, a temple built by the Soga, in the inscription recorded in *Gangōji engi*. Furthermore, as mentioned above, the same logographs are used for the names of rulers and their palaces in the Shūchō inscription, the inscription on the mandorla of the sixteen-foot Buddha from Gangōji, and the inscription on the pagoda finial. Additionally, the ties between the Soga and the *kinunui* are reflected by the fact that Asukadera was built on the land where the house of the ancestor of the Asuka *kinunui* once stood.[142]

THE *JŌGŪ SHŌTOKU HŌŌ TEISETSU*

Because the *Imperial Biography* is the first document to record the entire text of the Shūchō's inscription, it is necessary to understand the general schema of the document and the role that the inscription plays within it. The Shūchō's inscription was added together with the inscriptions on the mandorla of the Hōryūji Shaka triad and on the halo of the Hōryūji Yakushi image; their role in the narrative must be analyzed as well.

Ienaga Saburō has researched the *Imperial Biography*, analyzing it alongside other ancient documents with the main goal of providing a date for the text.[143] According to Ienaga, this document is a compilation of various manuscripts that took its current form in the late tenth or early eleventh century. It includes genealogies, events in the life of Prince Shōtoku, and inscriptions on monuments housed in Hōryūji. The *Imperial Biography* is also one of the earliest hagiographies of the prince believed to have been compiled by a monk from Hōryūji.

The manuscript is contained in a single scroll without subtitles or divisions, but Ienaga has divided it into five sections according to their contents. In his scheme, Section A includes genealogies related to the prince, mentioning his parents, his siblings from both parents and from his father, his children, his grandchildren, his siblings from his mother, and his ancestors (the rulers Kinmei, Bidatsu, Yōmei, Suiko, and Sushun). Section B narrates events in his life, emphasizing his role in the politics of the Asuka period and his sophisticated knowledge and patronage of Buddhism. This section includes references to the building of Gangōji and Shitennōji, and the establishment of the "cap ranks" system; his miraculous birth and all of his given names; his education and his teacher, Hyeja, as well as his erudition in Buddhism; the seven temples that he established; his lecture on the *Lion's Roar Sutra* and the establishment of Hōryūji; and his death, and Hyeja's promise to die a year later and meet him in a pure land.

Section C compiles inscriptions on objects housed at Hōryūji associated with the prince, and commentaries on these inscriptions. These include the inscriptions on the halo of the Yakushi image and on the mandorla of the Shaka triad (along with commentaries on the latter), the inscription on the Tenjukoku Shūchō (with commentaries), and three poems composed by Kose no Mitsue grieving Shōtoku's passing. Section D addresses events related to the Soga family and their role in the introduction and propagation of Buddhism in the Japanese islands. Events mentioned are the confrontation between Soga no Umako and the anti-Buddhist Mononobe no Moriya (d. 587), followed by the establishment of Shitennōji; the introduction of Buddhism and Umako's role; and the demise of Shōtoku's line through the killing of Prince Yamashiro and his family. Section E lists the dates of death and locations of the burial sites of the five rulers mentioned in Section A, as well as the prince. In addition, a text about Yamadadera, the temple in Sakurai (Nara Prefecture) commissioned by Soga no Kurayamada no Ishikawamaro, is recorded on the back of the manuscript.

Ienaga has indicated that the five sections were written at different times and brought together in the late tenth or early eleventh century.[144] Sections A and E, the genealogies and tomb locations, are the types of imperial records seen in *Kojiki*; as such, Ienaga considers them historically reliable, and dates them to the Taihō era (701–4). The information found in the genealogies, however, is different from that contained in the records in *Kojiki* and *Nihon shoki*. Ienaga thus has argued that the *Imperial Biography* relied on different sources from those used by *Kojiki*'s scribes. One clear example of this variation is the section of the genealogy on Shōtoku's wives and children. As discussed previously, this section contains the names of three wives of the prince, none of whom is mentioned in *Nihon shoki*.

Regarding Sections B and D (narratives about the life of the prince and others), Ienaga has suggested that some of the material is historical, but the vast majority is hagiographical. Most events are derived from accounts in *Hōryūji engi*, *Gangōji engi*, and the *Nihon shoki* narrative about the origins of Shitennōji. For this reason, Ienaga dates these sections to the period between the compilation of *Nihon shoki* in 720 and sometime after the compilation of the two *engi* in 747. The *Imperial Biography* includes information not mentioned in *Nihon shoki*, such as the list of the seven temples established by Shōtoku from *Hōryūji engi*. In addition, some narratives appear to "correct" the information given in *Nihon shoki*. For instance, regarding the date of the introduction of Buddhism to Japan, the *Imperial Biography* follows the date of 538 given in *Gangōji engi*, rather than 552 as recorded in *Nihon shoki*.

According to Ienaga, Sections A and B were probably joined together in the early eighth century, and Sections D and E were added sometime before the end of the eighth or beginning of the ninth century. He has called these four sections the "Old Version of the *Imperial Biography*."[145] As he explains, these four sections must have been combined before *Jōgū Shōtoku Taishi den hoketsuki* and *Shōtoku Taishi denryaku* were written, as most of the content of these two documents is derived from the Old Version. Section C, however, was added to correct information provided in the aforementioned hagiographies of the prince, particularly regarding his death. For example, in *Jōgū Shōtoku Taishi den hoketsuki*, Shōtoku's death is described as painless, but the inscription on the mandorla of the Shaka triad, included in Section C, states that the prince and one of his consorts died from a disease.[146] In the same way, *Shōtoku Taishi denryaku* states that the prince and a consort died on the same day, but the Shaka triad inscription indicates that Princess Kashiwade died on the twenty-first, and the prince, on the twenty-second. Because of these discrepancies, Ienaga has proposed that Section C was added after the compilation of *Shōtoku Taishi denryaku* in the tenth century.

With its inclusion in the *Imperial Biography* together with the inscriptions from the Shaka triad and the Yakushi image in Hōryūji's Golden Hall, the Shūchō inscription became associated with these two other texts, despite the fact that the original provenance of the Shūchō is unknown. Additionally, as discussed above, the Baekje-derived graphs used to record certain names in the Shūchō inscription are the same as those used in the inscriptions included in *Gangōji engi*. Notably, in the latter, Shōtoku is called by the names Umayado and/or Toyotomimi, rather than the Buddhist-related epithets found in the Hōryūji sources. For this reason, it is possible that the Shūchō was not made in the Ikaruga area, but in the Asuka region by people associated with the Soga kinship group. Somehow, the Shūchō ended up at Hōryūji, where its inscription was transcribed in the late tenth or early eleventh century.

Modern historians indicate that the content of the *Imperial Biography* complements the information recorded in *Nihon shoki*, giving a complete picture of the life (or hagiography) of the prince. Such a complete picture, however, is not found in hagiographies. Furthermore, it appears that the manuscript did not circulate. It seems to have been forgotten at Hōryūji, and only in the early thirteenth century did the Hōryūji monk Kenshin use the genealogy section of this document in his writings.

The next reference to the *Imperial Biography* is not found until 1695 (Genroku 8), when the *Dai Nihon shi* (Great History of Japan) was compiled.[147]

Although the exact provenance of the embroidered curtains is unknown, the evidence suggests that, by the late tenth or early eleventh century, the artifact was housed in a repository at Hōryūji, and its inscription was transcribed together with those on the mandorla of the Shaka triad and the halo of the Yakushi image there. When the three inscriptions and the poems (Ienaga's Section C) were added, the *Imperial Biography* became a new, more complete, evidence-based narrative, one that stressed the connections between Hōryūji and Prince Shōtoku. This new narrative suggested that Hōryūji was the first temple established by the prince, and also the only cultic center that housed memorials of his death. For instance, the Yakushi inscription indicates that Hōryūji was planned before any of the other temples established by Shōtoku. The inclusion of this inscription perhaps was meant to imply that the prince's campaign of building Buddhist temples did not begin with the construction of Shitennōji in 587, but started a year before, in 586, when he promised his ailing father, Great King Yōmei, to build a temple and enshrine in it an image of Yakushi.

Similarly, as noted by Ienaga, the inscription on the Shaka triad gives us an account of the circumstances of the deaths of the prince and his consort, Princess Kashiwade, that differs from the narratives found in *Jōgū Shōtoku Taishi den hoketsuki* and *Shōtoku Taishi denryaku*. The two commentaries that follow this inscription in the *Imperial Biography* focus on confirming the death dates of each of the people mentioned in the inscription: Queen Consort Anahobe, Princess Kashiwade, and the prince (621/12/21, 622/2/21, and 622/2/22, respectively).[148] Judging by the long discussion about these dates in the commentaries that precede the Shūchō inscription, it seems that one of the reasons for adding the latter was to provide further proof of the correct dates of the deaths of Shōtoku and Anahobe. These three inscriptions were included in the *Imperial Biography* as Hōryūji's "documentary evidence" of the prince's early Buddhist activities at the temple, and the circumstances of his death. Their addition to the manuscript, along with the poems by Kose no Mitsue, created a detailed narrative of the events associated with Shōtoku's death, including the memorials made for the next-in-line to rule, and even the funeral poetry recited in the prince's honor.

CONCLUSION

The inscription recomposed by Iida, using the *Imperial Biography* and later versions, has been accepted as the text originally embroidered on the Shūchō. Formerly it was believed to be a product of the early seventh century, but recent scholarship and archaeological discoveries have brought interesting new perspectives to issues that have long been the subject of scholarly debate. Most scholars now agree that the Shūchō's inscription was written in the middle or last quarter of the seventh century.

First, the discovery of *mokkan* at the Asuka pond site seems to have finally settled the nearly century-long dispute about the possible use of the term *tennō* in the early seventh century. Although it is not known what other evidence may lie underground, for now, the general consensus is that the term began to be used in the late seventh century during the reigns of Tenmu and Jitō. Second, if the inscription was composed at such a late date, then the use of Japanese-style posthumous names to refer to the rulers is not problematic; Wada's study provides a reasonable explanation for the inclusion of these terms by considering the ritual context in which the names were given.

Particularly revealing are the studies on the use of *man'yōgana*, or phonograms. Because they are not found in the official historical records produced by the Yamato court, these graphs, and their presence on the Shūchō, were considered problematic. Studies on *man'yōgana* have revealed that those recorded on the Shūchō were used by scribes from Baekje. Perhaps these were the same scribes, or scribes related to those who wrote the inscriptions on the pagoda finial and the sixteen-foot Buddha image from Gangōji (Asukadera). The three inscriptions share the same phonograms to record the rulers' Japanese-style posthumous names and the names of their respective palaces. In addition, these sources do not use the Buddhist epithet of Dharma King to refer to Prince Shōtoku, but give only the names that he apparently used during his lifetime: Umayado and Toyotomimi.

Likewise, the selective genealogy in the inscription was meant to show that Tachibana and Toyotomimi were direct descendants of the two most powerful families of the Asuka period, Kinmei's line and the Soga kinship group, which seems to have ruled side by side with the Yamato court since the time of Kinmei and Iname. In this genealogy, Kitashi hime is elevated to Senior Queen Consort, showing a clear Soga agenda. As Yoshie has pointed out, Tachibana, as a descendant of both sides, would have been the only person mentioned in the inscription who was interested in making these claims. She is portrayed as a grieving and dutiful wife and daughter-in-law who, with the support of her grandmother, Great King Suiko, was able to create a memorial for both her husband and his mother. Although we may assume that Tachibana was involved in the project, it is likely that Suiko was already dead when the creation of the Shūchō was carried out. Thus Tachibana must have strategically used her grandmother's name to give more authority to the statements in the inscription. If Tachibana were no longer alive, other supporters of the Kinmei–Soga line may have been interested in making the Shūchō. A close look at the kinship groups to which the supervisor and draftsmen belonged, the Hata and the Aya, shows that these groups not only were allied with the Kinmei–Soga line, but had control over the materials and labor force necessary to complete the project. The close involvement of these immigrant groups also explains the continental components of the visual evidence.[149]

The transcription of the Shūchō's inscription in the *Imperial Biography* may have changed its meaning, and therefore should be considered the second phase of the inscription's life. It is impossible to determine the extent of the modifications, deletions, or additions that may have been made to the original inscription on the Shūchō when it was transcribed in the *Imperial Biography* manuscript. By the late tenth or early eleventh century, the Shūchō was held in a repository at Hōryūji, and its inscription, together with those on the Shaka triad and Yakushi image at the temple, was added to the Old Version (to use Ienaga's term) of the text. At that moment, the original significance of the Shūchō's inscription was lost, and the three inscriptions, taken together, created a new narrative about Prince Shōtoku and his association with Hōryūji. This view is supported by the fact that the Shūchō's text does not show elements of the cult of the prince. Toyotomimi is presented just as a prince, not as the regent to Suiko. Although the Buddha is mentioned, the prince is not portrayed as particularly knowledgeable about Buddhism, and importantly, he is referenced only as Prince Toyotomimi, rather than the Dharma King or Prince Shōtoku. None of the epithets employed by the cult of the prince are seen here. For this reason, it is possible that the inscription was composed before "Prince Shōtoku" was created, probably by people associated with Gangōji and the Kinmei–Soga lineage in the Asuka region, and not in Ikaruga, which was a Kashiwade stronghold.

In the late tenth or early eleventh century, the Hōryūji monk who incorporated the Shūchō's inscription into the *Imperial Biography* gave it a new life. The inscription became evidence of the circumstances of the death of Prince Shōtoku. Already the scribe was puzzled by the term Tenjukoku, adding the comment that "Tenjukoku is a metaphor for heaven." The meaning of Tenjukoku at the time of the Shūchō's creation is tied to the politics, afterlife beliefs, and ritual practices that contributed to the production and reception of the embroidered curtains in seventh-century Japan.

3

Tenjukoku Shūchō in Seventh-Century Japan

THE PARTIAL RECONSTRUCTION of the Shūchō's iconographical program undertaken in this study has demonstrated that the subject matter was not Buddhist, as generally assumed, but associated with the funerary iconography then current in China and Korea. The vast majority of motifs can be traced back to Han-dynasty representations of the celestial realm; some of these were associated with divination practices and ideas of rulership. A few designs were the product of the interaction that occurred between Buddhism and indigenous Chinese beliefs in the fifth century. In addition, the inscription contains certain words (such as *minori* and *ōjō*) that might have a Buddhist meaning, but Tenjukoku as an afterlife abode does not appear in any of the canonical sutras. In order to understand this discrepancy, it is crucial to place the Shūchō within its historic and cultural context.

This chapter seeks to answer three questions. First, how was the Shūchō displayed? Second, what was the message that the patron or makers wanted to convey? Third, what was the meaning of the term Tenjukoku in seventh-century Japan? In order to fully explore these issues, seventh-century events, beliefs, and practices that might have had an impact on the creation of the Shūchō and the formulation of its inscription are analyzed. These include the use of embroidery as a pictorial medium, the role of curtains, the transmission of new Chinese ideas, the political situation, and the afterlife beliefs and funerary practices present in Japan at the time.

In the first section, "Embroidery as Pictorial Medium and Status Symbol," information about embroidery found in the earliest Japanese texts, which date to the eighth century, is discussed. Although most of the references address embroidered Buddhist icons, these passages are helpful for determining if the undertaking of a large-scale project like a pair of embroidered curtains was feasible at the time. Due to the scarcity of evidence in Japan, the second section, "Curtains in East Asia," relies on textual, archaeological, and pictorial evidence about the use of curtains in China and Korea, as well as Japan. The third section, "Infusion of New Ideas from China," examines the activities of the students in the first envoy to China, which left Japan in 608. Many of these students, who returned to Japan at various times in the following years, belonged to the Aya kinship group, which played a role in the making of the Shūchō.

Because the Shūchō's inscription and iconographical program seem to stress the right of the Kinmei–Soga line to rule, the fourth section, "Po-

Tamamushi Shrine, detail of fig. 33a.

litical Nuances in the Shūchō," addresses the problems with succession after the death of Prince Shōtoku and the struggles of the descendants of this line. In this period of political turmoil, the new leaders of the Soga clan, Emishi and Iruka, supported another royal line as contenders to the throne, and even made their own claims to rule. The fifth section, "Afterlife Beliefs and Funerary Practices," includes an analysis of the various options for such beliefs and practices as recorded in the textual and archaeological evidence. Because these beliefs and practices appear to have been based on continental ideas and models, in the sixth section, "Tenjukoku as an Afterlife Realm," pertinent aspects of Chinese culture between the fourth and sixth centuries, especially those derived from the interaction between Buddhism and indigenous religions, are analyzed.

EMBROIDERY AS PICTORIAL MEDIUM AND STATUS SYMBOL

The fragments of the Shūchō and the aforementioned banner from Hōryūji comprise the only material evidence of embroidered fabrics in ancient Japan. Yet entries in *Nihon shoki* and temple documents suggest that embroidery not only served as an indicator of sociopolitical status, but constituted the preferred pictorial medium used to make two-dimensional Buddhist images in the seventh and eighth centuries. The abundance of textual references to embroidered Buddhist images might be the reason that the fragments of the Shūchō were categorized as *shūbutsu*, in spite of the fact that the designs do not relate to Buddhist iconography.[1] The foregoing partial reconstruction of the Shūchō's iconographical program suggests that, in the seventh century, embroidery might not have been limited to the creation of Buddhist icons, but also may have been used for pictorial representations of other subjects.

Among the entries about embroidery in *Nihon shoki*, some refer to embroidered garments and caps. Two records suggest that embroidered garments were symbols of high social status. An entry from 608 describes the ensembles worn by the crown prince, princes, and ministers when an envoy visited from China. The text states that these elite individuals wore golden hair ornaments and clothing of brocade, purple, embroidered fabric, and multicolored patterned gauze.[2] The other entry is a sumptuary law from 681, which regulated the types of clothing and materials that could be worn by different segments of society from princes to commoners. The law contained ninety-two articles, although not all are recorded in *Nihon shoki*. The entry only mentions that the regulations addressed the use of gold, silver, jewels, purple, brocade, embroidery, twills, woolen carpets, headdresses, and girdles, as well as colored items.[3] Although the information in these entries cannot be verified against any other type of evidence, it can be assumed that embroidered fabrics were worn by members of the elite and were subject to regulation, perhaps following Chinese models. Purple—the color of the Shūchō's ground fabric—is the only color specifically mentioned in the two entries. This color, the dye for which was obtained from the roots of a variety of gromwell plant (genus *Lithospermum*), had been employed since the Han dynasty to indicate high rank.[4] Further evidence of the importance of fabric types and colors as status indicators is also evident in "cap ranks" systems. In these systems, the colors, embroidery, and fabric types used for official caps served as markers of the different politico-administrative ranks. In the three such systems recorded in *Nihon shoki* (647, 649, and 664), caps made with embroidered fabric correspond to the second highest rank.[5]

Nihon shoki also tells us that embroidery was the two-dimensional medium favored for making Buddhist images for the temples associated with the ruling elite.[6] Three of the so-called Four Great Temples (Asukadera, Kudara Ōdera, Kawaradera, and Yakushiji) in the Asuka area had embroidered Buddhist icons.[7] Information about the sizes of, and subjects represented on, the embroideries from Asukadera (Gangōji), Kudara Ōdera, and Yakushiji may help us to understand the possibilities of embroidery as a pictorial medium.

The first embroidered Buddhist icon mentioned in *Nihon shoki* was made for Asukadera, the first large-scale temple built in Japan, which was sponsored by the Soga kinship group. According to *Nihon shoki*, in 605, Great King Suiko ordered Prince Shōtoku, Soga no Umako, and other princes and ministers to vow to make a copper (*akagane*) Buddha image and an embroidered Buddha image, each measuring sixteen feet (the standard *jōroku* size, or one *jō*, six *shaku*).[8] A year later, both images had been completed, and were enshrined in the halls of the temple.[9] Although rather damaged and clumsily repaired, the Buddha sculpture (known as the Great Buddha of Asukadera) is still extant, but regrettably nothing is left of the embroidery. Excavations at the site of the temple have revealed that Asukadera had three Golden Halls; scholars thus have proposed a variety of theories regarding the placement of the two images, and also have suggested the possibility of the existence of a third icon. As the Great Buddha was housed in the northern Golden Hall, the embroidered icon could have been located either in the eastern or western Golden Hall.[10] These two icons are mentioned again in 645, in a message sent from Great King Kōtoku to the monks of Kudara Ōdera, conveying the ruler's support for Buddhism. Interestingly, the information about the icons' creation contained in this entry is slightly different from that found in the previous mentions. Rather than focusing on Suiko as the patron, the role of the Soga is emphasized, as Soga no Umako is given sole credit for commissioning the two Asukadera images.[11]

Kudara Ōdera (known subsequently as Takechi Ōdera, Daikandaiji, and Daianji), the second of the Four Great Temples to be built in the Asuka area, also had an embroidered Buddhist icon. The complex history of this temple is recorded in two sources: *Nihon shoki* and *Daianji engi narabi ni ruki shizaichō* (Account of the Establishment of Daianji and List of Accumulated Treasures), compiled in 747 (Tenpyō 19). Archaeological excavations suggest that the temple, established by Great King Jomei in 639, was located originally at the site of Kibi Pond. The temple was moved to Takechi (a currently unidentified location) in 673, renamed Daikandaiji in 677, and moved to the new capital of Nara in the early Nara period, with the name of Daianji.[12] *Nihon shoki* tells us that, in 650 (during Kōtoku's reign), a *jōroku* embroidered figure (*shuzo*) with attendant bodhisattvas and the Eight Classes of Beings (*hachibushū*), a total of thirty-six deities, was made; the project took five months to complete.[13] The day after the embroidery was finished, the Queen Dowager (who had ruled previously as Kōgyoku and would later rule as Saimei) offered a meager entertainment for the Ten Monks, monastic officials of high rank.[14] Because a similar entry appears in *Daianji engi*, it could be assumed that the embroidery was taken to the new capital.[15] As the entries in *Nihon shoki* indicate, the composition of the embroidery seems to have been complex, including a large number of Buddhist deities. The information in *Daianji engi* includes the size of the embroidered icon: two *jō*, two *shaku*, seven *sun* in height; and two *jō*, two *shaku*, four *sun* in width (for conversion of these measurements to the metric system, see Table 3 below). This text also states that the icon was commissioned by Enchi, a name for Saimei derived from the name of her tomb.[16] The dimensions listed contradict those given in *Nihon shoki*, where the term *jōroku* seems to be used to refer to a large image.

Daianji engi lists other embroideries in the temple's collection, such as an embroidered bodhisattva offered in the seventh month of 686 by the Queen Consort (probably Jitō) and the Crown Prince for the sake of the Kiyomihara palace's Heavenly Sovereign (probably Tenmu). Mizuno Ryūtarō has suggested that this offering relates to the *Nihon shoki* entry for the second day of the eighth month of 686 (Shuchō 1), which denotes the dedication of one hundred bodhisattvas within the palace, and the reading of two hundred volumes of the *Kannon Sutra* (Chapter Twenty-five of the *Lotus Sutra*).[17] The list also includes a set of embroideries for ordination ceremonies (S. *abhiṣeka*; J. *daikanjō*). Unfortunately, the components of the set are not mentioned, but we know that it was offered on the twenty-third day of the tenth month of 693 by the Kiyomihara palace's Heavenly Sovereign (Jitō) for the Benevolent Kings ceremony (*Ninnōe*). This ref-

Embroideries		jō	shaku	sun	26.8-cm shaku	29.8-cm shaku
Asukadera		1	6	-	4.29 m	4.77 m
Daianji (650)	Length	2	2	7	6.08 m	6.76 m
	Width	2	2	4	6.00 m	6.68 m
Daianji (742)	Length	2	-	-	5.36 m	5.96 m
	Width	1	8	-	4.82 m	5.36 m
Yakushiji	Length	3	-	-	8.04 m	8.94 m
	Width	2	1	7	5.82 m	6.47 m
Tōdaiji	Length	5	4	-	14.47 m	16.09 m
	Width	3	8	4	10.29 m	11.44 m

Table 3   Sizes of embroidered Buddhist icons. One *jō* equals ten *shaku*, and one *shaku* equals ten *sun*.

erence coincides with the lectures on the *Benevolent Kings Sutra* (*Ninnōkyō*) that were held in one hundred provinces for four days, as recorded in *Nihon shoki*.[18] Rulers were not the only people who presented embroidered icons at Daianji. In 742 (Tenpyō 14), the monk Dōji (d. 744), the head monk Kyōgi, and other monks offered two embroidered panels, each measuring two *jō* in height and one *jō*, eight *shaku* in width. The subjects were apparently derived from the *Flower Garland Sutra* and the *Greater Perfection of Wisdom Sutra* (S. *Mahāprajñāpāramitā sūtra*; J. *Daihannyakyō*).[19]

The third of the Four Great Temples that owned an embroidered Buddhist icon was Yakushiji. *Yakushiji engi* (Account of the Establishment of Yakushiji) lists an embroidered Buddhist icon housed in the Lecture Hall that measured three *jō* in height and two *jō*, one *shaku*, seven *sun* in width, with a representation of Amida, attendants, and heavenly beings, for a total of about one hundred embroidered figures.[20] A note on the temple's list of treasures states that Heavenly Sovereign Jitō dedicated this embroidered icon for the sake of Heavenly Sovereign Tenmu in 692.[21]

Apparently, the practice of making embroidered Buddhist icons continued into the eighth century. *Tōdaiji yōroku* (Records of Tōdaiji; compiled 1106) includes a record of three panels, each with an embroidered bodhisattva, hanging in the Great Buddha Hall on the day of the eye-opening ceremony for the gigantic bronze Buddha in 752 (Tenpyō shōhō 4). Each panel measured five *jō*, four *shaku* in height, and three *jō*, eight *shaku*, four *sun* in width. The text also lists two embroidered mandalas dedicated in 758 (Tenpyō hōji 2).[22] Panels with embroidered bodhisattvas at Tōdaiji are mentioned by Ōe no Chikamichi (d. 1151), who visited this temple as part of his pilgrimage to the Seven Great Temples of Nara. In *Shichidaiji nikki* (Diary of [the Pilgrimage to] the Seven Great Temples; ca. 1106), he recorded two embroidered panels with depictions of a Shō Kannon (S. Ārya Avalokiteśvara) and a twenty-armed Fukūkenjaku Kannon (S. Amoghapāśa Avalokiteśvara), each measuring about six *jō* in height.[23] It is difficult to determine if what Chikamichi saw were the eighth-century embroideries listed in *Tōdaiji yōroku* or later versions, although the dimensions are close enough to suggest that they might have been the former.

Embroidered fabrics from the Heian period have not survived, and only a few records contain references to embroidered Buddhist icons.[24] According to Ishida Mosaku, the main reason for the absence of embroidered Buddhist icons in this period is that painting replaced embroidery as the preferred medium.[25]

If the information about the sizes discussed above is correct, it can be surmised that embroidered Buddhist icons made in the seventh and eighth centuries were large, and that some featured complex compositions that included many Buddhist deities. Perhaps some of the compositions resembled the embroidered panel representing a *Buddha Preaching*, formerly at the temple Kajūji in Kyoto (see fig. 10).[26] The place and date of manufacture for this embroidery are controversial, as textual information about the piece is lacking. Some scholars argue that this embroidery was made in China, while others state that it was made in Japan; the dates proposed range from the mid-seventh to the late ninth century. The embroidery measures 2.08 by 1.58 meters, and includes fifty-six figures in the composition. Compared to the sizes of the aforementioned embroideries with Buddhist subjects recorded in ancient texts (listed in Table 3 below), the Kajūji image is small.

As indicated in Table 3, the length of a *shaku* varies according to the period. In this chart, the confirmed eighth-century length of 29.8 centimeters per *shaku*, and the proposed seventh-century length of 26.8 centimeters are used. Extant rulers confirm that the Nara-period *shaku* was equivalent to 29.8 centimeters.[27] Rulers from the seventh century have not survived, and for this reason, the length of the *shaku* at that time is controversial. The length of 26.8 centimeters has been proposed by Arai Hiroshi, who came up with this figure after measuring monuments and artifacts dated to the fourth through seventh centuries in Japan and Korea.[28]

The embroidered icons' dimensions, which range from four to sixteen meters, suggest that large-scale embroideries were made in the seventh and eighth centuries. If the measurements are accurate, then the production of a pair of embroidered curtains must have been feasible. These projects were not only large in terms of the sizes of the objects, but some of the embroideries seem to have had complex compositions, making it likely that the designers and manufacturers were specialized workers. If the embroidered icons for Asukadera and Kudara Odera were made in the first half of the seventh century, then their makers could have been the aforementioned *kinunuibe*, who specialized in needlework, in coordination with Buddhist monks who had knowledge of Buddhist iconography. References to specialized groups of workers, however, disappear after the Taika Reform of 645. The reason might be related to the abolishment of the *shinabe* (groups of skilled craftspeople) that were affiliated with immigrant kinship groups. As the court moved towards centralization, these specialized workers became subjects of the state.[29] Archaeological excavations suggest that the centralized-state system (*ritsuryō kokka*) was implemented during Tenmu's reign. For instance, the aforementioned excavations in 1991 at the Asuka pond site, southeast of Asukadera, revealed that, by the late seventh and early eighth centuries, workshops for glass, metal (gold, silver, and bronze), wooden and metal tools, lacquer, and tiles had been established, as well as the mint for the so-called Fuhon coins, which likely date from 683. In addition, *mokkan* found in the excavations reveal the management system in place for these workshops at the beginning of the centralized-state system.[30] If most craftspeople were integrated into this system, it is possible that the embroidered icons commissioned by Tenmu and Jitō were made by needlework specialists who were controlled by the state.

In sum, the vast majority of the textual evidence addressing embroidery relates to embroidered Buddhist icons, suggesting that the medium was used exclusively for this purpose. Yet the few entries about other types of embroidered objects indicate that the technique also was used to embellish fabrics, and that embroidered designs comprised markers of status. The abundance of references to embroidered Buddhist icons must be the reason for the classification of the fragments of the Tenjukoku Shūchō Mandara as such. This modern categorization was strengthened when the assemblage was displayed in the first exhibition dedicated exclusively to *shūbutsu*, held at Nara National Museum in 1964.[31] Following this exhibition, the Tenjukoku Shūchō Mandara was named the earliest example of this form of Buddhist art, and subsequently was exhibited and published under this description. The Shūchō's inscription, and the extant designs on the fragments, comprise evidence that embroidery as a pictorial medium was also used to create pictorial compositions on curtains. In order to further understand this topic, it is crucial to explore the use of curtains in ancient East Asia.

CURTAINS IN EAST ASIA

The *Imperial Biography*'s version of the Shūchō inscription clearly states that "two panels of embroidered curtains" (*shūchō nichō*) were made to represent Prince Shōtoku in Tenjukoku, upon the request of Princess Tachibana. When these curtains were discovered in the late thirteenth century, they were called a mandara. Due to this later nomenclature and the association of these fragments with Prince Shōtoku and the Buddhist nunnery of Chūgūji, modern scholars have assumed that the original artifact hung on a wall as a focus of worship, in the manner that painted Esoteric mandalas and Buddhist icons were displayed.[32] Furthermore, in English-language publications, the Shūchō is usually referred to as a "tapestry," a term that is also misleading as it refers to woven wall hangings with pictorial representations. Although some scholars had pointed out that the original embroidery served as curtains, in 1978, Ōhashi Katsuaki was the first scholar to explore the possible use of the artifact as such.[33] He determined that, in ancient Japan, curtains were used around beds that consisted of raised platforms with pillars, and also were employed to partially conceal Buddhist icons in shrines.[34] He romantically concluded that Princess Tachibana hung the Shūchō around her bed in the palace, in order to cherish the prince's memory. Although this might be an appropriate conclusion, when the elaborate iconographical program and the long genealogy embroidered on the curtains are taken into account, it is likely that the Shūchō must have been displayed to a selected, literate audience with the purpose of conveying a specific message.

Ōhashi's argument that curtains were used around beds is based on two entries in *Nihon shoki*. The first entry, from the chronicles of Great King Richū, tells us that the ruler wished to take Kurohime, the daughter of Hata no Yashiro no Sukune, as his concubine. He sent his younger brother, Prince Nakatsu, to announce his desires. Pretending to be Richū, Nakatsu proceeded to seduce Kurohime, and accidentally left his wrist-bells behind. The following day, Richū went to Kurohime's chamber; when he drew aside the curtain and sat down on the bed platform, he found his brother's wrist-bells, and realized that Nakatsu had been there the night before.[35] The other reference, from Kinmei's chronicles, narrates the story of the general Ōtomo no Sadehiko no Muraji looting the Goguryeo king's palace. The king managed to escape, but Sadehiko entered the palace and took many treasures, including a brocade curtain with threads of seven colors that hung in the king's private chambers.[36] These two entries certainly describe the use of curtains with beds, and the latter suggests that curtains were valuable objects that held worth as war booty. In addition to *Nihon shoki*, temple records were analyzed by Ōhashi to support his theory that curtains were used to cover Buddhist icons. Unfortunately, the evidence that he found does not provide information about specific materials or sizes, but only confirms that curtains were hung in shrines containing Buddhist icons.[37]

Besides the two functions proposed by Ōhashi, curtains were used to create temporary structures, and also were employed in funerary rituals. Two entries in *Nihon shoki* mention the use of curtains around tents where foreign envoys were entertained.[38] Curtains are among the funerary paraphernalia mentioned in regulations for funerals instated in 646 (Taika 2). These regulations indicate the sizes permitted for funerary mounds and the labor force allowed for the construction of tombs for princes and higher aristocrats, ministers, people of rank, and ordinary people as well. Importantly, the regulations also state that, for the interment of princes and those higher, white fabric should be used for the bier's curtains, and a hearse may be employed. For ministers, white fabric could be used for the bier, which had to be carried on men's shoulders. In short, according to these regulations, most people of rank could use white curtains around their biers, but common people were limited to coarse fabric. The regulations also forbade the construction of *mogari no miya*, the aforementioned temporary places of interment where specific ceremonies were held.[39]

In light of these regulations, and accepting an early-seventh-century date for the inscription, previously it seemed probable that the Shūchō had been part of the funerary paraphernalia of Prince Shōtoku and may have been used in his *mogari*, although no record of this exists. Furthermore, because the funerary regulations state that only white curtains should be used for the interment, it was theorized that colorful curtains, perhaps with pictorial decoration (such as the Shūchō), were employed in the entombment ritual and around the bier during the procession to transport the coffin to the tomb.[40] Considering the current understanding of the spread of literacy in seventh-century Japan, however, a later date for the manufacture of the Shūchō is more likely. If the Shūchō was not created for Shōtoku's burial ceremonies, it could have been hung inside the burial chamber at a later date, or used for a memorial service, as suggested by archaeological and textual evidence from China, Korea, and Japan.

In Japan and Korea, nails and metal fittings have been found on the walls of corridor-style tombs; these implements could have been used to hang fabrics or other kinds of fragile materials.[41] In China, white silk fabrics were found around the walls of the northern chamber of Tomb No. 1 at Mawangdui.[42] According to Wu Hung's research, such curtains might have held symbolic meaning; the bed chamber with curtains may have been a "spirit seat" (C. *ling zuo* or *shen wei*), a site that served to represent the invisible spirit of the deceased buried in the tomb.[43] In this chamber of Tomb No. 1, the silk cur-

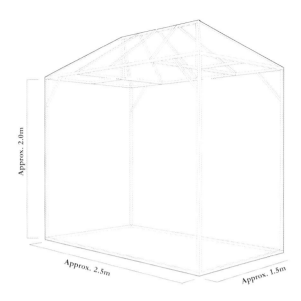

74 Reconstruction of a tent frame from the tomb of Liu Sheng. 113 BCE. Mancheng, Hebei Province. Line drawing by Summer Furzer.

tains cover the walls around a bamboo mat on the floor. A couch with thick cushions was found on top of the mat; additionally, a painted screen had been placed in the back. Lacquer vessels were found in front of the couch, as well as objects that obviously had belonged to the deceased female inhabitant, such as shoes, toilet boxes containing cosmetics, and a wig. Opposite to the couch was a group of wooden figurines representing singers, dancers, and musicians. These objects found nearby might have been offerings given to the deceased, whose spirit was believed to reside in the "spirit seat."

Other examples of "spirit seats" have been found in the tomb of Liu Sheng (dated to 113 BCE), in Mancheng, Hebei Province. Among the many objects found in the tomb were two sets of bronze brackets, which have been reassembled into two tent frames with gabled roofs. According to the reconstruction, each tent would have measured two and a half meters long, one and a half meters wide, and two meters tall (fig. 74).[44] Sets of vessels and figurines found aligned in front of the frames as offerings confirm that these tents also served as "spirit seats."[45] A third type is found in mural paintings in Eastern Han tombs. In these examples, a figure, usually identified as a portrait of the deceased, is depicted seated under a canopy with curtains tied to the poles. Because most of these portraits are painted on the wall behind a platform that served as an altar for offerings, Wu has argued that these figures are represented in their "spirit seats." Furthermore, the fact that most of the portraits are standardized has led Wu to suggest that the actual likeness of the deceased was irrelevant, as the main purpose of the image was to indicate the presence of the deceased's spirit.[46] Similar figures seated under canopies are found in Goguryeo tomb murals in Korea, such as Anak Tomb No. 3 (fig. 75) and Deokhungri. In these two tombs, as in their Chinese counterparts, the image of the deceased is seated under a canopy in front of a low screen. In all cases, the curtains are drawn or rolled, and tied to the top and side poles with bands or ribbons.

In addition to this material evidence, the placement of "spirit seats" in royal temples is recorded in Chinese documents. According to *Han jiu yi* (Old Ceremonies of the Han), by Wei Hong (act. 1st century), the Eastern Han royal temple in Luoyang housed an empty seat at its center, which represented Emperor Gaozu, the temple's main subject of worship.[47] The empty seat was sheltered by a canopy and embroidered curtains. Although the height of the canopy is not stated, its approximate size can be reconstructed based on the measurements given for the seat. This seat measured one *zhang* (J. *jō*) in length, and six *chi* (J. *shaku*) in width.[48] The Han *chi* was equivalent to about 23.5 centimeters; therefore, the perimeter of the seat was about seven and a half meters in total.[49] The seat was furnished with a table, and vessels inlaid with gold; food and wine were offered to the "spirit seat" during important sacrifices. The living emperor and his officials all knelt in front of it, paying their respects to Gaozu, the founder of the Han dynasty.[50] This reference in the *Old Ceremonies of the Han* is particularly relevant because it is the only text in China that refers specifically to embroidered curtains. Unfortunately, the subject embroidered on the curtains is not mentioned, but the seat's measurements suggest that the curtains covered a perimeter of seven and a half meters. These dimensions are similar to those of the reconstructed tents in Liu Sheng's tomb.

In contrast to these findings from China and Korea, little is known about memorial services or rituals for ancestor worship in ancient Japan. Archaeological excavations have not yet uncovered evidence that ancestral shrines (*sōbyō*) were built in ancient Japan.[51] Such sites are mentioned a few times in *Nihon shoki*, especially in conjunction with the shrines dedicated to the Earth and Grain, and in matters of succession. These entries suggest that safeguarding the ancestral shrines was the ruler's responsibility, and a measure of his success. For instance, before becoming Great King Jomei, Prince Tamura stated that he was too young and lacking in wisdom to accept the responsibility of keeping the ancestral shrines and the shrines to the Earth and Grain.[52] A similar narrative is recorded in the ascent of Great King Keitai (r. 507–31, in traditional reckoning).[53] Perhaps these entries reflect Chinese practices rather than actual events.

The only references associated with the remembrance of the dead in seventh-century Japan are those to the celebration of Ullambana (C. Yulanpen; J. Urabon), a Buddhist festival with Indian origins. In China, this festival was performed by both Buddhists and Daoists on the fifteenth day of the seventh month. Usually, donations were given to religious institutions to ensure the salvation of ancestors.[54] Two entries in *Nihon shoki*, from 606 and 657, make reference to the celebration of the Urabon festival in the seventh century. The first entry coincides with the year in which the sixteen-foot Buddha and embroidered Buddha were installed in Asukadera.[55] In addition, an entry of 659 states that the *Ullambana Sutra* was expounded in all temples of the capital for the sake of the ancestors for seven generations.[56]

Japanese textual evidence related to embroidered curtains usually involves the Tenjukoku Shūchō. In *Hōryūji engi*, however, a record of a pair of embroidered curtains not specifically identified as the Tenjukoku Shūchō does exist: "In the same group, [there are] two panels of embroidered cur-

75 Portrait of the deceased on the west wall of the west chamber, Anak Tomb No. 3. 357. Mural painting. South Hwanghae Province.

tains (*shūchō nichō*), twenty-two bands (*obi nijūni jō*), and 393 bells. Donated by Kiyomihara Gyō Tennō."[57] Because this entry appears in the section on Hōryūji's inventory, and because it is known that the Shūchō was at the temple when its inscription was transcribed in the tenth or eleventh century (as well as when it was rediscovered in 1274), it is possible that the entry does refer to the seventh-century Shūchō. The monk-scholar Kakuken (1764–1839) of Hōryūji, who compiled *Ikaruga koji binran* (Handbook of Ikaruga's Old Temples; 1836), was the first to draw attention to this entry in *Hōryūji engi*, and concluded that the Shūchō and the curtains referenced in the text were different objects.[58]

Modern scholars are split between those who accept that the *shūchō nichō* mentioned in *Hōryūji engi* refers to the seventh-century Shūchō, and those who do not. Those in the former group look to *Shōtoku Taishi denki* (Biography of Prince Shōtoku; 1317–19), a document narrating thirteenth-century events, which states that the mandara featured flat bands with golden bells.[59] These scholars argue that the fragmentary fabric bands with bells attached to chevron-shaped bronze plaques in Hōryūji's textile collection once formed part of the Shūchō. Because it is impossible to confirm if these bands were associated with the Shūchō since its manufacture in the seventh century, or if they were attached to the thirteenth-century artifact (the mandara), it cannot be determined if the description in *Shōtoku Taishi denki* refers to the Shūchō. Yet it is important to note that the embroidered curtains mentioned in *Hōryūji engi* were donated by the Kiyomihara Palace Heavenly Sovereign, which could refer to either Tenmu or Jitō. As discussed above, Jitō was actively involved in the commissioning and donation of embroidered goods. Therefore, it is possible that she commissioned a pair of embroidered curtains, and this entry in *Hōryūji engi* could comprise evidence that embroidered curtains other than the Tenjukoku Shūchō were made in ancient Japan.

Much like the motifs on the extant fragments of the Shūchō, the use of curtains might have been transmitted to Japan as one more Chinese practice. If that was the case, then the Shūchō could have been hung around a "spirit seat" to commemorate Prince Shōtoku and his mother, perhaps to celebrate the anniversaries of their deaths or to memorialize them during the Urabon festival. The pairing of mother and son in a mortuary setting is unusual in East Asian practice. The only explanation for commemorating the two of them together is that both were descendants of the Kinmei–Soga line who happened to die a few months apart.

INFUSION OF NEW IDEAS FROM CHINA

It is widely accepted that immigrants and Buddhist monks from China and the Korean peninsula played a role in the transmission of continental culture to Japan in the seventh century. In addition, Japanese students went to China, and returned to the islands after long stays. *Nihon shoki* tells us that the first group of students left in 608; most of them returned in the second quarter of the seventh century. As shown in Table 4, all but one of the students in this first envoy were related to the Aya kinship group.[60] Although *Nihon shoki* does not provide any details about their studies in China, the dates of their return show that some of the students stayed for more than three decades. This group arrived in China after its unification under the Sui dynasty (581–618), and witnessed the transition to the Tang. These students must have been exposed to many different aspects of Chinese culture. Upon their return to Japan, as the holders of continental knowledge, many of them were given administrative positions during Kōtoku's reign.

The activities of three members of this envoy

Students	Returned	Activities after return
Yamato no Aya no Atai Fukuin	623	Physician
Nara no Osa Emyō	No data	
Takamuku no Ayahito Kuromaro Genri	640	644 State Scholar 648 In charge of the Eight Departments of State 654 Member of envoy to China; dies in China
Imaki Ayahito Ōkuni	No data	
Monk-Scholars		
Imaki Ayahito Nichimon (Min)[61]	632	644 State Scholar 645 One of the Ten Professors 646 Temple head 648 In charge of the Eight Departments of State Omen interpretation
Minabuchi no Ayahito Shōan	640	Teacher of Prince Naka and Nakatomi no Kamatari
Shiga no Ayahito Eon	639	640, 652 Lectured on *Muryōjukyō* 646 Temple head
Imaki Ayahito Kōsai	No data	

Table 4 Members of the first envoy to China[62]

may help elucidate how the designs on the Shūchō were understood in seventh-century Japan. According to *Nihon shoki*, the first student to return was Fukuin. After studying Chinese medicine, he came back in 623 with another physician by the name of Enichi, and two Buddhist monks. They arrived with an envoy from Silla that brought Buddhist images, relics, and banners for Kōryūji (in Kyoto) and Shitennōji, two temples associated with Prince Shōtoku.[63] If Fukuin and Enichi studied Chinese medicine, they must have acquired knowledge about practices related to longevity and transcendence.[64]

Another member of the envoy, the monk Min, seems to have been particularly active as an interpreter of omens. Min returned to Japan in 632, and before becoming a State Scholar in 644, he explained certain signs in 637 and 639.[65] His role as an omen interpreter is highlighted in Kōtoku's chronicles. In 650, Min identified the appearance of a white pheasant as a good omen, which led to the naming of the Hakuchi (white pheasant) era (650–54). According to Min's interpretation, the white pheasant was seen when the ruler extended his influence to the four quarters and showed qualities such as frugal habits, the appropriate performance of sacrifices, wisdom, and compassion.[66] Kōtoku further explained that omens were a response from the heavens to a sage ruler, and mentioned the appearance of omens in China, and in Japan during the reigns of Ōjin (r. 270–310, in traditional reckoning) and Nintoku (r. 313–99, in traditional reckoning), who were emblematic of good sovereigns. Kōtoku seems to have been fond of Min, and visited the monk on his deathbed; after Min's death, the Great King, Queen Consort, and princes offered their condolences. In addition, Kōtoku ordered the making of paintings of Buddhas and bodhisattvas to be placed in Kawaradera.[67]

Min was not the first interpreter of omens to come to Japan. In 602, the monk Kwalluk (J. Kanroku) arrived from Baekje. The entry in *Nihon shoki* about his arrival states that he brought books on calendar-making, astronomy, geography, and the art of invisibility and magic.[68] In Japan, Kwalluk seems to have assumed the role of omen interpreter. According to Herman Ooms, during Suiko's reign, omens were used as a tool for political criticism between the ruling house and the Soga. Kwalluk read the portents for the Soga side.[69] Min and Kwalluk are both identified as monks, yet their activities mentioned in *Nihon shoki* suggest that they were trained in a variety of arts, with knowledge that was not limited to Buddhism. Although it is not possible to demonstrate that either Kwalluk or Min was directly involved in the design of the Shūchō, it is clear that belief in omens as messages from the heavens was prevalent in seventh- and eighth-century Japan.

A third member of the envoy, the monk Eon, returned to Japan in 639. According to *Nihon shoki*, he lectured on the *Buddha of Measureless Life Sutra* in 640 and 652.[70] This sutra describes Sukhāvatī, the Pure Land of Ultimate Bliss of the Buddha Amida. Because the entries do not specify the content of Eon's lectures, it is difficult to assert that he introduced the idea of birth in Amida's Pure Land to the Japanese court. It is conceivable that this sutra might have served instead as a vehicle for transmitting other ideas.

The few references in *Nihon shoki* to the returning students and immigrant monks suggest that they played an important role in the political and religious arenas of the mid-seventh century. Although they were called "monks," their activities were not limited to spreading Buddhist teachings. These men also played a role in the transmission of Chinese beliefs and practices, including divination methods used to verify good governance.

POLITICAL NUANCES IN THE SHŪCHŌ

In light of the seventh-century political situation after the death of Prince Shōtoku, as well as the new ideas being introduced from China, it is possible that the Shūchō conveyed two different messages when it was finished and displayed. On the one hand, the message was innocuous: as stated in the inscription, the curtains were made to commemorate the deaths of Prince Shōtoku and Queen Consort Anahobe, and to represent the prince in the afterlife realm known as Tenjukoku. On the other hand, political nuances may have been embedded in the embroidery. The long and selective genealogy carried by the turtle designs was surrounded by omen figures, suggesting that the creators might have aimed to glorify the Kinmei–Soga line amidst the problems of royal succession.

In order to understand the political message conveyed by the Tenjukoku Shūchō, the political events after Shōtoku's death that led to the end of the Kinmei–Soga line must be addressed. As narrated in *Nihon shoki*, this period witnessed the shift of political power from the descendants of Kinmei's line to those of Bidatsu's line. Prince Shōtoku's death in 622 was followed by the deaths of two other key figures of the Asuka period: Soga no Umako and Great King Suiko, who died in 626 and 628, respectively.[71] Umako had served as the head of the Soga kinship group since 570. When Bidatsu ascended the throne in 572, Umako was appointed senior minister (*ōomi*), and he continued to serve under the succeeding rulers Yōmei, Sushun, and Suiko. For more than fifty years, Umako controlled the politics of the Yamato court. Due to the fact that a well-established system of succession was not in place in the late sixth and early seventh centuries, conspiracy and bloodshed were common ways of solving disagreements. Umako always had the last word in the appointment of rulers, and achieved his goals by eliminating anyone who stood in his way.[72] He was an important patron of Buddhism who figured prominently in all episodes involving the establishment of the religion in Japan. He built Asukadera, the first large-scale Buddhist temple in Japan; construction of the temple began in 587 and culminated with the installation of the bronze and embroidered Buddhist icons in 609.[73] Although Umako is not mentioned in the genealogy on the Shūchō, as the son of Iname and the brother of two of Kinmei's wives, Kitashi hime and Oane, he was related to all eleven people recorded in it (see fig. 73).

After the deaths of Umako and Suiko, Umako's son Emishi was appointed senior minister. Entries in *Nihon shoki* suggest that a lack of agreement about the royal succession persisted within the Soga kinship group. *Nihon shoki* also tells us that Suiko's son, Prince Takeda, had died, as had the supposed next-in-line to the throne, Prince Shōtoku. Prince Yamashiro, Shōtoku's son, was the heir apparent, but no consensus could be reached to promote him to the throne. When the notables met to decide the matter, Emishi, alleging to follow Suiko's last request, appointed Prince Tamura, Bidatsu's grandson and a non-Soga, as the next Great King. Due to Emishi's recommendation of a non-Soga for the throne, discontent proliferated among the members of the Soga kinship group. Prince Yamashiro expressed his doubts about Suiko's alleged wishes from his residence in Ikaruga. Similarly, Sakaibe no Marise (d. 628), Umako's brother and an elder of the clan, did not agree with Emishi's decision and strongly expressed his dissent during a meeting held to discuss the building of Iname's tomb. Despite this lack of support from the members of the Soga clan, Emishi ensured that Prince Tamura took the throne as Great King Jomei, and took care of the opposing parties in the ruthless manner of his father. Sakaibe no Marise and his children were killed by Emishi's troops.[74]

Jomei ruled for about thirteen years, but *Nihon shoki* only records a few activities relevant to this study, such as his decree to build the Kudara Great Palace and Kudara Ōdera, the return of some of the students who went to China in 608, and the number of omens seen during his reign.[75] The other important figure during this time period was Princess Takara, also a descendant of Bidatsu's line. She was appointed Jomei's Senior Queen Consort in 630; after his death in 641, she ruled first as Great King Kōgyoku, and later as Saimei. Emishi served as Kōgyoku's senior minister, and his son, Iruka, also took charge of government.

From *Nihon shoki*, we gather that Emishi and Iruka outraged the royals by making blunt statements about their own political influence. Emishi created his own images of power; in 642, he erected an ancestral shrine in Takamiya (in Katsuragi, Nara Prefecture) and performed the eight-row dance.[76] According to Ooms, performance of this dance in the ancestral shrines was a privilege of the ruler.[77] Furthermore, Emishi ordered the construction of large-scale tombs for himself and Iruka, using Prince Yamashiro's laborers. This did not sit well with Yamashiro's wife, who was the eldest daughter of Shōtoku and Princess Kashiwade (see fig. 72).[78] Moreover, in 643, when Emishi was unable to attend court due to health problems, he appointed his son Iruka as senior minister. Using his newly acquired position, Iruka plotted to eliminate Prince Yamashiro and his descendants, and to make Furuhito (son of Jomei and Hotete no Iratsume, Emishi's sister) the new Great King. This marriage would have created strong ties between the royal family and the Soga once again.[79] As mentioned previously, Iruka succeeded in eliminating Prince Yamashiro and his family, who were forced to commit suicide in 643.[80] After this incident, the Soga furthered their claims of sovereignty by building two palaces on Amakashi Hill, and by styling their sons and daughters as princes and princesses. Living in fear of retaliation and attacks, they protected their palaces with palisades and an army. The demise of Iruka, however, happened at court: in 645, he was killed by Prince Naka no Ōe in front of Kōgyoku. Later, Naka ordered Emishi's execution as well.[81] In spite of their suspected treachery, the two Soga leaders were allowed a proper burial.

The deaths of Prince Shōtoku, Soga no Umako, and Great King Suiko led to the end of the Kinmei–Soga line. The individuals who commissioned the making of the Shūchō—Princess Tachibana, or her supporters—could have intended to make a statement about Prince Shōtoku's right to rule during this time of political turmoil. The selective genealogy accompanied by figures of omens might have been a statement about the just reign of the Kinmei–Soga line, and an assertion that Prince Shōtoku and Princess Tachibana were its direct and rightful descendants. In this genealogy, the deceased Prince Shōtoku appears as a direct descendant of both Kinmei and the Soga through his parents, Great King Yōmei and Queen Consort Anahobe. Princess Tachibana's mother is not listed in any genealogy, but her omission might have been intended to secure the focus on Tachibana not only as a descendant of the past dominant lineage (as a great-granddaughter of Kinmei and granddaughter of Suiko), but also as someone with links to the ruling one: both Tachibana and Great King Jomei were grandchildren of Bidatsu.

Emishi and Iruka had denied Prince Yamashiro the right to rule and supported Prince Tamura (Jomei), who was descended from Bidatsu's line. The princes and princesses from Kinmei's line were outraged by this circumstance, and expressions of their discontent are found in *Nihon shoki*. When Prince Tamura was being considered for the throne, Prince Hatsuse, son of Shōtoku and Princess Kashiwade, sent the following message: "Both my father and I spring from the Soga family, as is well known to the world. We, therefore, rely on it as on a high mountain. I pray, therefore, that the succession to the Dignity be not lightly spoken of."[82] Even more significantly, Emishi and Iruka later seemed to be making their own claims to the throne. One of Shōtoku's daughters, Princess Tsukishine, who was also Yamashiro's wife, had strong words about Emishi: "Soga Emishi usurps the government of the land and does outrageous things. In heaven there are not two suns, in a state there cannot be two sovereigns."[83] If Tachibana was still alive when the Shūchō was made, its inscription and iconographical program might have been a way for her to express similar feelings. If she was not alive, then the supporters of the Kinmei–Soga line may have used the Shūchō for the same purposes.

The time period when Soga no Emishi and Iruka were making their claims to the throne marked the twentieth anniversary of the deaths of Shōtoku and his mother. Could it be possible that Princess Tachibana, as the wife and daughter-in-law of the two individuals commemorated by the Shūchō, planned a memorial service and displayed the curtains around a "spirit seat?" The conspicuousness of the genealogy suggests that the intended audience must have been the literate elite, a group aware of the lineage issues and problems of succession happening at the time. Despite the political nuances implicit in the message, Tachibana also was explicitly remembering Shōtoku and Anahobe, and expressing her wish to see her late husband in Tenjukoku. If the Shūchō was made in the late seventh century, as suggested by the current scholarly consensus, the curtains still could have served as a memorial for the prince and the Queen Consort, descendants of a glorious ruling lineage of the past.

AFTERLIFE BELIEFS AND FUNERARY PRACTICES

It is generally assumed that the Asuka period saw the Buddhist transformation of Japan. The religion certainly spread, but it did not significantly influence beliefs about the afterlife, or burial practices. A multifaceted picture of afterlife beliefs is offered in the earliest textual sources, and Tenjukoku—which clearly refers to an afterlife realm—adds one more option. Eighth-century sources such as *Kojiki* and *Nihon shoki* refer to two afterlife abodes, both of which generally are acknowledged as Chinese in origin: Yomi no kuni and Tokoyo no kuni. The first is written with the same characters used for Huangquan (Yellow Springs), or the underworld; and the description of the second evokes the lands of the immortals.[84] Scholarship regarding these two realms is split. Some scholars argue that the presence of these terms comprises evidence of the arrival of Daoist beliefs in early Japan, whereas others claim that the terms were simply "deposited" by the compilers of *Nihon shoki* because, at the time of the compilation, people were interested in things Chinese.[85]

Poems in *Man'yōshū* suggest other afterlife options. In certain poems, the deceased are portrayed as sleeping, while in others, they are said to have gone to another land, a distant place, or the heavens. Princes were believed to go to the High Heavens (Takama no Hara), the realm of Amaterasu, the sun goddess; or to ascend to the celestial realm like the gods. Other poems suggest that the dead went to the mountains or beyond the sea, or secluded themselves in rocks.[86]

In addition, the Buddhist belief of being transported to a pure land also seems to appear, providing another afterlife destination. In *Nihon shoki*, the only reference to this Buddhist afterlife abode involves Prince Shōtoku's teacher, the monk Hyeja, who promised to meet the prince a year after his death in a pure land.[87] Besides this reference, a few inscribed bronze Buddhist icons, dated as early as 594, further support the spread of this belief in ancient Japan.[88]

It is clear that afterlife beliefs were not homogeneous. In the midst of this diversity, the creation of Tenjukoku as another afterlife option would not have been unusual. In order to understand the meaning of Tenjukoku as an afterlife abode, two things must be considered: Tachibana's grief-stricken words as evidence of the introduction of the Chinese practice of pictorializing the afterlife realm, and burial ceremonies in ancient Japan.

Based solely on the Shūchō's inscription, previous studies have assumed that Shōtoku and Tachibana were both devout Buddhists, and that Tenjukoku was a Buddhist pure land where the prince was reborn. Because the Shūchō's iconographical program is not coherently Buddhist, however, the inscription may not align exclusively with Buddhist beliefs. Tachibana's words might reflect the implicit worldview portrayed by the iconographical program, which might relate to the transmission of new Chinese ideas. To reiterate Tachibana's purported words,

> My prince said, "This world is empty; the only truth is the Buddha" (*seken wa munashi, tada hotoke nomi kore makoto nari*). He appreciated this *minori*. As a reward, my prince must have been born in "The Land of Heavenly Lifespan" (Tenjukoku). But, I cannot visualize that land. Please, somehow create an illustration of the place to which my prince was transported (or where he resides).[89]

As mentioned previously, this portion of the inscription contains words allegedly uttered by Prince Shōtoku that reveal his Buddhist beliefs, or perhaps beliefs associated with Princess Tachibana. From context, the word *minori*, which has multiple meanings, has been assumed to denote the Buddhist Dharma.[90] Based on these interpretations, the logical conclusion is that Tenjukoku signifies the Buddhist pure land where the prince was reborn. As a consequence of this interpretation, the fragments of the Shūchō have been categorized as the remains of the first pictorial representation of a Buddhist pure land in Japan.[91]

The last sentence of the quote, "Please, somehow create an illustration of the place to which my prince was transported (or where he resides)," deserves special attention. The final four-character phrase is transcribed as 往生之状 in the Chion'in version of the *Imperial Biography*; as 位生之状 in *Chūgūji engi*; and as 住生之状 in documents recounting the thirteenth-century events surrounding the rediscovery of the Shūchō. As discussed previously, in Pure Land Buddhism, the term 往生 (*ōjō*) refers to being reborn in Sukhāvatī, Amitābha's Pure Land of Ultimate Bliss; thus the last phrase is usually translated as "the place where he was reborn," assuming a Buddhist context for the inscription.

In his study of the various versions of the inscription, Iida Mizuho has noted the latter two transcriptions of the final four-character phrase in the documents dating to the thirteenth century.[92] He has argued that, at that time, the inscription was copied directly from the embroidery, rather than from the *Imperial Biography*. Certainly, the thirteenth-century scribe could have copied the phrase accurately, or written what he considered appropriate. Yet, if the scribe was able to copy the inscription directly from the embroidered artifact, it must have been in a state of preservation that allowed the reading of most of the graphs. If that had been the case, then the surrounding designs must have been in good condition as well. The thirteenth-century scribe might have noted that the designs were not related to representations of an Amitābha "transformation tableau" (C. *bianxiang*; J. *hensō*), diagrams or paintings of Amitābha's Pure Land that became popular in the early thirteenth century.[93] For this reason, the scribe might have opted for 住生之状.

Two conclusions may be reached on the two different renderings of the phrase. First, if the phrase was 往生之状, as recorded in the *Imperial Biography*, then the lack of coherence between the text and the iconographical program suggests that, when the idea of being transported to a pure land arrived in Japan, this concept did not come accompanied by pictorial representations of those Buddhist realms. Second, if the phrase was 位生之状 or 住生之状, as recorded in the thirteenth-century documents, then an exploration of the other afterlife options that may have been current at the time is warranted. Tachibana's words reveal her uncertainty about a world unknown to her. On the one hand, she could not visualize Tenjukoku, because, as Barbara Ruch has suggested, the idea of this world after death must have been new to her.[94] On the other hand, the remaining designs from the Shūchō, along with Tachibana's request to have a visual representation of this world made, suggest that she (or her supporters) might have been familiar with Chinese practices of pictorializing afterlife realms. The Takamatsuzuka and Kitora tombs provide evidence that such practices were introduced in the late seventh or early eighth century. More importantly, if the phrase was 住生之状, "the place where my prince resides," it could be argued that Tenjukoku was conceived as another land or place of residence.

Based on the extant designs and the reconstruction of the iconographical program proposed in this study, the Shūchō and its portrayal of Tenjukoku likely were aligned with traditions of Chinese funerary art, and should be considered as evidence of the transmission of the practice of creating pictorial representations of personalized afterlife worlds. As mentioned previously, in his comprehensive study on Chinese funerary art, Wu Hung has indicated that funerary art never developed a standard iconography because tombs belonged to individuals who expressed personal desires. Yet tomb decoration and funerary artifacts utilized certain common designs, especially for representing the "tripartite universe" of the heavens, the earthly realm, and paradise.[95] He also has pointed out that, as religious beliefs multiplied in China, deities and motifs associated with the new beliefs were incorporated into funerary iconography. The Queen Mother of the West, derived from the immortality cult; Taiyi, a

Daoist god; and the Buddha are all found in the iconographical programs of certain tombs. A specific Buddhist or Daoist funerary iconography, however, never developed. Buddhist and Daoist designs served to enrich the iconographical program of the afterlife as an ideal paradise; such designs never were meant to represent a specific Buddhist or Daoist afterlife abode. According to Wu, after the fifth century, the influence of Buddhism in the funerary arts of China decreased, while Daoism's impact increased, as demonstrated especially by the popularity of representations of two of the Four Divinities, the dragon and tiger, in tombs and sarcophagi.[96] Evidence of the transmission of the subject of the Four Divinities is found in seventh-century tombs from Goguryeo and Baekje in Korea, and in the late-seventh or early-eighth-century Takamatsuzuka and Kitora tombs in Japan.[97]

Archaeological and textual materials also show that the burial practices and rituals found in Japan followed Chinese and Korean models. The Takamatsuzuka and Kitora tombs yield confirmation of the transmission of the practice of building burial chambers covered by earthen mounds, the adoption of the iconography of the Four Divinities, and the representation of the constellations. The dating of these tombs suggests that, although Buddhism was introduced in the mid-sixth century, the burial practices established in the Kofun period (ca. 250–ca. 550) persisted. In fact, the first sovereign to be cremated in accordance with a Buddhist ritual was Jitō, who died in 702 (Taihō 2) and was cremated in 703 (Taihō 3) in Asuka.[98] Furthermore, mortuary rituals of the time did not include ceremonies specific to any one religion. Records of funerary rites in *Nihon shoki* reveal that the services performed were political in nature, and were not necessarily meant to ease the transition of the deceased from this world into the next.

As mentioned previously, after the death of a ruler or member of the elite, a temporary burial place, the *mogari no miya*, was built as the locus of the funerary rituals until the permanent interment of the corpse in the tomb.[99] The *mogari* rite was based on the Chinese *bin* ritual recorded in the *Liji* (Book of Rites; compiled Western Han dynasty), although the performance of the rite was adapted to suit Japanese needs.[100] Most of the *mogari* recorded are those performed for rulers, and although the details vary, the main service was the presentation of eulogies (*shinobigoto*) by ministers and members of the court.[101] Bidatsu's *mogari* is the first for which the presentation of eulogies is detailed. On this occasion, Senior Minister Soga no Umako and Mononobe no Moriya, senior *muraji* and head of the rival Mononobe clan, not only presented their eulogies for Bidatsu, but also took the opportunity to express their mutual hatred of one another.[102] When Suiko died, the records state that all of the ministers presented eulogies, but the names of these ministers are not recorded.[103] Some *mogari* included the participation of envoys from the Korean peninsula. For example, in Jomei's "great Baekje *mogari*," the heir apparent, Prince Hirakasu wake (the future Great King Tenji), recited the eulogies, and envoys from Baekje, Goguryeo, and Silla all offered their condolences.[104] The presentation of eulogies in Jomei's *mogari* also reveals that eulogies may not have been delivered personally, but could be stated on behalf of others; a certain *omi* presented eulogies on behalf of the princes, and a *muraji*, on behalf of the senior minister.[105]

The record of Tenmu's *mogari* is the longest and most detailed, and reveals features of the newly established centralized state. Everyone from the crown prince, members of the court, ministers and functionaries, Buddhist monks and nuns, to commoners participated in this lengthy *mogari*. A series of entries records the different groups going to the temporary burial place and presenting eulogies, lamentations, and offerings of food, song, and dance. On the day of the final interment, the last eulogy included a recitation of the imperial genealogy. Importantly, the role of the Buddhist monks and nuns was limited to the presentation of lamentations, and sutra readings or Buddhist offerings were not part of the ceremony.[106] Tenmu's *mogari* is also the only example that notes offerings of food for the deceased. Yet archaeological evidence suggests that, since the fifth century, when immigrant groups introduced the corridor-style tomb, offerings of food and drink must have been part of the rituals, as evidenced by the vessels found inside most burial chambers.[107]

The few entries in *Nihon shoki* associated with the organization of *mogari* suggest that the Haji, an immigrant kinship group, served the Yamato court as supervisors of both pottery manufacture and funerals.[108] Although it cannot be confirmed, the Haji claimed that their ancestor Nomi no Sukune invented *haniwa* to replace human sacrifices during funerals.[109] Like the Aya, the Haji were one of the service nobility groups in charge of specialized workers, and as such received the honorary title of *muraji*. Unfortunately, only three records in *Nihon shoki* refer to the participation of the Haji in the organization of *mogari*. When Prince Kume, Shōtoku's brother, was appointed to lead the invasion of Silla in 602, he fell ill and died in Tsukushi (Kyushu) before carrying out the expedition. His *mogari* was organized by the Haji no Muraji from Saba in Suō Province (present-day Yamaguchi Prefecture).[110] Another Haji no Muraji was put in charge of the burial of Kōgyoku's grandmother in 643, and also of Kōtoku's burial in 654.[111] According to Wada Atsumu, the duties performed by the Haji were not limited to the construction of the temporary place for mourning and the funerary mound, but also included the presentation of offerings at the *mogari no miya*, the organization of the funerary procession, and the supervision of the burial site.[112]

As these records attest, the Haji were in charge of the logistics of funerals, but they were not religious specialists. Funerals, especially those of rulers, were political events at which clan leaders showed their allegiance to the ruler or to the other members of the ruling elite, in order to ensure a good relationship with the appointed successor. Jomei's *mogari* was particularly noteworthy as it was attended by envoys from the three Korean kingdoms, who showed their support for his newly established ruling lineage.

The evidence discussed above strongly suggests that, by the time Prince Shōtoku died, Buddhist ideas about rebirth in a pure land were not widespread, even though Buddhism had been introduced to Japan more than eighty years earlier. The variety of afterlife realms mentioned in eighth-century sources indicates that a common view about the afterlife may not have existed. In addition, Wu has demonstrated that funerary iconographical programs in China did not aim to represent a world after death specific to any religion, but a personalized selection of elements. For this reason, the Shūchō might not have portrayed a Buddhist pure land or a Daoist heaven, which would also explain why the term Tenjukoku does not appear among the pure lands described in the Buddhist sutras or the multiple heavens listed in the Daoist scriptures.[113] Tenjukoku seems to have been one more destination for the dead among the many that coexisted in ancient Japanese belief.

TENJUKOKU AS AN AFTERLIFE REALM

The English translation of the term Tenjukoku, "Land of Heavenly Lifespan," certainly evokes images of the heavens, and thus seems fitting for an afterlife realm. Although the term Tenjukoku does not appear in any Buddhist or Daoist texts, the composite *tenju* (C. *tianshou*), "heavenly lifespan," appears in both. In a certain Daoist text, the term is specifically related to the Chinese belief that heaven grants each person an allotted lifespan. This term seems to have been used in Chinese translations of Buddhist sutras to express the idea that life in Buddhist pure lands was longer than life on earth. The interaction between Buddhism and Daoism that took place in China likely had bearing on the use and understanding of terms such as *tianshou*.

From the fifth century onward, Daoist priests and Buddhist monks were involved in debates that resulted in changes in both religions. The most notable of these changes were the adoption of some Buddhist beliefs by Daoists, the use of Daoist concepts in the translation of Buddhist sutras, and the writing of Daoist and Buddhist scriptures with similar content.[114] Erik Zürcher has argued that the Buddhist sutras of the Mahāyāna tradition, the form of Buddhism most prevalent in East Asia, influenced the writing of Daoist scriptures in style and terminology. Finding Buddhist elements in Daoist scriptures, he has concluded that Buddhism was seen as complementary to Daoism.[115] In addition, the interaction between these religions, especially during the fifth century, led to the incorporation of Buddhist ideas into Daoism. For instance, the concepts of karma and rebirth were adopted by the Celestial Masters (C. Tianshi) and Numinous Treasure (C. Lingbao) schools of Daoism.[116] The Celestial Masters adepts venerated Laozi (ca. 5th–4th century BCE, in traditional reckoning), the founder of philosophical Daoism, and linked him to the Buddha, even claiming that Laozi became the Buddha. They adopted certain Mahāyāna concepts such as the ideas of hell and rebirth, and the veneration of scriptures. Followers of the Celestial Masters were required to observe a set of rules for proper behavior; abuse and disobedience were punished, not only on earth, but also through rebirth in hell or a lower realm of existence. Although these and other Buddhist concepts were adopted by the Celestial Masters, Daoist ideas prevailed, especially the beliefs that all people had the potential to achieve immortality, and that good behavior could lead the follower to attain the higher levels of the heavens.[117]

A number of studies have demonstrated that Daoist terminology was used in the translation of some Buddhist sutras. Among these is the study by Fukunaga Mitsuji on the aforementioned *Buddha of Measureless Life Sutra* (C. *Wuliangshou jing*), a sutra that describes the Pure Land of Ultimate Bliss of the Buddha Amitābha. This sutra was translated into Chinese between 250 and 400.[118] Fukunaga has found a number of Daoist ideas and terms in the translation, and has argued that these elements were used to make the sutra accessible and easy to understand for the Chinese.[119] For example, the Sanskrit title of the text, *Sukhāvatīvyūha sūtra*, translates into English as "The Sutra on the Display of the [World of] Bliss" or "The Sutra Displaying the [World of] Bliss." Yet the Chinese rendering of the title, *Wuliangshou jing*, literally translates as "Sutra of Measureless Lifespan." Rather than making a literal translation of the Sanskrit title, the translator retitled the sutra, choosing another name for the Buddha Amitābha: Amitāyus, meaning "measureless lifespan." According to Fukunaga, this title allowed the Chinese people to understand the idea of rebirth in the Land of Bliss through comparison to the Chinese concept of longevity, a cornerstone of the immortality cult and Daoism.[120] Following Fukunaga's theory, it is possible that people not versed in Buddhism may have seen this scripture as a manual for the achievement of longevity or immortality. Fukunaga has found many other instances where Daoist concepts were used in the translation of this sutra, even noting that the term *daojiao* (J. *dōkyō*), "teachings of the Dao," was used to refer to Amitābha's teachings.[121] Fukunaga's observations raise questions about the reception and understanding of Buddhism in China, and more importantly, about the reception and understanding of Buddhism as transmitted from China to other regions of Asia.

As mentioned above, the compound *tianshou* is found in Buddhist sutras and a Daoist scripture. Fukui Kōjun, a scholar of Daoism, has studied the *Shūchō* inscription from the premise that the artifact is a mandara representing the pure land where Shōtoku was reborn. Although he has not taken the visual evidence into account, as a specialist in Chinese Daoism, Fukui has noted certain Daoist or Chinese elements. His argument that Tenjukoku represents a Buddhist pure land where Shōtoku achieved an endless lifespan is based on his study of the four Agama sutras (J. *Agongyō*). In these texts, Fukui has found that the term "heavenly lifespan" was used to express the idea that life in heaven was long, as exemplified in phrases such as "heavenly lifespan, thousand years" or "heavenly lifespan, five thousand years."[122] He has concluded that, in these Buddhist sutras, "heavenly lifespan" was used to indicate that a lifetime in heaven was much longer than a human lifespan. Fukui also has found the compound "heavenly lifespan" in the Maitreya sutras, and has asserted that Tenjukoku refers to an endless lifetime in heaven. And if Tenjukoku is a heaven, it could be Maitreya's Tuṣita Heaven.[123]

The Daoist text in which the compound *tianshou* is found is the *Taiping jing* (Scripture of the Great Peace), which has a long and complicated history.[124] It is believed that the *Taiping jing* originated in the Han dynasty, around the second century. The text was transmitted by the Celestial Masters from the third through fifth centuries, but its current form took shape in the sixth century.[125] In his study of the *Taiping jing*, Max Kaltenmark discusses the ideas about longevity and immortality contained in the text. In brief, the text states that a person cannot live forever; each person has an allotment of life that must be lived before the person can turn into a happy spirit beyond the grave.[126] According to the text's classification of the lifespans granted by heaven, the highest form is the "heavenly longevity" 天壽 of one hundred and twenty years; "earthly longevity" 地壽 measures one hundred years; "human longevity," 人壽 eighty; the "hegemon's longevity" 霸壽 is sixty; and the "longevity of the neighborhood group of five" measures fifty years.[127] This classification suggests that the compound "heavenly longevity" refers specifically to the longest lifespan granted by heaven: one hundred and twenty years.

Barbara Hendrischke, who has translated the *Taiping jing*, offers a more complete explanation of the section in which this classification of lifespans is recorded. Titled "How to Work Hard and Do Good," this section deals with personal accountability for one's deeds. In Daoist belief, a person's accountability does not end with death, but extends to the next world. Good deeds bring longevity and assure a happy life in the netherworld, and in some special cases, death can even be avoided. Thus, a connection exists between longevity and morality.[128]

Although further research is necessary, based on the evidence, the compound "heavenly lifespan" likely was a Chinese idea recorded in the Daoist text *Taiping jing*. Because the compound referred to a long span of time, it was incorporated into the translation of Buddhist sutras to refer to eternal life in the Buddhist pure lands. The compound *tianshou* could have arrived in Japan via the official introduction of Sinicized Buddhism, or it could have been brought by immigrants from China or the Korean peninsula, or even the returning Japanese students.[129] It is difficult to determine if the concept is Daoist or Buddhist in origin; at the time, however, such distinctions may have been irrelevant. Recent research on Buddhist and Daoist texts has demonstrated that both religions produced scriptures that addressed similar themes in order to satisfy the needs of devotees.

Christine Mollier has studied a group of texts produced in China between the fifth and eighth centuries, which traditionally have been classified as false or suspect sutras. These texts are not Chinese translations of Indian or Central Asian sutras, but were written in Chinese; in contemporary scholarship, they are known as Buddhist apocrypha. Studies have revealed that these texts are the product of Sinicized Buddhism, created to appeal to the Chinese laity and rulers, and address their religious needs. Mollier has found scriptures that occur in both Daoist and Buddhist form, however, and has discovered that Buddhist and Daoist beliefs often mirrored each other.[130] Especially relevant here is her study of two texts—one Buddhist and one Daoist—that deal with the prolongation of life. The *Yisuan jing* (Sutra to Increase the Account) is classified as a "suspect sutra" in Buddhist catalogues of the Tang dynasty. Mollier has found this sutra in both Buddhist and Daoist versions. The Buddhist sutra is titled *Foshuo qiqian fo shenfu yisuan jing* (Sutra of the Divine Talismans of the Seven Thousand Buddhas to Increase the Account, Preached by the Buddha); and the Daoist scripture, *Taishang Laojun shuo changsheng yisuan miaojing* (Marvelous Scripture for Prolonging Life and for Increasing the Account, Revealed by the Most High Lord Lao). These two texts contain the same incantations and talismans aimed to protect and prolong the lives of the faithful. Mollier has demonstrated that the Buddhist sutra is a replica of the Daoist scripture.[131]

The foregoing evidence suggests that the religious beliefs and practices transmitted from China to Korea and Japan were not as clearly differentiated and categorized as modern scholarship would like to expect. The Sinicized Buddhism that arrived in Japan included many Chinese beliefs and concepts, some of which could have been Daoist. The term Tenjukoku, derived from the compound "heavenly longevity," was related specifically to the longest lifespan granted by heaven. Princess Tachibana wished to represent Prince Shōtoku in an afterlife "land" (*koku*) where he would be granted a longer lifespan than he could have had on earth as a reward for his good deeds.

CONCLUSION

This chapter has aimed to answer three questions: how the Shūchō was displayed, the nature of the message that the patron or makers wanted to convey, and the meaning of the term Tenjukoku in seventh-century Japan. An analysis of textual, pictorial, and archaeological evidence from China, Korea, and Japan has revealed that the Shūchō could have been hung in a temporary structure similar to the Chinese "spirit seats," which were used to enshrine the spirits of the deceased. As such, the Shūchō could have been used for a memorial service to commemorate the anniversaries of the deaths of Prince Shōtoku and his mother. This practice could have been introduced by immigrants, Buddhist monks, or students returning from China.

Taking into account the long, selective genealogy recorded on the Shūchō and the embroidered omen designs, as well as the events after the death of Prince Shōtoku that led to the end of the Kinmei–Soga line, it seems possible that the Shūchō was not made exclusively to represent Prince Shōtoku in Tenjukoku, but that it also might have conveyed a political subtext. If Princess Tachibana was still alive when the Shūchō was made (likely in the second half of the seventh century), the curtains could have been produced to convey a message of discontent to the new ruling lineage. Tachibana even could have been claiming that she was the rightful heir to the throne. If she was no longer alive, then anyone related to the Kinmei–Soga line, or perhaps the supporters of this royal line, may have created the Shūchō with the desire to remember the prince and the lost lineage.

The transmission of continental culture, especially religious beliefs, is a complex matter, because religions in practice were not clearly categorized, and interaction between the different religions and popular beliefs took place. An overview of the interaction between Buddhism and Daoism in China between the third and fifth centuries has revealed that these two religions borrowed from each other. Certain Buddhist ideas were adopted into Daoism, some Daoist terms were used in the translation of the sutras, and many of the same popular concerns of devotees were addressed by both Buddhist monks and Daoist priests. Although more research on all of these topics is necessary, the evidence suggests that Tenjukoku might be related to the compound *tianshou* recorded in the Daoist *Taiping jing*. According to this text, *tianshou* refers to the longest lifespan granted by heaven, of one hundred and twenty years. This compound of Daoist origins seems to have been used in the translation of Buddhist sutras to express the idea of the long lifespans enjoyed in the Buddhist heavens or pure lands. Although it is impossible to determine exactly how the term arrived in Japan, based on the evidence, Tenjukoku does not appear to have referred to a heavenly realm (as the name suggests), but to an afterlife land where a lifespan of one hundred and twenty years could be experienced. Tenjukoku was neither Buddhist nor Daoist, but an afterlife destination derived from Chinese beliefs.

4

From Shūchō to Tenjukoku Mandara

IN 1274, THE NUN SHINNYO rediscovered the Shūchō during her campaign to restore the nunnery of Chūgūji. Extensive documentary evidence allows us to reconstruct the circumstances of this rediscovery in detail. These documents refer to the embroidery as a "mandara," and mention its dedication as the "Tenjukoku Mandara" in a Buddhist ceremony held in 1275. A close analysis of the textual material, especially the liturgical text used in the dedication ceremony, reveals the significance of the Tenjukoku Mandara at the time. The monk Jōen, who wrote the liturgy, identified Prince Shōtoku as an incarnation of Guze Kannon. He went on to state that the prince's mother, Queen Consort Anahobe, was Amida, and that the prince's wife was the bodhisattva Seishi (S. Mahāsthāmaprāpta). The identification of these three royals as deities associated with the Pure Land school relates to a form of devotion, known as the "Amida triad in one tomb with three remains" (*sankotsu ichibyō no Amida sanzon*), that developed at Shōtoku's tomb at Shinaga.[1] This belief led Jōen to refer to the embroidery as an Amida mandara representing Muryōju Tenju (Measureless Lifespan, Heavenly Lifespan).[2] Modern scholars have pointed to these phrases as evidence that, in the seventh century, Tenjukoku was the name used for Amida's Pure Land; yet these scholars do not take into account the whole content of the liturgical text or the historical context for its composition.[3]

From a comprehensive analysis of the documents associated with the Tenjukoku Mandara, and the developments in the cult of the prince during the medieval period, it appears that the search for the Shūchō began with Shinnyo's quest to restore Chūgūji. Once the artifact was discovered and its inscription read, however, the nun and other Shōtoku devotees used the found embroidery to promote the Amida triad belief from Shinaga. The unusual designs on the embroidery—especially the turtles with ancient script bearing the names of the prince and his mother—and the identification of the pictorial subject as an afterlife realm known as Tenjukoku were particularly fitting to this belief. Textual and visual evidence indicates that the belief had reached Hōryūji, a temple closely associated with Chūgūji, by the mid-thirteenth century. With this belief already in place, the discovery of the embroidery representing Shōtoku and his mother in Tenjukoku might have prompted the nuns of Chūgūji to incorporate Pure Land beliefs into their worship and practice.

In order to understand the events associated with the rediscovery of the Shūchō and its transformation into the Tenjukoku Mandara, it is crucial to

Shōkō Mandara, detail of fig. 83.

reconstruct the religious context for the Shōtoku cult in the medieval period. The first section of this chapter, "Pure Land Buddhism and the Cult of the Prince," includes an analysis of the status of the cult in the late Heian and Kamakura periods, especially its incorporation of Pure Land beliefs. Because Prince Shōtoku was believed to be an incarnation of Kannon (often grouped with Amida as one of this Buddha's attendant bodhisattvas), certain temples and sites associated with him constructed stories to convince devotees that a visit to these sites would grant them rebirth in Amida's Pure Land. Among these sites, the temple Shitennōji, Shōtoku's tomb at Shinaga, and the temple Hōryūji became important cultic centers that propagated these ideas.

The second section of the chapter, "Chūgūji and the Nun Shinnyo," focuses on the history of the nunnery and the nun, as both took center stage in the events associated with the Tenjukoku Mandara. The early history of the nunnery is shrouded in mystery; certain documents reveal that Chūgūji was first associated with Prince Shōtoku, but that later the association shifted to his mother, Queen Consort Anahobe. A biographical account of Shinnyo is also included. Although the nun is usually associated with the monk Eison (1201–1290), founder of the Shingon Ritsu school, records also show that she was a Shōtoku devotee, and as such, closely associated with Hōryūji. Part of the reason for Shinnyo's fame was her rediscovery of the ancient artifact depicting the prince's afterlife.

The third section, "From Shūchō to Tenjukoku Mandara," is dedicated to an analysis of the relevant documents from the late thirteenth century. By analyzing the documents within the context of the medieval Shōtoku cult, it becomes clear that the search for the mandara began with Shinnyo's quest to restore Chūgūji; when the artifact was discovered, however, this was seen as a miraculous event in the thriving cult of the prince. The Chūgūji nuns thus used the Tenjukoku Mandara as a means of incorporating the Pure Land promise of salvation into the practice at their nunnery.

PURE LAND BUDDHISM AND THE CULT OF THE PRINCE

Interestingly, devotion to Prince Shōtoku was integrated into the various schools of Japanese Buddhism.[4] With the belief in the prince as an incarnation of Guze Kannon in the Heian period, and with Kannon's connection to Amida as one of the latter's attendant bodhisattvas, Shōtoku's identification as Kannon created an easy path for incorporating Pure Land beliefs into the prince's cult during the Kamakura period. In order to attract more devotees, some of the temples allegedly established by Shōtoku created stories that associated him with Amida's Pure Land and the promise of rebirth there.[5] These stories must have been disseminated widely; by the early twelfth century, members of the imperial family, aristocrats, Buddhist monks, and people from all levels of society made pilgrimages to Shitennōji and Hōryūji, two of the seven temples said to have been established by the prince. Later records and memoirs suggest that, by the late twelfth century, Shōtoku's tomb at Shinaga was also added to this pilgrimage route.

A discussion of the integration of the Pure Land faith at Shitennōji, the prince's tomb at Shinaga, and Hōryūji will serve to demonstrate the prevalence of these beliefs. For the sake of clarity, each of these cultic centers is discussed separately, but it is important to note that all of these sites were intertwined, due largely to the key role played by *hijiri* (itinerant monks) in the popularization of Pure Land beliefs and the propagation of the Shōtoku cult.

Shitennōji

As recorded in *Nihon shoki* and hagiographies related to Shōtoku, Shitennōji was the first temple established by the prince. According to the story, in 587, during the battle between the pro-Buddhist faction led by Soga no Umako and the anti-Buddhist faction led by Mononobe no Moriya, Shōtoku carved wooden images of the Four Heavenly Kings (Shitennō) and vowed to build a temple dedicated to them if the pro-Buddhist group was granted victory. After the Mononobe were defeated, the prince

76 West Gate of Shitennōji. Stone gateway in the foreground, and Great West Gate in the background. Osaka. Important Cultural Property.

built Shitennōji in Settsu Province in 593.[6] Other than this brief account, not much is known about the early history of the temple as it was destroyed and rebuilt multiple times. In fact, the current temple was built after the previous complex was destroyed in World War II.[7]

In the eleventh century, Shitennōji was the first of Shōtoku's cultic centers to successfully add a Pure Land component. Based on a message allegedly left by Prince Shōtoku at the temple, Shitennōji claimed to be an entrance to the Pure Land on earth. Recorded in *Arahakadera gote in engi* (Account of the Origins of Arahakadera with the [Prince's] Handprints; compiled 11th century), also known as *Shitennōji engi* (Account of the Origins of Shitennōji), the prince's message explains that the space between the pagoda and the Golden Hall on the temple's grounds corresponded to the center of the Eastern Gate of the Pure Land (fig. 76).[8] As the message indicates the specific location of the gate that could lead to the Land of Bliss, the spot became a site for the practice of *nenbutsu*, the recitation of Amida's name as a prayer for rebirth in this land. A postscript states that the scroll was discovered in 1007 (Kankō 4) by the monk Jiren in the temple's Golden Hall. To enhance the credibility of the story, the temple asserted not only that the scroll was written by the prince himself, but also that it included his alleged handprints. This message from Shōtoku was one of many "discovered" in medieval times. Known as "Messages for the Future Left by the Prince" (*Taishi no miraiki*), these narratives, constructed by parties interested in promoting his cult, emerged as vital components of the lore of the medieval cult of Shōtoku.[9]

The story of the miraculous discovery of the scroll and the merits of the site must have spread, as emperors and aristocrats included Shitennōji in their religious pilgrimage routes. Fujiwara no Michinaga (966–1028), the eminent politician and power broker, visited the temple during his pilgrimage of 1023 (Jian 3). He began in Kii Province (present-day Wakayama and southern Mie Prefectures) with a visit to Kongōbuji and the tomb of Kūkai (774–835), founder of the Shingon school; and then visited the Seven Great Temples: Tōdaiji, Kōfukuji, Gangōji, and Daianji in Nara; and Yamadadera, Moto Gangōji, and Tachibanadera in Asuka. On the way back, he visited Hōryūji, Kawachi Dōmyōji, and Shitennōji. Ono Kazuyuki has indicated that Michinaga did not go to Shōtoku's tomb, as the whereabouts of the tomb were unknown at the time.[10]

According to the lore, *hijiri* from the temple Zenkōji in Nagano, traveling in the greater capital region, supposedly functioned as pilgrims' guides, and created connections between Shitennōji, Prince Shōtoku, and the cult of the Zenkōji Amida triad. These Zenkōji *hijiri* played a major role in the popularization of Pure Land beliefs, especially the Zenkōji cult, which also held connections to Shitennōji.[11] Central to the Zenkōji cult was a narrative about a miraculous icon, an Amida triad that was brought (or that "came") from Baekje and stayed for many years in the Naniwa Canal in Settsu Province, where Shitennōji is located. Before reaching Japan, this icon had made a long journey through India and Korea. Based on an analysis of the various extant versions of *Zenkōji engi* (Account of the Origins of Zenkōji), Donald McCallum has concluded that the earliest version of the

Zenkōji Amida legend was created in the early twelfth century. Although this early version did not include the prince, he is mentioned in later versions from the Kamakura period.[12] In these later accounts, the basic story from *Nihon shoki* about Shōtoku's prayer to the Four Heavenly Kings to ensure victory against the Mononobe, and his vow to build Shitennōji, was woven into the Zenkōji narrative. According to this new version, after the defeat of the Mononobe, Shōtoku went to the Naniwa Canal and invited Amida to come to the palace, but Amida declined the prince's offer, as the triad was waiting for someone else.[13] In addition to this conversation between Amida and Shōtoku recorded in *Zenkōji engi*, a series of letters exchanged between the prince and Amida are also "documented."[14] Shimaguchi Yoshiaki has argued that these stories of communication between Amida and Prince Shōtoku would have been seen as proof of their strong connection, and were used by the Zenkōji *hijiri* to spread faith in this Buddha and the prince.[15]

In the eleventh century, with the alleged discovery of a message from Prince Shōtoku at Shitennōji claiming that a gate to the Pure Land existed at the temple, Shitennōji upgraded its popularity from a temple dedicated to devotion to the prince to a site that also offered the possibility of salvation in Amida's Land of Bliss. As such, it became an important pilgrimage destination for devotees of both Shōtoku and Pure Land Buddhism. At the same time, Shitennōji and the prince were also integrated into the story of the Zenkōji Amida triad, enhancing this cult. This synthesis of ideas benefited all parties involved, as *hijiri* associated with the Pure Land school spread these different beliefs far and wide.

The Tomb at Shinaga

Located on the grounds of the Buddhist temple Eifukuji in Minami Kawachi (Osaka), the tomb at Shinaga has been identified as the burial site of Prince Shōtoku since the eighth century (fig. 77).[16] *Nihon shoki* states that the prince was buried in the royal tomb at Shinaga (Shinaga Misasagi).[17] The same information is found in later hagiographic narratives, such as the *Imperial Biography*, *Jōgū Shōtoku Taishi den hoketsuki*, and *Shōtoku Taishi denryaku*.[18] Shinaga is also listed as the tomb of the prince in *Engishiki* (Regulations of the Engi Era; 927), in the section corresponding to the imperial tombs.[19] Ono Kazuyuki has stated that the inclusion of the tomb in *Engishiki* suggests that the site was under the supervision of the state, and that perhaps ceremonies were performed there.[20] Archaeologists, however, disagree about the designation of the site as the actual burial place of the prince.[21]

The origins of Eifukuji, the temple at the tomb site, are similarly controversial. The temple claims that, when Shōtoku died, Great King Suiko ordered the construction of a hut for a monk to protect the tomb; and that, during the reign of Emperor Shōmu, a temple complex was built in 724 (Jinki 1) in the prince's memory.[22] Archaeological excavations at the site have not yielded any evidence to support such claims that the temple was established in the seventh or eighth century. Temple structures, such as the pagoda and the Main Hall, were probably built in the thirteenth century after the visits of the monks Chōgen (1121–1206), the solicitor for the fundraising campaign to restore Tōdaiji; and Ippen (1239–1289), the founder of the Jishū sect of the Pure Land school. Furthermore, the name Eifukuji only appeared in the fifteenth century.[23] While these issues should be noted, they are not crucial here, as they do not appear to have much bearing on how the site of Shinaga became a devotional center that offered the possibility of transport to Amida's Land of Bliss.

A particularly important event that transformed the tomb into a devotional site was the discovery of a message from the prince in the eleventh century. As in the case of Shitennōji, this was designated as a "Message for the Future Left by the Prince." The story is recorded in *Kojidan* (Talks about Ancient Matters; 1212–15), a collection of *setsuwa*, myths or folktales often with Buddhist content, compiled by Minamoto no Akikane (1160–1215). Entitled "The Discovery of Prince Shōtoku's Message for the Future," the story relates that, on the twentieth day of the ninth month of 1054 (Tengi 2), a slab with an inscription written by the prince himself was discovered near his tomb; at the time, a stone pagoda

77   Entrance to the tomb of Prince Shōtoku. Eifukuji, Minami Kawachi, Osaka.

was being built. The *Kojidan* story also states that the abbot of Shitennōji, Kanshun (978–1057), after hearing about this miraculous event, visited the tomb site and then had a dream in which he was told that a temple had to be built there.[24]

The message on the slab narrates Shōtoku's efforts for the propagation of Buddhism, such as the war against Mononobe no Moriya, the establishment of forty-six temples, the ordination of more than thirteen hundred monks and nuns, and his lectures and commentaries on three sutras. Notably, the prince predicts that, four hundred and thirty years or so after his death, the inscribed slab would be found at Shinaga, and that a temple would be constructed for the prosperity of Buddhism. Because the *Kojidan* story mentions specifically an abbot from Shitennōji visiting the temple, it is possible that monks from Shitennōji were involved in the tale's creation. This theory is supported by the fact that the same story is recorded in a document at Shitennōji, *Tennōji hiketsu* (Shitennōji's Secret Decisions; 1227), in which the monk that discovered the slab is identified as Chūzen.[25]

Although archaeological evidence has not confirmed that a temple was built at the site in the eleventh century, textual evidence suggests that, by the late twelfth century, the tomb site was visited. The monk Jien (1155–1225), who served as abbot of Shitennōji between 1213 and 1225, visited Shitennōji and the prince's burial site in 1191 (Kenkyū 3). In *Shūgyokushū* (Collection of Gathered Jewels; 1236), a compilation of poems, Jien writes about his visit to the "funerary mound of the Prince of the Upper Palace" (Jōgū Taishi no kofun) after stopping at Shitennōji.[26] Because he mentions only a funerary mound and not a temple, it is not likely that a Buddhist temple existed yet at the site, although the tomb already seems to have been a place visited by devotees.

The sources discussed above suggest that Shitennōji's monks were exploring the tomb as early as the mid-eleventh century. Records at Hōryūji, however, indicate that Hōryūji's monks had access to the tomb even earlier. The most important source for understanding Hōryūji's claims to the prince's tomb are the writings of the monk-scholar Kenshin, who was the master (*inju*) of the Shōryōin, a hall at Hōryūji dedicated to honoring Shōtoku's spirit.[27] Although Kenshin's life dates are unknown, documents suggest that he was active in the mid-thirteenth century. He wrote *Shōtoku Taishi den shiki* (Private Record of the Biography of Prince Shōtoku), also known as *Taishi den kokon mokurokusho* (Selection from Ancient and Modern Records of the Prince), a key document for understanding the Shōtoku cult in the Kamakura period. In addition to this manuscript, an inscription on a wooden image of the bodhisattva Nyoirin Kannon at Hōryūji gives us some information about his activities.[28] This inscription records a repair to the image carried out in 1258 (Shōka 2). Kenshin's name appears together with that of the monk Eison, the aforementioned founder of the Shingon Ritsu sect. In his records, Eison states his involvement in the repairs and ceremonies associated with the Nyoirin Kannon at Hōryūji, and also mentions a visit to Hōryūji and the tomb at Shinaga.[29] Strangely, although the names of the two monks are the only names recorded in the Nyoirin Kannon inscription, Kenshin and Eison do not mention each other in their respective writings.

Kenshin's writings show that, as a monk-scholar, he was dedicated to the study of Hōryūji and Prince Shōtoku. *Shōtoku Taishi den shiki* reveals his knowledge of documents, as well as oral traditions, associated with the prince and his cult at the time. Kenshin's manuscript consists of two scrolls; although no date is recorded on them, the events documented suggest that the first scroll was written in 1238 (Katei 4), and the second, between 1239 and 1247.[30] *Shōtoku Taishi den shiki* contains notes and commentaries about Hōryūji's Eastern Compound, the inscriptions on the images in the Golden Hall, the temples established by Shōtoku, a calendar of yearly activities, and more. All of this information is found in a series of undated and sometimes contradictory notes written on both sides of the scrolls. Certain entries clearly reveal that Kenshin had studied documents such as the *Imperial Biography* and *Shōtoku Taishi denryaku*. Kenshin asserts that he is the keeper of various secrets related to the prince, which were transmitted orally in his family from generation to generation, because he is a descendant of Chōshimaru, Shōtoku's alleged servant.[31]

Kenshin records different events associated with the tomb at Shinaga, with the aims of confirming the number of people in the burial chamber, and more importantly, with connecting the tomb to Hōryūji.[32] First, he refers to the aforementioned legend of the discovery of the prince's message on an inscribed slab in 1054. In one entry, he states that the monk Chūzen entered the tomb, as recorded in *Tennōji hiketsu*; in another, he writes that it was a *hijiri* who entered, and experienced something extraordinary there. Another set of entries seems to have been written to question the established tradition and create a connection between the tomb and Hōryūji. Kenshin claims that, because someone had broken into the tomb and perhaps stolen some of the prince's remains, an imperial order was issued to inspect the tomb. This task was assigned to the Hōryūji monk Kōnin, who reported that the tomb held two or three coffins. Significantly, Kenshin states that Kōnin entered the tomb in 994, sixty years before the 1054 discovery of the message. Moreover, Kenshin claims that Kōnin is one of his ancestors, as attested by a detailed genealogy. As Nishiguchi Junko has suggested, by the mid-eleventh century, the site at Shinaga likely was being explored by monks from Shitennōji; for this reason, Kenshin included a monk from Hōryūji in his version of the story to create an even earlier connection between the tomb and his own temple.[33] A third set of entries about the tomb relates to the number of coffins and their occupants. Kenshin states, "In the tomb, there are three coffins. The northern one is the mother's, the eastern one is the prince's, and the western one is the princess's."[34]

Kenshin also includes a verse that is crucial to understanding the transformation of the tomb at Shinaga into a cultic center dedicated to Prince Shōtoku. This verse purportedly came from a document now lost, *Shōshisen* (Narratives of Matsuko), compiled by Ōtoribe Aya no Matsuko, a devotee of the Shōtoku cult. The verse is known today as *Byōkutsuge* (Verse of the Tomb Chamber), but in *Shōtoku Taishi den shiki*, it appears with the title "The Inscription Written by the Prince Himself on the Stone Slab Found in his Tomb."[35] As suggested by this title, the verse is another of the "Messages for the Future Left by the Prince." In this passage, the prince explains his original vow of great compassion and mercy for all sentient beings, and states that he was born in Japan to spread Buddhist teachings. As he proclaims,

> I am Guze Kannon, my wife Jōe [Princess Kashiwade] is Dai Seishi, and my compassionate mother is the master of the Western Pure Land, Amida. The worldly truth and the ultimate truth are rooted in the same body; one body manifesting as three, but they are the same body.

The verse also states that the prince fulfilled his duty and returned to the Western Pure Land, but that "the Amida triad in the tomb with three remains" stayed (at Shinaga) for the sake of future generations of sentient beings in this age of the end of the Dharma (*mappō*, a degenerate age thought to have begun in 1052). Importantly, at the end of the verse, the site is identified as the place where the Seven Buddhas of the Past preached the Dharma; the text encourages people to visit this tomb once, as these visitors will then be free from evil and transported to the Land of Bliss.[36] In addition to its appearance in *Shōtoku Taishi den shiki*, this verse also is included in *Jōgū Taishi gyoki* (Record of the Prince of the Upper Palace), written in 1257 by Shinran (1173–1263), the founder of the True Pure Land sect.[37]

Perhaps to lend credibility and an early date to belief in the Shinaga Amida triad, Kenshin also includes a narrative involving Kūkai, the aforementioned founder of the Shingon school in Japan. According to Kenshin, in 810 (Kōnin 1), Kūkai confined himself in the tomb for one hundred days. On the ninety-sixth day, he had a vision in which he saw a bright light and heard the voice of the prince saying, "I am the manifestation (*suijaku*) of Kannon, my mother is the Buddha of Measureless Lifespan (Muryōju), and my wife is the manifestation of Seishi."[38] This story does not appear in any of Kūkai's records. As it is recorded only in *Shōtoku Taishi den shiki*, it is possible that Kenshin added this incident to certify that the three royals buried in Shinaga were incarnations of Amida, Kannon, and Seishi, and that Kūkai was witness to this miraculous manifestation.

While it is impossible to determine who composed the "Verse of the Tomb Chamber," its contents are crucial to understanding how Pure Land belief was cleverly introduced at the tomb site. Because three people were buried in a tomb at Shinaga, and because Shōtoku was believed to be an incarnation of Kannon, the other two individuals were assigned their respective Buddhist incarnations as deities associated with the Western Pure Land. The addition of a story about Kūkai's experience at the tomb served as confirmation that the three royals did reside there as incarnations of Amida, Kannon, and Seishi. A wooden relief carving of Amida flanked by Kannon and Seishi riding on puffy clouds hangs above the entrance gate to the funerary mound as a reminder of its occupants (fig. 78).[39]

Records from the thirteenth century show that the tomb site had become a full-fledged cultic center visited by aristocrats and figures associated with Kamakura Buddhism, such as Chōgen, Eison, and Ippen. In his memoirs, *Namu Amida Butsu sazenshū* (Benevolent Deeds of Namu-Amidabutsu; ca. 1206), Chōgen states that the Buddhist sculptor Kaikei (act. 1183–1236), who seems to have been a Pure Land devotee, erected a hall at the tomb of the prince.[40] This passage comprises the first evidence of a building at the site. Furthermore, an incident involving Chōgen suggests that relics might have been obtained from the tomb. As recorded in the Kamakura-period history *Hyakurenshō* (One Hundred Selected Refinements), in the Genkyū era (1204–6), the monks Jōkai and Kenkō entered the

78 Amida triad relief at the entrance to the tomb of Prince Shōtoku. Eifukuji, Minami Kawachi, Osaka.

tomb and took a tooth, which was then given to Chōgen.[41] Kenshin also records this event, stating that the relic was placed inside the Jūichimen Kannon image at Shin Daibutsuji in Iga (Mie Prefecture), a temple built by Chōgen.[42] Although the veracity of this incident cannot be corroborated, as Imao Fumiaki has suggested, the *Hyakurenshō* story reveals that, in the thirteenth century, it was possible to enter the tomb.[43] The other important religious figure who visited the site was Ippen, who confined himself in the tomb in 1286 (Kōan 9), after visiting Shitennōji. This visit is recorded and pictorialized in the eighth scroll of *Ippen shōnin eden* (Pictorial Biography of the Monk Ippen; 13th century). In the painting, Ippen prays in front of a funerary mound covered with trees. After Shinaga, Ippen went to Taimadera (Nara), suggesting that this temple was also part of the circuit that involved Pure Land belief and the Shōtoku cult.[44]

Large crowds also seem to have visited the tomb site, as attested by a ceremony held in 1246 (Kangen 4), in which Eison administered the bodhisattva precepts (a set of moral codes often given to laypeople) to five hundred and two attendees.[45] Eison also records that, on the sixth day of the tenth month of 1258 (Shōka 2), he had spent the night at the shrine of the prince at Shinaga, performing a continuous Nyoirin Kannon *darani* (S. *dhāraṇī*; a mystical incantation).[46]

Members of the imperial family and aristocrats also visited the tomb at Shinaga. In 1271 (Bun'ei 8), Retired Emperor Go-Saga (r. 1242–46) and his Empress Ōmiyain (Fujiwara no Kitsushi; 1225–1292) traveled from Shitennōji to Shinaga. Significantly, two years after her death, in 1294, Ōmiyain's remains were buried in front of the prince's tomb.[47] Lady Nijō (1258–after 1307), a concubine of Emperor Go-Fukakusa (r. 1246–60) known for her diary, *Towazugatari* (An Unasked-for Tale, commonly

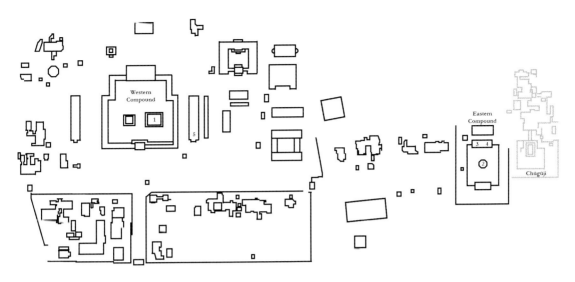

79   Plan of Hōryūji indicating precincts dedicated to Prince Shōtoku. 1. Golden Hall; 2. Yumedono; 3. Painting Hall; 4. Relic Hall; 5. Shōryōin. Diagram by Ken C. Pradel.

translated as *The Confessions of Lady Nijō*; ca. 1304–7), visited Chūgūji, Hōryūji, Taimadera, and the prince's tomb in 1290. In her account, she comments on the skillfully arranged rocks, and notes that she had offered a small-sleeved gown at the tomb.[48]

Although these records of pilgrimage do not confirm that devotees visited the site because of belief in the Shinaga Amida triad, these accounts suggest that, by the late twelfth century and into the thirteenth, the tomb at Shinaga, together with Shitennōji, Hōryūji, and Taimadera—sites associated with Prince Shōtoku and the Pure Land school—were part of a pilgrimage route traveled by aristocrats and important figures of Kamakura-period Buddhism.

Hōryūji
As the second temple allegedly built by the prince, in 607, Hōryūji in Ikaruga is another site dedicated to devotion to Shōtoku. The early history of this temple is controversial, but by the twelfth century, Hōryūji had three precincts dedicated to the prince, and ceremonies in his honor were performed in two of them. In addition, evidence indicates that belief in the Shinaga Amida triad had reached this temple, and that efforts were made to propagate it there.

Among the places dedicated to Prince Shōtoku at Hōryūji (fig. 79), the oldest is the Golden Hall in the Western Compound, which houses the famous bronze Shaka triad made after the death of the prince, his mother, and one of his wives (probably Princess Kashiwade). No evidence exists, however, to confirm that a ceremony in Shōtoku's honor was ever performed in this hall.[49] The second precinct includes three halls dated to the eighth century, all dedicated to the prince's veneration, and located in the Jōgūin, known today as the Eastern Compound. Shōtoku was worshipped as an incarnation of Kannon at the Yumedono; the relic held by the prince at the age of two is housed in the Relic Hall; and narrative paintings depicting scenes of his life were once in the Painting Hall.[50] The Shōryō-e (a memorial service for the saintly spirit of the prince) had been performed in the Jōgūin since the eighth century, but unfortunately the exact hall where this service took place is not mentioned.[51] The third structure dedicated to the prince was constructed in 1121. The Shōryōin (Hall of the [Prince's] Saintly Spirit) was built in the eastern area of the Western Compound, and dedicated to the worship of Prince Shōtoku as Regent. As mentioned previously, the monk Kenshin was the master of this hall in the mid-thirteenth century.[52] Currently, the Shōryō-e is performed each year at the Shōryōin from March twenty-second through twenty-fourth.[53]

Regarding the introduction of Pure Land beliefs at Hōryūji, temple records suggest that Pure Land practices were introduced in 1072 (Enkyū 4) by the monk Shō (or Sei), who established a meditation hall (sanmaidō) housing an Amida image for practice of nenbutsu. He asked Hōryūji's officials for permission to establish the subtemple (bessho) of Konkōin. Shō's devotions included the practice of jōgyō sanmai, the "constantly walking meditation"; the chanting of the Lotus Sutra; and the performance of welcoming ceremonies for Amida. Nishiguchi Junko has maintained that Shō's disciples were active preachers.[54]

In addition to the establishment of a hall dedicated to nenbutsu practice, Kenshin's writings indicate that other forms of Pure Land faith also reached Hōryūji. In Shōtoku Taishi den shiki, Kenshin refers to communications between the Zenkōji Amida and Prince Shōtoku.[55] Importantly, one of the letters allegedly sent from the Zenkōji Amida to the prince is now held among the temple's treasures. The letter is in a box, covered in brocade fabric, that contains two brocade bags and a smaller box holding the message. According to the legend, when Great King Yōmei died, the grieving prince performed nenbutsu for seven days and seven nights. Afterwards, in order to verify if his father had benefitted from this deed, Shōtoku sent a letter to the Zenkōji Amida with a messenger named Abe no Omi, who returned with Amida's response, the letter currently preserved in the box. All of the fabrics on and in the box date from the seventh century, further supporting the legend's claim.[56]

In the early thirteenth century, bronze images of Amida and two attendant bodhisattvas were added to the altar platform in the Golden Hall, joining the Shaka triad, the Yakushi image, and many others. The Amida image was made to match the Shaka and Yakushi images, with the robe hanging over the pedestal in the style characteristic of the Asuka period. An inscription on the back of the halo explains the circumstances of this Amida's manufacture. The inscription states that, in the Jōtoku era (1097–99), the Amida image that originally occupied the pedestal was stolen. The monks were devastated; with the empty pedestal as a reminder of the loss, eventually a fundraising campaign was organized to fill the space left by the stolen image. The manufacture of the new triad began in the third month of 1231 (Kangi 3), and an eye-opening ceremony was performed in the eighth month of 1232 (Jōei 1). The sculptor in charge was Kōshō (act. 1198–1233), who held the honorable title of Bridge of the Dharma (hokkyō), and was one of the six sons of the famous sculptor Unkei (ca. 1150–1223). The bronze was cast by Taira no Kunitomo (fig. 80).[57] Since the time of its manufacture, the Amida image has sat on a square wooden pedestal in the western bay of the hall, flanked by two smaller bronze images of Seishi and Kannon to form a triad (figs. 81, 82).[58] Although the inscription states that the previous Amida icon was stolen, it is highly likely that this portion of the inscription is a fabrication. An inventory recorded in Kondō nikki (Diary of the Golden Hall), dated 1078 (Jōryaku 2), lists eighteen small Buddhist icons on the wooden platform in the western bay, and later inventories make no reference to an Amida triad being stolen.[59]

Kenshin commented on the Golden Hall's Amida triad, but his notes are contradictory. First, he seems to acknowledge that this triad represents the incarnations of the three royals: "The Amida triad in the western bay comprises the original bodies (hontai) of Empress Anahobe, Prince Shōtoku, and Princess Kashiwade. These are their origin images (konpon sonzō)."[60] This statement clearly relates to belief in the Shinaga Amida triad. In another entry, however, he suggests that the images in the Golden Hall were made to honor deceased members of the royal family:

> The Yakushi image was made for the sake of Emperor Yōmei; the Amida, for the sake of Empress Anahobe; Kannon, for the sake of the prince; and Seishi, for the sake of the princess. This triad of the west is made for the benefit of all living beings in Japan. The Shaka triad located in the eastern bay was made to commemorate the prince's entrance into nirvana (go nyūmetsu).[61]

FROM SHŪCHŌ TO TENJUKOKU MANDARA

80 Kōshō (act. 1198–1233). The Buddha Amida from the Golden Hall Amida triad. 1232. Bronze. H. 64.6 cm. Golden Hall, Hōryūji, Nara. Important Cultural Property.

81 Kōshō. Seishi from the Golden Hall Amida triad. 1232. Bronze. H. 55.2 cm. Originally from Hōryūji. Musée des Arts Asiatiques-Guimet, Paris, France.

82 Kōshō. Kannon from the Golden Hall Amida triad. 1232. Bronze. H. 55.4 cm. Great Treasure Hall, Hōryūji, Nara. Important Cultural Property.

In this case, Kenshin's comments about the Yakushi image and the Shaka triad are based on the inscriptions on each image. As none of the imperial family members is mentioned in the inscription on Amida's halo, it is likely that, when Kenshin wrote that the Amida image was made for the sake of Empress Anahobe, he meant that the Amida icon is Empress Anahobe, the Kannon is Prince Shōtoku, and the Seishi is Princess Kashiwade. The sentence "This triad of the west is made for the benefit of all living beings in Japan" supports this claim, as it bears a similar message to the "Verse of the Tomb Chamber."

Further evidence of Kenshin's involvement in the spread of belief in the Shinaga Amida triad is the *Shōkō mandara* (Mandala of the Eminent Prince), a painting designed by him and dedicated in 1254 (fig. 83). The work is currently housed in the Shōryōin. Although this painting is not mentioned in *Shōtoku Taishi den shiki*, Kenshin's notes reveal his involvement in its planning.[62] The complex iconography and composition of the work reflect the state of the Shōtoku cult by the mid-thirteenth century, as seen by Kenshin. He created this painting out of his belief in the necessity of having a work that included the prince's previous and later reincarnations, as well as portraits of his family and others associated with him.[63]

The painting includes portraits of selected members of the prince's family, but the composition reveals that Kenshin had the Shinaga Amida triad in mind when he designed it. Queen Consort Anahobe is in the center of the composition, flanked by Prince Shōtoku to her left and Princess Kashiwade to her right. The three are aligned as human incarnations of Amida and his attendant bodhisattvas. These three figures are surrounded by twenty-five princes and princesses: Shōtoku's siblings, his children from his three wives, and his grandchildren (the children of Prince Yamashiro). Notes in *Shōtoku Taishi den shiki* indicate that Kenshin might have intended this painting as an Amida *raigō* (a welcoming descent of Amida to usher believers to the Western Pure Land); hence he may have included the princes and princesses as the standard number of twenty-five bodhisattvas. Realizing, however, that twenty-seven bodhisattvas (including Kannon/Shōtoku and Seishi/Kashiwade) appear in the composition in total, he wrote, "If there were twenty-three princes and grandchildren related to the prince, [in addition] to Prince [Shōtoku] and Princess [Kashiwade], they would make a total of twenty-five people who could be the incarnations [of the bodhisattva retinue] from the Western Pure Land."[64] Notably, the upper left section of the painting also includes a pictorial representation of a funerary mound, a golden Amida triad, and Kūkai. The golden Amida triad in the center appears to be emerging from the small white hemisphere that represents the funerary mound to the left of the triad. In addition, Kūkai sits to the left of the mound, as a reference to the story from *Shōtoku Taishi den shiki* in which he allegedly heard a message from the prince, confirming the residence of the triad in the tomb. This painting is proof that belief in the Shinaga Amida triad reached Hōryūji, where the work was also used to explain the multiple facets of the cult of Prince Shōtoku.

Evidence of Pure Land devotion, the cult of the prince, and belief in the Zenkōji Amida at the three cultic sites connected with Shōtoku—Shitennōji, the tomb at Shinaga, and Hōryūji—demonstrates the intricate associations between these cultic centers. The Pure Land form of the Shōtoku cult included three components. The first of these was the discovery of "Messages for the Future Left by the Prince," such as those found at Shitennōji and Shinaga. The second was evidence of communication between Shōtoku and Amida, such as the letter kept at Hōryūji and the episode in the Zenkōji narrative. Third was the promise of salvation in Amida's Pure Land to those who visited these sites. The already popular belief in Shōtoku as an incarnation of Kannon was used to support the Pure Land aspect of the cult of the prince, especially at the tomb at Shinaga. The three sets of remains buried in the tomb were identified as those of Prince Shōtoku, his mother, and his wife, and because Shōtoku was believed to be Kannon, the other two royals occupying the tomb were deified

83 Shōkō Mandara. 1254. Hanging scroll, color on silk. 163.5 x 117 cm. Shōryōin, Hōryūji, Nara.

as incarnations of Amida and Seishi. Although no evidence that this belief reached Shitennōji has been found, Kenshin's writings, the *Shōkō mandara*, and the Golden Hall's Amida triad reveal that belief in the Shinaga Amida triad was propagated at Hōryūji. This circumstance is crucial for understanding the developments associated with Chūgūji and the Tenjukoku Mandara in the late thirteenth century.

CHŪGŪJI AND THE NUN SHINNYO

Before addressing the reappearance of the Shūchō in the late thirteenth century, it is important to discuss the early history of Chūgūji, as well as the nun Shinnyo. The origins of the nunnery are unknown; as mentioned previously, the patron assigned to the nunnery changed over time from Prince Shōtoku to his mother, Queen Consort Anahobe. This change was probably related to the evolving cult of the prince and the deification of his mother. The nun Shinnyo is usually associated with the monk Eison from the Shingon Ritsu lineage, but she also had close connections with Hōryūji, which may have led to her discovery of the embroidery at that temple.

Chūgūji

The evidence associated with Chūgūji is scant. In the early sixteenth century, the nunnery was moved to the northeast corner of Hōryūji's Eastern Compound, where it stands today (see fig. 79). The original temple was five hundred meters to the east of its present location. Archaeological excavations of this original site in 1963 and 1984 revealed a Golden Hall and a pagoda aligned on a north-south axis. In addition, it is speculated that a Lecture Hall may have stood to the north of the Golden Hall. Tiles found at the site date to the Asuka, Hakuhō, and Nara periods, which led to the conclusion that a small temple—probably a clan temple—built before the mid-eighth century existed at this location.[65] Along with this archaeological data, records of repairs found in Hōryūji documents suggest that, in the twelfth century, Hōryūji supported the nunnery.[66]

With regard to the nunnery's patronage, at first Chūgūji (or the original temple at the site) was believed to be one of the seven temples established by Prince Shōtoku; then, the palace of the prince's mother, which had been transformed into a temple; and lastly, the nunnery established by Anahobe. The first mention of Chūgūji appears in *Hōryūji engi*, one of the early hagiographic sources associated with the prince. In this document, Great King Suiko and Tōgū Jōgū Shōtoku Hōō are acknowledged as the founders of seven temples: Hōryūji gakumonji, Shitennōji, Chūgū nunnery (*niji*), Tachibana nunnery, Hachiokadera (Kōryūji), Ikejiri nunnery (Hokkiji), and Katsuragi nunnery.[67] Moreover, Chūgūji is identified as the place where the prince lectured on the *Lotus* and *Lion's Roar Sutras* on the fifteenth day of the fourth month of 598.[68] In the *Imperial Biography*, the prince is the sole figure recorded as the founder of the same seven temples.[69]

By the ninth century, in *Shōtoku Taishi denryaku*, Chūgūji is identified as "the palace of Empress Hashihito Anahobe, which became a temple after her death." The site is listed among the eleven temples associated with Prince Shōtoku.[70] The list includes Chūgūji twice: as the palace of Anahobe, and also as a temple called Hōkōji, known as the nunnery of Ikaruga (Ikaruga niji).[71] Based on this evidence, it is believed that these three names—Chūgūji, Hōkōji, and Ikaruga niji—were used to refer to the nunnery. Similarly, in the late-eleventh- or twelfth-century *Fusō ryakki*, two entries refer to the temple, and in both cases, the prince's mother is mentioned. An entry from 606 (Suiko 14) states, "Chūgūji is the palace of the prince's mother"; and another from 622 (Suiko 30) notes, "Chūgū, the palace of the mother-empress, becomes a temple."[72] Ōhashi has argued that, in the Heian period, Chūgūji might have been identified as Anahobe's palace because the term *chūgū* was used at the time to refer to an empress consort.[73] The association of Chūgūji specifically with Anahobe might be related to the active role ascribed to her in the prince's cult, as reflected in the hagiographies (particularly *Shōtoku Taishi denryaku*). According to these accounts, Anahobe dreamed about a golden monk who claimed to be Guze Kannon and asked to dwell in her womb, and after a year, Prince Shōtoku was born.[74]

Some factual information about the nunnery can be gathered from documents at Hōryūji. Entries in *Hōryūji bettō shidai* (Record of Hōryūji's Abbots) record that the pagoda at Chūgūji was repaired between 1101 and 1108 (Kōwa 3 and Tennin 1); the Golden Hall, between 1109 and 1131 (Tennin 2 and Tenshō 1); and that twelve Buddhist icons were painted, and the pagoda was repaired again, in 1164 (Chōkan 2).[75] These entries suggest that the nunnery was under Hōryūji's protection in the twelfth century. Kenshin's writings also include some annotations about Chūgūji. The monk seems to have studied the available manuscripts; his notes on Chūgūji reveal that he had read *Shōtoku Taishi denryaku*, and was confused about all of the temple's names: "Chūgūji was the palace of the mother of the prince, Empress Anahobe. The temple is called the nunnery of Ikaruga, also Chūgūji. The temple is also called Hōkōji. So many names, that [the situation] is doubtful."[76] Kenshin's statements on the second scroll are completely different, as they stress the active role of Anahobe. As he states, "Chūgūji was established by the empress. The temple's name *chūgū* probably relates to the founder or perhaps to its location."[77] Furthermore, another note confirms that the Queen Consort was the founder: "When the prince was sixteen years old, on the first day of the first month, the empress erected the central pillar of the pagoda of Chūgūji."[78] It is impossible to determine if Kenshin fabricated these statements, or if he recorded oral traditions of the Ikaruga region, but it is clear that, by the mid-thirteenth century, Anahobe was acknowledged as the founder of Chūgūji.

In conclusion, based on the archaeological evidence, we can surmise that a small temple near Hōryūji, with the name of Chūgūji, was added to the list of the seven temples established by Prince Shōtoku by the mid-eighth century. As the prince's mother was given an active role in the hagiographical accounts of his life, by the late ninth century, the temple became associated with Anahobe. By the thirteenth century, after Anahobe had been deified as an incarnation of Amida, she was recognized as the founder of Chūgūji. It was within this religious context that the nun Shinnyo took center stage in her campaign to restore the nunnery.

Shinnyo

Shinnyo's activities and accomplishments are recorded in documents from the Kamakura, Muromachi (1336–1573), and Edo periods associated with Hōryūji, Chūgūji, and Saidaiji (Nara). From these documents, we gather that the nun held connections to important members of the Buddhist establishment, as well as the aristocracy. Shinnyo is particularly prominent in sources associated with Eison and the Shingon Ritsu sect. Although her activities within this movement were important, her dealings with Hōryūji were primarily what led to her popularity in the Kamakura period. Foremost among these dealings were her discovery of the Shūchō, an ancient object associated with Prince Shōtoku, and its transformation into the Tenjukoku Mandara.[79]

Shinnyo's life is recorded in the biographical collections of the Ritsu lineage, in documents such as *Ritsuon sōbōden* (Vinaya Cloister Saṃgha Jewel Hagiographies; 1689) and *Shōdai senzai denki* (Tōshōdaiji Millenary Anniversary Hagiographies; 1701).[80] She is also mentioned in documents from the Kamakura period such as *Shasekishū* (Sand and Pebbles; 1279–83), a collection of Buddhist parables written by the monk Mujū Ichien (1226–1312); and texts from Saidaiji, the main temple of the Shingon Ritsu sect.[81]

Shinnyo was the daughter of the monk-scholar Shōen of Kōfukuji, a disciple of Jōkei (1155–1213) of the Hossō school.[82] Apparently the nun was a disciple of Ze-amidabutsu of Shōryakuji (in southeastern Nara Prefecture). According to Ritsu documents, Shinnyo's interest in becoming a fully ordained nun led her to search for the leaders of the Ritsu lineage, Eison and Kakujō (1193–1249). In his autobiography, Eison writes that, in 1243 (Kangen 1), he met "the woman who would become the nun

Shinnyo of Chūgūji" when she visited Saidaiji to attend an ordination ceremony.[83] Shinnyo was moved by the ceremony and asked to be ordained fully as a nun, but the community of Ritsu monks was undecided. The following year, she visited Kakujō at Tōshōdaiji, a Ritsu-sect temple in Nara, to request her ordination. After further setbacks, she was finally ordained as a *bikuni* (nun) between 1244 and 1249. Details about her ordination are recorded in *Shōyoshō* ([Monk] Shōyo's Notes; 1394–1428).[84] This document states that Shinnyo, who was known in all circles, had been the abbess (*chōrō*) of three nunneries in Nara: Hokkeji, Shōbōji, and Chūgūji.[85] Lori Meeks has demonstrated that the records of her ordination and the events associated with the discovery of the Tenjukoku Mandara were compiled by Ritsu monks. For this reason, these texts emphasize the role of this lineage in the life of the nun and the revival of Chūgūji.[86]

Shinnyo's *ganmon* (dedication prayer; dated 1281), documents at Hōryūji, and texts associated with the discovery of the Tenjukoku Shūchō demonstrate that the nun had strong connections with Hōryūji, and enjoyed the support of the temple's monks. Her connections with Hōryūji extend back to the early thirteenth century. Shinnyo's name appears in *Hōryūji bettō shidai* in an entry from 1234 (Tenpuku 2) that lists the participants in the dedication ceremony for a portrait of Shōtoku in the Jōgūin. The portrait in question is the famous painting known as the *Portrait of Prince Shōtoku and Two Attendants*, which was located formerly in the Relic Hall and is currently in the Imperial Collection.[87] The text states that Shinnyo's father, Shōen, was in charge of the dedication ceremony, and that the monk Keisei (act. 13th century) and "a Fujiwara woman named nun (*ama*) Shinnyo" were the sponsors of the painting.[88] Keisei, together with Kenshin, played a key role in the revamping of the cult of the prince at Hōryūji. He identified this painting as "the image of the prince that appeared in front of Prince Asa from Baekje," and by so doing, turned it into a cultic object.[89] If Shinnyo was active in Hōryūji circles and met Keisei, it is highly probable that she met Kenshin as well. If that was the case, perhaps she was already acquainted with the deification of Anahobe and Princess Kashiwade, and also with the new role of Anahobe as the founder of Chūgūji. Shinnyo's close connection with Hōryūji explains how all of these elements were interwoven in the events related to the revival of the nunnery.

It is not known exactly when Shinnyo went to Chūgūji, but a manuscript of the nunnery's calendar of annual rituals and ceremonies (*Ryōjusen'in nenjū gyōji*), written by the "bodhisattva-precept nun" (*bosatsukai bikuni*) Shinnyo, is dated 1262 (Kōchō 2), which gives us an approximate date for her residence there.[90] The subsequent events of her life were all related to her campaign to restore the nunnery, and to the miraculous discovery of a mandara in 1274.[91] Other sources give us information about her later years and activities. Shinnyo lived a long life; she was seventy-one years old (in traditional reckoning) when she wrote her *ganmon* in 1281.[92] The following year, she added punctuation (*katen*) and notes (*okugaki*) to a copy of *Yugashijiron* (S. *Yogācāra-bhūmi śāstra*, Discourse on the Stages of Concentration Practice; ca. 4th century). The last known reference to Shinnyo is the aforementioned account in the diary of Emperor Gofukakusa's consort, Lady Nijō, who visited Chūgūji in 1290. Lady Nijō met Shinnyo, the head of the cloister, and recalled that she had seen the nun once at the palace.[93] Shinnyo must have been eighty years old at the time of Nijō's visit to the nunnery.

FROM SHŪCHŌ TO TENJUKOKU MANDARA

Reconstructing the history of the transformation of the Shūchō into the Tenjukoku Mandara is possible due to the number of extant texts that narrate the events of the late thirteenth century. These events are recorded in documents dated from the thirteenth through the nineteenth century. While scholars have used this whole corpus of material to reconstruct the events associated with the Tenjukoku Mandara, a consideration of the context for the compilation of each text is essential for evaluating any document's validity. For this reason, and because this study follows the "biographical method," the documents are analyzed chronologically here. In so doing, it becomes clear that Shinnyo's quest began with the aim of finding out the date of the death of the nunnery's founder, but that once the artifact was brought to light, the Shūchō acquired a new life. The unusual embroidery representing Tenjukoku, the afterlife realm inhabited by Prince Shōtoku and his mother, was associated with belief in the Shinaga Amida triad and used to propagate the Pure Land form of the cult of the prince.

The first document to be discussed, *Chūgūji engi*, recounts Shinnyo's wish to restore Chūgūji, her quest to find the mandara, and the miraculous discovery. The second, *Tenjukoku (shin) mandara uragaki* (Facts about the (New) Tenjukoku Mandara; 1275), tells of a fundraising and eye-opening ceremony held to dedicate the mandara. The third and final document, *Taishi mandara kōshiki* (Liturgy for the Prince's Mandala; 1275), is the text of a separate dedication ceremony, which not only gives a brief description of the format and composition of the work, but more importantly, explains how the artifact was perceived at the time. Variations of these narratives are found in later sources as well.[94]

Discovering the Mandara: *Chūgūji engi*

The 1274 *Chūgūji engi* is a short document that narrates Shinnyo's quest to reestablish Chūgūji, the reasons behind her search for the mandara, and the dream that led to its miraculous discovery.[95] The first section of this document contains a transcription of the Shūchō's inscription, followed by a narrative in vernacular Japanese:

> A nun called Shinnyo followed the five hundred Buddhist precepts and faithfully practiced the two-hundred-year-old Buddhist mercy. She pledged to restore the dilapidated pagoda and temple of Chūgūji, [but] the date of the death anniversary of the nunnery's patron, the empress [Anahobe no Hashihito], was unknown. The nun thought that prayer would help. On the fifteenth day of the second month of 1273, Shinnyo and other nuns secluded themselves for an eight-day, eight-night–long Shaka *nenbutsu* in the pagoda of Chūgūji.[96] Their intention was to finish the prayer on the date of the anniversary of the prince's death [the twenty-second]. On the night of the twentieth, the nun Hosshin had a dream in which she saw the monk Eikaku from Hōryūji bringing a mandara that had a portrait and the date of the death of the empress. This mandara was in a repository at Hōryūji, together with other treasures that belonged to the empress, as well as documents from Chūgūji. Shinnyo was sure that the dream was true, a response from the Buddha. She went to Hōryūji to find the monk Eikaku, and asked Abbot Genga for authorization to search in the repository, but he refused to allow it.[97] The months and days passed by; the nuns just waited for an opportunity to gain access to the repository. This year [Bun'ei 11 (1274)], on the twentieth day of the first month, a thief broke into the repository and took many treasures. In the second month, the thief was caught, and on the twenty-fifth day, the abbot opened the repository to put back the objects taken. Shinnyo rejoiced, because she was allowed to search for the mandara that the nun Hosshin had seen in her dream. Ten trunks were in the repository, and Shinnyo began to open them one by one. When she opened the last of the trunks, which contained dance costumes, she stumbled upon the mandara. The nun was deeply moved upon seeing that the death date of [Chūgūji's] patron was indeed in the inscription, and she cried. The abbot and the monks of Hōryūji were also filled with joy; notice of the finding spread rapidly among the laity. This event truly became testimony of the wonderful powers of the means of Amida and Kannon over the defiled world for the years to come. On the top [section] of the mandara, there are turtles and a moon disk. There are a hundred [turtles]; each circle has four embroidered characters placed [corresponding to] the four directions. The nun tried to read and copy the characters, but she was afraid of making mistakes. [For this reason,] on the thirteenth day of the fourth month of Bun'ei 11 (1274), the nun took the mandara from Nanto [Nara] to Higashiyama [in Kyoto], and after the inscription was read, she returned to Nara on the fifteenth day.

The contents of this document are rather straightforward. The nun Shinnyo had vowed to restore Chūgūji, and needed the date of death of its alleged founder, Queen Consort Anahobe. A group of nuns performed the Shaka *nenbutsu* ritual, and one of them, Hosshin, had a revealing dream about a mandara that included the empress's portrait and date of death, and was housed in a repository at Hōryūji. After inquiring multiple times, Shinnyo was allowed into the repository, where she found the mandara. The only fact in this narrative that can be corroborated in other historical sources is the robbery of Hōryūji's repository. This event is recorded in *Hōryūji bettō shidai* under Abbot Genga, on the twentieth day of the first month of 1274.[98]

The events narrated in *Chūgūji engi* became the basic story of Shinnyo's quest to restore the nunnery and the miraculous discovery of the mandara; later versions contain additions and enhancements. An interesting point in this narrative is that credit for the miraculous finding is given to Amida and Kannon. This could comprise evidence of the spread of Pure Land beliefs at Hōryūji and Chūgūji, or perhaps may be a reference to the belief in Anahobe and Shōtoku as incarnations of these deities. Moreover, this is also the first document to mention the very distinctive design of one hundred turtles with four characters each at the top of the mandara. Although Shinnyo was literate, the story states that she was afraid of making mistakes when transcribing the inscription. She obviously was not familiar with the graphs used by the scribes from Baekje in the seventh century, and needed the help of people with knowledge of ancient script. In addition, because the embroidery was probably damaged, it may have been missing characters that had to be filled in. For these reasons, Shinnyo took the mandara to Kyoto, the capital, where the inscription was transcribed.

Later documents include the names of people involved in the reading of the inscription.[99] These individuals might have taken an interest in this rare inscription after the story of the discovery became well known, but they did not participate directly. The monk Jōen, who is mentioned in the next two documents, was closely involved in the revamping of the Tenjukoku Shūchō, and it is very likely that he read the inscription (and perhaps also wrote *Chūgūji engi*).

Fundraising and Eye-Opening Ceremony: *Uragaki*

The observations and events that followed the discovery of the mandara, such as the damaged condition of the artifact and the eye-opening ceremony held for it, are documented in *Tenjukoku (shin) mandara uragaki* (hereafter, *Uragaki*). An *uragaki* is a text written to comment on or certify the authenticity of a scroll, painting, or text, usually written on the back of the scroll. The text of this *Uragaki* has been transcribed in various documents at Hōryūji, such as the aforementioned *Shōyoshō* and *Ikaruga koji binran*.[100] While these documents are from later periods, based on the role of an *uragaki* and its contents, it is safe to assume that this text was written after work of some sort on the artifact, or even a new mandara, was finished in 1275.

In brief, *Uragaki* includes a shortened account of Shinnyo's journey to restore Chūgūji and the discovery of the mandara, with some small variations from the narrative in *Chūgūji engi*. Shinnyo's reason for searching for the artifact is the same: the need to know the date of the death of Queen Consort Anahobe. In *Uragaki*, however, Shinnyo herself has the dream (and also finds the mandara). The date of the discovery is given as one day after the date recorded in *Chūgūji engi*. The whole text reads as follows:

> The nun Shinnyo from Jishōin, near Kōfukuji, had pledged to restore Chūgūji, but she did not know the date of the death anniversary of the mother of the prince. While praying, she had a dream, and on the twenty-sixth day of the second month of Bun'ei 11 (1274), she found an embroidered mandara in Hōryūji's treasure repository. The mandara had two panels with an inscription with the death date of the [temple] patron. Seeing that the mandara's threads had decayed, the nun suffered. In the third month of the following year [Bun'ei 12, or 1275], the mandara was taken to Kyoto, and with support from

people of all levels of society, an embroidered copy was made. The calligrapher was Jōkan; the designer, Hōgen Ryōchi; and the embroiderers, Fujii Kuniyoshi and his children, Kunikami and Ankoku. The mandara was finished on the second day of the eighth month of Kenji 1 [also 1275] and dedicated on the twenty-second at Chōkōdō with an eye-opening ceremony.[101] The retired emperors [Gofukakusa and Kameyama] and their mother [Ōmiyain] attended the ceremony, and all of them rejoiced. The ceremony was performed by Jōen, Seal of the Dharma Great Tendai Buddhist Master (*hōin daikashōi gon dai sōzu*). Today's offering of a textile was unusual. Fujiwara no Sadamitsu was in charge of the documentation and recorded this.

Uragaki gives us some interesting information about the production of embroideries in the thirteenth century, and about the people involved in the eye-opening ceremony. One of the interesting aspects of *Uragaki* is that the names of the craftsmen involved in the manufacture of the Tenjukoku Mandara are listed, which is unusual in the Kamakura period. Extant embroidered Buddhist icons from the Kamakura and Muromachi periods do not include inscriptions or records of the donors or craftspeople. Perhaps because the names of the supervisor and designers were recorded in the Shūchō's inscription, the craftsmen decided to imitate their predecessors. These craftsmen are mentioned only in *Uragaki*, and their specific roles as recorded give us an idea of the division of labor in the production of embroidered textiles. Thus it is known that a calligrapher and a designer were involved; and significantly, embroidery seems to have been a family business and a male activity, as a father and his two sons are listed as the embroiderers. This is an interesting point, as needlework usually is argued to have been women's work.[102]

More information about the embroidery process can be gathered from this text, such as the time needed to finish the project. This point requires some explanation, as the dates recorded are confusing. *Uragaki* states that the mandara was taken to Kyoto in the third month of Bun'ei 12, and that the replica was finished in the eighth month of Kenji 1.

As recorded, it would seem that the project took about a year and a half to complete, but as Hayashi Mikiya has explained, the Kenji era began on the twenty-fifth day of the fourth month of Bun'ei 12. Therefore, the eighth month of Kenji 1 would have been only five months after the third month of Bun'ei 12.[103] Hayashi also has suggested that the presence of the retired emperors Gofukakusa and Kameyama (r. 1259–74) indicates that these royals must have supported the project financially.[104] It is important to remember that Ōmiyain, the mother of both retired emperors, was a Shōtoku devotee who not only visited Hōryūji, but was also buried near the tomb at Shinaga. The involvement of members of the imperial family might also explain why the monk Jōen performed the eye-opening ceremony at Chōkōdō. The complete name of this temple, a private temple of Emperor Goshirakawa (r. 1155–58) in Kyoto, is Hokke Chōkō Amida Sanmaidō. The site was used for performance of *Hokke zanmai* (*Lotus* meditation), a confession rite for the sake of deceased ancestors.[105] As both Queen Consort Anahobe and Prince Shōtoku were ancestors of members of the imperial family, it might not be a coincidence that the ceremony was performed on the twenty-second, as that is the date of the prince's death.

To focus on a problematic portion of the text, the phrase "an embroidered copy (寫繡) was made" has been the subject of debate. Some scholars argue that a new mandara was produced; others state that the Shūchō was repaired; and some hold that the Shūchō was repaired, and a new work also was made. The extant physical evidence can support any of these theories. Certainly, the *shin* (new) in the title of the document could be used to support the theory that a "new" mandara, or a replica of the Shūchō, was produced in 1275. In the facsimile of *Uragaki* contained in *Shōyoshō*, however, the graph *shin* appears to be an addition written smaller than the rest of the text. Therefore, it is possible that the original title did not include the word "new."[106]

The last section of *Uragaki* emphasizes that the offering of a textile was an unusual event.[107] This sentence might explain why Shinnyo's discovery of the mandara was considered such an extraordinary occurrence. Although we will never know how much of the Shūchō had survived, the fact that such fragile material had endured for some six centuries, with bright colors and well-preserved images, might have indeed made an impact. The Shūchō was not the only fabric icon to be revamped in the Kamakura period. The Taima Mandara, located at Taimadera, was also being promoted at the time through replication. This eighth-century work is a tapestry representing a *hensō*, or transformation tableau, of Amida's *Visualization Sutra* (S. *Amitāyurdhyāna Sūtra*; J. *Kanmuryōjukyō*). From the early thirteenth century onward, multiple painted copies of the Taima Mandara were made as Pure Land beliefs became popular.[108]

To recap, *Chūgūji engi* and *Uragaki* suggest the following sequence of events. The Shūchō was discovered in the second month of 1274. In the fourth month, Shinnyo took it to Kyoto for the first time; she must have had the embroidered inscription transcribed, and *Chūgūji engi* composed. This *engi* was probably used for a fundraising campaign, which appears to have been successful, as retired emperors and people from all strata of society seem to have contributed. Then, in the third month of 1275, she took the Shūchō back to Kyoto, and five months later, after the completion of the mandara, Buddhist ceremonies were performed before the work was taken to Chūgūji. Although we do not know the details of the eye-opening ceremony, the liturgical text used for another ceremony provides insight into how the Shūchō was perceived at the time.

Explaining the Tenjukoku Mandara: *Taishi mandara kōshiki*

The day before the eye-opening ceremony, a service was performed at the Shakadō of Ryōzenji, a temple of the Tendai school located in Kyoto's Higashiyama district.[109] Details of this service are documented in *Taishi mandara kōshiki*, a liturgical text composed by the monk Jōen especially for the Tenjukoku Mandara.[110] This long text, which is the first to use the composite "Tenjukoku Mandara," was clearly intended to weave the embroidered artifact into the thriving Shōtoku cult. Jōen understood Tenjukoku to be Amida's Pure Land, where Anahobe, Shōtoku, and Princess Kashiwade resided as incarnations of the Amida triad.

A *kōshiki* is a liturgical text that promotes devotion to a particular Buddha, bodhisattva, or patriarch; when used in ritual, such texts generate a karmic connection (*kechien*) between the participants and the object of devotion. According to James Foard, in a ritual based on a *kōshiki* text, ten or twelve monks and a number of lay practitioners would gather to recite the text before the image of the featured deity. The aim of the ritual was to create a bond among a group of devotees seeking to further their understanding and faith. Although *kōshiki* are written in *kanbun* (classical Chinese, used for official texts in Japan from ancient through early-modern times), these texts were recited in vernacular Japanese or a Sino-Japanese hybrid. In short, *kōshiki* comprised a form of worship, propagation, and teaching that took shape between the tenth and thirteenth centuries. In most cases, the performance of *kōshiki* served to explain the object of devotion.[111]

The contents of *Taishi mandara kōshiki* give detailed explanations about Prince Shōtoku, the embroidered mandara, and the liturgy itself. As *kōshiki* usually were performed in front of an image of the deity, it is likely that the embroidered mandara, as the focus of the liturgy, was hung in view of all participants. Indeed, certain passages in the *kōshiki* suggest that the priest leading the liturgy pointed to specific motifs, the inscription, or sections of the composition.[112] The text begins with a ceremony of communal obeisance (*sōrei*), followed by explanations and hymns of praise (S. *gāthā*; J. *kada*), and ends with transfer of merit (*ekō*). The explanations touch upon the prince's original state (*honji*) and manifestation (*suijaku*), as well as the mandara. Sections that contain explanations of the content of the liturgy are helpful for understanding the reception of the discovered mandara.

In brief, *Taishi mandara kōshiki* focuses on the hagiographic events of Shōtoku's life and his afterlife in Tenjukoku. Jōen narrates important events in the life of the prince based on popular hagiographic accounts, and also uses quotes from the "Verse of the Tomb Chamber" and the inscription on the Shūchō to explain the meaning of the discovered mandara. In essence, this text reveals Jōen's interpretation of the Shūchō's inscription and imagery grounded on his knowledge of the Shōtoku cult and Buddhism in Japan.

The opening of *Taishi mandara kōshiki* indicates that the subject is the prince and the discovered mandara. It begins with a hymn of praise to the Three Jewels—the Buddha, the Dharma, and the Saṃgha (the Buddhist community)—and the prince, "the Dharma King of the Upper Palace who continues the mission of the great teachers that transmitted the Dharma all through the three kingdoms." After the hymn, Jōen asks the participants "to bow to this mandara showing his birth in the Pure Land (*ōjō no mandara*)." The participants are also encouraged "to praise the main image [the mandara] by setting up vases with flowers and burning incense." These offerings are repeated multiple times in the ceremony.

Next is the offering of the three acts (verbal, mental, and physical) with the purpose of gaining happiness from the Dharma. Jōen continues with the first section of the ceremony, which is divided into two segments: praising Shōtoku's *suijaku*, followed by his *honji*. Narration of the prince's *suijaku*, his manifestation on this earth, includes his miraculous conception, his prayer to the Buddha when he was two years old, his journey to China on a cart pulled by a blue dragon, and many other events. The text also refers to Shōtoku's political role as heir to the throne during Suiko's time and his promulgation of the Seventeen-Article Constitution, as well as his Buddhist deeds, such as his lectures and commentaries on sutras, the battle against the opponents of Buddhism, the forty-six temples established by him, and the creation of the Eastern Gate to the Pure Land at Shitennōji. Jōen also mentions Hyeja's death on the first anniversary of the death of the prince; the admiration for the prince's teachings felt by Saichō (767–822), the founder of the Tendai school in Japan; and how Kūkai ascended to the third level of enlightenment when he visited the tomb. This explanation of Shōtoku's *suijaku* is followed by another hymn of praise, exalting the prince's *honji* as Kannon:

> Our respect to Guze Kannon, the Prince of Japan (*zokusan ō*), who transmitted the flame to the kings of the east;
> He was born from the western direction and began to propound the wondrous Dharma to save all sentient beings;
> I take refuge in the transmitter of the Buddhist Law, the Saintly Spirit of the Prince of the Upper Palace, so that I definitely attain what I hope in my heart.

This hymn, which must be repeated three times (as specified in the text), serves as an introduction to the next segment about Shōtoku's *honji* as Kannon. This section is particularly important, because it reveals that Jōen had knowledge of the Pure Land form of the Shōtoku cult. In fact, the liturgy includes a quote from the "Verse of the Tomb Chamber," in which the prince proclaims his divinity, and that of his mother and wife:

> I am Guze Kannon; my wife and companion Jōe is Dai Seishi; and my compassionate mother, who bore and raised me, is the lord Amida, the teacher and master of the Western Paradise.

Jōen emphasizes how these three members of the royal family "hid their true selves [as incarnations of Buddhist deities], and together they teach and benefit humans." To further confirm the *honji* of the prince as Kannon, he mentions the miraculous events narrated in the hagiographic sources, such as Shōtoku's encounter with Prince Asa and the monk Nichira from Baekje, both of whom recognized him as Guze Kannon. Jōen then explains the benefits of worshipping Guze Kannon, "who resides in the Land of Bliss, but also is the Kannon of this world, who made the universal vow that all people will reach enlightenment." After this, Jōen addresses the audience: "You must know that this bodhisattva [Shōtoku] has made a great vow, and that all people have a relationship with this bodhisattva."

The second section of the ceremony focuses on the mandara, which must have hung in front of the participants. The liturgy is organized and clear, and for each segment, Jōen explains its specific purpose. The segment below is particularly relevant for understanding his view of the mandara:

> [I will explain] the history of its origins (*engi*) followed by a description of it. First [I will explain] the history of its discovery. This mandara represents the life story of the Prince of the Upper Palace through his birth in the Pure Land. It is a representation of a *hensō* embroidered by the ladies-in-waiting at the command of Heavenly Sovereign Suiko.

When Jōen spoke these words, referring in part to the inscription, he must have pointed to the turtles that carried the ideograms for Suiko and the ladies-in-waiting. Mentioning Suiko must have helped to confirm the antiquity of the object in the minds of the participants.

Next, Jōen explains how the object had been deteriorating at Hōryūji, and that nobody knew of its existence until Shinnyo decided to restore Chūgūji:

> But then there was a nun who was devoted to the Prince of the Upper Palace. She cried upon seeing that the old temple of Chūgūji was dilapidated, and promised to repair the temple and build a new hall.

After a brief description of Shinnyo's struggles to revamp Chūgūji, Jōen explains,

> The prince built this hall for his mother. The nun wanted to reopen the temple for the anniversary of her death and hold a memorial, but she did not know the date. She prayed to know the day and the month. She asked for a sign, but there was none. She wanted a record, but there was no record. Just believe in the unseen Three Jewels and pray with all your heart.

This last sentence serves as a transition to the recounting of the nun's performance of the Shaka *nenbutsu* "to solidify her devotion to the prince," which she was scheduled to finish "on the day of the anniversary of the death of the prince." Jōen then relates the dream that led to the discovery of the mandara, and the discovery itself on the twenty-sixth day of the second month of Bun'ei 11, after robbers had entered the temple.

> As expected, among the four hundred characters on the numinous turtles, the date of the death—the twenty-first day of the twelfth month—was found quickly. Everyone was moved to the core, and their chests were moistened by their tears of joy.

As in *Chūgūji engi*, the discovery is seen as "the *hōben* (product of the techniques) of Amida and Kannon, an extraordinary sign in this time of the latter age (*mappō*)." Jōen emphasizes that Shinnyo was motivated by her profound devotion to Prince Shōtoku, which surely yielded positive results. During the ceremony, when the "numinous turtles" and the date were mentioned, it is likely that attention was drawn to the specific turtles bearing that information.

After another hymn of praise, the monk continues by explaining the meaning of Tenjukoku. This portion of *Taishi mandara kōshiki* is the most pertinent to elucidating Jōen's interpretation of the mandara. What the monk expounds here had a strong impact not only in the medieval world, but also for modern historiography. Jōen writes, "The next discussion is about the circumstances of the creation of the place of the Great Incarnation (i.e. Tenjukoku)," and continues,

> Now, let's offer praise to the object [mandara] and its significance. First, regarding the object, this is a transformation scene of the Pure Land of Supreme Bliss (*Gokuraku jōdo*). Amida and Kannon, the teacher and disciple of this comfortable land, manifested compassion and came to our world of suffering; Anahobe and Umayado [came to this world and] suffered as mother and son before they returned to their original land.

Here, Jōen identifies the pictorial representation as Amida's Pure Land. He explains that Anahobe and Shōtoku were in our world, but because they are incarnations of Amida and Kannon, they have returned to their place of origin: the Pure Land. The sentences that follow indicate that Jōen aims to convince the members of his audience that they are in front of an unusual visual representation of Amida's Pure Land:

> In some cases, our Pure Land of the West (Saihō jōdo) is a house existing in the west, and sometimes it is the record of the place where they returned. As already indicated, this place where they live, how can it not be the Pure Land?

Jōen continues with an explanation of the rebirth process: "The principle of human and heavenly rebirth; people receiving the body of a Buddha after being transformed in a lotus, which has the bliss of supernatural power." At this moment of the service, he must have pointed to the designs of a figure emerging from a lotus, the only motif among the fragments that relates to the idea of being transported to Amida's Pure Land (see figs. 11, 13, 17).

Jōen's explanation of the term Tenju, and of the meaning of the mandara, further reflects his own interpretation:

> The Pure Land's adornment is an infinite, empty space. For example, this picture, its name is Muryōju Tenju. What is the meaning of this Amida mandara? Now I will explain its significance. [This mandara] is the land of the eternal and tranquil light (jōjakōdo) that strangely merges together. The inscription [on the mandara] says, "My Great King [Shōtoku] said, 'This world is empty, the Buddha is the only truth'; he appreciated the Buddhist teachings, [therefore] I say my Great King's reward is within Tenjukoku." Reflecting upon these words, they are profound. Things are perceived in their original state (hōju hōi); the nature of the forms of existence, impermanence, and eternality are one. The ultimate knowledge of the Buddha's ultimate reality appears in the secular world, without equal. Emptiness is true and real; apart from the true and real, there is no emptiness. The prince thoroughly penetrated the teaching of the Buddhist Law and was reborn in Tenjukoku. Not having attained the lakṣaṇas (special attributes) of the wondrous body, how can we attain the essence of awakening in the Dharma realm and the conditions in the other world? The inscription [from the tomb] says, "the worldly truth and the ultimate reality are one essence; one essence that manifests as three, which are the same single body."[113] This body manifests in three locations. Is it not in the fourth land of the non-dual eternal and tranquil light? Now, the meaning of ten 天 is the first principle (dai ichigi); the meaning of ju 寿 is the everlasting truth that the eight events of the Buddha's life took place in this land, and the benefits of three generations. According to this, previous Buddha, later Buddha, they attain this body. It is a pure land, and it is [also] an impure land. Return to this land! This is the place where the eternally abiding, blissful capacity of manifesting oneself, and doing anything free of defilement are perfected.

In the long segment above, Jōen explains that the embroidered artifact is an Amida mandara representing the land of the eternal and tranquil light, the land of the Dharma-body Buddha (one of the four lands theorized by the Tendai school).[114] To further emphasize the Amidist component of the work, he relates Tenju to Muryōju, another name for Amida. Additionally, in interpreting the meaning of Tenjukoku, he relies on Shōtoku's words as recorded in the Shūchō's inscription, and comments on the Buddhist concepts mentioned. As Jōen explains, due to the prince's deep understanding of the Buddhist teachings, he was reborn in Tenjukoku, but he did not attain the marks of Buddhahood (the special bodily attributes, or lakṣaṇas, that distinguish a Buddha). Here Jōen clearly indicates that a figure recognizable as a Buddha does not appear in the embroidery. For him, tenju is nirvana, the ultimate reality attained by Śākyamuni. Essentially, Jōen suggests that Prince Shōtoku reached enlightenment in Tenjukoku, a place that was a pure land, but at the same time, an impure land; a place where a Buddha has yet to appear, a place of possibilities.

Following this explanation of the mandara's significance is a brief visual description:

[We can] see in each of the four levels of the palace [or superimposed four palaces] that men and women, birds and beasts are not separated. … two circles for the sun and the moon, both shine the light of meditation and wisdom; there are a bell and a gong on each side, to startle [us from] the illusion of the cycles of transmigration.[115]

Jōen's description includes some of the motifs discussed previously, such as men and women, birds and animals, and the sun and moon. The presence of these elements confirms that the Tenjukoku Mandara featured at least some of the designs from the original artifact.

Although *Chūgūji engi* emphasizes the need to find the mandara for the purpose of determining the date of Anahobe's death, Jōen's statements in the last section of *Taishi mandara kōshiki* reveal that, by the time of its dedication, this purpose was no longer relevant: "For forty-nine years [Shōtoku] practiced the Dharma, [and] we still can encounter those conditions as he returns, after six hundred years, with the discovery of the mandara." This sentence clearly indicates that, at this point in time, the discovery of the mandara was a miracle associated with the prince and his desire to continue supporting Buddhism. The discovery of such a fragile and dazzling embroidery, made after the deaths of Shōtoku and his mother, must have amazed the devotees who participated in the ceremony.

The last part of *Taishi mandara kōshiki* is the transfer of merit, after which is a postscript that gives information about the dedication of the mandara and the ceremony in which the liturgical text was used:

The new embroidered Tenjukoku Mandara was dedicated in the Shakadō of Ryōzenji in Rakutō [Kyoto] in autumn, in the eighth month of the first year of the Kenji era [1275]. There were lectures on the *Lotus Sutra* and the *Lion's Roar Sutra*, as well as daily praises, and people worshipped it. After a while the nun [Shinnyo], who prayed and yearned for the saintly spirit of the prince, concentrated on the abridged version of a five-part ceremony creating a karmic connection with the three deities. It was a graceful work, but wordy and difficult to follow. On the twenty-first day of the same year and month, the date of the death of the empress, this ceremony was successfully [performed] in front of this mandara, written by the Tendai Lotus School Seal of the Dharma Great Master (*hōin gon daisōzu*) Jōen.

As evidenced by the text, *Taishi mandara kōshiki* is undoubtedly a document associated with the Shōtoku cult. Its contents reveal that the discovery of the Shūchō was believed to be a miraculous event similar to the discovery of the scroll at Shitennōji, or the inscribed slab at the tomb at Shinaga. As in these two previous cases, the artifact contained words uttered by the prince. Notably, due to the spread of belief in the Shinaga Amida triad, Jōen identified Tenjukoku as Amida's Pure Land, where Shōtoku and his mother attained nirvana and resided as Kannon and Amida, respectively. For this reason, the monk identified the mandara as an Amida mandara. The ceremonies performed honored the two royals. The dates of the ceremonies, the eye-opening ceremony (or dedication) on the twenty-second day and the *kōshiki* on the twenty-first day of the eighth month, correspond to the anniversaries of the deaths of the prince and Anahobe, respectively. Both deified royals were honored using an ancient artifact made to memorialize them more than six hundred years earlier.

A Vow Fulfilled

After discovering the Tenjukoku Mandara, Shinnyo fulfilled her vow to restore Chūgūji, as noted in various sources. Hōryūji's involvement seems to have continued, as records in *Hōryūji bettō shidai* indicate work being done at the nunnery. A couple of years after the dedication of the Tenjukoku Mandara, in 1277 (Kenji 3), a ridgepole-raising ceremony for an unspecified hall was performed, and in 1280 (Kōan 3), Abbot Genga led the completion ceremony.[116] After this rite, Shinnyo wrote her *ganmon* in the first month of Kōan 4 (1281). In this document, Shinnyo tells us about her desire to restore Chūgūji, which she describes as a temple having a two-storied Golden Hall with three bays, and a three-storied pagoda. After detailing the dilapidated state of the nunnery, she recounts her discovery of the mandara, and the new prosperity of Chūgūji.[117]

The nunnery must have thrived while the nun was alive, as records suggest that aristocrats visited the site. As mentioned previously, in 1290 Lady Nijō went to Chūgūji, as well as the prince's tomb. She mentions in her diary that her intention was to learn more about the nunnery's connection to Prince Shōtoku and his consort, and that she recognized Shinnyo, whom she had seen in the palace.[118] Unfortunately, Nijō does not mention the Tenjukoku Mandara at all. In contrast, in the account of her visit to Taimadera, she briefly refers to the *Taima mandara engi* (Account of the Origins of the Taima Mandala, early 13th century), although she does not mention seeing or worshipping the mandara.[119]

By the fourteenth century, Chūgūji had declined once again. *Hōryūji bettō shidai* states that the living quarters were destroyed by fire in 1309 (Enkyō 2) and then rebuilt, but destroyed again in 1311 (Ōchō 1).[120] After these entries, Chūgūji is not mentioned in any records from Hōryūji until the sixteenth century. The story of Shinnyo and the Tenjukoku Mandara is retold with slight variations in other texts.[121]

CONCLUSION

As belief in Amida and the promise of salvation in the Western Pure Land spread through Japan, Pure Land faith was woven into the worship of Prince Shōtoku at Shitennōji, Hōryūji, and the tomb at Shinaga. Because the prince already was believed to be an incarnation of Kannon, one of the bodhisattvas inhabiting Amida's Pure Land, the path for his assimilation into this faith was straightforward. The belief that developed at the tomb at Shinaga, known as the "Amida triad in one tomb with three remains," is fundamental to understanding the meaning given to the seventh-century embroidered artifact upon its rediscovery. According to this belief, Shōtoku, Anahobe, and Princess Kashiwade, who were believed to be buried in the same tomb, inhabited the site as incarnations of Kannon, Amida, and Seishi, respectively. This belief in the deified royals reached Hōryūji, as evidenced by the Amida triad in the Golden Hall, completed in 1232, and the *Shōkō mandara*, made in 1254. Because this temple had strong connections with Chūgūji, it must have played a role in the transmission of this belief. Shinnyo, who usually is associated with Eison and the revival of the Ritsu lineage, was also a devotee of Prince Shōtoku, and had been associated with Hōryūji since the early thirteenth century (even before she met Eison).

By studying the relevant documents and taking into account their dates of compilation and their content, it becomes clear that Shinnyo's original mission changed after the Shūchō was discovered. Her initial intention was to restore the nunnery and to hold a memorial for its founder, Queen Consort Anahobe. In order to achieve her goal, she needed to know the date of Anahobe's death. In 1274, the nun found the seventh-century embroidery in a repository at Hōryūji and took it to Kyoto, where she met the monk Jōen, who transcribed the difficult-to-read inscription and wrote *Chūgūji engi*.

At this point, the nun began to formulate other plans, including the repair of the damaged embroidery. It is likely that she went back to the capital multiple times to seek support, using the *engi* in the fundraising campaign, which successfully culminated in the dedication of the mandara in 1275. Jōen composed and performed the *Taishi mandara kōshiki*, as well as the eye-opening ceremony. In this document, the composite "Tenjukoku Mandara" is used for the first time. Importantly, *Taishi mandara kōshiki* reveals that the discovery of the seventh-century artifact made for Shōtoku and his mother was seen as a miraculous event associated with the benevolence of the prince. Although the *kōshiki* was performed on the twenty-first day, Anahobe's death anniversary, the prince's mother is not the focus of the liturgy, but plays a role subordinate to that of the prince. This document also reveals that Jōen associated the Shūchō with belief in the Shinaga Amida triad. The unusual pictorial representation, which was identified on the artifact itself as a depiction of Tenjukoku, the place where Shōtoku was reborn (or where he resides), was perfectly suited to the contention that Tenjukoku is a pure land and also an impure land, where the three royals live as incarnations of Kannon, Amida, and Seishi.

Based on the contents of *Taishi mandara kōshiki*, it is clear that the discovery of the embroidered curtains must have been one of the highlights in the development of the Shōtoku cult during the Kamakura period. Temple precincts such as the Jōgūin of Hōryūji displayed a number of objects associated with the prince, and other sites, such as Shitennōji and the tomb at Shinaga, claimed to have found his messages for the future. The unexpected discovery of the mandara aligned with these popular trends. Like *Shitennōji engi*, the stone slab found at Shinaga, and the "Verse of the Tomb Chamber," the dazzling and colorful embroidered curtains not only contained information about the prince, but more importantly, recorded words uttered by him about Buddhism. Moreover, this discovery must have seemed particularly exceptional due to the fact that silk fabric is such a fragile material. The Shūchō had not merely survived for more than six hundred and fifty years, but still showed designs and an inscription in bright and well-preserved colors. To convince devotees of the truth of this miraculous finding, the remains of the Shūchō had to be displayed. For this reason, although *Uragaki* states that a copy was made, it is highly likely that the Shūchō instead was repaired.

5

The Restoration, Fragmentation, and Secularization of the Tenjukoku Mandara

Textual sources from the fourteenth through nineteenth centuries show that the restored embroidery continued to be known as the Tenjukoku Mandara. More importantly, these sources allow us to trace the history of the fragmentation of the artifact and its changing significance through time. The goal of this chapter is to propose a reconstruction of the repaired mandara after analyzing the remaining corpus of documents associated with it. The content of each document will be analyzed in order to determine the context for its compilation and its reliability as evidence for proposing a reconstruction. The chronological and contextual analysis of these documents allows us not only to assess the sources themselves, but also to trace the reasons for the fragmentation of the mandara and its changing significance, especially during the Edo period.

The first section, "The Tenjukoku Mandara in the Lore of the Shōtoku Cult," is focused on the documents dated to the fourteenth and fifteenth centuries that demonstrate that the narratives about the discovery of the Shūchō and its transformation into the Tenjukoku Mandara were incorporated into the tradition of devotion to the prince. During this time, the core narrative of Shinnyo's story was modified according to specific agendas, particularly by the Shingon Ritsu school. Evidence for the reasons behind the mandara's fragmentation is also discussed briefly. In the second section, "The Edo Period: From Religious Icon to Antique," documents from the eighteenth and nineteenth centuries are analyzed. In this period, interest in antiquities led monk-scholars and antiquarians to visit temples and shrines to study ancient documents, epigraphs, and icons. For this reason, the Shūchō's inscription, as recorded in the *Imperial Biography* and other documents, and especially the surviving turtles bearing characters, attracted the attention of scholars. Their records reveal that the fragments were no longer seen as religious objects, but rather as the remains of an ancient artifact and epigraph.

After evaluating the sources, the last section, "Reconstructing the Tenjukoku Mandara," includes an analysis of the designs on the thirteenth-century fragments, and proposes a tentative reconstruction of the artifact's dimensions, the placement of the one hundred turtles, and the composition. Because this study argues that the seventh-century Shūchō was repaired (rather than duplicated in full), the reconstruction is based on seventh-century parameters. In contrast to previous studies, the reconstruction proposed here takes into account the manufacture and design processes that may have been employed in the seventh century.

Monk in belfry, Tenjukoku Shūchō Mandara, detail of fig. 88.

THE TENJUKOKU MANDARA IN THE LORE OF THE SHŌTOKU CULT

Shinnyo's quest to find the mandara began with two purposes: to know the date of the death of the nunnery's founder, and to restore Chūgūji. When the new mandara was dedicated, however, the artifact was seen as one of Prince Shōtoku's messages for the future, and as such, was integrated into the lore of the Shōtoku cult. Three documents of the fourteenth and fifteenth centuries attest to this fact: *Shōtoku Taishi denki*, *Shōyoshō*, and *Chūgūji engi* (1463 version). The first two documents are annotated versions of, or commentaries on, *Shōtoku Taishi denryaku*.[1] Writing commentaries on the most popular hagiographical account of the prince's life was common practice in medieval Japan; Kenshin's *Shōtoku Taishi den shiki* also fits into this category. These first two sources include enhanced versions of the thirteenth-century account, and incorporate people connected to the Shingon Ritsu school. Thus it is likely that Shingon Ritsu monks transformed the basic account to include aspects pertinent to their agenda, especially in relation to the salvation of women and their need to rely on male Ritsu priests.[2] As indicated by its title, the third document is an account of the history of Chūgūji. Its contents, however, are derived from the prince's hagiography, especially those elements associated with Pure Land beliefs.

These three documents reveal that the Tenjukoku Mandara had become an integral part of the lore of the Shōtoku cult and Chūgūji. Each includes the standard hagiographical account of the prince's life, as well as events associated with Shinnyo and the Tenjukoku Mandara, with some interesting twists.

Shōtoku Taishi denki

Dated to the Bunpō era (1317–19), *Shōtoku Taishi denki* is a long document that comments on the hagiographical events included in *Shōtoku Taishi denryaku*. The text is organized chronologically according to the prince's age.[3] The story of the mandara is included in the episode in which Shōtoku, at fifty years old, endures the death of his mother. According to *Shōtoku Taishi denki*, the prince knelt in front of his mother's tomb, mourning her passing, for seven days and seven nights. During this time, he revealed his mother's true identity and explained that her *honji* was Amida, the founder of the Land of Peace and Nurturance (Annyō, a synonym for the Land of Bliss). Because of her great compassion for saving beings, she left her lotus throne in the Pure Land to mingle with the beings that wander through the six realms of existence (i.e., the continuous cycle of death and rebirth), dwelling with them in this land of dust. When her karmic connection to this realm ended, she did not return to the Pure Land, but decided to continue to help sentient beings. The prince did not know the land where she was reborn, so he felt uneasy. He wondered if she was in an impure land or a pure land; therefore, he prayed to see the place where his mother lived. On the seventh night, a heavenly woman appeared from the tomb bringing a message from his mother. She explained that Anahobe would not return to the Western Pure Land, but would remain in this defiled world. She would be born in Tenjukoku, located to the southwest of India, a pure land in the impure land for those with heavy karmic obstacles.[4]

Then Anahobe, framed by rays of light, made herself visible in Tenjukoku and described this land to her son. The language used in this segment is consistent with descriptions of pure lands in Mahāyāna texts.

> [There are] pagodas and palaces that glitter like jewels, with many gates and multi-storied buildings the color of agate and amber; treasure ponds with banks of golden sand that glow and shine; jeweled lotus flowers of many colors; everything enveloped by the fragrance of spindle trees. The pond waters are clear and pure, birds frolic by the waterside, and sacred birds sing peacefully the Dharma. People gather, talk, and listen in between the jeweled trees that spread the Dharma in this pure land. Near the treasure pond, the waves preach the principle of selflessness. [In this land,] there is no spring or autumn, flowers and fruits bloom all year because it is neither cold nor hot. Just touching the grass comforts body and heart. Just as in the Land of Bliss, the land is lapis lazuli, the

road has golden ropes, and there are beautiful canopies with flowers and jeweled banners. In the center of this land there is a four-storied palace (or four superimposed palaces). I [Anahobe] am in the fourth palace, and bells and gongs stand to the left and right.[5]

The story continues by explaining that Shōtoku then drew a picture of Tenjukoku with his own hands, and later showed his sketch to Heavenly Sovereign Suiko, who ordered the imperial consorts and ladies-in-waiting to create the embroidered artifact.[6] In addition to his detailed description of Tenjukoku as a place, the compiler of *Shōtoku Taishi denki* describes the object as constructed from "three panels of twill (*aya katabira*), carefully embroidered with threads of five colors in a loose and broad manner. At the four edges were flat bands with golden bells."[7]

The passage about the origins of the mandara is followed by Shinnyo's campaign to revive Chūgūji, and the mandara's discovery. The nun's role, however, is diminished by the inclusion of a Shingon Ritsu monk. According to the text, the abbot of Sairinji (in present-day Osaka), Nichijō Shōnin (or Sōji; 1233–1312), Eison's disciple and nephew, began the campaign to restore the nunnery, but in a dream Prince Shōtoku told him that, because Chūgūji was a nunnery, it had to be reestablished by a nun. Heartbroken, Nichijō went to see the abbot of Saidaiji, Shien (another of Eison's names), who decided to choose among the Ritsu nuns at the nunnery; Shien selected Shinnyo.[8] As the new abbess of Chūgūji, Shinnyo deemed it important to know the date of the death of the institution's patron. She asked the elder monks, but nobody could give her an answer.[9]

What follows in *Shōtoku Taishi denki* are the events narrated in the 1274 version of *Chūgūji engi*: the performance of the Shaka *nenbutsu*, and the dream about the location of the mandara. In the fourteenth-century text, however, the story about the discovery is elaborated to include more details, such as the information that the mandara was found inside a red Chinese trunk that contained seven brocade bags: "The big mandara was inside one of the bags; it has flat bands with golden bells; it is made of silk fabric and can be stretched across three bays. When the nun found the Chinese trunk and moved the bags, she heard the sound of bells."[10]

After the mandara's discovery, a multitude of people worshiped the artifact at Hōryūji, and an imperial envoy was organized to take it to the capital. Whereas no mention is made in either the 1274 *Chūgūji engi* or *Uragaki* of any specific person helping the nun to read the inscription, in *Shōtoku Taishi denki* it is reported that a priest from Kyoto's Hirano Shrine, the Confucianist Kanesuke, transcribed and annotated the inscription written on the turtles' shells.[11] The text also states that Jōen performed the Hokke Sanjikkō ceremony at Ryōzenji with the participation of the retired emperors. This ceremony, which consisted of thirty lectures held over thirty days, included the twenty-eight chapters of the *Lotus Sutra*, the *Sutra of Immeasurable Meanings* (S. *Ananta nirdeśa sūtra*; C. *Wuliang yi jing*; J. *Muryōgikyō*) as the introduction, and the *Samantabhadra Meditation Sutra* (J. *Fugen kangyō*) as the conclusion.[12] Moreover, the document states that, after this ceremony, the "new mandara [and] the copied mandara" were both taken back to Chūgūji, where Jōen composed the three-part *Taishi mandara kōshiki*.[13]

Compared to the thirteenth-century narratives, the passage from *Shōtoku Taishi denki* pertaining to the Tenjukoku Mandara and the nun Shinnyo includes extraordinary events, making the story more appealing. This text highlights the Pure Land beliefs associated with the artifact, particularly in the episode that finds Anahobe appearing in Tenjukoku as Amida and describing this land to Prince Shōtoku, who sketches it and shows it to Suiko. The passage also emphasizes the supportive role of Shingon Ritsu monks, particularly Sōji and Eison, in the revival of Chūgūji. As discussed previously, however, the 1274 *Chūgūji engi* demonstrates that, in the early stages of Shinnyo's quest, Hōryūji played an important role in Shinnyo's campaign to restore Chūgūji and in her discovery of the mandara. Furthermore, the priest Kanesuke from Hirano Shrine is included in the later account as the person who read the inscription. *Shōtoku Taishi denki*, which clearly presents an enhanced version of the late-thirteenth-century events, was written with the specific purpose of stressing the role of the Shingon Ritsu school in Chūgūji's revival. The Ritsu monks seem to have tried to benefit from the popularity that Shinnyo gained from her alleged discovery of the Tenjukoku Mandara.

Shōyoshō

Shōyoshō was written by the monk Shōyo from Hōryūji. Although the details of his life are unknown, his name appears in a document dated to 1406, which states that he was fifty-seven years old at the time. For this reason, as well as certain facts recorded in the manuscript, it is believed that the text was written during the Ōei era (1394–1428). The oldest extant version, however, is a copy dated to 1547 (Tenbun 16). *Shōyoshō* includes commentaries on Shōtoku's life events, with particular attention given to the temples founded by him. These commentaries are based on Shōyo's study of documents and oral traditions.[14] Chūgūji, the nun Shinnyo, and the Tenjukoku Mandara are addressed in the last section of the manuscript.[15] This section includes a transcription of *Uragaki*, a commentary on the prince's wives, a long discussion about the revival of the Ritsu school and Shinnyo's discovery of the mandara, a record of the dates of death of Anahobe and Shōtoku, a confirmation of the accuracy of these dates based on the Shūchō's inscription, and an interpretation of the term Tenjukoku.

After the transcription of *Uragaki*, the portion dedicated to Shōtoku's wives reveals that Shōyo had access to manuscripts such as *Kuji hongi* (or *Kujiki*; dated to the Heian period), *Nihon shoki*, and *Shōtoku Taishi denryaku*. He writes about the discrepancies between the sources, highlighting Tachibana's appearance in the Tenjukoku Mandara's inscription.[16] Following this portion are the intertwined accounts about the Tenjukoku Mandara and Shinnyo. These begin with the mandara's origins in the seventh century, mentioning Anahobe's appearance to the prince in a dream and how he sketched Tenjukoku and showed it to Suiko, who ordered the making of the artifact.[17] This passage clearly is derived from *Shōtoku Taishi denki*, but Shōyō does not mention the source.

Shōyo's manuscript also addresses Shinnyo's biography. Hosokawa Ryōichi and Lori Meeks have discussed this section at length, particularly the nun's ordination and her association with the Shingon Ritsu school.[18] Regarding Chūgūji, Shōyo writes that the nunnery was one of the forty-six temples built by the prince, but was founded by Anahobe. He evidently researched records associated with Shōtoku and his mother, focusing on the date of Anahobe's death. To clarify this issue, Shōyo revisits the inscription on the mandorla of the Shaka triad at Hōryūji, and comments on the importance of finding the mandara to determine this significant date.

As in *Shōtoku Taishi denki*, Shōyo mentions the sound of the bells as an important incident in the mandara's discovery. Yet, according to his account, when Shinnyo went to Kyoto, she searched for learned men to read the inscription, and found Kazan'in Chūnagon (Counselor of the Center) Fujiwara Morotsugu (1222–1281) and Jōen, who both read it. Shōyo does not mention the priest from Hirano Shrine. Clearly Jōen played a key role in the events after Shinnyo's discovery of the mandara, but it is not clear why Shōyo included Morotsugu. Information about this man is scant. A court noble who specialized in ancient customs, he became Naidaijin (Inner Minister or Minister of the Center) in 1271.[19] If he was filling the lesser post of Chūnagon by the time of the events surrounding the mandara, as recorded by Shōyo, then it seems that he had been demoted, or that the monk's information is not accurate. Due to the lack of knowledge about Morotsugu, it is impossible to determine if he read the inscription, or why Shōyo chose to include him in his account.

The document also contains an entry entitled "Shūchō's inscription accurate dates," which reveals that one of Shōyo's goals was to determine the dates of the deaths of the prince and his mother. Additionally, the monk mentions that, after Shinnyo found out the date of Anahobe's death in 1274, every year the Queen Consort had been remembered properly. To close the segment about Chūgūji,

Shōyo notes his interpretation of Tenjukoku, stating that this place was "Muryōjukoku, the Land of Bliss in the West, one of the three levels of the nine grades [of rebirth]."[20] His creation of the composite "Muryōjukoku" was based perhaps on the artifact's association with Pure Land beliefs, or on Jōen's association of Tenju with Muryōju.

Shōyo's writings about Chūgūji, Shinnyo, and the Tenjukoku Mandara reveal that, in the fifteenth century, the nun and the artifact figured prominently in Chūgūji's history, but more importantly, they were part of the lore of the Shōtoku cult. Although Shōyo does not mention *Shōtoku Taishi denki* in his manuscript, he must have been familiar with the text, as he highlights the role of Shingon Ritsu monks in the revival of Chūgūji, the appearance of Anahobe in Tenjukoku, and the sound of the bells when the mandara was discovered. And while he does not equate Anahobe with an incarnation of Amida, his interpretation of Tenjukoku is clearly based on Pure Land beliefs. In short, by the late fourteenth or early fifteenth century, such enhanced narratives about the origins of the Tenjukoku Mandara must have been widespread.

Chūgūji engi

The fifteenth-century *Chūgūji engi* is an expanded version of the document of the same title from 1274. A postscript indicates that the original manuscript was written by a certain Tōrin in 1463 (Kanshō 4), although the earliest extant copy dates from the Edo period.[21] This *engi* comprises an elaborate account of the nunnery's origins and an homage to Shōtoku and his parents. The halls of Chūgūji are described as Buddhist pure lands, and the prince, his father Yōmei, and his mother Anahobe are identified as deities who can help devotees to reach these Buddhist lands. Key elements related to the Pure Land form of the Shōtoku cult are included, with a focus on the role of the Tenjukoku Mandara's discovery within this context.

Whereas the 1274 *Chūgūji engi* is centered on the events related to Shinnyo and the discovery of the mandara, the longer 1463 version includes a hagiography of Shōtoku. This portion begins with the arrival of the Zenkōji Amida and Buddhist sutras from Goguryeo during Kinmei's reign.[22] Like the other hagiographic accounts, the text refers to Shōtoku's miraculous birth and lists his religious and political accomplishments, as well as his miraculous deeds.[23] The document includes an explanation of the prince's *honji* as Kannon, which was recognized by Prince Asa and the monk Nichira from Baekje. Then the focus shifts to the forty-six temples allegedly established by the prince, and Chūgūji. Over time, the number of temples supposedly founded by Shōtoku increased from seven to eleven, and finally to forty-six; this account numbers Chūgūji among the forty-six temples, but also includes it as one of the original seven, clarifying that Chūgūji is Hōkōji, a temple built for the prince's mother that was known as the central palace (*chūgū*) due to its location in the center of the palace complex.[24]

A detailed and extremely glamorized description of the various buildings and icons of Chūgūji is presented. The nunnery is portrayed as a grandiose temple complex with southern and central gates, a Golden Hall, and a three-storied pagoda. The complex also had a lecture hall, bell tower, sutra repository, gallery, bath house, and monks' quarters.[25] This description fits more the current layout of Hōryūji's Western Compound than the archaeological remains of Chūgūji.[26]

The 1463 *engi* claims that the Golden Hall housed an image of Nyoirin Kannon, the *honji* of the prince; sculptures of the Four Heavenly Kings; and paintings of the lands of the Four Buddhas, figures of *arhats*, bodhisattvas, and celestial beings. The Lecture Hall contained a sculpture of the Buddha Yakushi, the *honji* of Yōmei, flanked by the bodhisattvas Nikkō (S. Suryaprabha) and Gakkō (S. Candraprabha). The Tenjukoku Mandara, measuring one *jō* and six *shaku*, was displayed at the back of the Lecture Hall. The *engi* explains that "Tenjukoku is Muryōjukoku," and that Queen Consort Anahobe, as an incarnation of Amida, is the master of the Land of Bliss. To assert that Anahobe is Amida, the *engi*'s compiler includes the complete "Verse of the Tomb Chamber" under the title of the "Verse Found in the Tomb of the Dharma King Shōtoku," followed by the Shūchō's inscription (but without the genealogy).[27] Interestingly, the *engi* states that the mandara was stolen from Chūgūji by a monk from Ikarugadera (Hōryūji), who hid it in a trunk in the temple's treasure repository.[28] The writer was certainly versed in the lore of the Shōtoku cult, especially its Pure Land aspects. The statement that "Tenjukoku is Muryōjukoku" suggests that the writer was familiar with *Shōyoshō*, or perhaps this was simply the prevalent belief at the time. Certain points, particularly the description of Chūgūji as an extravagant temple complex and the negative portrayal of the Hōryūji monk as a thief, evidently formed part of the writer's agenda of diminishing the role of Hōryūji and its support of the nunnery.

Following the description of the nunnery and its icons is the story about Shinnyo's quest to find the mandara, as narrated in the 1274 *Chūgūji engi* with some omissions, such as the names of the nun that had the dream and the abbot of Hōryūji, Genga, who was an early supporter of Shinnyo.[29] This latter omission is further evidence that Hōryūji's support was downplayed or erased in the later document. The 1463 *engi* also equates the discovery of the Tenjukoku Mandara with the return of the prince, stating that, thanks to this miracle, Chūgūji had returned to its former glory. At the end of the manuscript is a short passage about the alleged role of Prince Shōtoku in the ordination of five hundred nuns, who made Chūgūji their main temple.[30]

Shōtoku Taishi denki, *Shōyoshō*, and the 1463 *Chūgūji engi* confirm that the Tenjukoku Mandara became an important item within the Shōtoku cult. In contrast to the accounts found in thirteenth-century documents, the role of the nun Shinnyo in the revival of Chūgūji is diminished in favor of that of the Shingon Ritsu monks (especially in *Shōtoku Taishi denki* and *Shōyoshō*). These documents suggest that, if not for the involvement of priests from the Ritsu school, the nun would not have been able to accomplish her deed. In addition, the 1463 *Chūgūji engi* portrays Hōryūji in a negative light and omits the active role of the temple as recorded in the earlier documents. This *engi* also demonstrates that, in the fifteenth century, the "Verse of the Tomb Chamber" and the inscription on the Shūchō served as evidence to support the belief that Anahobe and Shōtoku resided as incarnations of Amida and Kannon, respectively, in Tenjukoku. All three documents show that the Tenjukoku Mandara had become integrated into the hagiography of Shōtoku and tied with the Shingon Ritsu school and Pure Land Buddhism.

THE EDO PERIOD: FROM RELIGIOUS ICON TO ANTIQUE

The restored Tenjukoku Mandara was a large-scale artifact in the thirteenth century, but by the eighteenth, only fragments of it remained. While a variety of factors could have caused the mandara's deterioration, it seems that its popularity might have been the main reason for its disrepair. Notes written by Jōjun Shōnin (1389–1457) from the temple Takada Honzan Senjuji (Mie Prefecture) suggest that pilgrims who went to Chūgūji took pieces of the embroidery as tokens of their visit. In 1413 (Ōei 20), Jōjun went on a pilgrimage to Shitennōji and Chūgūji; from the former, he brought back to Senjuji a fragment of the prince's *kesa* (monk's surplice), and from the latter, he took a fragment of the Tenjukoku Mandara.[31] If this was common practice, the few remains included in the assemblage suggest that many devotees must have visited the nunnery and left with pieces of the artifact.

Senjuji is a Pure Land temple allegedly established by Shinran, the aforementioned founder of the True Pure Land sect; the fact that a monk from this temple visited Chūgūji and Shitennōji demonstrates that the connection between Pure Land beliefs and the Shōtoku cult persisted through the fifteenth century. The success of Shinnyo and her associates in promoting the Tenjukoku Mandara as an artifact related to Pure Land faith and the prince might have led devotees to take pieces of this miraculous object. These fragments may have served as souvenirs of pilgrimages to Chūgūji, or the pieces may have been thought to have miraculous powers, as with similar examples in European religious history.[32]

In the Edo period, the inscription and remains of the Shūchō Mandara attracted the attention of monk-scholars and antiquarians. During this time, monks studied ancient documents housed in their temples, and scholars and artists interested in Japan's past visited temples and shrines searching for ancient documents, inscriptions, and objects, keeping records of their observations.[33] Some of these records include line drawings of the objects observed. These Edo-period documents reveal that the Tenjukoku Mandara was no longer esteemed as a religious icon, but as a historical artifact and ancient epigraph.

The first document from this period to include a reference to the Tenjukoku Mandara is *Yamato meishoki* (Records of Famous Places of Yamato), also known as *Washū kyūseki yūkō* (Thoughts about Historical Places in Yamato), written by Hayashi Sōho (1623–ca. 1694) and published in 1681 (Enpō 9).[34] Hayashi traveled around the Yamato region compiling the histories, stories, and poems of its famous places and remains. He visited Chūgūji, and his notes about the nunnery seem to be based on the narrative recorded in *Shōtoku Taishi denki*. Hayashi mentions the roles played by Nichijō Shōnin of Sairinji and Eison of Saidaiji in the revival of the nunnery, as well as Shinnyo's role as the abbess. Referring to the Tenjukoku Mandara as one of the important objects belonging to the nunnery, he states that "the one hundred turtles [are] placed around it (*meguri ni*)." This statement has been used by modern scholars in theorizing the arrangement of the turtles on the original embroidery. Yet, when Hayashi visited the nunnery, the Tenjukoku Mandara was probably already in fragments.

In the early eighteenth century, the monk Ryōkin (1694–1742) from Hōryūji made the first textual and visual record of the fragmented Tenjukoku Mandara. Ryōkin surveyed, repaired, and transcribed manuscripts and inscriptions in Hōryūji's collection.[35] As part of his duties, in the Kyōhō era (1716–36), he compiled *Hōryūji Ryōkin homōshū* (Collection of Notes by Ryōkin of Hōryūji), in which he recorded objects, treasures, and documents at the temple.[36] The text includes mention of a *mushiharai* held at Chūgūji on the second day of the seventh month of 1731 (Kyōhō 16). *Mushiharai* is the airing of documents and clothing during mid-summer to prevent mildew and insect damage. The title of the brief entry, "The Turtle Designs of the Tenjukoku Mandara's Inscription at Chūgūji" (*Chūgūji Tenjukoku Mandara mei kikkō no zu*), indicates that what interested Ryōkin during this *mushiharai* was the inscription and the remaining turtle designs on the mandara. Ryōkin carefully records the size of each turtle shell (one *sun*, three *bun*), and also provides detailed drawings of the three most visible turtles, with notations about the colors on the different parts of each and on the moon design. His notes include the graphs on each of the three turtles and a comment about the fourth turtle being badly damaged. He also specifies that fifty or sixty fragments with people, Buddhist images, a demon-like figure, and the motif of the moon with a rabbit had been preserved. Ryōkin's notes suggest that he saw the fragments present in the current assemblage.

In addition to *Hōryūji Ryōkin homōshū*, the monk also compiled *Hōryūji tōin engi* (Account of the Origins of Hōryūji's Eastern Compound) in 1736 (Genbun 1). In this manuscript, Ryōkin records the text of the "Inscription on Chūgūji's Tenjukoku Mandara" (*Chūgūji Tenjukoku Mandara mei*), *Uragaki*, and other documents associated with Prince Shōtoku.[37]

Two documents from the nineteenth century give further information about scholars' interest in the Tenjukoku Mandara: the aforementioned *Ikaruga koji binran*, compiled by the monk Kakuken in 1836 (Tenpō 7); and *Kanko zatsujō* (Booklet about Miscellaneous Antiquities) by Hoida Tadatomo (1791–1847), published in 1841 (Tenpō 12). *Ikaruga koji binran* is a collection of notes and commentaries on inscriptions that appear on icons and manuscripts at Hōryūji.[38] The document is divided into sections on the following items: icons and monuments, documents, books, main icons, shrines, and miscellaneous. In the documents section, Kakuken records the "Tenjukoku Mandara's inscription," and also *Uragaki*. As in *Hōryūji Ryōkin homōshū*, the monk includes drawings of the three turtles, but Kakuken also notes the size of the original mandara (one *jō*, six *shaku*), and states that only about four *shaku* have survived.

Kakuken's interest in the inscription appears to have been purely historical, and he researched other documents to validate it. He explains that the inscription is found in the *Imperial Biography*, which recently had been annotated by Kariya Ekisai (1775–1835), and that it also is recorded in another document at Hōryūji.[39] Based on Kakuken's notes, the latter document was probably Ryōkin's *Hōryūji tōin engi* or *Hōryūji Ryōkin homōshū*. He also notes that "a pair of embroidered curtains with twenty-two bands and 393 bells donated by the *tennō* of the Kiyomihara Palace" is listed in *Hōryūji engi*, but doubts that this artifact is the Tenjukoku Mandara. Kakuken also refers to Hayashi's *Yamato meishoki* and the detail about the one hundred turtles around the mandara. To close his discussion of the Tenjukoku Mandara's inscription, he writes, "From Suiko 30 to Tenpō 7, a total of 1215 years of history."

Kakuken then records the text of *Uragaki*, which also had been transcribed in *Shōyoshō* and *Hōryūji tōin engi*. Perhaps based on his research of these and other documents, Kakuken adds a sentence to his version of *Uragaki*: "The inscription was read by Kazan'in Chūnagon Fujiwara Morotsugu, the monk Jōen from Onjōji, and a priest from Hirano Shrine." As mentioned above, Jōen is included in most documents associated with the Tenjukoku Mandara, but Morotsugu and the priest Kanesuke of Hirano Shrine are listed in *Shōyoshō* and *Shōtoku Taishi denki*, respectively, as the people who read the inscription. Kakuken obviously had access to a number of documents and compiled information from them. To close his comments about *Uragaki*, he states that this document records the history of the mandara's origins at Chūgūji; that Jōen confined himself at the nunnery and offered a song; and that, according to *Shōyoshō*, Tenjukoku is a Pure Land realm (Gokurakukai). His last sentence about *Uragaki* takes the same format as his final thought on the mandara's inscription: "From Bun'ei 11 to Tenpō 7, a total of 563 years of history." Kakuken evidently was attempting to determine the antiquity of these two texts.

Kakuken knew the antiquarian Hoida Tadatomo, a scholar from Kyoto who traveled in the Yamato region. As a specialist in ancient objects and manuscripts, Hoida was put in charge of restoring documents in the Shōsōin between 1833 and 1836. During that time, he investigated ancient objects and artifacts, and published some of them.[40] In fact, Hoida was the first to publish about the Tenjukoku Mandara, and he included information that, as he acknowledged, was given to him by Kakuken. His study on the Tenjukoku Mandara is included in *Kanko zatsujō*, a pictorial record of ten antiquities dating from the Nara period (according to Hoida). This woodblock-printed publication includes drawings of the objects, documents related to them, and Hoida's explanations.[41] In the text, the inscription on the mandara is divided into one hundred sets of four characters each; Hoida was the first scholar to devise this arrangement. He also includes drawings of the four surviving turtles with graphs, the moon design, the red bird, the sprouting-bud motif, two of the three monks, and the metamorphosis design.[42]

Regarding the inscription, Hoida explains that, while the remains of the ancient text can be seen on the few extant turtles, the whole text is recorded in the *Imperial Biography*. He also indicates that the events of the mandara's discovery are narrated in *Shōyoshō* and Hayashi's *Yamato meishoki*. Hoida evidently was assessing the sources, because he questioned the validity of Shinnyo's dream of finding the mandara. As he argues, the story must have been a construction, as the *Imperial Biography* clearly states that the "embroidered curtains" were at Hōryūji. Similarly, he points out discrepancies between the dates of Shōtoku's death as recorded in *Dai Nihon shi* and the *Imperial Biography*, as well as problems with Anahobe's dates.[43] In addition, Hoida states that Kakuken had informed him that, in the An'ei era (1772–81), the fragments of the Tenjukoku Mandara were pasted on a hanging scroll that measured two *shaku*, nine *sun* in length and two *shaku*, seven *sun* in width; and that white silk heads were added to the headless bodies at this time. Hoida's reliance on information from Kakuken is not surprising, as scholars and antiquarians commonly depended on the knowledge of the monks at the temples that they visited. Fortunately for Hoida, Kakuken was well versed in the documents housed in the temples of the Ikaruga area.

Due to the interest in ancient objects and inscriptions that arose during the Edo period, the fragmented Tenjukoku Mandara, its inscription, and *Uragaki* were brought to light. As one of the oldest epigraphs in Japan, the Shūchō's inscription attracted the attention of scholars, who carefully studied its contents by means of other sources. At the time, however, the text was acknowledged as the "Tenjukoku Mandara inscription," making it clear that the thirteenth-century identification of the artifact prevailed. (This usage would continue through the modern era.) The unusual way of recording the inscription on the embroidered turtles certainly added to its historical importance. Some of the documents written by scholars such as Hayashi and Hoida were published in booklets, and might have reached the audience interested in antiquities. These documents compiled in the Edo period by monk-scholars and antiquarians became the foundation for the modern studies of the Tenjukoku Shūchō Mandara that began to appear in the Meiji period (1868–1912).

RECONSTRUCTING THE TENJUKOKU MANDARA

Modern scholars studying the Tenjukoku Shūchō Mandara assemblage have relied on all of the sources discussed in this study for interpreting the assemblage and proposing reconstructions of the original artifact. Yet an evaluation of these sources has revealed that, although they are useful for recreating the artifact's biography (particularly its changing significance), their reliability as sources for reconstructing the dimensions and composition of the embroidery is limited. Therefore, the reconstruction proposed here is based on the material and visual evidence, as well as the manufacture and design processes that were likely employed in the seventh century.

This section begins with an analysis of the designs on the thirteenth-century fragments, with the premise that the seventh-century embroidered curtains were repaired using purple twill, with a horizontal band of white silk added to the top of the repaired artifact. For the sake of clarity, these designs are sorted into two main groups: those on the purple twill, and those on the white silk. This analysis of the designs is followed by a tentative reconstruction of the dimensions of the artifact and the placement of the turtles and other motifs in the composition. Because this study claims that the seventh-century Shūchō was repaired rather than duplicated, the restored Tenjukoku Mandara might have preserved the original dimensions and arrangement of the hundred turtles. For this reason, the reconstruction is based on the design process, fabrics, and measurement system in use during the seventh century. Needless to say, because the evidence is scant, the proposed reconstruction is partial and tentative.

Analysis of the Motifs on the Thirteenth-Century Fragments

Without doubt, some designs found on the thirteenth-century purple twill and white silk are copies of those from the seventh-century artifact. The vast majority, however, do not have counterparts on the Shūchō. As mentioned above, the designs are divided in two groups, taking into account their ground fabrics and their relationship to the designs on the earlier fragments. The first group, which comprises the designs on purple twill, is divided into three sub-groups: first, the motifs that evidently were copied from the Shūchō, where their counterparts survive; second, motifs that do not have extant counterparts on the seventh-century fragments, but that might have been copied; and third, those with origins that are difficult to determine. The second group comprises the designs on white plain-weave silk.

Designs on Purple Twill with Seventh-Century Counterparts

Some of the designs on purple twill that were copied from the original composition are the same size and shape as their counterparts on the purple gauze of the seventh century, such as the turtle motif, the figure emerging from a lotus, the zigzag lines representing water, and the small lotus flowers.

As mentioned in Chapter One, only one turtle (A-6, or turtle no. 26 in the inscription) and some five isolated characters survive from the seventh-century artifact (see figs. 2, 11). More turtles have survived from the thirteenth century. Three of these later turtles appear on the assemblage (fig. 84), and an additional turtle with the characters 利令者椋 was found in 1920 in the Shōsōin; this fragment is currently in the Chūgūji collection (see fig. 4).[44] The height of each turtle is about eight centimeters.[45] Among the three turtles on the assemblage, two contain legible characters: 千時多至 (D-13, or turtle no. 65), and 皇前日啓 (A-17, or turtle no. 69). The third turtle (C-15) is damaged, but in 1940, Ishida Mosaku identified the characters on this turtle as 佛是真玩 (turtle no. 78).[46] Ōhashi Katsuaki has noted that a small fragment from the Shūchō with the character 佛, the first character of the four as identified by Ishida, was among the pieces in the Shōsōin collection (see fig. 2). As this character appears only once in the inscription, Ōhashi has argued that the presence of the character in both seventh-century and thirteenth-century fragments demonstrates that a replica of the Shūchō was produced in the thirteenth century.[47] Nevertheless, in 2008, when Mita Kakuyuki analyzed the fragments with a digital microscope, he concluded that the characters on this turtle are 斯歸斯麻 (turtle no. 1).[48] Mita's observation thus debunked Ōhashi's theory of the existence of a replica. If the Shūchō was repaired, and if only five turtles from the hundred, and twenty-five graphs from the four hundred graphs of the inscription have survived, then only about five or six percent of the embroidered inscription is extant. This low percentage certainly poses a challenge for an accurate reconstruction.

The other design copied from the original composition is the figure emerging from a lotus, which measures about fifteen centimeters in height (D-1).[49] Among the three thirteenth-century figures on purple twill (fig. 85), two are similar to the seventh-century design (A-12 and D-14). These figures wear robes with wide sleeves that flare outwards, hold their hands in a gesture of prayer, and wear headpieces that are difficult to identify. The third figure has a bare torso, wears a necklace, and holds a tray-like object in the right hand (B-12). In addition, an arc-shaped form, probably the scarf, frames the head, and the trumpet-shaped skirt is not as wide as that seen on the other figures. These subtle variations indicate that more than one type of figure emerging from a lotus was portrayed on the Tenjukoku Mandara. As discussed previously, motifs of the figure emerging from a lotus likely alternated with flaming flowers, and were located between scenes of the celestial and earthly realms. The surviving thirteenth-century designs reveal that the composition was not repetitive, with at least two different types of figures emerging from lotuses interposed between the flaming-flower designs.

The triangular design with a lotus flower and leaf on a seventh-century fragment (D-8; see figs. 17, 18) seems to fit into a portion of the pond motif with zigzag design on a thirteenth-century fragment (C-11; see figs. 15, 16). Furthermore, the small flower (C-10) is similar in size and shape to the only surviving seventh-century small flower (B-6; see figs. 13, 14). All of these designs likely were part of a lotus pond, a reconstruction of which has been proposed (see fig. 69).

This analysis of the visual evidence confirms that certain designs on the Shūchō were represented multiple times. Because the composition must have followed a rhythmic pattern, the missing designs could easily be replaced by using a purple ground fabric to match the color of the original ground fabric. The fact that the sizes and shapes of the thirteenth-century motifs are nearly identical to those of their seventh-century counterparts suggests that the later designs were traced directly from the originals.

84 Turtles, Tenjukoku Shūchō Mandara (A-6, D-13, A-17, C-15), details of figs. 11, 15, 17.

85 Figures emerging from a lotus, Tenjukoku Shūchō Mandara (D-1, A-12, B-12, D-14), details of figs. 11, 13, 17.

86 Tenjukoku Shūchō Mandara (section E), detail of figure 1.

Designs on Purple Twill Probably Originating from the Seventh-Century Artifact

Among the designs on purple twill without seventh-century counterparts, some might have been copied from the original, such as the male and female figures, the Buddhist monk in the belfry, the so-called "demon figure," and the borders. This supposition is based mainly on formal and stylistic features of the designs, and on comparison to the designs seen on some of the monuments and works discussed previously as possible precursors or sources for the Shūchō.

Excluding the representations of Buddhist monks, a total of fourteen figures appears on the purple twill. Although the colors of the threads used to embroider these figures have faded, the figures still may be discerned. One partial figure may have been a flying being holding a tray with offerings (B-13), and the rest are either men, women, or children. Although the male and female figures are not as well preserved as the seventh-century examples, they share common stylistic features with the earlier figures, especially in the clothing. Most of the figures are seated; the vast majority face to the left (B-14, B-15, B-16, B-17, B-18, D-17), and a couple to the right (C-8, C-9); many of them hold flowers in their hands (B-15, B-18, C-8, C-9, D-17). The images B-17 and B-18 can be identified as female figures because of their wider jackets and full skirts, garments that look similar to those on the better

87 Line drawing of Tenjukoku Shūchō Mandara (section E). Line drawing by Cheryl Laner.

preserved female figures wearing the long pleated skirts on the white silk fragment (E-5; figs. 86, 87).[50] In addition to the seated figures are a small figure, perhaps a child, offering an unidentified object (B-9); a kneeling figure with hands held in a gesture of prayer (D-16); and a dancing figure (D-15). This last figure has been pasted onto the assemblage diagonally, yet the direction of the warp indicates that the dancer originally stood upright. The garments worn by this figure are similar to those of the seventh-century standing figure (B-5). Both wear a long jacket, *hirami*, pants, and pointy shoes. The similarities in the style of the garments worn by the seventh-century and thirteenth-century figures strongly indicate that the later figures were copied.

Motifs from the Tenjukoku Mandara
E-1   Upper border with circles
E-2   Lower border with circles
E-3   Incomplete architectural setting with three standing and two kneeling monks
E-4   Tree
E-5   Incomplete architectural setting with two monks and three seated figures
E-6   *Hengeshō* or metamorphosis phase
E-7   Unidentified, perhaps canopies

88 Tenjukoku Shūchō Mandara (section F), detail of figure 1.

In addition, it appears that they were drawn using a similar scale. The torsos of the seventh-century seated figure (B-4) and the thirteenth-century examples (B-17, B-18, C-9), as measured from the neckline to the waist (marked by the belt), all measure about 2.6 centimeters.

One of the largest purple twill fragments contains the figure of a monk in a belfry striking a bell (F-2; figs. 88–90). The belfry is represented in a schematic manner, but the style of the roof and the bell itself suggests that these might have been copied from the Shūchō. The belfry's roof seems to be a hip-and-gable roof (*irimoya*), but a closer looks reveals that it is a *shikorobuki*. The hip-and-gable roof is characterized by a continuous flow from the ridge to the eaves on the two longer sides that do not have gables, but in the *shikorobuki* form, a step appears midway between the ridge and eaves. One of the earliest examples of *shikorobuki* is the roof of the aforementioned Tamamushi Shrine at Hōryūji (see fig. 33). In the fragment, the roof at the front of the belfry (to the left) shows the triangular gable and the hip delineated with green threads. The sloping hip section features parallel lines in yellow, perhaps representing tiles. The view of the long side also shows parallel lines that break where the step appears, emphasizing the two planes of the roof. In addition, horn-shaped roof ornaments known as *shibi* are located at the ends of the ridge. Three columns supporting the roof are visible, and below them, the platform consists of three stacked levels. The lowest level bears a checkered motif; the middle level is blue; and the top, green. Besides this Japanese depiction of a *shikorobuki* roof, an almost identical repre-

89 Line drawing of Tenjukoku Shūchō Mandara (section F). Line drawing by Cheryl Laner.

sentation, including *shibi*, appears on a fragment of a pictorial tile from Baekje, dated to the early seventh century and housed in the National Museum of Korea (fig. 91).⁵¹ On the tile, the line that separates the two planes of the roof appears on both the short (gabled) side and the long side. Moreover, two parallel lines at the bottom suggest a three-level platform.

In addition to the belfry's roof, the features of the bell also suggest an ancient style. The bell hangs from a frame with an arch-shaped support; suspended from a flower-shaped hook, the bell exhibits three horizontal bands extending around its body at top, middle, and bottom. A vertical band divides the surface facing the viewer into four sections of roughly equal size, with an x-shaped motif marking the intersecting point. As Sugiyama Hiroshi has explained, the earliest examples of Buddhist bells fea-

Motifs from the Tenjukoku Mandara
F-1 Border with spade-shaped motifs
F-2 Belfry with monk striking bell
F-3 Three male figures, two holding walking sticks and wearing straw coats
F-4 Border with circles

90 Monk striking a bell, Tenjukoku Mandara (F-2), detail of fig. 88.

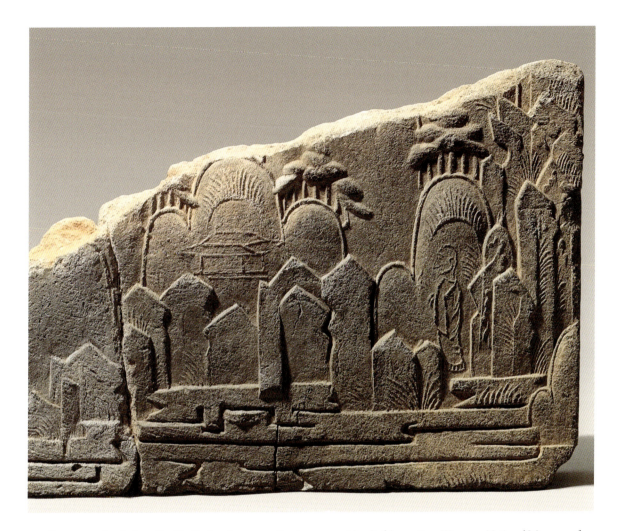

91 Fragment of a tile from Baekje. Early 7th century. Earthenware with relief decoration. W. 25 cm. National Museum of Korea, Seoul.

ture a striking point at the center of the bell's surface, as seen in the embroidery. In later bells, the striking point is located closer to the bottom.[52]

A perplexing design on purple twill is the figure with a bare torso, seated cross-legged, and wearing a short skirt with flaring ribbons on the arms (C-13). This motif was identified as a "demon-like figure" by the monk Ryōkin in the eighteenth century.[53] Meiji-period scholars used the same terminology until the 1950s, when Hayashi Mikiya proposed that this figure was a Niō, or Benevolent King, a protector of Buddhism. Of the types of Niō, Hayashi con-

cluded that this example represents a Kongō Rikishi because the figure holds a staff in his right hand and his left hand is lowered with the fingers outspread, which corresponds to the iconography of this deity.[54] Ōhashi agrees with this identification, explaining that the grotesque facial features and garments certainly match those of a Kongō Rikishi; yet, the seated posture of this figure is unusual, as guardian figures of this type usually are depicted standing.[55]

Similar seated figures with naked torsos, short skirts, and flowing scarves are portrayed within circles and ovals framed by palmette designs in Chi-

92 Fragment of a tapestry border with spade and zig-zag designs. 7th century. Silk. 5 x 15 cm. The Gallery of Hōryūji Treasures, Tokyo National Museum.

nese monuments and artifacts from the Northern and Southern Dynasties period. Such motifs usually are combined with half-palmettes and other designs used in the fifth century. For instance, on the stone pole base found in the tomb of Sima Jinlong, two of the sides feature a design of oval-shaped frames, with every other frame inhabited by a seated figure of this type (see fig. 58). Similar figures also are depicted on a lintel at an entrance to Yungang Cave No. 10, also dated to the fifth century. In this case, the seated figures face each other within the oval-shaped frames with half-palmettes. The design of the oval, however, is more complex, with each divided by a vertical line in the center, which also forms one side of a hexagon design that overlaps the oval frames. A comparable design is found on the aforementioned lacquered coffin from Guyuan; in addition to the pattern of hexagons dividing the circles and the two seated figures facing each other, a border with circles accentuates the lines of the hexagons and fantastic animals.[56] In all cases, the figures are seated, with their fluttering scarves suggesting a celestial atmosphere. As these seated figures are repeated in all three of the Chinese works discussed, it is possible that the Tenjukoku Mandara's composition also included multiple figures of this type.

In addition to the figural motifs, decorative designs also appeared on the Shūchō. Two different designs on the thirteenth-century fragments are repeated in narrow horizontal bands, which perhaps were used as borders to frame or differentiate scenes or segments of the composition. One border

The spade-shaped pattern is less common than the circles, and the only evidence that this design might have been part of the original artifact is a small fragment of a fabric with woven design in the Hōryūji collection, dated to the seventh century (fig. 92).[58] With regard to the assemblage, Ōhashi has observed that the two different borders are adjacent to each other in section B (B-7, B-8), and has suggested that the border with spade-shaped designs surrounded the one with circles.[59] Mita's analysis, however, has revealed that this specific fragment with the spade design is not attached to the border with circles, and in addition, the direction of the warps does not coincide. A small fragment at Tokyo National Museum, however, shows the two borders together.[60] Based on the extant border segments, it is probable that, in certain areas, the two borders were adjacent, but in others, only the border with circles was used to frame sections of the work. These borders must have served to divide the composition into registers or cells.

Designs on Purple Twill of Indeterminate Origin

Among the designs on purple twill, it is difficult to determine if the two incomplete lotus pedestals (C-12, C-14) and the two fragments with three seated monks (C-6 and the fragment in fig. 4) were based on parts of the original composition, or added as new elements during the repairs. Considering the facts that only portions of these lotus pedestals, which exhibit no characteristics of any distinctive period style, have survived; and that the fragments with three seated monks show generic representations, establishing the likelihood of counterparts on the Shūchō poses a challenge.

Of the two incomplete lotus pedestals, the example next to the water motif features reversed petals (C-12), and the other shows upright petals (C-14). Both of them include some remains of the subject or object that once sat upon them, but these are difficult to discern. Because lotus pedestals are usually associated with Buddhist images, scholars have suggested that these pedestals are evidence that a Buddha image was represented in Tenju-

includes circles (B-8, E-2, F-4), and the other, a pattern of spade-shaped forms (B-7, F-1). The three extant borders with circles on purple twill are sewn to the white silk fabric. The motif of repeated circles or pearls came into use in Central Asia as early as the first century BCE; this design was introduced into the Chinese decorative vocabulary during the Han dynasty, and used through the Tang.[57] In Cave No. 150 at Dunhuang (dated to the early seventh century), for example, borders with circles are used to divide the composition into cells. In addition, textile fragments in the Shōsōin and Hōryūji collections include designs framed by a circular band of continuous pearl motifs. A similar arrangement is found on the halos of the Shaka triad and the Yakushi image in Hōryūji's Golden Hall.

koku.⁶¹ Yet *Taishi mandara kōshiki*, the liturgical text by Jōen used for the dedication of the Tenjukoku Mandara, does not include any reference to a Buddha presiding in Tenjukoku. As mentioned previously, Jōen clearly states that the prince "penetrated the teaching of the Buddhist Law and was reborn in Tenjukoku, [but did not attain] the *lakṣaṇas*," which are the distinctive marks that identify a Buddha. Moreover, he describes Tenjukoku as a place where a Buddha has yet to appear. These two statements from Jōen demonstrate that the Tenjukoku Mandara did not include a Buddha presiding over the composition. Due to the larger size of these pedestals, perhaps they supported the palaces mentioned in *Taishi mandara kōshiki* and *Shōtoku Taishi denki*. These palaces might have looked like those depicted on one of the panels of the aforementioned bronze banner from Hōryūji, which shows double-roofed pavilions resting on double lotus pedestals (fig. 93).⁶² The other open-work bronze panels contain seated Buddha images, heavenly beings, flaming jewels, and a design that could be a reliquary or pagoda decorated with palmette motifs. The function of the banner, and the subjects represented, seem to suggest that the imagery depicts a heavenly realm or a Buddhist paradise.⁶³

The three seated Buddhist monks on two similar fragments may be recognized by their monk's robes and shaven heads. One group appears on the assemblage (C-6), and the other is found on a fragment in the Chūgūji collection (see fig. 4). In the latter, a two-tiered object overlaps the figures. A similar object is also affixed just below the three monks on the assemblage (C-7); this item has been identified as an incense burner due to its resemblance to the burner depicted in the "Worship of Relics" scene on the lower front panel of the Tamamushi Shrine (fig. 94). Of the two fragments, the three monks on the assemblage are preserved in better condition. The monks on the left side and in the center wear an undergarment, indicated by a diagonal line crossing the torso, and a robe covering both shoulders. They hold the ends of their robes in front of their chests. The monk on the right wears his robe covering only one shoulder, and holds an

93   Panel No. 1 from Hōryūji bronze banner, detail of fig. 34.

object difficult to identify in his left hand, and a stick-like item in his right.⁶⁴

In the "Worship of Relics" scene on the Tamamushi Shrine, two celestial beings descend on clouds toward the incense burner at center, which is being worshipped by two monks who hold small incense burners in their hands. Ōhashi has pointed out that the two monks in this scene, although rep-

94 "Worship of Relics." Lower front panel of Tamamushi shrine, fig. 33.

resented in profile, both hold the ends of their robes, much like the monks on the fragment. Furthermore, he has found a similar representation of a seated monk with the end of his robe gathered in his lap in Cave No. 285 at Dunhuang. Ōhashi has concluded that these two examples from the Tamamushi Shrine and Dunhuang serve as evidence that figures of monks created in the seventh century can be identified by this feature.[65] Although more research is necessary, Ōhashi's hypothesis seems to be correct. Among the Buddhist monks in extant portraits from later periods, none holds the end of his robe in front of his chest.[66]

Designs on White Silk

Only three fragments of white plain-weave silk remain on the assemblage (B-11, E, F-3). A distinctive characteristic of the designs on these fragments is that they are embroidered following the direction of the weft, whereas the designs on purple twill, as well as those on purple gauze, are embroidered following the direction of the warp (see fig. 7). Another feature common to these three fragments is that all are sewn to a purple twill border with a design of repeated circles. The fragment in section E, which is the most complete of the three, also shows a border with circles at top, but this border segment does not overlap with purple twill. Because the purple twill is found at the bottom portions of these fragments, Mita has concluded that a white silk band was sewn to the upper section of the repaired artifact.[67] *Shōtoku Taishi denki* states that the Tenjukoku Mandara was made by sewing "three panels of twill."[68] If this information is correct, this phrase could be interpreted to mean that the two panels of the original artifact were sewn together and a horizontal band of white silk was added to the top of the purple fabric as part of the thirteenth-century repairs.

Section E comprises the biggest piece of white silk, and preserves a discernible composition in spite of being damaged (see figs. 86, 87). This large piece contains depictions of two incomplete double-roofed pavilions with people inside. It is likely that both structures originally were shown with three bays. The building on the left includes (from right to

95 Prince Shōtoku lecturing on the *Lion's Roar Sutra*. Kamakura period (1185–1333). Hanging scroll, color on silk. 195.5 x 225 cm. Ikarugadera, Hyōgo Prefecture.

left) a standing monk and a seated monk holding the ends of their robes in the first bay, and three seated figures holding offerings in the second bay (E-5). The seated woman at right holds a lotus flower, the male figure in the center holds a box, and the other woman at left holds an incense burner. All of the figures appear large in proportion to the size of the building. A tree with few leaves stands between the two buildings (E-4). The structure to the right is also incomplete, and bears a design of reversed lotus petals at the foundation, perhaps to indicate a different type of building. Inside the structure, three monks stand and two kneel in front of an incomplete altar (E-3). A lotus flower (E-6, similar to B-2) and three canopies (E-7) hover above the roof of the building at left, hinting at a celestial realm.

Scholars have suggested that these images represent scenes from the life of Prince Shōtoku.[69] Ishida Mosaku has argued that this scene in section E depicts Shōtoku lecturing on the *Lion's Roar Sutra*, one of the established forms for representing the prince in the Kamakura period. As he points out, when the prince lectured on the sutra, lotus petals supposedly fell from heaven. Lotus petals are conspicuous in the example from the Kamakura period (fig. 95), but not as prominent on the mandara fragment. According to Ishida, the comma-shaped designs that appear below the structure with the five monks represent lotus petals.[70] The standard iconography of Shōtoku lecturing on the *Lion's Roar Sutra* (as seen in fig. 95), however, also includes Prince Yamashiro, the politician and diplomat Ono no Imoko (act. early 7th century), Soga no Umako, Hyeja, and Gakka (a Confucian scholar and Shōtoku's teacher of traditions other than Buddhism), none of whom seems to be present in the scene on the mandara fragment.[71]

In the fragment in section F (see figs. 88, 89), two figures walk in an outdoor setting, as suggested by the plants and rocks (F-3). One holds a walking stick, and both appear to wear straw raincoats. Above them, to the left, another figure stands. Ōhashi has identified these figures as travelers, but Mita has argued that this imagery represents a scene from the *Sutra of Maitreya's Great Buddhist Accomplishments* (*Miroku taisei bukkyō*), in which two old men pray at a shrine.[72] The visual evidence is not clear enough to determine the subject represented.

The smallest fragment of white silk is the only one with a direct counterpart among the seventh-century fragments of purple gauze. The three seated figures on this fragment, which are probably male (B-11), are similar in composition to the three headless figures from the seventh century (D-6), but slightly smaller in size. In fact, all of the figures on the white silk fragments are smaller than those on purple twill or purple gauze. It could be assumed that some of these designs were traced directly from the originals, but due to the softness of the fabric, were not reproduced to the exact same size. These scenes correspond to the descriptions in *Taishi mandara kōshiki* and *Shōtoku Taishi denki* of "people gathering."

Although a precise identification of the subjects depicted in section E and fragment F-3 is not possible based only on the visual evidence, in light of the long introductory section of *Taishi mandara kōshiki* narrating the hagiography of the prince, it is possible that these scenes were related to the events of this hagiography. Selected scenes may have been created by copying the surviving figures from the original embroidery on a smaller scale, in a wide register framed by borders filled with circles. The unrecognizable garments and the different style, distinct from those used in Kamakura-period hanging scrolls depicting the life of the prince, would have validated the antiquity of the representations for thirteenth-century viewers.

The Restored Tenjukoku Mandara

The reconstruction of the restored Tenjukoku Mandara is based on a determination of its dimensions and the placement of the one hundred turtles. Three documents provide brief descriptions of the Tenjukoku Mandara: *Taishi mandara kōshiki*, Shinnyo's *ganmon*, and *Shōtoku Taishi denki*. Shinnyo's *ganmon* only mentions the embroidered turtles (and possibly a dragon), while the other two texts refer to the same elements: a four-storied palace (or four superimposed palaces), men and women, birds and animals, the sun and moon, and a bell and a gong on each side. The only additional information regarding the composition is found in *Shōtoku Taishi denki*, which indicates that the four superimposed palaces or four-storied palace was located in the center of the work.[73] Regrettably, except for mention of this element and the bell and gong to each side, the descriptions do not give any hint about the placement of the other designs in the composition. For this reason, their value as evidence for reconstructing the artifact is limited.

Similarly, the hundred turtles carrying the inscription are mentioned in many documents associated with the events of the thirteenth century, but the information about their placement differs. For instance, the 1274 *Chūgūji engi* states that the turtles and the moon were "*sono ue ni*," which can be interpreted to mean "on the mandara" or "at the top of the mandara." The fourteenth-century *Shōtoku Taishi denki* is even more vague, stating only that the turtles were "on a section (*zashiki*) of the mandara"; and *Shōyoshō*, from the late fourteenth or early fifteenth century, indicates that the turtles were "at the bottom" (*shita ni*). In addition, in the seventeenth century, Hayashi explained in *Yamato*

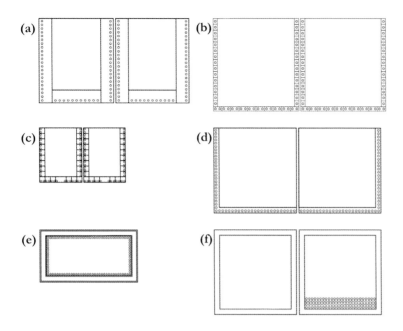

96 Reconstructions of the placement of the turtles on the Tenjukoku Shūchō Mandara. Diagrams by Ken C. Pradel, adapted from Ōhashi Katsuaki, *Tenjukoku Shūchō no kenkyū*, 94.

96a, 96b. Ōno Genmyō.
96c. Ishida Mosaku.
96d. Adachi Kō.
96e. Hayashi Mikiya.
96f. Hori Yukio.

meishoki that the mandara was nicely decorated with one hundred turtle shells "around" it (*meguri ni*).[74] The last two sources were likely compiled when the mandara was already fragmentary, and therefore are not reliable.

The textual information about the dimensions of the artifact is also controversial. As *Shōtoku Taishi denki* states, "it was a big mandara, which stretched across three *ken*."[75] A measurement of one *jō*, six *shaku* (about sixteen feet) is recorded in two sources, the 1463 *Chūgūji engi* and the early-nineteenth-century *Ikaruga koji binran*.[76] In a fourth document, the aforementioned *Shōdai senzai denki* of 1701, the Tenjukoku Mandara is mentioned in Shinnyo's biography; this text states that the mandara measured two *jō*.[77] *Ken* is a unit of measurement used for buildings and land. One *ken* equals six *shaku* (about six feet), and also refers to a bay, or the space between pillars in a building. If *ken* as used in *Shōtoku Taishi denki* refers to a measurement equaling six *shaku*, and if the mandara stretched across three *ken*, then the artifact measured eighteen *shaku* in width. As for the other measurements given, one *jō*, six *shaku* (or *jōroku*) equals sixteen *shaku*, and two *jō* equals twenty *shaku*. Thus, the textual evidence suggests that the size of the mandara was somewhere between sixteen and twenty *shaku* (or about sixteen and twenty feet). One problem with the information is that, with the exception of *Shōtoku Taishi denki*, the documents do not specify if these measurements refer to the length or the width of the mandara. Another problem is the late dates of *Shōdai senzai denki* and *Ikaruga koji binran*. It is likely that the measurements recorded in these two documents were based on oral traditions or copied from other sources.

The measurement of one *jō*, six *shaku*, or *jōroku*, given in the 1463 *Chūgūji engi* may not have been an exact measurement, but a canonical size. *Jōroku* generally is used to refer to the height of Buddhist icons. A *jōroku* image is sixteen *shaku* high, but seated images that are eight *shaku* in height are also called *jōroku*.[78] Records of the exact length and width exist for most of the embroidered Buddhist icons mentioned previously in this study, except for the embroidered icon of Asukadera, which also is recorded as a *jōroku* image.[79] It is possible that these *jōroku* dimensions refer simply to a canonical measurement.

Based on the information about the location of the turtles in the aforementioned sources, scholars have proposed a variety of arrangements for the one hundred turtles on the Tenjukoku Mandara.

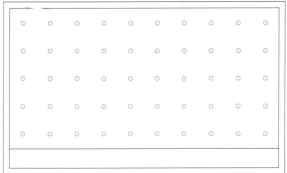 

97 Reconstruction of the placement of the turtles on the Tenjukoku Shūchō Mandara by Ōhashi Katsuaki. Diagram by Ken C. Pradel, adapted from Ōhashi Katsuaki, *Tenjukoku Shūchō no kenkyū*, 120.

The first scholar to propose a reconstruction of the placement of the turtles was Ōno Genmyō, who bases his reconstruction on the assumption that the Tenjukoku Mandara was a Pure Land mandara representing a *hensō*. Therefore, Ōno states that the mandara included outer bands on both sides and at the bottom, a format typical of *hensō*. Moreover, because *hensō* usually are accompanied by texts on the outer border, he concludes that the turtles bearing the inscription were placed on the outer bands, and offers two different arrangements (figs. 96a, 96b).[80] Ishida Mosaku, Adachi Kō, and Hayashi Mikiya have created their reconstructions based on Hayashi Sōho's record in *Yamato meishoki*, which states that the turtles were placed around the mandara. Ishida has proposed an arrangement similar to Ōno's. According to Ishida, the turtles were arranged on the sides and bottom of each panel, with fifty turtles on each (fig. 96c).[81] Adachi also has followed the same general idea of the turtles placed on an outer band, but he has suggested that the turtles were located on the left side of the left panel, on the right side of the right panel, and on the bottoms of both (fig. 96d).[82] Hayashi, theorizing an outer band surrounding the entire work, has stated that the turtles were placed inside this band rather than on it (fig. 96e).[83]

A different arrangement has been proposed by Hori Yukio, following information in *Shōtoku Taishi denki* and *Shōyoshō*. The first source states that the turtles were "on a section," and the second places them "at the bottom." Therefore, Hori suggests that the turtles were arranged in four rows of twenty-five turtles each, or five rows of twenty turtles each, at the bottom of one panel (fig. 96f).[84] Taking a completely different approach, Ōhashi bases his reconstruction on an analysis of the fragments. Noticing that the only turtle from the seventh century is found on the largest extant fragment, which shows the relationship between the different designs on the composition, Ōhashi concludes that the turtles mingled with the other designs (see fig. 26). Because the turtles carried the inscription, they had to be placed systematically so that the inscription could be read easily. As mentioned previously, the characters were arranged to be read in the following order: top, right, left, bottom. For this reason, Ōhashi has proposed that fifty turtles were spread evenly across each panel of the Shūchō, arranged in twenty columns of five turtles each. For his reconstruction, he uses the *komajaku* (*shaku* derived from Goguryeo), which measures 35.5 centimeters (fig. 97).[85] Although Ōhashi's theory that the turtles with characters mingled with the other designs in the composition is convincing, other methods of reconstructing the size and arrangement of the turtles are also possible.

The theories presented, especially that proposed by Ōhashi, suggest that it is important to take into account other variables. For this reason, in this study, in addition to the visual and material evidence, aspects of textile production and the design process also are taken into consideration. Because the evidence strongly suggests that the seventh-century artifact was repaired, it is assumed that the seventh-century designers determined the composition. Another factor to consider is the size of the bolts of fabric, which would determine how many were needed in order to create the two panels of curtains.

Ōhashi has suggested that *Shōtoku Taishi denki* is the most reliable source for reconstructing the dimensions of the artifact, as the writer must have seen the Tenjukoku Mandara in Chūgūji's Golden Hall.[86] Although it is not possible to corroborate that the writer positively saw the mandara, because the document was compiled about forty years after the Tenjukoku Mandara was taken to Chūgūji, the artifact still somehow may have remained intact at the nunnery. In addition, Ōhashi posits that *ken*, in this case, refers to the spaces between the bays, and states that the 1963 excavations at the original site of Chūgūji revealed that the Golden Hall was five bays in width and four bays in length (fig. 98).[87] The excavation report specifies a space between the pillars of about 2.6 meters; therefore, Ōhashi has concluded that the Tenjukoku Mandara must have been 7.8 meters wide. It is important to note that this width corresponds to the tentative dimensions established for the Chinese curtains discussed previously, namely those that hung from tent frames in Liu Sheng's tomb (with an approximate width of eight meters), and those that surrounded the "spirit seat" referenced in *Old Ceremonies of the Han* (approximately seven and a half meters). If the Tenjukoku Mandara was as wide as suggested, many bolts of fabric, sewn together, would have been needed to create the two panels of embroidered curtains. In order to determine the number of bolts required, the width of the bolts produced in the seventh century and also the size of the unit of length used at the time must be identified.

As mentioned previously, the traditional unit of length in Japan was the *shaku*. The size of a *shaku* was not standardized in the ancient period and changed over time. The length of the modern *shaku*

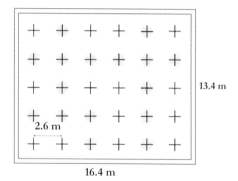

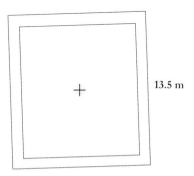

98 Plan of the former Chūgūji, showing the Golden Hall (top) and pagoda. Diagram by Ken C. Pradel, adapted from Nara Kokuritsu Hakubutsukan, *Yamato Ikaruga Chūgūji no bi*, 12.

(*kanejaku*) was defined in the Meiji period to equal 30.3 centimeters, which is roughly one foot in U.S. and Imperial units (30.48 cm). The fractional units of the *shaku* are decimal based (e.g., one *shaku* is divided into ten *sun*; one *sun* is divided into ten *bu*; and so on), as exemplified by the earliest extant rulers, which date to the eighth century (fig. 99). The sizes of the rulers preserved in the Shōsōin and Hōryūji collections range between 29.5 and 30.5 centimeters.[88] In addition to the existing physical evidence, textual sources indicate that the measuring system used in China during the Tang dynasty was adopted in Japan in the eighth century.

Based on references found in the Taihō Code, a legal and administrative system enacted in 703; and *Ryō no shūge* (Collection of Theories on the Administrative Code; mid-ninth century), it is gener-

THE RESTORATION, FRAGMENTATION, AND SECULARIZATION OF THE TENJUKOKU MANDARA

99 Four *shaku*-length rulers. 8th century. Stained ivory. From left to right: 29.8 x 2.5 x .9 cm; 30.5 x 3 x 1 cm; 29.8 x 2.6 x .7 cm; 30.3 x 3 x 1 cm. Shōsōin, Nara Prefecture.

189

	Japanese unit	**Chinese unit**	**Equivalence in cm.**
Group A	Taihō Code short *shaku*	Tang short *shaku*	24.7
	Taihō Code long *shaku*	Tang long *shaku*	29.7
	Komajaku	1.2 × Code long *shaku*	35.6
Group B	Taihō Code short *shaku*	Tang long *shaku*	29.7
	Taihō Code long *shaku*	1.2 × Tang long *shaku*	35.6
	Komajaku	Code long *shaku*	35.6

Table 5   Proposed equivalences for the Taihō Code shaku[89]

ally believed that the Tang *shaku*, which measured 29.7 centimeters, was used in the Nara period, and that the *komajaku* was used in the seventh century. These references to the *shaku* can be confusing, as the Taihō Code mentions two different *shaku*, the "long *shaku*" and the "short *shaku*," with the long *shaku* being equivalent to the short *shaku* multiplied by 1.2. Furthermore, the phrase "six long *shaku* equals five *komajaku*" in *Ryō no shūge* led to the assumption that the unit from Goguryeo, measuring 1.2 long *shaku*, was used in the seventh century. Depending on which *shaku* corresponds to the size of 29.7 centimeters, the equivalences in Table 5 have been proposed.

A particularly important study about the length of the *shaku* in the seventh century was carried out by Arai Hiroshi. In the 1990s, Arai demonstrated that the 35.6-centimeter *komajaku* unit of measurement had never been used by builders and artisans, but had been applied ahistorically to measure ancient monuments. In order to determine the length of the *shaku* used in the seventh century, Arai measured tombs, temple plans, and artifacts dating from the fourth to late seventh century in Japan and the Korean peninsula. After measuring about fifty monuments, he used their average size to determine the unit of measurement that was employed. He concluded that the *shaku* in the seventh century was equivalent to 26.8 centimeters.[90] Because this unit is found in both the Korean peninsula and Japan, he proposed naming it the "ancient Korean-Japanese *shaku*," or the "ancient Japanese-Korean *shaku*," but settled with *kokanjaku*, or "ancient Korean *shaku*," acknowledging the peninsular origins of the unit.[91] A study by Kashima Masaru has confirmed that a *shaku* corresponding to Arai's proposed length was used in the making of the bronze banner from Hōryūji (see fig. 34).[92] In addition, as mentioned above, the space between columns at the original, seventh-century site of Chūgūji was 2.6 meters, roughly ten *kokanjaku*.

Accepting Arai's theory, the 26.8-centimeter (or roughly ten-inch) *shaku* is used in this study for the reconstruction of the restored mandara. Furthermore, it is assumed that the designs must have been laid out using a grid system, in which each unit or cell measured 2.68 centimeters (or approximately an inch) per side.[93] Before the reconstruction is proposed, however, the width of the bolts of fabric must be determined by analyzing the existing evidence in China and Japan, particularly for gauze fabrics. The extant records indicate that the width of a bolt of fabric was about two *shaku*. For example, an inscription found on a silk fabric from Dunhuang states that "one bolt is two *chi* (*shaku*), two *cun* (*sun*) wide; and four *zhang* (*jō*) long."[94] Similar dimensions are found in Japanese sources. *Nihon shoki* records the measurements of fabrics used for tax purposes, and while the length of the bolts could be either one or four *jō*, the width remained constant at two and a half *shaku*.[95] In a later source, the aforementioned *Engishiki* of 927, in the Oribe (Weavers' Guild) section, the measurements for each type of fabric, including two different types of gauze, are recorded. Bolts of the first type of gauze, used for headgear, measured four *jō* long and two *shaku*, six *sun* wide.

Source	Measurements Length	Measurements Width	Using the 26.8 cm-shaku Length	Using the 26.8 cm-shaku Width	Using the 29.7 cm-shaku Length	Using the 29.7 cm-shaku Width
Dunhuang inscription	4 *jō*	2 *shaku*, 2 *sun*	10.72 m	0.58 m	11.88 m	0.65 m
Nihon shoki	1 or 4 *jō*	2.5 *shaku*	2.68 or 10.72 m	0.67 m	2.97 or 11.88 m	0.74 m
Engishiki (headgear)	4 *jō*	2 *shaku*, 6 *sun*	10.72 m	0.69 m	11.88 m	0.77 m
Engishiki (misc.)	4 *jō*	2 *shaku*	10.72 m	0.53 m	11.88 m	0.59 m

Table 6 Measurements of bolts of fabric with metric equivalents

Bolts of the other type, used for miscellaneous purposes, measured four *jō* in length and two *shaku* in width.[96] In all cases, it is clear that the width of the bolt was determined by the ideal working width for the weaver. Table 6 shows the equivalent lengths in the metric system for each of these examples when both the 26.8- and 29.7-centimeter units are used.

In addition to the textual evidence, gauze fabrics from the late seventh and early eighth centuries are found in the collections of Shōsōin and Hōryūji. A few examples preserve both side selvages, and a number of the fabrics are about fifty centimeters wide, which is approximately two *shaku*. As the span between the bays of Chūgūji measured about 2.6 meters or roughly ten *shaku* (using the 26.8-centimeter *shaku*), and the mandara "stretched across three *ken* (bays)," according to *Shōtoku Taishi denki*, then the mandara was thirty *shaku* wide. If the bolts of fabric measured two *shaku* in width, then fifteen bolts were needed to span three bays. If the bolts of fabric instead measured two and a half *shaku* wide, only twelve bolts would have been needed. Judging from modern times, when curtain sizes generally are standardized and panels usually are symmetrical, the first case requiring an odd number of bolts does not seem appropriate, as one panel would have consisted of seven pieces, and the other, eight. In the second case, requiring an even number of bolts, each panel would have consisted of six pieces sewn together. Before any conclusion is drawn regarding the number of bolts, however, the layout of the designs, particularly the one hundred turtles carrying the inscription, also must be taken into account.

As noted previously, the one hundred turtles had to be laid out in an organized manner so that the inscription could be read easily. This study follows Ōhashi's theory that the turtles were spread evenly across each panel, but using the 26.8-centimeter *shaku* (as opposed to Ōhashi's 35.5-centimeter *komajaku*). Mita has noted that, in Ōhashi's proposed arrangement, the turtles corresponding to the name of Toyotomimi (Shōtoku), or the turtles numbered 49 through 52, are split between the two curtains, with 49 and 50 at the bottom of the first panel, and 51 and 52 at the top of the second. Mita has proposed that the names of Anahobe, Shōtoku, and Tachibana must have been placed carefully in the center of the composition due to the importance of these three royal figures. According to Mita's theory, the four turtles carrying the name of Anahobe (No. 45 through No. 47) and the four carrying Tachibana (No. 54 through No. 55) were aligned in columns flanking the name of Shōtoku. He further argues that the intention was to create a group of three, much like the Shaka triad at Hōryūji, where the inscription mentions the prince, his mother, and one of his wives.[97]

Unfortunately, none of the manuscripts that record the inscription provide a clue about the possible grouping of the four hundred characters. No reference to the number of characters per column or the four-character groupings in the original com-

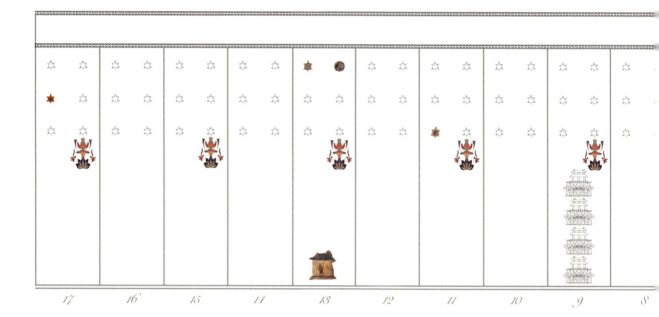

position exists.⁹⁸ For this reason, to determine the layout of the one hundred turtles, it is crucial to consider the size of the fabrics. As indicated previously, based on the width of the Tenjukoku Mandara as suggested by *Shōtoku Taishi denki*, either twelve or fifteen bolts of fabric were needed to make an artifact spanning three bays. The one hundred turtles must have been placed in a rhythmic and orderly fashion in order to facilitate reading of the inscription. Yet one hundred cannot be divided equally into twelve or fifteen groups.

Earlier in this study, it was proposed that the turtles carrying the inscription represent omen figures that appear in the celestial realm, which also includes the sun and moon. As noted previously, the 1274 *Chūgūji engi* states that the turtles and the moon were "at the top" (*sono ue ni*); if these two circular designs are added to the one hundred turtles, a total of 102 round designs were part of the section of the composition depicting the celestial realm. To distribute these 102 designs evenly, they must be arranged in groups of three or six. Therefore, if a fabric measuring two *shaku* in width was used, six round designs likely were included on each piece, arranged in two columns of three turtles/circles

each (see fig. 70). If this was the case, then seventeen bolts were needed to lay out the 102 designs (fig. 100a). As mentioned previously, the odd number of bolts might be problematic if the original artifact consisted of two panels, as stated in the *Imperial Biography*. It may be important to remember that the seventh-century iconographical program included some designs associated with yin-yang beliefs. Following this belief system, a curtain consisting of eight panels and another of nine would not have been without justification, as the numbers are significant: even numbers are associated with yin, and odd numbers, with yang.⁹⁹ Continuing further with this concept, the moon, being yin, would have been located on the eight-paneled curtain; and the sun, being yang, on the nine-paneled piece.¹⁰⁰ In the seventh century, both panels would have been draped around a "spirit seat" (fig. 100b). The names of Anahobe (turtles No 45 and No 46), Toyotomimi (turtles No 50 through No 52), and Tachibana (turtles No 54 and No 55) would have been in the center, especially when the panels were sewn together as part of the thirteenth-century restoration (see fig. 70).

The seventh-century Shūchō was a large-scale project, and its repaired version, the Tenjukoku

THE RESTORATION, FRAGMENTATION, AND SECULARIZATION OF THE TENJUKOKU MANDARA

100a Reconstruction of the Tenjukoku Mandara by Chari Pradel. Reconstruction by Cheryl Laner and Summer Furzer.

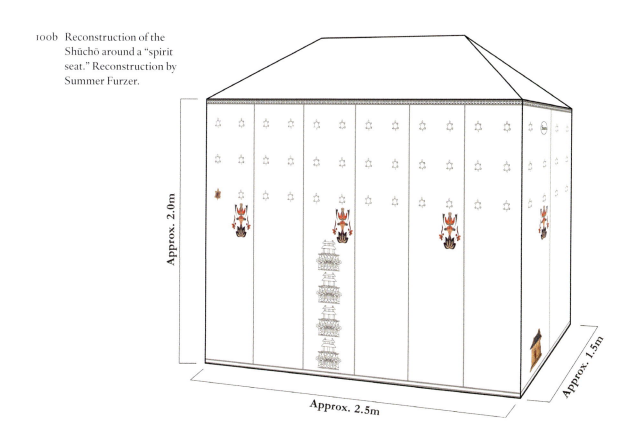

100b Reconstruction of the Shūchō around a "spirit seat." Reconstruction by Summer Furzer.

Mandara, maintained the size of the original and its layout of the turtles carrying the inscription. Because *Shōtoku Taishi denki* states that the Tenjukoku Mandara consisted of three pieces of twill sewn together, it is likely that the two panels of the Shūchō were joined, and a third piece added. This third piece was the white plain-weave silk, which contained genre scenes, probably related to the hagiography of Shōtoku. The repaired Tenjukoku Mandara must have been more than eight meters wide and about two and a half meters high. This proposed reconstruction is wider than the expanse of the three bays of Chūgūji's Golden Hall, yet fabric is a supple material that can be adjusted easily.

CONCLUSION

The physical, visual, textual, and contextual evidence suggests that the Tenjukoku Mandara was a repaired version of the seventh-century Shūchō. Displaying the seventh-century artifact, or what remained of it, was crucial for convincing Shōtoku's devotees of Shinnyo's miraculous finding. Seeing that the inscription recorded on the turtles was transcribed at this time, it is likely that a good percentage of the original embroidery had survived, but that portions of it were damaged. Certain designs on the thirteenth-century fragments of purple twill appear to be direct copies of the seventh-century designs, suggesting that the Shūchō was repaired. Purple twill was used to replace the damaged sections likely in order to match the color of the original artifact. The fact that the designs on white silk are rendered in the seventh-century style, but on a slightly smaller scale, suggests that this section with scenes from the prince's hagiography was added to match the liturgical text used for the dedication of the Tenjukoku Mandara.

The restored Tenjukoku Mandara was certainly large, as stated in the texts, but preserved the original seventh-century features of the Shūchō. The one hundred turtles, an important element of the composition, must have been arranged symmetrically (probably using a grid) to facilitate reading of the inscription. The restored mandara was about eight meters wide and two and a half meters long. In the seventh century, one panel of the curtains was made using eight bolts of fabric, and the other, nine bolts; each bolt contained six turtles arranged in two columns of three turtles each. The similar round designs of the sun and moon completed the representation of the celestial realm with its omen figures. When the two panels were sewn together in the thirteenth century, the names of Prince Shōtoku and his mother (as well as Princess Tachibana) occupied the center of the composition, fitting the narratives disseminated at the time.

The descriptions of the Tenjukoku Mandara in two documents dated to the late thirteenth and early fourteenth century, respectively, mention the one hundred turtles, the sun and moon, people and animals, four palaces, and a bell and gong. The extant designs confirm that these motifs were part of the composition, yet a complete reconstruction of the work is an impossible task due to the small number of extant fragments. As mentioned above, the extant pieces comprise only about five percent of the complete artifact. While a variety of compositions could be proposed, we know for certain that the celestial realm with the sun, moon, and the one hundred turtles surrounded by fantastic animals and soaring celestial beings was included. Motifs of a figure emerging from a lotus divided the heavenly realm from the earthly realm. As suggested by the sources, four palaces were depicted in the center of the composition, and a bell and gong appeared on the right and left sides (fig. 100a). Perhaps the male and female figures walked towards the palaces, and somewhere in the large composition lotus ponds and people participating in gatherings were shown. As suggested by *Taishi mandara kōshiki*, the restored Tenjukoku Mandara must have included scenes from the hagiographic account of Shōtoku's life, which were represented on the white silk band added to the top of the mandara. If the current state of the fragments is any indication, the restored Tenjukoku Mandara likely was not as striking as the seventh-century embroidered curtains, yet it contained the remains of the six-hundred-year-old embroidered fabrics. Their bright colors and state of preservation must have made a strong impact on devotees, and served to promote Tenjukoku as a special pure land. Displaying the ancient artifact, or at least parts of it, was crucial for supporting the story of its miraculous discovery.

The corpus of surviving textual material dating from the fourteenth to the nineteenth century allows us to follow the biography of the fragments. Documents from the fourteenth and fifteenth centuries show that the Tenjukoku Mandara became a key element in the Shōtoku cult, as the events surrounding the Shūchō's discovery and the dedication of the mandara were added to the hagiographic accounts of the prince's life. It seems that the popularity of the mandara in medieval Japan might have been the cause of its fragmentation, as pilgrims took pieces of the artifact as souvenirs of their visits to Chūgūji. Documents from the eighteenth and nineteenth centuries, however, show that the Tenjukoku Mandara, by this time, was sought not as a religious icon, but as an ancient object and epigraph worthy of historical research. Records by monk-scholars and academics who studied the available documents emphasize the Buddhist life of the artifact, which actually began in the thirteenth century with the discovery of the seventh-century embroidered curtains. These Edo-period documents became the source for the modern scholarship carried out in the Meiji period. The fascination and appeal of the Tenjukoku Shūchō Mandara, and the questions surrounding it, have endured as long as any legend of the prince.

Epilogue

TENJUKOKU SHŪCHŌ MANDARA AS AN ART-HISTORICAL OBJECT

In the Meiji period, the Tenjukoku Mandara was included in the first officially sanctioned text of Japanese art history, which was published in 1900 and sponsored by the government. Satō Dōshin has argued convincingly that this history had a political agenda.[1] The main purpose of the text was to support the imperial system based on the belief that "Japan's history and tradition were maintained by the succession of emperors."[2] The incorporation of the Tenjukoku Shūchō Mandara into the official art historical canon determined its designation as a National Treasure and also framed the ensuing modern and contemporary studies about the artifact.

In the late nineteenth century, a number of Buddhist institutions suffered the consequences of *shinbutsu bunri*, a policy promulgated in 1868 that mandated the separation between Shinto and Buddhism. Chūgūji and the other temples in the Ikaruga region were not affected; rather, they benefitted from the antiquities preservation campaign that followed the destruction of Buddhist icons and paraphernalia.[3] In 1871, the Grand Council of State (Dajōkan) promulgated the Laws for Preserving Antiquities (*Kokikyūbutsu hozon kata*), and in 1872, the Exposition Office (Hakurankai Jimukyoku) was established. This office asked the prefectural governments to submit lists of their antiquities, with owners. After temples and shrines submitted their lists, the members of the Exposition Office visited these religious institutions to examine the objects, especially in the cities of Nagoya, Ise, Kyoto, and Nara. Later, expositions (*hakurankai*) were organized to display these antiquities. The Tenjukoku Mandara was exhibited in the Second Nara Hakurankai held in 1876 (Meiji 9) at the Great Buddha Hall of Tōdaiji.[4] These surveys of treasures not only served to protect the art, but also formed the basic database of art works for the study of art history.[5] Especially important was the survey of antiquities carried out by Ernest Fenollosa (1853–1908) and Okakura Tenshin (1862–1913), two men who played an important role in the establishment of the discipline of art history in Japan. Their numerous activities were closely intertwined with the political agenda of the Meiji government.[6]

The Tenjukoku Mandara was incorporated into the first official art history of Japan due to the activities of Fenollosa and Okakura. Both began their survey of antiquities in 1880 (Meiji 13), and in 1886 (Meiji 19), they investigated Hōryūji and the neighboring Chūgūji, Hōrinji, and Hokkiji. Shinkawa Tokio has argued that the development of the discipline of art history was influential in shaping the image of Prince Shōtoku.[7] The objects and inscriptions found at Hōryūji and the neighboring temples, complemented by the narratives in *Nihon shoki*, undoubtedly created the desired imperial image of past rulers, especially Shōtoku. In addition to surveying

Detail from the 1982 replica of the Tenjukoku Shūchō Mandara, detail of fig. 101.

ancient objects, Okakura and Fenollosa were the first instructors of art history at the Tokyo School of Fine Arts, which opened in 1889 (Meiji 22). Okakura delivered a series of lectures about Japanese art at this school between 1890 and 1892 (Meiji 23–25); the resulting publication reveals that Okakura included the Tenjukoku Mandara as a pictorial work of the so-called "Suiko period."[8] Okakura's other activities included the founding of the art-history journal *Kokka* (Flowers of the Nation) in 1889. According to Satō, this journal "served to integrate the fine arts into the framework of the state structure."[9]

The Tenjukoku Mandara was featured twice in *Kokka* in 1896. First, the scholar Kurokawa Mayori (1829–1906), an official during the Meiji period, included the Tenjukoku Mandara in his three-part account of the "History of Painting of This Country."[10] Kurokawa's main goal was to assert that the embroidered fragments essentially comprised an example of painting of the "Suiko period," as the designs were embroidered over a base of drawings. Hence he concluded that painting during this period was characterized by the use of five colors; he also recognized the influential role played by immigrants from Goguryeo. Using the inscription in the *Imperial Biography*, Kurokawa explained that the ladies-in-waiting embroidered curtains that became known as the Tenjukoku Mandara, which represented a pure land. The article is accompanied by a drawing of a detail of section C that includes the figure emerging from a lotus, a turtle, women, the three headless seated figures, and a lotus plant.[11]

The second article in *Kokka*, written by Kosugi Sugimura (1834–1910), a scholar who specialized in ancient documents, is dedicated entirely to the Tenjukoku Mandara. The article includes woodblock-printed illustrations of the mandara.[12] Kosugi's history of the Tenjukoku Mandara is based on the information contained in the documents available to him: the inscription in the *Imperial Biography* and *Tenjukoku mandara uragaki*, as recorded in *Shōyoshō* and *Hōryūji tōin engi*. Because he read *Shōyoshō*, he identified Tenjukoku as the Pure Land of Ultimate Bliss; he used the information in *Hōryūji tōin engi* as supporting evidence of Prince Shōtoku's activities. Kosugi acknowledged the research carried out in the Edo period by the monk Ryōkin, Kariya Ekisai, and Hoida Tadatomo. Basically, he wrote the history of the Tenjukoku Mandara based on the facts stated in the documents mentioned, which certainly created a coherent historical account.

The works of these two Meiji-period scholars determined the importance of the Tenjukoku Mandara in the development of the history of Japanese art. The documents associated with the mandara known at the time, especially the Shūchō's inscription and *Uragaki*, served as the primary sources for writing the history of the artifact; these sources highlighted the role of the imperial line as patrons of the arts in the early seventh century. Although these documents are not discussed or cited in *Histoire de l'art du Japon*, published in 1900 for the Paris Exposition Universelle, the contents of this French publication indicate that the account of the Tenjukoku Mandara contained therein was based on these early documents, as evidenced by the association of the embroidered artifact with members of the imperial family: Prince Shōtoku, Empress Suiko, Princess Tachibana, and Empress Anahobe, all of whom are emphasized. In addition, this text highlights the role of royal women and their association with the art of embroidery by discussing the embroidered banner fragments from Hōryūji, which have been attributed, by temple tradition, to the hands of Anahobe and Princess Kashiwade.[13] Furthermore, because the early seventh century was seen as the time of the Buddhist transformation of Japan, the fragments and the inscription were considered under the rubric of Buddhist art, and the corpus of textual material about the thirteenth-century artifact was used to support this assumption.

For more than a century, most Japanese scholars from a variety of disciplines, whether or not they have been aware of the imperialistic connotations, have studied the fragments and the Shūchō's inscription within these parameters, as a work of the Asuka period made under the patronage of Empress Suiko to represent the Buddhist pure land where Prince Shōtoku was reborn. The Tenjukoku Mandara and its related documents were used to fabricate the prince's Buddhist afterlives and to construct his Buddhist persona.

PRESERVING AND REPRODUCING THE TENJUKOKU SHŪCHŌ MANDARA

For centuries, monks and textile specialists have made efforts to preserve the fragments of the Tenjukoku Shūchō Mandara. The embroidered fragments were pasted on paper in the late eighteenth century, surrounded by pieces of undecorated fabric to protect them, and framed with brocade as a hanging scroll. Temple records indicate that, in the late 1910s (Taishō 8 or 9), this hanging scroll was placed in a glass case.

By the 1970s, the assemblage was deteriorating. Takeuchi Shozō, a specialist in ancient textiles, decided to put together a team to create a replica of the Tenjukoku Shūchō Mandara. In 1976, Takeuchi recruited Kitagawa Heirō (1898–1988), a Living National Treasure with knowledge of ancient weaving techniques, to weave the ground fabrics. Kirimura Kyōko, listed as a disciple of a certain Sanuki Kyōichi, was put in charge of the embroidery work; and Usami Naoyuki of Kyoto National Museum mounted the replica. The piece was finished in May of 1982 and placed in the Main Hall of Chūgūji, where it can be seen today (fig. 101).[14] The original assemblage was taken to Nara National Museum for preservation.

In addition to the 1982 replica, another was made in 2010 by the Nishijin Bijutsuori Kōbō (Nishijin Textile Art Atelier) in Kyoto (fig. 102).[15] This example is woven using the brocade technique; measuring 70 by 65 centimeters, it is slightly smaller than the original assemblage. The unidentified weaver spent four months completing it.

As this study has shown, the importance of the Tenjukoku Shūchō Mandara is not limited to the moment of its creation in the seventh century. Rather, the assemblage of fragments and its corpus of textual material reveal the changing and enduring significance of the embroidered pieces in Japanese history. This book has retraced the history of the fragments and their perception from the manufacture of the artifact in the late seventh century to its incorporation into the Japanese art historical canon. The vast majority of modern studies have used the textual evidence associated with the fragments to support a Buddhist interpretation of the seventh-century artifact, yet this study, by considering the period and historical context of the compilation of each of the sources, has reached a different conclusion. In addition, benefitting from new archaeological discoveries in Japan and East Asia, as well as from innovative scholarship in the field of East Asian studies, the creation of a partial reconstruction of the iconographical program has been possible.

Based on these methods, a new interpretation of the original artifact and a new date for its manufacture have been proposed. As demonstrated in these pages, the subject represented on the pair of embroidered curtains was not Buddhist, but was associated with the visual vocabulary of funerary art from China and the Korean peninsula. Because the subject was not Buddhist, the term Tenjukoku might have been related to popular Chinese religious practices, which arrived with immigrants from China and Korea. Tenjukoku was one of the many afterlife destinations envisioned in ancient Japan, a land where a person could receive the longest lifespan granted by the heavens. It is likely that the curtains were used in a memorial service around a "spirit seat" to commemorate Prince Shōtoku and his mother years after their deaths. For this reason, the embroidered curtains should be categorized as an example of funerary art in ancient Japan, rather than as the remains of a *shūbutsu* or an embroidery with a Buddhist subject. Furthermore, as a likely product of the late seventh century, the curtains might have carried a political subtext and included a message to support the Kinmei–Soga line and its descendants at a time when the royal succession was under dispute. Importantly, members of immigrant kinship groups, who had control over the materials, technology, and labor force, might have been actively involved in the creation of the Shūchō.

FABRICATING THE *TENJUKOKU SHŪCHŌ MANDARA* AND PRINCE SHŌTOKU'S AFTERLIVES

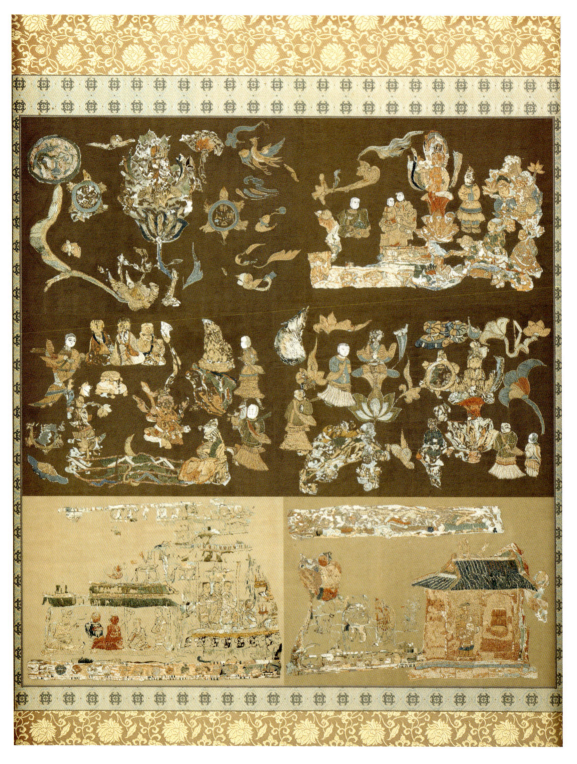

101   Kitagawa Heirō (1898–1988), Kirimura Kyōko, and Usami Naoyuki. Tenjukoku Shūchō Mandara (replica). 1982. Embroidered silk. 88.8 x 82.7 cm. Chūgūji, Nara Prefecture.

EPILOGUE

102   Nishijin Bijutsuori Kōbō. Tenjukoku Shūchō Mandara (replica). 2010. Brocade. 70 x 65 cm. Chūgūji, Nara Prefecture.

The subsequent events in the life of the Shūchō and its inscription were intertwined with the development of the cult of Prince Shōtoku, leading to the transformation of this funerary object into a Buddhist icon. In the late tenth or early eleventh century, the Shūchō was located at Hōryūji, where a monk transcribed the embroidered inscription into a manuscript, the *Imperial Biography*. This document, a hagiographical account of the life of Prince Shōtoku, was compiled to construct the image of the prince as a Dharma King, stressing his role in the propagation of Buddhism. The Shūchō's inscription, separated from its source, took on a life of its own when it was recorded together with the inscriptions on the mandorla of the Shaka triad and the halo of the Yakushi image in Hōryūji's Golden Hall. These three inscriptions created an evidence-based narrative about Shōtoku's Buddhist activities. In addition, the inscriptions from the Shūchō and the Shaka triad contained the wishes for the prince's afterlife expressed by his close associates. Because Tenjukoku, the afterlife destination cited on the Shūchō, was unknown to the *Imperial Biography*'s scribe, he wrote that it must be heaven.

In keeping with the transformation of a funerary object into a Buddhist work, in the late thirteenth century the embroidered curtains were rediscovered at Hōryūji and given a new life as a Buddhist mandara at the nunnery of Chūgūji. In 1274, the nun Shinnyo began her quest to find the mandara, which she believed to include the date of death of the nunnery's alleged founder, Queen Consort Anahobe. Yet, shifting from this focus on Anahobe, in 1275 Shinnyo and the monk Jōen dedicated the found Shūchō as the Tenjukoku Mandara, seen as a transformation tableau of Amida's Pure Land where the prince and his mother resided as incarnations of Kannon and Amida, respectively. This identification was associated with a Pure Land form of the Shōtoku cult that originated at the prince's tomb at Shinaga and spread to Hōryūji. Interpreted as an Amida transformation tableau, the unusual pictorial program embroidered on the curtains was particularly fitting for this newly established form of the cult. Shinnyo became famous in religious circles due to her discovery of an ancient artifact associated with Prince Shōtoku, which supposedly contained words uttered by him. The Tenjukoku Mandara was then incorporated into the lore of the Shōtoku cult. In the Edo period, the fragmented artifact and its inscription, still identified as the Tenjukoku Mandara, attracted the attention of monk-scholars and scholars interested in ancient objects and epigraphs. Due to its accrued Buddhist identity, the Tenjukoku Mandara entered the modern art historical cannon as a Buddhist icon.

The aim of this book has been to tell the complete history of the Tenjukoku Shūchō Mandara by considering the changing significance of the artifact as narrated in sources previously referenced to support its Buddhist import. The use of the biographical method has allowed us to unravel the complex history of the embroidered fragments from the moment of the curtains' creation, to the role of the mandara within the context of the cult of the prince, to the assemblage as an antiquity and art-historical object supporting the imperial ideology of the Meiji period.

Appendix
Fabrics and Stitches

DUE TO THE FRAGILITY of the medium, the history of textiles in Japan is as fragmentary as the evidence itself. Loom parts and weaving tools found at archaeological sites in Kyushu and Nara show that fabrics had been woven since the Yayoi period (ca. 400 BCE–ca. 250 CE). Small pieces of fabric attached to the surfaces of bronze mirrors and bells, along with imprints on ceramic shards, confirm that most fabrics were plain weave. The situation is similar for the Kofun period (ca. 250–ca. 550 CE), although the extant remains show a greater variety of fabrics, including luxurious woven silks. In tombs dated to the fourth and fifth centuries, most of the remains are plain-weave fabrics, but in the sixth century, twills and brocades are also found, and in seventh-century tombs, tapestries and brocades with gold and silver threads appear.[1] The oldest extant textiles of considerable size are held in the collections of Hōryūji and the Shōsōin at Tōdaiji.[2] These collections contain textiles dated to the late seventh through the mid-eighth century, some made in Japan and others imported from China. The earliest extant examples of embroidered textiles associated with an inscription are the fragments found in the Tenjukoku Shūchō Mandara assemblage.

The embroidered fragments of the seventh-century Shūchō and the thirteenth-century Mandara were pasted alongside pieces of undecorated fabric.

Right side of section B, Tenjukoku Shūchō Mandara, detail of fig. 13.

Information about the rationale for this arrangement apparently does not exist. The different types of undecorated fabric used to fill in the open spaces create distinguishable rectangular sections of slightly different sizes (fig. 103). As a result, the assemblage is divided into six well-defined sections that may be differentiated (see figs. 11–18, 86–89). In addition to the pieces on the assemblage, others are scattered among various collections (see figs. 2–6).[3]

The first technical analysis of the Tenjukoku assemblage, treating the undecorated fabric, ground fabric, and embroidery stitches, was published in 1923 by Nakagawa Tadayori and a group from the Kawashima Orimonojo (Kawashima Weaving Studio) in Kyoto's Nishijin district, a historic site of textile production. This study was followed by research by Ishida Mosaku (1940), Ōta Hidezō (1948), Mōri Noboru (1953, 1963), Nishimura Hyōbu (1964), Yamabe Tomoyuki and Dōmyō Mihoko (1977), Sawada Mutsuyo (1992), and Mita Kakuyuki (2008).[4] This last study by Mita was performed using a digital microscope, and contains the most detailed information about the fibers, fabric structures, and stitches. Each of these scholars focused on the technical aspects of the fabrics, and most of them proposed their own reconstructions of the format and iconography of the seventh-century artifact. Many facets of their analyses overlap, and because some of the early opinions have been replaced by new ideas, the current consensus regarding the technical aspects of the fragments is presented here. In spite of the controver-

FABRICATING THE *TENJUKOKU SHŪCHŌ MANDARA* AND PRINCE SHŌTOKU'S AFTERLIVES

103 Diagram of undecorated fabrics on the Tenjukoku Shūchō Mandara. Diagram courtesy of Mita Kakuyuki.

APPENDIX

104 White plain weave, Tenjukoku Mandara (section E), detail of fig. 86.

105 Paper with black outlines and needle holes underneath white plain weave, from the head of the figure at far left in E-5, detail of fig. 86.

106 Twill weave, Tenjukoku Mandara (upper right side of section F), detail of fig. 88.

sies surrounding the inscription (discussed in Chapter Two), many of the scholars mentioned above based their conclusions on the inscription, and have supported the theories that the Shūchō was made in the early seventh century (during the Asuka period), and that the subject represented was a Buddhist Pure Land.

GROUND FABRICS

Analyzing the assemblage, textile specialists found embroidered designs on four different fabrics, all woven with silk fibers: white plain weave, purple twill, purple gauze, and purple plain weave (see fig. 7; arrows indicate the direction of the warp). In terms of fabric structures, however, these four materials comprise only three types: plain weave (*hiraori*), twill (*aya*), and gauze (*ra*).[5]

Plain weave is the simplest form of weaving, in which weft threads (the transverse element) are passed alternately over and under each warp thread (the longitudinal element) across the loom. In this case, the fabric is a balanced plain weave, because the warp and the weft are the same size and equally spaced (fig. 104).[6] White plain weave is found in section B under the three seated figures (B-11); in section E under the scenes in architectural structures, including the upper border with circles; and in section F, under the three walking figures and the border with circles (F-3). Nakagawa also noticed white paper with black outlines punctured by needle holes underneath the white plain-weave fabric, and concluded that the designs were drawn on the paper and then embroidered together with the ground fabric (fig. 105).[7] The thinness and translucency of the silk must have allowed the designs on the paper underneath to show through.

In contrast to plain weave, which exhibits a consistent alternation of the warp and weft threads, in twill structures, diagonal patterns are created by deviating from this consistent alternation, creating skips or "floats" (fig. 106). Used in an organized fashion, floats create patterns and texture variations.[8] Unfortunately, the remains of the twill are

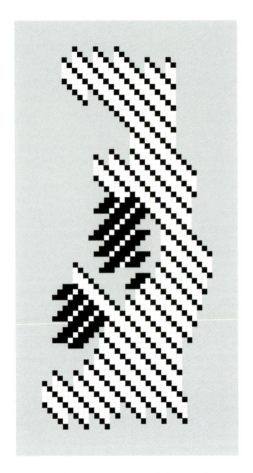

107 Diagram of twill pattern, Tenjukoku Mandara. Diagram courtesy of Mita Kakuyuki.

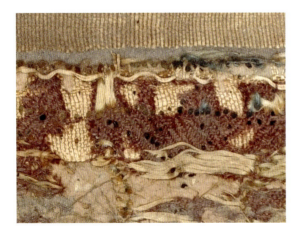

108 Purple twill sewn to white plain weave, Tenjukoku Mandara (bottom of E-2), detail of fig. 86.

109 Complex-gauze weave, Shūchō, detail of fig. 26.

too damaged to see any complete pattern, but in some sections a geometric form can be discerned (fig. 107). Similar to the white plain weave, the purple-twill fragments are embroidered over paper. In sections B-11, E, and F-3, the bottom border with circle motifs is a purple-twill fragment sewn to the white plain-weave fabric (fig. 108).

The third type of fabric structure is complex gauze (*ra*). In textile terminology, gauze (*ro*) may be any thin, light, transparent fabric. It also is defined as a fabric with a cross-warp structure (*sha*), in which a pair of warps or groups of warps are crossed and then interlaced with the weft, re-crossing before the next weft or at some later point (fig. 109).[9] Patterns are created by alternating the crossing of different groups of warps. In the case of the assemblage fragments, groups of three warp elements are crossed in alternation, producing diamond-shaped patterns (fig. 110).[10] Sawada found purple plain-weave fabric coupled with the purple gauze (fig. 111), and concluded that the purple plain weave was used in a similar fashion to the paper found underneath the white plain weave and purple twill.[11] In addition to the purple gauze, some scholars have claimed that a small piece of a paler gauze fragment comprises the ground fabric of D-6 alone. While some white threads can be detected among the embroidery stitches, because the embroidered threads cover the whole surface of this

APPENDIX

110 Diagram of complex-gauze pattern, Shūchō. Diagram courtesy of Mita Kakuyuki.

111 Purple plain weave and gauze, Shūchō (D-8), detail of fig. 17.

design, and the fragment is pasted onto the paper backing, it is impossible to see the ground fabric of this fragment.[12]

In addition to the ground fabrics, the threads and stitches used for the embroidered designs provide further information.

EMBROIDERY THREADS AND STITCHES

Embroidery is a pictorial medium. Colorful designs with an array of textures are created through the use of different stitches and types of thread. Stitches both delineate and fill in the designs. In the case of the fragments on the assemblage, textile specialists have been able to further classify the remains based on the technical aspects of the embroidery.

The analysis of the embroidery stitches on the fragments by Ōta Hidezō, published in 1948, is the authoritative study regarding this feature. Ōta was the first to notice that the designs embroidered on the purple-gauze fabric were all created using backstitch, with the threads exhibiting a strong Z-twist; and that, on the purple-twill and white plain-weave fragments, a variety of embroidery stitches were employed, using a loose S-twisted thread.[13] This difference in embroidery threads and stitches further supports the division of the fabrics into two groups from two different periods. By comparing these features to other extant embroidered textiles, along with the information provided by the inscription and textual sources, Ōta concluded that the gauze fragments dated to the Asuka and Hakuhō periods, and the others, to the Heian or Kamakura period.[14] According to Ōta's observations, the fragments with bright colors and well-preserved embroidery threads comprise the remnants of the seventh-century Shūchō, and those fragments with faded and damaged threads were produced in the thirteenth century. The reason for the better preservation of the older embroidery is the tight twisting of the threads. With silk threads, a tighter twist creates abrasion resistance and aids retention of the material's luster.

FABRICATING THE *TENJUKOKU SHŪCHŌ MANDARA* AND PRINCE SHŌTOKU'S AFTERLIVES

112 Outline stitch, from the right shoulder of the figure in B-5, detail of fig. 13.

113 Stem stitch, from tasuki and clothing of the figure in D-3, detail of fig. 17.

114 Satin stitch, from the head of the monk at right in C-6, detail of fig. 15.

115 Surface satin stitch, from the back of the figure at upper left in F-3, detail of fig. 88.

116 Long-and-short stitch, from a petal of the lotus in A-12, detail of fig. 11.

117 Long stem stitch, from a line in the pond design in C-11, detail of fig. 15.

APPENDIX

118 Couching, from the roof of the belfry in F-2, detail of fig. 88.

119 Fancy couching, from the frame of the band with circles in E-2, detail of fig. 86.

Bright red, green, yellow, white, navy, and black threads are used on the purple-gauze fragments. The motifs are embroidered using two variations of backstitch: outline stitch (*matsuinui*; fig. 112); and stem stitch (*kaeshinui*) employed in contiguous rows to cover the surface of the designs (fig. 113).[15] Backstitch forms a single unbroken line of stitching by moving the thread forward and then backward along a line. It is used for practical as well as decorative purposes. The difference between stem stitch and outline stitch is that, in the former, the thread is placed below the needle when stitching, whereas in the latter, the thread is kept above the needle.[16]

On the purple twill and white plain weave, a variety of embroidery stitches are used to delineate and fill in the design surfaces. Among the filling stitches are satin stitch (*hiranui*), surface satin stitch (*omote hiranui*), and long-and-short stitch (*sashinui* or *shusuzashi*). Satin stitch is formed by working the needle alternately in and out of the fabric to create a series of flat, parallel stitches on both faces. In satin-stitched fabrics, the front and the back look the same. In the fragments, satin stitch is used for people's hair and clothing, as well as the circular shape of the turtles (fig. 114).[17]

Surface satin stitch is used for the circle- and spade-shaped motifs on the borders of designs, the human figures, and hems of clothing (fig. 115). It looks similar to satin stitch on the front face, but when the thread is pulled through to the reverse of the fabric, the needle only takes a small portion of the fabric at the edge of the design, and returns to the front. This stitch is used to save thread, as only one side of the fabric is covered.[18] Long-and-short stitch is another variation of satin stitch in which rows of stitches of different lengths fill in the surface of the design, as in the belfry structure (F-2). If the stitches are embroidered in radiating lines and threads of different colors are interspersed, as in the petals of the figures emerging from lotuses, the technique is called *ungenzashi* (fig. 116).[19]

In addition to these filling stitches, two different outlining stitches are found on the fragments. Standard outline stitches (*matsuinui*), discussed above, are used for people's heads, and long stem stitches (*naga kaeshinui*) are employed for the parallel lines of the lotus pond (C-11; fig. 117). A variation of outline stitches is couching (*komanui*), in which a thread or group of threads is fastened to the fabric with stitches. For instance, the yellow lines of the roof of the belfry are single threads that are held to the fabric by small diagonal stitches (fig. 118).[20] Lastly we find a variation of couching called fancy couching (*tabanenui*), in which multiple threads are laid to create a foundation that is held in place by perpendicular stitches of alternating colors. This technique is used to create the wide parallel lines framing the band with circles in section E (fig. 119).[21]

211

UNDECORATED FABRIC

When the assemblage was put together in the late eighteenth century, pieces of fabric were cut to fit in between the fragments with designs. For lack of a technical term, these are referred to here as undecorated fabrics (see fig. 103). According to Sawada, previous scholars have classified these pieces as crepe (*chijimi*), a plain-weave fabric that employs tightly twisted warp and weft threads to create a textured surface.[22] Sawada noticed, however, that not all of these fabrics were the same. The fabric used in sections B, C, D, and E is a very thin plain weave, woven with dark threads. Because the thickness of the warp and weft threads is different, this material seems to be a crepe. But due to the thinness of these pieces, she has suggested the composite name of "plain-woven gauze" (*ro heiken*) for the fabric. In addition, Sawada has pointed out that this type of fabric is found among the textiles in the Hōryūji collection, which date to the late seventh and eighth centuries, and also in Buddhist paintings of the medieval period. Because sections B, C, D, and E use the same type of undecorated fabric, she has stated that these sections must have been assembled at the same time.

Sections A and F include fabrics that are different from those mentioned above. Section F shows a dark twill fabric that is distinguishable from the thirteenth-century purple twill, and also some pieces of plain-woven gauze. Section A includes a purple plain weave and one small piece of dark plain weave on the left side. According to Sawada, these two fabrics in section A indicate that a motif probably fell off, and the darker piece was added to cover the empty spot. She has concluded that the different types of undecorated fabric constitute evidence of the many attempts to preserve the embroidered fragments before they were pasted in their current form during the An'ei era (1772–81), when the white heads of certain figures were also painted in (fig. 120).[23]

120   Painted white head from the An'ei era (1772–81) on the figure in D-3, detail of fig. 17.

OTHER FRAGMENTS

In addition to the assemblage, other remains from the Tenjukoku Shūchō Mandara are scattered in the collections of Chūgūji, Hōryūji, Tokyo National Museum, and the Shōsōin.[24] Chūgūji, home to the assemblage, also holds two thirteenth-century fragments, one showing three seated monks and an incense burner (similar to the scene depicted on section C) and the other featuring a turtle with the characters 利令者椋 (see fig. 4). About forty small fragments from the seventh-century Shūchō are found in the Shōsōin. They include pieces with the characters 奈, 甘, 居, 佛, and 娶, incomplete turtles, a number of lotus flowers, a lotus sprouting from a zig-zag motif, and a couple of bud motifs. Some of these fragments are sewn onto white fabric (see fig. 2).[25] In addition, Hōryūji holds a small fragment depicting the upper body of a figure from the seventh-century Shūchō (see fig. 3), and Tokyo National Museum contains pieces with part of a turtle, a flower, an s-shaped motif, and an elongated leaf motif (see figs. 5, 6).

The reason that these fragments of the Tenjukoku Shūchō Mandara are in these different collections has to do with Hōryūji's donation to the Imperial Household in 1877 (Meiji 10). Some fragments had been kept at Hōryūji after the dis-

121 Incomplete seated figure from the Shūchō among fragments of an embroidered banner with design of celestial beings. 7th century. Silk. Hōryūji, Nara Prefecture.

covery of the artifact in the thirteenth century, and must have been given as part of the donation. Because the donated goods were stored temporarily in the Shōsōin before they were taken to Tokyo, some fragments must have been left there. These pieces were rediscovered in 1920, whereupon the Imperial Household returned the two aforementioned thirteenth-century fragments (group of monks and turtle) to Chūgūji, and kept the other fragments in the Shōsōin.[26] The incomplete seated figure held by Hōryūji was found among the remains of the banner with celestial beings in the temple's textile collection in the late 60s or early 70s (fig. 121).[27] And the fragments now found in Tokyo National Museum were part of Hōryūji's donation of textiles to the Imperial Household.

Other than these remains, a small thirteenth-century fragment of a border with spade-shaped motifs is held by the Kawashima Orimono Kenkyūjo (Kawashima Weaving Research Institute) in Kyoto. Furthermore, some pieces of doubt-ful provenance from the Fujita Museum in Osaka are published as remnants of the Tenjukoku Shūchō Mandara. One fragment shows a turtle with the characters 天下生名, and another, a flying celestial being. Although the characters on the turtle certainly correspond to the inscription, the ground fabric and embroidery techniques differ from those exhibited by the other fragments. Moreover, the flying celestial being is identical to the figure depicted on the fourth panel of the bronze banner (kanjōban) in the Hōryūji collection.[28] Similarly, for a 2009 exhibition at the University Art Museum, Tokyo University of the Arts, Tokyo's Nezu Museum lent two fragments purportedly from the Tenjukoku Shūchō Mandara that share the same color scheme as the assemblage.[29] These fragments, however, include metallic threads; although such threads are found on embroidered textiles dating to the sixth and seventh centuries, they are not found among the fragments of the Tenjukoku Shūchō Mandara.

Endnotes

Prologue

1. The many names of this prince are discussed in detail in Chapter Two.
2. Most existing studies take the form of articles published in Japanese scholarly journals. A book by Ōhashi Katsuaki, *Tenjukoku Shūchō no kenkyū* (Tokyo: Yoshikawa Kōbunkan, 1995), compiles the articles published by the author on the topic between 1977 and 1994. His study focuses on explaining the piece as a Buddhist artifact of the Asuka period (ca. 550–645). Although he addresses the events associated with the discovery of the mandara in the thirteenth century, he does not provide a contextual analysis of these events.
3. Bunkazai Kyōkai, *Kokuhō zuroku* (Tokyo: Bunkazai Kyōkai, 1952), 34–35; Bunkazai Hogo Iinkai, *Kokuhō*, vol. 1 (Tokyo: Mainichi Shinbunsha, 1963–67).
4. The title *tennō* (literally, "heavenly sovereign"; usually translated into English as "emperor" or "empress") likely was not used until the late seventh century. The contemporary designation for earlier monarchs, such as Kinmei and Suiko, probably would have been *ōkimi*, or "Great King." In English, "Great King" has been used conventionally to designate both male and female rulers, to avoid confusion with "queen" meaning the wife of the reigning monarch.
5. For a discussion of these scholars' positions, see Yoshida Kazuhiko, "Kindai rekishigaku to Shōtoku Taishi kenkyū," in *Shōtoku Taishi no shinjitsu*, ed. Ōyama Seiichi (Tokyo: Heibonsha, 2004), 19–44. See also Shinkawa Tokio, *Shōtoku Taishi no rekishigaku: Kioku to sōzō no sen-yonhyakunen* (Tokyo: Kōdansha, 2007), 60–99.
6. Ōyama Seiichi, *Shōtoku Taishi no "tanjō"* (Tokyo: Yoshikawa Kōbunkan, 1999). For a short discussion in English, see Yoshida Kazuhiko, "The Thesis That Prince Shōtoku Did Not Exist," *Acta Asiatica* 91 (2006): 1–20.
7. Hayashi Mikiya, *Taishi shinkō: Sono hassei to hatten* (Tokyo: Hyōronsha, 1972), and *Taishi shinkō no kenkyū* (Tokyo: Yoshikawa Kōbunkan, 1980). For a discussion in English, see Kevin Gray Carr, *Plotting the Prince: Shōtoku Cults and the Mapping of Medieval Japanese Buddhism* (Honolulu: University of Hawai'i Press, 2012), 23–103.
8. Ōyama Seiichi, ed., *Shōtoku Taishi no shinjitsu* (2003; reprint, Tokyo: Heibonsha, 2004); Yoshida Kazuhiko, ed., *Henbōsuru Shōtoku Taishi: Nihonjin wa Shōtoku Taishi o donoyō ni shinkō shite kita ka* (Tokyo: Heibonsha, 2011). In the present study, the prince is called "Shōtoku" for the sake of clarity.
9. Carr, *Plotting the Prince*, 6–8.
10. For a discussion of Shōtoku as Guze Kannon, see Fujii Yukiko, *Shōtoku Taishi no denshō: Imēji no saisei to shinkō* (Tokyo: Yoshikawa Kōbunkan, 1999), 12–35. See also "'Guze Kannon' no seiritsu: Reigenka sareta Shōtoku Taishi," in Ōyama, *Shōtoku Taishi no shinjitsu*, 317–39. On his multiple reincarnations, see Carr, ibid., 47–69; and Chari Pradel, "Shōkō Mandara and the Cult of Prince Shōtoku in the Kamakura Period," *Artibus Asiae* 68, no. 2 (2008): 215–46.
11. All of these forms are reproduced in Shitennōji no Hōmotsu to Shōtoku Taishi Shinkōten Jikkō Iinkai, *Shitennōji no hōmotsu to Shōtoku Taishi shinkō: Kaisō sen-yonhyakunen kinen* (Osaka: Shitennōji no Hōmotsu to Shōtoku Taishi Shinkōten Jikkō Iinkai, 1992). See also Ishida Mosaku, "Shōtoku Taishi zō no kusagusa sō," in *STZ*, vol. 4, ed. Shōtoku Taishi Hōsankai Kanshū (Kyoto: Rinsen Shoten, 1988), 8–25.
12. For a summary of the various interpretations of the term Tenjukoku, see Maria del Rosario Pradel, "The Fragments of the Tenjukoku Shūchō Mandara: Reconstruction of the Iconography and the Historical Contexts" (Ph.D. dissertation, University of California, Los Angeles, 1997), 61–105.
13. Tsuji Zennosuke, "Wakayama-ken oyobi Kyōto-fu e kenkyū ryokō ho (shōzen)," *Shigaku zasshi* 12, no. 2 (1901): 100–101.
14. Matsumoto Bunzaburō, *Miroku jōdo ron: Gokuraku jōdo ron* (Tokyo: Heibonsha, 2006).
15. Shigematsu Akihisa, *Nihon Jōdokyō seiritsu katei no kenkyū* (Kyoto: Heirakuji Shoten, 1964), 66.
16. Ōya Tōru, *Kana genryū kō* (Tokyo: Kokutei Kyōkasho Kyōdo Hanbaijo, 1911), 60–62.
17. Ōya Tokujō, "Tenjukoku Shūchō kō," *Shūkyō kenkyū* 5, nos. 4, 5 (1928): 55–70, 73–85; also "Tenjukoku to wa nanzoya," *Yumedono* 4 (1931): 20–34. The dating of the Shaka triad to 623 is controversial. For a comprehensive study of this icon, see Akiko Walley, *Constructing the Dharma King: The Hōryūji Shaka Triad and the Birth of the Prince Shōtoku Cult* (Leiden and Boston: Brill, 2015).
18. The theories are too numerous to discuss here. For a summary in English, see Pradel, "Fragments," 63–76.
19. Kosugi Sugimura (1834–1910) was the first of many scholars to use these documents. See his "Suiko mikado jidai no bijutsu kōgeihin: Tenjukoku no mandara to iu mono," *Shigaku zasshi* 12, no. 1 (1901): 69–74.
20. These documents are discussed in Chapters Four and Five.

21 In 1939, Tokiwa Daijō (1870–1945) found the phrase "Saihō Tenjukoku" in the postscript on a sutra scroll belonging to the Mitsui family. Ōya Tokujō questioned Tokiwa's reading, but agreed that Tenjukoku could be the Western Pure Land. See Tokiwa Daijō, "Tenjukoku ni tsuite," in *Shina Bukkyō no kenkyū*, vol. 1 (Tokyo: Shunjūsha, 1939), 37–51; and Ōya Tokujō, "Saikin no Tenjukoku mondai ni tsuite," *Mikkyō kenkyū* 70 (1939): 37–51. In 1959, Okabe Chōshō (b. 1909) analyzed the evidence again and agreed with Tokiwa's reading. In recent research, however, Takase Tamon concluded that the scribe did not write Tenjukoku. See Okabe Chōshō, "Mitsui-kezō *Kegon kyō* okusho no soku butsuteki kōsatsu," *Nihon rekishi* 120 (1958): 76–80; and Takase Tamon, "Mitsui Bunko hon *Kegon kyō* bun ni mieru 'Tenjukoku' ni tsuite: Shinshiryō no shōkai to 'ten' ji no sai kentō," *Sagami joshi daigaku kiyō* 64A (2000): 13–22. For a summary of the first three interpretations in English, see Pradel, "Fragments," 69–72.

22 Ōhashi, *Tenjukoku Shūchō no kenkyū*, 135.

23 See Pradel, "Fragments," 87–92.

24 Mochizuki Shinjō, "Tenjukoku Shūchō no saikō," in *Nihon jōdai bunka no kenkyū*, ed. Yoshida Kakuin (Nara: Hōsōshu Kangakuin Dōsōkai, 1941), 393–408; Fukui Kōjun, "Tenjukoku Mandara no shisōteki seikaku," in Fukui Kōjun, *Tōyō shisō no kenkyū* (Tokyo: Risōsha, 1955), 128–52; Shimomise Shizuichi, "Tenjukoku Mandara ni tsuite," in Shimomise Shizuichi, *Yamatoe shi kenkyū* (Tokyo: Fuzanbō, 1956), 97–130.

25 Igor Kopytoff, "The Cultural Biography of Things: Commodization as Process," in *The Social Life of Things: Commodities in Cultural Perspective*, ed. Arjun Appadurai (Cambridge: Cambridge University Press, 1986), 64–94; Richard Davis, *Lives of Indian Images* (Princeton, NJ: Princeton University Press, 1997).

26 Kopytoff, ibid., 66–67.

27 Davis, *Lives of Indian Images*, 8–10.

28 Ibid., 7.

29 Ibid., 11.

30 Michael Como, *Shōtoku: Ethnicity, Ritual and Violence in the Japanese Buddhist Tradition* (Oxford: Oxford University Press, 2008).

31 I paraphrase the term "popular Chinese cultic practices" from Michael Como, who has demonstrated that such practices, especially those associated with the festival calendar, played a key role in the shaping of Japanese religion. See his *Weaving and Binding: Immigrant Gods and Female Immortals in Ancient Japan* (Honolulu: University of Hawai'i Press, 2010), especially the introduction.

32 The issue of the transmission of Daoism to Japan is controversial. No evidence has been found for the existence of Daoism as an organized religion in Japan, but it is likely that elements of yin yang and the Five Phases (C. *wu xing*), which were later incorporated into Daoism in China, were transmitted by Chinese and Korean immigrants. See Ana Seidel, "Chronicle of Taoist Studies in the West 1950–1990," *Cahiers d'Extrême Asie* 5 (1989–90): 223–348; Livia Kohn, "Taoism in Japan: Positions and Evaluations," *Cahiers d'Extrême Asie* 8, no. 1 (1995): 389–413; David Bialock, *Eccentric Spaces, Hidden Histories: Narrative, Ritual and Royal Authority from* The Chronicles of Japan *to* The Tale of Genji (Stanford, CA: Stanford University Press, 2007), 17–110; and Herman Ooms, *Imperial Politics and Symbolics in Ancient Japan: The Tenmu Dynasty, 650–800* (Honolulu: University of Hawai'i Press, 2009), 132–53. For the role of immigrants in the transmission of continental beliefs, see Shimode Sekiyo, "Toraijin no shinkō to Dōkyō," *Rekishi kōron* 6 (1976): 88–101.

I

1 The designs on the Tenjukoku Mandara are analyzed in Chapter Five, after an examination of the corresponding textual material in Chapter Four.

2 For important research on the technical aspects of the Tenjukoku Shūchō Mandara, see Nakagawa Tadayori, "Tenjukoku Mandara ni tsuite," *Shisō* 20 (1923): 333–41; Ishida Mosaku, "Kokuhō Tenjukoku Mandara Shūchō," in *Chūgūji ōkagami, Hokkiji ōkagami*, ed. Ishida Mosaku (Tokyo: Ōtsuka Kōgeisha, 1940), 6–10; Ōta Hidezō, "Tenjukoku Mandara no shūgi to Kenji shūri ni tsuite," *Shiseki to bijutsu* 188 (1948): 161–76; Mōri Noboru, "Tenjukoku Shūchō," *Museum*, no. 13 (1952): 22–24, and "Tenjukoku Shūchō ni tsuite—Shūchō no genpon to Kenji saikō no Shūchō ni tsuite," *Kobijutsu* 11 (1965): 27–38; Nishimura Hyōbu, "Zuhan kaisetsu—Tenjukoku Shūchō," in NKH, *Shūbutsu* (Tokyo: Kadokawa Shoten, 1964), 12–18; Yamabe Tomoyuki and Domyo Mihoko, "Tenjukoku Shūchō," in *YKT*, ed. Ōta Hirotarō, vol. 1 (Tokyo: Iwanami Shoten, 1977), 70–77; Sawada Mutsuyo, "Tenjukoku Shūchō no genjō," *Museum*, no. 495 (1992): 4–25; and Mita Kakuyuki, "Gihō kara mita Tenjukoku Shūchō," *Fuirokaria* 25 (2008): 67–98. See also the Appendix for illustrations of fabric details.

3 The white heads that appear on certain figures are eighteenth-century additions; see Chapter Five.

4 For fabrics in both collections, see Sawada Mutsuyo, *Jōdai-gire shūsei: Kofun shutsudo no sen'i kara Hōryūji Shōsōin-gire made* (Tokyo: Chūō Kōron Bijutsu Shuppan, 2001); and Matsumoto Kaneo, *Jōdai-gire: Shōsōin-gire to Asuka Tenpyō no senshoku* (Kyoto: Shikisha, 1984).

5 For fabrics in the Hōryūji collection, see Hōryūji, *Hōryūji to shiruku rōdo bukkyō bunka* (Nara: Hōryūji, 1989), 136–59.

6 In addition to the banner fragments in the Hōryūji collection, others are housed in the Fujita Art Museum, Osaka; Yamato Bunkakan, Nara; Nezu Museum, Tokyo;

the collection of Tokyo University of the Arts (Tokyo Geijutsu Daigaku); and Eifukuji, Osaka.

7   All pieces are reproduced in Sawada, *Jōdai-gire shūsei*, plates III-ii-2–III-ii-7, IV-iii-29–IV-iii-236. They also are reproduced in NKH, *Shūbutsu*, 34–41.

8   For running stitch, see Irene Emery, *The Primary Structures of Fabrics: An Illustrated Classification* (Washington, DC: The Textile Museum, 1966), 234–35.

9   Ōta, "Tenjukoku Mandara no shūgi," 167; Sawada, *Jōdai-gire shūsei*, 180–84.

10 Archaeological evidence suggests that the embroidery technique used in the two sets of remains might have already been known in the sixth century. Kirihata Ken has noted that a quiver found in the mid-sixth-century Nishimiyayama funerary mound (Tatsuno-shi, Hyōgo Prefecture) showed small pieces of gauze over a plain-weave lining and traces of embroidery with tightly twisted threads. Despite the difficulty of analyzing the fabric attached to the surface of the quiver, he could distinguish between the tightly twisted threads, the gauze fabric, and the plain weave. Kirihata also has noticed that the fibers from these fragments were thicker than those of the Shūchō, and that golden and silver threads were used to delineate the unidentified designs. Kirihata Ken, "Nishimiyayama kofun shutsudohin chōsa o shuppatsu to shite: Tenjukoku Shūchō no saku kisetsu kansō," *Ōtemae daigaku shigaku kenkyūjō kiyō* 5 (2005): 19.

11 Small fragments found in 1956 at Tōshōdaiji, Nara Prefecture, confirmed that this style of embroidery was prevalent in the eighth century. The findings included about a dozen fragments (no larger than about 5 cm) of plain weave and twill embroidered with stitches similar to those found in the Shōsōin examples. See NKH, *Shūbutsu*, 41–42; and Itō Shinji, *Shūbutsu*, Nihon no bijutsu, no. 470 (Tokyo: Shibundō, 2005), 22–23.

12 The Kajūji embroidered icon previously was considered to have been made in Japan. See NKH, *Shūbutsu*, 18–21. Now it is generally accepted to be an import, but no agreement has been reached regarding the Buddha represented; see Itō, *Shūbutsu*, 74–75. For a discussion of the subject matter on the Kajūji embroidery, see Hida Romi, "Kajūji shūbutsu saikō," *Bukkyō geijutsu*, no. 212 (1944): 62–88. For the British Museum embroidery, see Roderick Whitfield, *The Art of Central Asia: The Stein Collection in the British Museum*, vol. 3 (Tokyo: Kodansha, 1982–85), 281–84. The Kajūji icon measures 208 x 158 cm, and the British Museum icon, 241.0 x 159.5 cm.

13 Mita Kakuyuki, "Hōryūji denrai: Shūbutsu retsu no bunrui to kisoteki kōsatsu," *Museum*, no. 637 (2012): 7–29.

14 For Takamatsuzuka tomb, see J. Edward Kidder, "The Newly Discovered Takamatsuzuka Tomb," *Monumenta Nipponica* 27 (1972): 245–51; "Takamatsuzuka hekiga kofun tokushō," *Bukkyō geijutsu*, no. 87 (1972); Takamatsuzuka Kofun Sōgō Gakujutsu Chōsakai, *Takamatsuzuka kofun hekiga chōsa hōkokusho* (Kyoto: Benridō, 1974); and NBK, *Takamatsuzuka kofun hekiga foto mappu shiryō* (Nara: Nara Bunkazai Kenkyūjo, 2009). For Kitora tomb, see Donohashi Akio, "Kitora kofun no shijinzu: Shujaku no shutsugen," *Bukkyō geijutsu*, no. 258 (2001): 13–17; Sugaya Fuminori, "Kitora kofun hekiga no shujakuzō," *Higashi Ajia no kodai bunka*, no. 108 (2002): 95–107; Asukamura Kyōiku Iinkai, *Kitora kofun to hekiga* (Asuka: Asuka Kokyō Kenshōkai, 2001); Aboshi Yoshinori, "Nihon Takamatsu, Kitora kofun no hekiga," *Higashi Ajia no kodai bunka*, no. 124 (2005): 2–10; and Bunkachō, TKH, and NBK, *Kitora kofun hekiga: Tokubetsuten* (Tokyo: Asahi Shinbunsha, 2014).

15 For a short discussion of the Korean connection, see William W. Farris, *Sacred Texts and Buried Treasures: Issues in the Historical Archaeology of Ancient Japan* (Honolulu: University of Hawai'i Press, 1998), 55–122. For detailed studies in English, see Como, *Shōtoku* and *Weaving and Binding*.

16 For illustrations, see *Kōkuri kofun hekiga* (Tokyo: Chōsen Gahōsha, 1985) and *Koguryŏ kobun pyŏkhwa* (Seoul: Yŏnhap Nyusŭ, 2006). Publications in English include Chŏn Ho-t'ae (Jeon Ho-Tae), *The Dreams of the Living and Hopes of the Dead: Goguryeo Tomb Murals* (Seoul: Seoul National University Press, 2007); and two excellent dissertations that address the connections between Chinese and Goguryeo funerary art: Ah-Rim Park, "Tomb of the Dancers: Koguryo Tombs in East Asian Funerary Art" (Ph.D. diss., University of Pennsylvania, 2002); and Miwa Stevenson, "Webs of Signification: Representation as Social Transformation in Muraled Tombs of Koguryo" (Ph.D. diss., Columbia University, 1999).

17 This chronology is based on Chŏn, ibid., 51–112.

18 Stevenson, "Webs of Signification." The third and fourth chapters of this dissertation present a comprehensive study of Han tombs and the Goguryeo tombs of Anak and Deokhungri. For a brief overview of Chinese influence in Goguryeo tombs, see Chŏn, ibid., 41–50.

19 Chŏn, ibid., 62–112. See also *Kōkuri kofun hekiga*.

20 Stevenson, "Webs of Signification," especially Chapters Three and Four.

21 Wu Hung, *The Art of the Yellow Springs: Understanding Chinese Tombs* (Honolulu: University of Hawai'i Press, 2010). For a general overview of Han tomb painting, see Wu Hung, "The Origins of Chinese Painting: Paleolithic Period to Tang Dynasty," in *Three Thousand Years of Chinese Painting*, ed. Yang Xin et al. (New Haven and London: Yale University Press, 1997), 22–34.

22 Wu, *Art of the Yellow Springs*, 34–63.

23 Ibid., 35.

24 For *hirami*, see Sekine Shinryū, *Nara-chō fukushoku no kenkyū* (Tokyo: Yoshikawa Kōbunkan, 1974), 247–55. A garment from the Shōsōin collection identified as a *hirami* is reproduced in figure 50.

25 Mōri Noboru has stated that the fabric used in the seventh century is not purple like the rest of the fragments, but white. See his "Tenjukoku Shuchō ni tsuite," 33. Mita Kakuyuki has pointed out that, while the fabric is of a lighter color, it is difficult to confirm that the gauze was originally white. Mita, "Gihō," 68.

26 Both pleated and ruffled skirts are found in the Shōsōin collection. See NKH, Shōsōin ten mokuroku (Nara: Nara Kokuritsu Hakubutsukan, 1998, 1999), 62 and 66, respectively.

27 For tasuki, see Sekine, Nara-chō fukushoku, 164–65. Ōhashi identifies this item in the Shūchō fragments as tasuki, a sash or cord used for holding up bunched sleeves when working. The cord passes over the shoulders and under the armpits, and crosses in the back. See Ōhashi, Tenjukoku Shūchō no kenkyū, 42–43. The item worn by these women, however, does not correspond to Ōhashi's description. Some haniwa identified as miko (female shamans) wear a similar bag-like element to the side; a closer look reveals that this is not a piece of fabric that crosses the chest, but a garment covering the whole upper body. See Tatsumi Kazuhiro et al., "Seikatsu," in Seikatsu to saishi, vol. 3 of Kofun jidai no kenkyū, ed. Ishino Hironobu et al. (Tokyo: Yūzankaku Shuppan, 1990–93), 29–32, plate 1.

28 For illustrations of these tomb murals, see Kōkuri kofun hekiga, plates 97, 105, 107, 108.

29 Lena Kim, "Goguryo People Wearing Jougwan in Tang Chinese Art," The International Journal of Korean Art and Archaeology 2 (2008): 94. See also Wontack Hong, Paekche of Korea and the Origins of Yamato Japan (Seoul: Kudara International, 1994), 156–60. Hong cites Chinese and Japanese sources that address the similarities between the clothing of the Three Kingdoms period and Yamato Japan.

30 As cited by Tanaka Fumio, Wakoku to toraijin: Kōsakusuru "uchi" to "soto" (Tokyo: Yoshikawa Kōbunkan, 2005), 49.

31 Ōhashi Katsuaki, "Tenjukoku Shūchō no genkei," Bukkyō geijutsu, no. 117 (1978): 64.

32 For processions in tombs of the Southern Qi dynasty (479–502), see Audrey Spiro, Contemplating the Ancients: Aesthetics and Social Issues in Early Chinese Portraiture (Berkeley, Los Angeles, and Oxford: University of California Press, 1990), 138–52. For processions in the Buddhist cave temples at Dunhuang, Longmen, and Gongxian, see Tonkō Bunbutsu Kenkyūjo, ed., Tonkō bakukōkutsu, vol. 1 (Tokyo: Heibonsha, 1980–82), plates 113, 122–24, 128; Ryūmon Bunbutsu Hokanjo and Pekin Daigaku Kōkokei, eds., Ryūmon sekkutsu, vol. 1 (Tokyo: Heibonsha, 1987–88), plates 39, 59, 71, 72, 142, 167; and Kananshō Bunbutsu Kenkyūjo, ed., Kyōken sekkutsuji (Tokyo: Heibonsha, 1983), plates 4, 40, 41.

33 NBK, Takamatsuzuka kofun hekiga.

34 Mary Fong, "Four Chinese Royal Tombs of the Early Eighth Century," Artibus Asiae 35, no. 4 (1973): 322; Tonia Eckfeld, Imperial Tombs in Tang China, 618–907: The Politics of Paradise (London and New York: RoutledgeCurzon, 2005).

35 Entries from Nihon shoki (hereafter, NS) cited in this volume are referenced from W.G. Aston, trans., Nihongi: Chronicles of Japan from the Earliest Times to A.D. 697 (Rutland, VT and Tokyo: Charles E. Tuttle Co., 1988); and Nihon shoki, Nihon koten bungaku taikei, vols. 67, 68 (Tokyo: Iwanami Shoten, 1965; hereafter, NKBT). See the NS entry for Suiko 13/7/1: Aston, Nihongi, part 2, 134; NKBT, vol. 68, 186.

36 NS entry for Tenmu 11/2/28: Aston, Nihongi, part 2, 354; NKBT, vol. 68, 451.

37 Ōhashi was the first scholar to point out this important feature. Ōhashi, Tenjukoku Shūchō no kenkyū, 35–37.

38 See Lillian Lan-ying Tseng, Picturing Heaven in Early China (Cambridge, MA: Harvard University Asia Center, 2011). See also Wu, Art of the Yellow Springs, 47–53, 151–63.

39 See Saitō Rieko, "Tonkō dai 249 kutsu tenjō ni okeru Chūgokuteki zuzō no juyō keitai," Bukkyō geijutsu, no. 218 (1995): 39–56. For the introduction of Indian-derived flying beings, see Chari Pradel, "Winged Immortals and Heavenly Beings Across the East Asian Skies," in Spirits in Transcultural Skies—Essays on the Interactions and Iconography of Protective Winged Beings in Art and Architecture, ed. Niels Gustchow and Katharina Weiler (Heidelberg: Springer Transcultural Research Books Series, 2015), 99–124.

40 Chŏn Ho-t'ae (Jeon Ho-Tae), "Artistic Creation, Borrowing, Adaptation, and Assimilation in Koguryo Tomb Murals of the Fourth to Seventh Century," Archives of Asian Art 56 (2006): 81–104, and Dreams of the Living.

41 For a detailed discussion of the origins of the representations of the sun and moon in China, see Tseng, Picturing Heaven, 277–97. See also Michael Loewe, Ways to Paradise: The Chinese Quest for Immortality (London and Boston: George Allen and Unwin, 1979), 127–35.

42 For the Mawangdui banner, see A.G. Bulling, "The Guide of the Souls Picture in the Western Han Tomb in Ma-wang-tui near Ch'ang-sha," Oriental Art 20, no. 2 (1974): 158–73. See also Wu Hung, "Art in a Ritual Context: Rethinking Mawangdui," Early China 17 (1992): 111–44. The painting from Jinqueshan is reproduced in Wu Hung, The Wu Liang Shrine: The Ideology of Early Chinese Pictorial Art (Stanford, CA: Stanford University Press, 1989), 114.

43 Bulling, ibid., 166.

44 Sun Zuoyun, "An Analysis of the Western Han Murals in the Luoyang Tomb of Bo Qianqiu," trans. Suzanne Cahill, Chinese Studies in Archaeology 1, no. 2 (1979): 44–78; Jona-

45 Sun, ibid., 63.

46 For the lacquered coffin, see Luo Feng, "Lacquer Painting on a Northern Wei Coffin," *Orientations* 21, no. 7 (1990): 18–29; Patricia E. Karetzky and Alexander Soper, "A Northern Wei Painted Coffin," *Artibus Asiae* 51, nos. 1, 2 (1991): 5–28; and Annette Juliano and Judith Lerner, *Monks and Merchants: Silk Road Treasures of Northwest China* (New York: Harry N. Abrams with The Asia Society, 2001), 77–81. For a survey of the Queen Mother's early history, see Suzanne Cahill, *Transcendence and Divine Passion: The Queen Mother of the West in Medieval China* (Stanford, CA: Stanford University Press, 1993), 11–65. For a visual representation of the Queen Mother of the West in her paradise, see Robert Bagley, *Ancient Sichuan: Treasures from a Lost Civilization* (Princeton, NJ: Princeton University Press, 2001), 295–96.

47 For tombs of the Southern Dynasties, see Nanjing Museum, "Two Tombs of the Southern Dynasties at Huqiao and Jianshan in Danyang County, Jiangsu Province," trans. Barry Till and Paula Swart, *Chinese Studies in Archaeology* 1, no. 3 (1979–80): 74–124, and "A Large Tomb of the Southern Dynasties Period with Decorated Bricks at Huqiao, Danyang, Jiangsu," *Wenwu* 2 (1974): 44–52, also published in Albert E. Dien, Jeffrey K. Riegel, and Nancy T. Price, eds., *Chinese Archaeological Abstracts 4, Post Han* (Los Angeles: Institute of Archaeology, University of California, Los Angeles, 1985), 1484–93.

48 Nanjing Museum, "Two Tombs," 87–88.

49 Reproduced in Spiro, *Contemplating the Ancients*, plates 36, 37.

50 For influences from the Southern Dynasties on Baekje's pictorial tiles, see Sekino Tadashi, "Sen yori mitaru Kudara to Shina Nanchō toku ni Ryō to no bunka kankei," *Hōun* 10 (1934): 23–33. See also Susan Bush, "Some Parallels between Chinese and Korean Ornamental Motifs of the Late Fifth and Early Sixth Centuries A.D," *Archives of Asian Art* 37 (1984): 60–78.

51 See Aboshi Yoshinori, "Kankoku no hekiga kofun," *Bukkyō geijutsu*, no. 89 (1972): 4–9. See also Kim Ki-ung, *Kudara no kofun* (Kyoto: Gakuseisha, 1976), 123–29.

52 The murals in Kitora tomb were discovered between 1983 and 2001. First a fiber scope was introduced, followed later by digital cameras. For illustrations, see Asukamura Kyōiku Iinkai, *Kitora kofun to hekiga*. For a short history of the nondestructive excavation, and approximate measurements of the murals, see Sugaya, "Kitora kofun hekiga." See also Donohashi, "Kitora kofun no shijinzu."

53 Aboshi Yoshinori, "Nihon Takamatsu, Kitora kofun no hekiga," *Higashi Ajia no kodai bunka*, no. 124 (2005): 3.

54 For a comprehensive study of the Tamamushi Shrine, see Uehara Kazu, *Tamamushi zushi no kenkyū: Asuka, Hakuhō bijutsu yōshiki shiron* (Tokyo: Yoshikawa Kōbunkan, 1991).

55 A detail is reproduced in TKH, *Hōryūji kennō hōmotsu* (Tokyo: Tokyo Kokuritsu Hakubutsukan, 1975), 215. See also TKH, *Kanjōban. Hōryūji kennō hōmotsu tokubetsu chōsa gaihō 11* (Tokyo: Tokyo Kokuritsu Hakubutsukan, 1991).

56 For a brief discussion in English, see Jessica Rawson, *Chinese Ornament: The Lotus and the Dragon*, 1984 (Reprint, London: British Museum Publications, 1990), 99–107. For a catalogue raisonné of the red bird motif in East Asia, see Aboshi Yoshinori, "Kofun hekiga, boshi nado ni miru shujaku, hōō no zuzō," in Aboshi Yoshinori, *Hekiga kofun no kenkyū* (Tokyo: Gakuseisha, 2006), 152–91. For the red bird in Korea and Japan, see Yoshitaka Ariga, "Korean Elements in Japanese Pictorial Representation in the Early Asuka Period," in Washizuka Hiromitsu et al., *Transmitting the Forms of Divinity: Early Buddhist Art from Korea and Japan* (New York: Japan Society, 2003), 96–105. In this essay, both red birds are translated as "phoenix," which is misleading due to the Western connotations of the term.

57 Stephen Little with Shawn Eichman, *Taoism and the Arts of China* (Chicago and Berkeley, CA: Art Institute of Chicago and University of California Press, 2000), 129.

58 Wu, "Origins of Chinese Painting," 29.

59 For a discussion of the origins of the Four Divinities, see Tseng, *Picturing Heaven*, 236–64.

60 Aboshi, "Kankoku no hekiga kofun," 4–9.

61 The animals discovered are the rat, ox, tiger, horse, dog, and wild boar. See Bunkachō, TKH, and NBK, *Kitora kofun hekiga*.

62 For Yakushiji's Yakushi triad, see Yui Suzuki, *Medicine Master Buddha: The Iconic Worship of Yakushi in Heian Japan* (Leiden and Boston: Brill, 2012), 16–22. For illustrations of the pedestal, see Nara Rokudaiji Taikan Kankōkai, ed., *Nara rokudaiji taikan* (hereafter, *NRT*), vol. 6, *Yakushiji* (Tokyo: Iwanami Shoten, 1999–2001), 62–63.

63 Meeks has argued that the mention of dragons indicates that "the mandala had been made and/or used by the royal family." Lori Meeks, *Hokkeji and the Reemergence of Female Monastic Orders in Premodern Japan*, Studies in East Asian Buddhism, vol. 23 (Honolulu: University of Hawai'i Press, 2010), 294.

64 For a detailed discussion of omens, see Tseng, *Picturing Heaven*, 89–148.

65 Wu, *Wu Liang Shrine*, 73–107.

66 For the Dunhuang scroll, see Matsumoto Eiichi, "Tonkō hon zuiō zukan," *Bijutsu kenkyū*, no. 184 (1956): 241–58.

67 Wu, *Wu Liang Shrine*, 73–107.

68 Tseng, *Picturing Heaven*, 111–16.
69 For a detailed description of the Deokhungri tomb, see Stevenson, "Webs of Signification," 113–34; for the identification of the motifs on the ceiling, see pages 127–29.
70 Ibid., 267–70.
71 Wu, *Art of the Yellow Springs*, 52–53.
72 Fu Juyou and Chen Songchang, *A Comprehensive Introduction about the Cultural Relics Unearthed from the Han Tombs at Mawangdui*, trans. Zhou Shiyi and Chen Kefeng (Changsha: Hunan Publishing House, 1992), 40.
73 Susan Bush, "Thunder Monsters, Auspicious Animals, and Floral Ornament in Early Sixth-Century China," *Ars Orientalis* 10 (1975): 20–22.
74 The first scholar to point out this association was Kosugi Kazuo. See his "Zōkei ni mirareru kame to moji to no kankei," in *Fukui hakushi shōju kinen tōyō shisō ronshū* (Tokyo: Fukui Hakushi Shōju Kinen Ronbunshū Kankōkai, 1960), 236–42.
75 Michael Saso, "What Is the 'Ho-T'u'?," *History of Religions* 17, nos. 3, 4 (1978): 401.
76 Schuyler Cammann, "Some Early Chinese Symbols of Duality," *History of Religions* 24, no. 3 (1985): 215–54. See also Peng Yoke Ho, *Chinese Mathematical Astrology: Reaching Out for the Stars* (London and New York: RoutledgeCurzon, 2003).
77 For extensive discussion of the Shūchō turtle and the Asuka turtle, see Ōhashi Katsuaki, "Shin hakken no sekizō kamegata suiban ni tsuite," *Bukkyō geijutsu*, no. 250 (2000): 122–32; and Ueda Masaaki, "Kameishi to shūchō," *Asuka kaze* 75 (2000): 5–9.
78 For details on the excavation and a description of the site, see Asukamura Kyōiku Iinkai, *Kamegata sekizō butsu ikō* (Asuka: Asuka Kokyō Kenshōkai, 2000). See also Senda Minoru and Uno Takao, *Kame no kodaigaku* (Osaka: Tohō Shuppan, 2001).
79 Ueda Masaaki, in "Kameishi to shūchō," has pointed out that the way in which these two stone receptacles connect is similar to the connections between waterways seen in Anapji (Anap Pond) in Gyeongju, built by King Munmu (r. 661–81) in 674.
80 A similar turtle-shaped receptacle exists at Shitennōji in Osaka. This receptacle is associated with another, more naturalistic stone turtle that serves as a spout. Not much is known about this receptacle at Shitennōji; currently, ceremonies are performed at the site to send the spirits of the dead to Amida's Pure Land. See *Shitennōji, Koji o meguru: Oshie, bi, rekishi*, vol. 25 (Tokyo: Shōgakkan, 2008), 18.
81 NS entry for Saimei 2/9: Aston, *Nihongi*, part 2, 250–51; NKBT, vol. 68, 328–29.
82 The character *shin* is one of the twelve branches, a system developed in ancient China for reckoning time.
83 NS entry for Tenji 9/6: Aston, *Nihongi*, part 2, 293–94; NKBT, vol. 68, 374.

84 For the complete poem in Japanese, with English translation and analysis, see Torquil Duthie, *Man'yōshū and the Imperial Imagination in Early Japan* (Leiden: Brill, 2014), 391–98.
85 *Shoku Nihongi* entry for Tenpyō 1/6/20, in *Shoku Nihongi*, Shin Nihon koten bungaku taikei, vol. 13 (Tokyo: Iwanami Shoten, 1990), 213–15. One *sun* is approximately equivalent to 1 3/16 inch, or 30 millimeters; one *bu* is one tenth of one *sun*. These units of measurement originated in ancient China.
86 For a discussion of omens in eighth-century Japan, see Ross Bender, "Auspicious Omens in the Reign of the Last Empress of Nara Japan, 749–770," *Japanese Journal of Religious Studies* 40, no. 1 (2013): 45–76.
87 *Shoku Nihongi* entry for Jingo-keiun 2/9/1, in *Shoku Nihongi*, vol. 13, 213–15. See also Bender, ibid., 68.
88 See Pradel, "Winged Immortals."
89 Robert F. Campany, *To Live as Long as Heaven and Earth: A Translation and Study of Ge Hong's* Traditions of Divine Transcendence (Berkeley, CA: University of California Press, 2002), 3–5. For descriptions of *xian*, see Robert F. Campany, *Making Transcendents: Ascetics and Social Memory in Early Medieval China* (Honolulu: University of Hawai'i Press, 2009), 3–4.
90 Yoshimura Rei, "Ryūmon Hoku Gi kutsu ni okeru tennin tanjō no hyōgen," *Bijutsushi*, no. 69 (1968): 1–12; "Kyōken sekkutsu ni okeru keshō no zuzō ni tsuite," *Waseda daigaku daigakuin bungaku kenkyūka kiyo* 21 (1976): 115–26; "Nanchō tennin zuzō no Hokuchō oyobi shūhen shokoku e no denba," *Bukkyō geijutsu*, no. 159 (1985): 11–29; and "Mogao sekkutsu ni okeru tennin zō no keifu," *Kokka*, no. 1177 (1993): 3–17. For a summarized version of Yoshimura's research, see his "Nanchōteki tennin no Nihon e no denba," in *Hōryūji kara Yakushiji e: Asuka Nara no kenchiku, chōkoku*, ed. Mizuno Keizaburō et al. (Tokyo: Kōdansha, 1990), 171–77. See also Yoshimura, "Tenjukoku Shūchō to Kondō Kanjōban ni mirareru tennin tanjō no zuzō," *Museum*, no. 354 (1979): 4–17.
91 Yoshimura, "Nanchō tennin zuzō."
92 For a detailed discussion of the Guyang Cave and its donors, see Amy McNair, *Donors of Longmen: Faith, Politics, and Patronage in Medieval Chinese Buddhist Sculpture* (Honolulu: University of Hawai'i Press, 2007), 7–30. McNair has suggested 502 as the date for the introduction of the southern type of Buddhist heavenly being in the north.
93 Yoshimura, "Ryūmon," 10.
94 Yoshimura, "Nanchō tennin zuzō," 20–21.
95 The sprouting-bud design is included in the complex compositions of engraved sarcophagi from the early sixth century found in Luoyang (Henan Province), such as one example from Shangyao in the Luoyang Museum, and one in the Minneapolis Institute of Art;

and also the late-sixth-century sarcophagus for Li Ho (d. 582) from Shaanxi Province. For the Shangyao and Li Ho sarcophagi, see Patricia Karetzky, "A Scene of the Taoist Afterlife on a Sixth Century Sarcophagus Discovered in Loyang," *Artibus Asiae* 44, no. 1 (1983): 5–20, and "The Engraved Designs on the Late Sixth Century Sarcophagus of Li Ho," *Artibus Asiae* 47, no. 2 (1986): 81–108. For the Minneapolis sarcophagus, see Eugene Y. Wang, "Coffins and Confucianism: The Northern Wei Sarcophagus in the Minneapolis Institute of Arts," *Orientations* 30, no. 6 (1999): 56–64. Unfortunately, none of these studies addresses the sprouting-bud motif.

96 Yoshimura, "Nanchō tennin zuzō," 12–13.

97 Audrey Spiro, "Shaping the Wind: Taste and Tradition in Fifth-Century South China," *Ars Orientalis* 21 (1991): 102; http://www.jstor.org/stable/4629415 (last accessed June 12, 2011).

98 Isabelle Robinet, *Taoism: Growth of a Religion*, trans. Phyllis Brooks (Stanford, CA: Stanford University Press, 1997), 100–103.

99 Isabelle Robinet, "Metamorphosis and Deliverance of the Corpse in Taoism," *History of Religions* 19, no. 1 (1979): 43–44.

100 Yoshimura had noticed that, on the sides of the stele of Xiao Hong, the bud motif accompanies monsters and fantastic animals, but no transformation process is depicted. He concluded that these monsters and animals, as inhabitants of the celestial realm, must also have transformed from the celestial lotus or bud motif. Yoshimura, "Nanchō tennin zuzō," 13–14.

101 For the representation of *yunqi* in Han art, see Wu Hung, "A Sanpan Shan Chariot Ornament and the Xiangrui Design in Western Han Art," *Archives of Asian Art* 37 (1984): 47–48. For the theory of the combination of floral motifs and *yunqi*, see Sakai Atsuko, "Chūgoku Nanbokuchō jidai ni okeru shokubutsu unki mon ni tsuite," *Bijutsushi* 49, no. 1 (1999): 66–81. The idea of floral motifs as *qi* is also addressed briefly by Inoue Tadashi in "Rengemon: Sōzō to keshō no sekai," in Uehara Mahito, *Rengemon*, Nihon no bijutsu, no. 359 (Tokyo: Shibundō, 1996), 87–98.

102 For a chart including all of the monuments studied and the variations on the bud design, see Sakai, ibid., 80–81.

103 For floral designs, see Bush, "Thunder Monsters, Auspicious Animals," and "Floral Motifs and Vine Scrolls in Chinese Art of the Late Fifth to Early Sixth Centuries A.D.," *Artibus Asiae* 38, no. 1 (1976): 49–83.

104 Sakai, "Chūgoku Nanbokuchō jidai," 77–78.

105 Inoue, "Rengemon."

106 Ibid., 94. For an English translation, see John S. Major, *Heaven and Earth in Early Han Thought: Chapters Three, Four and Five of the Huainanzi* (Albany, NY: State University of New York Press, 1993), 62.

107 For the pictorial representation of *qi*, see Inoue, ibid., 95–97. See also Wu, "Sanpan Shan Chariot Ornament."

108 For photographs of this ceiling, see *Koguryŏ kobun pyŏkhwa*, 196–211.

109 The top of the wooden pillow measures 44.2 cm in length (from end to end); the bottom, 40 cm; and it is 33.7 cm high and 12.2 cm deep. For a detailed discussion of this object, see Yoshimura Rei, "Kudara Mutei ōhi ki makura ni egakareta tennin tanjō zu," in Yoshimura Rei, *Chūgoku bukkyō zuzō no kenkyū* (Tokyo: Tōhō Shoten, 1983), 117–35; first published in *Bijutsushi kenkyū* 14 (1977).

110 Yoshimura, "Tenjukoku Shūchō," 6. Yoshimura has reconstructed the sequence as follows: A-10 (an incomplete motif), A-5 (bud motif), and F-6 (motif on a thirteenth-century fragment); he also considers B-1 and B-2 as another step of the process. This sequence differs from the reconstruction proposed here.

111 More evidence that the Southern-style celestial being was known in Japan has been discovered. An ink sketch of such a being was found in the wooden pedestal of the Yakushi image in the Golden Hall at Hōryūji. See TKH, *Kokuhō Hōryūji ten: Hōryūji Shōwa shizaishō chōsa kansei kinen* (Tokyo: Shogakkan, 1994), 100–101.

112 For the origins of the palmette design and its evolution in China, see Rawson, *Chinese Ornament*, 35–88. For a brief overview of important artistic changes in China, see James C.Y. Watt, "Art and History in China from the Third to the Eighth Century," in James C.Y. Watt et al., *China: Dawn of the Golden Age, 200–750 AD* (New York, New Haven, and London: The Metropolitan Museum of Art and Yale University Press, 2004), 3–45. Watt argues that the palmette is derived from a foliage motif introduced in China with Buddhism in the fifth century.

113 Bush, "Thunder Monsters, Auspicious Animals" and "Floral Motifs and Vine Scrolls."

114 For the evolution of the acanthus motif into the palmette, see Rawson, *Chinese Ornament*, 35–56.

115 For the transformation of the palmette design into peony scrolls, see ibid., 69–88. In Japanese, the term *karakusamon* (plant motif from the Tang dynasty) is used to refer to the plant-derived scrolling design that consists of stems, vines, leaves, and flowers repeated rhythmically, usually within a band or border. See Yamamoto Tadanao, *Karakusamon*, Nihon no bijutsu, no. 358 (Tokyo: Shibundō, 1996).

116 Rawson, *Chinese Ornament*, 64–69.

117 For the palmette in India and East Asia, see Hayashi Ryōichi, "Parumetto," in Hayashi Ryōichi, *Tōyō bijutsu no sōshoku mon'yō* (Kyoto: Dōhōsha, 1992), 147–224.

118 For more about the lacquered coffin, see Luo, "Lacquer Painting"; Karetzky and Soper, "Northern Wei Painted Coffin"; and Juliano and Lerner, *Monks and Merchants*, 77–81.

119 Reproduced in Watt et al., *China: Dawn of the Golden Age*, 162.
120 Alexander Soper, "South Chinese Influence on the Buddhist Art of the Six Dynasties Period," *Museum of Far Eastern Antiquities Bulletin* 32 (1960): 47–107.
121 The most comprehensive study of these tombs is Annette Juliano, *Teng-hsien: An Important Six Dynasties Tomb*, Artibus Asiae Supplementum, vol. 37 (Ascona: Artibus Asiae Publishers, 1980). For the dating of the tomb, see page 68 of Juliano's study.
122 Bush, "Thunder Monsters, Auspicious Animals," 20–22.
123 For the Gongxian caves, see Kananshō Bunbutsu Kenkyūjo, *Kyōken sekkutsuji*; and Yoshimura, "Kyōken sekkutsu." For Dunhuang Cave No. 285, see Yoshimura, "Nanchō tennin zuzō."
124 For the palmette design on the Korean peninsula, see Hayashi, "Parumetto," in Hayashi, *Tōyō bijutsu*, 192–205. See also Bush, "Some Parallels," 60–78.
125 For the palmette design in Japan, see Hayashi, ibid., 205–24.
126 This imagery also is found on the engraved sarcophagus from the Northern Wei period in the Minneapolis Institute of Art. See Wang, "Coffins and Confucianism."
127 Further evidence that Japanese representations of the celestial realm included auspicious clouds, celestial beings, and fantastic animals is offered by the panel from the Tamamushi Shrine that bears depictions of the sun and moon. In addition to these two motifs, clouds, celestial flowers, celestial beings, transcendents riding flying beasts, three birds, and a heavenly horse surround Mount Sumeru (see the frontispiece to Chapter Three). See Uehara, *Tamamushi zushi no kenkyū*. As discussed in the section on "People," depictions of men and women involved in processions or gatherings likely were placed below imagery of the celestial realm.
128 In the reconstruction of the embroidered artifact (fig. 100), the figure emerging from the lotus has been overlapped with A-8 on panel 3.
129 For "birth by transformation in a lotus," see the following publications by Yoshimura Rei: "Unkō ni okeru renge keshō no hyōgen," in Yoshimura Rei, *Chūgoku bukkyō zuzō no kenkyū* (Tokyo: Tōhō Shoten, 1983), 35–53; "Unkō ni okeru renge sōshoku no igi," in Yoshimura, *Chūgoku bukkyō zuzō no kenkyū*, 55–73; "Kyōken sekkutsu"; "Nihon no bukkyō bijutsu to shiruku rōdo: Renge keshōzo no keifu," *Rekishi kōron* 12, no. 4 (1978): 130–37; and "Tenjukoku Shūchō."
130 For the Indian origins of the motif, see Yoshimura, "Nihon no bukkyō bijutsu," 130–32.
131 All of the different variations on this process as seen at Yungang are discussed in Yoshimura, "Unkō ni okeru renge keshō."
132 Ibid., 35. This translation is from Leon Hurvitz, trans., *Scripture of the Lotus Blossom of the Fine Dharma* (New York: Columbia University Press, 1976), 197–98. Italics have been added here for emphasis.
133 For a translation and comprehensive study of the three Amitābha sutras (including the *Sukhāvatīvyūha Sūtra*), see Luis O. Gómez, *The Land of Bliss: The Paradise of the Buddha of Measureless Light* (Honolulu: University of Hawai'i Press, 1996). This quote is found on page 187.
134 To support his idea, Yoshimura also has referred to the screen behind the Amida triad in the Tachibana Shrine at Hōryūji (early 8th century), where five figures are seated on open lotuses, with lotus flowers, lotus leaves, flaming lotuses, and a bud motif between them. Yoshimura, "Tenjukoku Shūchō," 8. In this case, the figures doubtless represent the beings born in the pond of Amida's Western Paradise.
135 Yoshimura, "Kyōken sekkutsu," 115–26.
136 Just below this register, a valance-like element consisting of a row of contiguous V-shaped designs with circles at the points is represented. This design is similar to those seen on the wooden canopies in Hōryūji's Golden Hall and the Tachibana Shrine. Wooden sculptures of auspicious birds and heavenly musicians with flowing scarves, seated on lotus flowers, are attached to the wooden canopies in the Golden Hall, likely representing the idea of the celestial realm. See NKH, *Hōryūji*, and Asahi Shinbunsha, *Kokuhō Hōryūji Kondō ten* (Tokyo: Asahi Shinbunsha, 2008), 102–13.
137 Yoshimura, "Nihon no bukkyō bijutsu," 136.
138 For a complete discussion of this tomb, see Nancy Steinhardt, "Changchuan Tomb No. 1 and Its North Asian Context," *Journal of East Asian Archaeology* 4, nos. 1, 2 (2003): 225–92.
139 Yoshimura, "Tenjukoku Shūchō," 8.
140 Ōhashi, *Tenjukoku Shūchō no kenkyū*, 112–15.
141 This reconstruction has been made by replicating and reversing the following designs: A-5, B-6, C-5, C-10, C-11, D-2, D-7, D-8, and D-9.
142 Among the designs that are difficult to identify, some appear to be foliage, such as A-9, B-1, and B-3. The remains of these motifs are not complete enough to propose any possible reconstruction. Similarly, the long and narrow curved piece in two colors (A-11) is reminiscent of the scarves of the heavenly figures on the Hōryūji embroidered banner, but it is risky to assert that similar figures were part of the Shūchō's composition.
143 Ōhashi, *Tenjukoku Shūchō no kenkyū*, 109–10.

2

1. *Jōgū Shōtoku hōō teisetsu* is reproduced in *DNBZ*, vol. 71 (Tokyo: Suzuki Gakujutsu Zaidan, 1972), 119–21. For versions with commentaries, see Ienaga Saburō, *Jōgū Shōtoku hōō teisetsu no kenkyū* (Tokyo: Sanseidō, 1972); and Ienaga Saburō et al., *Shōtoku Taishi shū* (Tokyo: Iwanami Shoten, 1975). The present study has made use of Okimori Takuya, *Jōgū Shōtoku hōō teisetsu: Chūshaku to kenkyū* (Tokyo: Yoshikawa Kōbunkan, 2005). For English translations, see William A. Deal, "Hagiography and History: The Image of Prince Shōtoku," in *Religions of Japan in Practice*, ed. George J. Tanabe (Princeton, NJ: Princeton University Press, 1999), 316–33; and John Bentley, *Historiographical Trends in Early Japan* (Lewiston, NY: Edwin Mellen Press, 2002), 103–16.

2. One of these documents is *Chūgūji engi: Chūgūji mandara ama Shinnyo kishō tō no koto* (The Chūgūji Account: About the Prayer of the Nun Shinnyo and the Mandara of Chūgūji), dated to 1274, which is discussed in detail in Chapter Four. The other is *Tenjukoku Mandara Shūchō engi kantenbun* (Annotated Tenjukoku Mandara Shūchō Account), written by Urabe Kanebumi (act. 13th century). Urabe analyzes the inscription by comparing its contents to *Nihon shoki*, *Kojiki*, *Shōtoku Taishi den*, and *Shinsen shōjiroku*. For a detailed study of the annotated version, see Iida Mizuho, "'Tenjukoku Mandara Shūchō engi kantenbun' ni tsuite," *Shoryōbu kiyō* 16 (1964): 41–59; and Nishizaki Tooru, "Shoryōbu zō 'Tenjukoku Mandara Shūchō engi kantenbun' shakubun narabi ni kenkyū," *Mukogawa kokubun* 67 (2006): 46–56. The inscription is also transcribed in documents compiled at Hōryūji between the sixteenth and nineteenth century, such as *Shōyoshō* (1547), *Hōryūji tōin engi narabi ni Chūgūji Tenjukoku Mandara meibun* (1737), and *Ikaruga koji binran* (or *benran*; 1836).

3. See Iida, ibid. See also Iida Mizuho, "Tenjukoku Shūchō mei o megutte," *Kobijutsu* 11 (1965): 39–49, and "Tenjukoku Shūchō mei no fukugen ni tsuite," *Chūō daigaku bungakubu kiyō shigakuka* 11 (1966): 23–43. These articles are also published in Iida Mizuho, *Shōtoku Taishi den no kenkyū*, vol. 1 of *Iida Mizuho chosakushū* (Tokyo: Yoshikawa Kōbunkan, 2000). For a comprehensive list of the documents in which a version of the inscription is recorded, see Iida, "Tenjukoku Mandara Shūchō," 43–49, and "Tenjukoku Shūchō mei no fukugen," 24–33.

4. For example, see Edwin A. Cranston, "Asuka and Nara Culture: Literacy, Literature and Music," in *The Cambridge History of Japan*, ed. John W. Hall et al., vol. 1 (Cambridge: Cambridge University Press, 1997), 453–86.

5. For the Seventeen-Article Constitution, see the *NS* entry for Suikō 12 (604)/4/3: Aston, *Nihongi*, part 2, 128–33; *NKBT*, vol. 68, 180–86. For the sutra lectures, see the *NS* entry for Suikō 14 (606)/7: Aston, *Nihongi*, part 2, 135; *NKBT*, vol. 68, 188. For the records, see the *NS* entry for Suikō 28 (620): Aston, *Nihongi*, part 2, 45; *NKBT*, vol. 68, 203.

6. This is recorded in *Hōryūji garan engi narabi ni ruki shizaichō* (Account of the Establishment of Hōryūji and List of Accumulated Treasures, 747). See *Hōryūji garan engi narabi ni ruki shizaichō*, in *HSS*, vol. 1 (Tokyo: Wakō Shuppan, 1985), 18–19.

7. For an English translation, see Miwa Stevenson, "The Founding of the Monastery Gangōji and a List of Its Treasures," in *Religions of Japan in Practice*, ed. George J. Tanabe (Princeton, NJ: Princeton University Press, 1999), 304. For an annotated Japanese-language version of *Gangōji engi*, see *Jisha engi*, ed. Sakurai Tokutarō et al. Nihon shisō taikei, vol. 20 (Tokyo: Iwanami Shoten, 1978).

8. Ōya Tōru, *Kana genryū kō*. For a good discussion in English of the contents and issues of these texts, see David B. Lurie, "The Origins of Writing in Early Japan: From the 1st to the 8th Century C.E." (Ph.D. dissertation, Columbia University, 2001), 399–422.

9. John Bentley, "The Origin of Man'yōgana," *Bulletin of the School of Oriental and African Studies* 64, no. 1 (2001): 59–73.

10. Ibid., 62–64.

11. Ibid., 71–72.

12. The number of works addressing the problems associated with these inscriptions is vast. For a detailed discussion of the issues with the Gangōji inscriptions, see Donald McCallum, *The Four Great Temples: Buddhist Archaeology, Architecture, and Icons of Seventh-Century Japan* (Honolulu: University of Hawai'i Press, 2009), 23–82.

13. Yoshida Kazuhiko, "'Gangōji garan engi narabi ni ruki shizaichō' no shinyōsei," in *Shōtoku Taishi no shinjitsu*, ed. Ōyama Seiichi (Tokyo: Heibonsha, 2004), 120–22.

14. David B. Lurie, *Realms of Literacy: Early Japan and the History of Writing* (Cambridge, MA: Harvard University Press, 2011).

15. Ibid., 68–120.

16. Ibid., 131–50.

17. David B. Lurie, "The Subterranean Archives of Early Japan: Recently Discovered Sources for the Study of Writing and Literacy," in *Books in Numbers*, ed. Wilt L. Idema (Cambridge, MA: Harvard-Yenching Library and Harvard University, 2007), 99–101.

18. Lurie, "Origins of Writing," 105. See also Bentley, "Origin of Man'yōgana."

19. For a detailed discussion of this issue, see Lurie, ibid., 235–42.

20. Lurie, *Realms of Literacy*, 88–104.

21. For the postscript, see Okimori, *Jōgū Shōtoku*, 107, 109.

22. For details on the dating of this manuscript to the mid-eleventh-century, see Ogino Minahiko, "*Hōō teisetsu* shosha nendai ni kansuru shin shiryō," in Ogino Minahiko, *Nihon komonjogaku to chūsei bunkashi* (Tokyo:

Yoshikawa Kōbunkan, 1995), 412–16. See also Ienaga et al., *Shōtoku Taishi shū*, 545–46. It seems that this document was taken to Chion'in in 1874 (Meiji 7); see Ienaga et al., *Shōtoku Taishi shū*, 147.

23 For a very readable chart listing the main differences, see Iida, "Tenjukoku Mandara Shūchō," 46.

24 Iida, "Tenjukoku Shūchō mei o megutte," 45–46.

25 Okimori Takuya, "Jōgū Shōtoku hōō teisetsu no man'yōgana hyōki," in Okimori, *Jōgū Shōtoku*, 168–69.

26 Okimori, *Jōgū Shōtoku*, 106–17. For a rendering in Classical Japanese, see Iida, "Tenjukoku Shūchō mei o megutte," 46–47. The rationale behind the arrangement of three turtles per column shown in figure 70 is discussed in Chapter Five.

27 In the surviving sections of a work of calligraphy (*kohitsugire*) attributed to Minamoto Kaneyuki (Heian period), each column contains twelve graphs from the Shūchō inscription. A total of eight columns (ninety-six graphs) survives. Judging by the style of the writing, this piece of calligraphy has been dated to the early Kamakura period. See Tanaka Toyozō, "Tenjukoku Shūchō engi bun ihon no danpen," *Gasetsu* 4, no. 7 (1940): 583–92. If the dating of these calligraphy pieces is correct, it is possible that the Shūchō inscription—or the *Imperial Biography* document—was circulating before the discovery of the Shūchō in the late thirteenth century. For a discussion of this possibility, see Hayashi Mikiya, "Tenjukoku Shūchō ni kansuru ichi, ni no mondai," *Shigaku zasshi* 66, no. 9 (1957): 44–54. For a photograph of the calligraphy, see Iida, ibid., 44.

28 Hoida Tadatomo, *Kanko zatsujō*, *NKZ*, ed. Yosano Hiroshi et al., vol. 3 (Tokyo: Nihon Koten Zenshū Kankōkai, 1928). See also http://kindai.ndl.go.jp/info:ndljp/pid/1051975 (last accessed December 23, 2015). For more on this text, see Chapter Five.

29 *Tenka*, meaning "all under heaven," was the name of a specific and unique polity, an empire that included satellite, tribute-paying border kingdoms. Ooms, *Imperial Politics*, 36.

30 In *NS*, Kitashi hime is not Kinmei's Senior Queen Consort, but is listed as the third of five concubines. *NS* entry for Kinmei 2 (541)/3: Aston, *Nihongi*, part 2, 39–41; *NKBT*, vol. 68, 64–66. Her status was probably elevated when she was reburied with Kinmei in 612. *NS* entry for Suiko 20/2/28: Aston, *Nihongi*, part 2, 143; *NKBT*, vol. 68, 196. See Kondō Ariyoshi, "Tenjukoku Shūchō no seisaku jiki ni tsuite: Shūchō meibun ni yoru kentō," *Bijutsushi kenkyū* 47 (2009): 131–48.

31 Translations of royal and aristocratic titles are from the glossary in Joan Piggott, *The Emergence of Japanese Kingship* (Stanford, CA: Stanford University Press, 1997), 305–29.

32 For a discussion about the use of *ōkimi* to refer to Prince Toyotomimi and Prince Owari, and *hime miko* for Anahobe, see Nomiyama Yuka, "Tenjukoku Shūchō no seiritsu nendai ni tsuite," *Arena* 5 (2008): 250–58.

33 The term *minori*, or *hō*, is used to refer to the Buddhist Dharma, and also to the system of state law and imperial bureaucracy imported to Japan from Korea and China.

34 Okimori, *Jōgū Shōtoku*, 116–17.

35 Tōno Haruyuki, "Tennō gō no seiritsu nendai ni tsuite," in Tōno Haruyuki, *Shōsōin monjo to mokkan no kenkyū* (Tokyo: Hanawa Shobō, 1977), 410.

36 Wada Atsumu, "Wafū shigō no seiritsu to kōtōfu," in *Zemināru Nihon kodai shi ge*, ed. Ueda Masaaki et al. (Tokyo: Kōbunsha, 1980), 327–28.

37 Ōyama Seiichi, "Shōtoku Taishi no seiritsu to Ritsuryō kokka," in Ōyama Seiichi, *Nagayaōke mokkan to kinsekibun* (Tokyo: Yoshikawa Kōbunkan, 1998), 221.

38 *NS* entry for Yōmei 1 (586)/1/1: Aston, *Nihongi*, part 2, 107; *NKBT*, vol. 68, 155. Akiko Walley has suggested that Soga no Umako constructed the political persona of Prince Umayado as the Dharma King and that the inscription on the mandorla of the Shaka triad at Hōryūji is the earliest textual evidence of this construction. Walley, *Constructing the Dharma King*, 1-15 and 109-124.

39 *Hōryūji garan engi*, 8.

40 Okimori, *Jōgū Shōtoku*, 81.

41 Ōyama, "Shōtoku Taishi no seiritsu," 269.

42 This ability is listed in the entry corresponding to the day on which the prince was appointed Prince Imperial (*kōtaishi*). *NS* entry for Suiko 1 (593)/4/10: Aston, *Nihongi*, part 2, 122; *NKBT*, vol. 68, 173.

43 Shinkawa, *Shōtoku Taishi no rekishigaku*, 22–23.

44 In *Kojiki*, Shōtoku is called Prince Kamitsumiya Umayado Toyotomimi, but in *Nihon shoki*, different names are used in the twenty-two entries that refer to him. He is called Shōtoku only twice, as the husband of Uji no Kaidako, first daughter of Suiko (entry for Bidatsu 3/3/10); and in the genealogy of Princess Anahobe Hashihito and Great King Yōmei (entry for Yōmei 1 (586)/1/1), where all of his names are listed. He is referred to as Prince Umayado in the battle against the anti-Buddhist faction at court, the Mononobe (Sujun 1/7), but called Prince Umayado Toyotomimi when he is appointed Crown Prince by Great King Suiko (Suiko 1 (593)/4/10), with his extraordinary virtues listed. After this entry, in those that record his political and religious activities, he simply is called Crown Prince. He is referred to again as Prince Umayado Toyotomimi in the entry corresponding to his death (Suiko 29 (621)/2/5), and as Prince Kamitsumiya in the entry about his burial (Suiko 29/2).

45 *NS* entry for Bidatsu 5/3/10: Aston, *Nihongi*, part 2, 95; *NKBT*, vol. 68, 140.

46 Okimori, *Jōgū Shōtoku*, 67–72. For more on the prince's wives, see Maekawa Akihisa, "Shōtoku Taishi kisaki jūdai no shiteki haikei," Chapter 1 of Maekawa Akihisa,

Nihon kodai seiji no tenkai (Tokyo: Hōsei Daigaku Shuppankyoku, 1991), 3–16; and Takioto Yoshiyuki, "Shōtoku Taishi no tsumatachi," in *Shōtoku Taishi jiten*, ed. Mayuzumi Hiromichi and Takemitsu Makoto (Tokyo: Shin Jinbutsu Ōraisha, 1991), 80–84.

47 Ōyama Seiichi, "'Jōgūki' no seiritsu," in *Shōtoku Taishi no shinjitsu*, ed. Ōyama, 146–47.

48 Takioto, "Shōtoku Taishi," 80.

49 Maeda Haruto, "Kashiwade uji," in *Shōtoku Taishi jiten*, ed. Mayuzumi and Takemitsu, 214–17. Under the Baekje administrative system established in the Yamato court in the late fifth century, the *tomo no miyatsuko* were service functionaries in charge of the *be* or *tomo*, groups that provided services to the court. Gina L. Barnes, "The Role of the *Be* in the Formation of the Yamato State," in *Specialization, Exchange, and Complex Societies*, ed. Elizabeth M. Brumfiel and Timothy K. Earle (Cambridge and New York: Cambridge University Press, 1987), 87–89.

50 NS entries for Kinmei 31/5 and Sushun 1/7: Aston, *Nihongi*, part 2, 88, 113; *NKBT*, vol. 68, 128, 162. The Soga–Mononobe conflict, a political and military dispute of some three decades between the pro-Buddhist Soga clan and pro-Shinto Mononobe, supposedly culminated in 587 with a Soga victory in a decisive battle near Mount Shigi (Nara Prefecture).

51 For the Kashiwade, see Ishida Hisatoyo, ed., *Shōtoku Taishi jiten* (Tokyo: Kashiwa Shobō, 1997), s.v. "Kashiwade uji."

52 Tamura Enchō, *Kodai Chōsen bukkyō to Nihon bukkyō* (Tokyo: Yoshikawa Kōbunkan, 1980), 145–47.

53 See Okimori, *Jōgū Shōtoku*, 98.

54 Ibid., 104–5. For the issues surrounding the identification of the consort, see Inoue Kazutoshi, "Hōryūji Kondō Shaka sanzonzō kōhai mei o yomu," *Bunka shigaku* 62 (2006): 1–24.

55 Takioto, "Shōtoku Taishi," 84.

56 For the genealogy in *Jōgūki* (Record of the Prince of the Upper Palace; 7th century), see Ōyama, ed., *Shōtoku Taishi no shinjitsu*, 136; and for the *Imperial Biography*'s genealogy, see Okimori, *Jōgū Shōtoku*, 67. For the Inabe, see Saeki Arikiyo, ed., *Nihon kodai shizoku jiten* (Tokyo: Yūzankaku, 1994), s.v. "Inabe." Hirano Kunio has argued that Inabe was added to the princess's name likely because a member of the group might have been her wet nurse, or perhaps because some blood relation between the princess and the group existed. He also has stated that it is significant that the Hata, another immigrant clan from the continent, and the Inabe lived near each other. See Hirano Kunio, "Hata-shi no kenkyū," *Shigaku zasshi* 70, no. 3 (1961): 37–38. Michael Como has used Hirano's interpretations to support his theory that the Hata were involved in the creation of the Tenjukoku concept. Como, *Shōtoku*, 48.

57 Kumagai Kimio, "Tennō no shutsugen," in Kumagai Kimio, *Ōkimi kara tennō e* (Tokyo: Kōdansha, 2001), 337.

58 Herman Ooms has demonstrated that this new concept of rulership was rooted in Daoist beliefs. See Ooms, *Imperial Politics*, 154–56. See also Senda Minoru, "'Tennō' gō seiritsu Suiko chō setsu no keifu: Mō hitotsu no Yamataikoku ronsōteki jōkyō," *Nihon kenkyū* 35 (2007): 405–6.

59 Senda, ibid., 406–8.

60 Tsuda Sōkichi, "Tennō kō," in Tsuda Sōkichi, *Nihon jōdaishi no kenkyū* (Tokyo: Iwanami Shoten, 1949), 474–91. First published in *Tōyō gakuhō* (1920).

61 Fukuyama Toshio, "Hōryūji no kinsekibun ni kansuru ni, san no mondai," *Yumedono* 13 (1935): 48–57.

62 NS entry for Tenmu 9/11/12: Aston, *Nihongi*, part 2, 348; *NKBT*, vol. 68, 444. For Yakushiji, see McCallum, *Four Great Temples*, 201–36. On Yakushi belief, see Suzuki, *Medicine Master Buddha*.

63 Seiichi Mizuno, *Asuka Buddhist Art: Hōryūji*, trans. Richard L. Gage (New York and Tokyo: Weatherhill/Heibonsha, 1974), 30–39.

64 For a detailed discussion of the discovered *mokkan*, see Masuo Shin'ichirō, "Tennō gō no seiritsu to Higashi Ajia," in *Shōtoku Taishi no shinjitsu*, ed. Ōyama, 47.

65 Tōno, "Tennō gō no seiritsu," 404–9.

66 Hayashi Mikiya, "Jōdai no tennō no yobina," *Shikan* 45 (1955): 32–44.

67 Iida Mizuho, "Tenjukoku Shūchō to Asuka bukkyō," in *Ronshō Nihon bukkyō shi*, ed. Kawagishi Kokyō (Tokyo: Yūzankaku Shuppan, 1989), 190.

68 For *mogari*, see Wada Atsumu, "Mogari no kisoteki kōsatsu," in *Shumatsuki kofun: Ronshū*, ed. Mori Kōichi (Tokyo: Hanawa Shobō, 1973), 285–386; François Macé, *La Mort et les Funérailles dans le Japon Ancien* (Paris: Publications Orientalistes de France, 1986); and Gary L. Ebersole, *Ritual Poetry and the Politics of Death in Early Japan* (Princeton, NJ: Princeton University Press, 1989), 123–215. This topic is discussed in further detail in Chapter Three.

69 Wada, ibid., 332–33.

70 Yamada Hideo, "Kodai tennō no okurina ni tsuite," in Yamada Hideo, *Nihon kodaishi kō* (Tokyo: Iwanami Shoten, 1987), 125–26.

71 Okimori, *Jōgū Shōtoku*, 166–67.

72 For texts of the inscriptions in *Gangōji engi*, see *Jisha engi*, 19–21, 332–33. For a translation of the finial inscription, see Stevenson, "Founding," 314–15. For a discussion of the issues with *Gangōji engi*, see McCallum, *Four Great Temples*, 32–40.

73 McCallum, ibid., 35.

74 Sema Masayuki, "Suiko chō ibun no saikentō," in *Shōtoku Taishi no shinjitsu*, ed. Ōyama, 82.

75 Ibid., 84–89.

76 Yoshida Kazuhiko, "Tenjukoku Mandara Shūchō meibun no jinmei hyōki," *Arena* 5 (2008): 238–39.
77 The commentaries on the Shūchō inscription in the *Imperial Biography* explain the readings of these two graphs. Okimori, *Jōgū Shōtoku*, 116.
78 Yoshida, "Tenjukoku Mandara Shūchō," 242–47.
79 Saeki, ed., *Nihon kodai shizoku jiten*, s.v. "Fumibe."
80 For the role played by craftsmen and priests from Baekje in the construction of Asukadera (Gangōji), see McCallum, *Four Great Temples*, 40–42.
81 NS entry for Suiko 29/5/2: Aston, *Nihongi*, part 2, 148; *NKBT*, vol. 68, 204.
82 Ōyama, "Shōtoku Taishi no seiritsu," 296–301.
83 Kariya Ekisai and Hoida Tadatomo, scholars who lived during the Edo period, had already noticed this discrepancy. See Miyata Toshihiko, "Tenjukoku Shūchō mei seiritsu shikō," *Shigaku zasshi* 47, no. 7 (1936): 913.
84 Ibid., 925.
85 Iida, "Tenjukoku Shūchō mei o megutte," 47. No information about this calendrical system has been found by the present author.
86 NS entry for Jitō 4/11/11: Aston, *Nihongi*, part 2, 400; *NKBT*, vol. 68, 506. The Yuanjia calendar was created in 443 in South China during the Liu Song dynasty (421–79) and transmitted through Baekje; the Yifeng calendar was created during China's Tang dynasty in 665, and transmitted to Silla in the Yifeng era (676–78).
87 For a detailed explanation of his calculations, see Kanazawa Hideyuki, "Tenjukoku Shūchō mei no seiritsu nendai ni tsuite: Gihōreki ni yoru keisan kekka kara," *Kokugo to kokubungaku* 78, no. 11 (2001): 37–38.
88 Ibid., 40–41.
89 For examples, see Miyata, "Tenjukoku Shūchō mei seiritsu," 910–27; and Fukui, "Tenjukoku Mandara," 131.
90 Iida, "Tenjukoku Shucho mei no fukugen," 41.
91 Ibid.
92 For use of the term *dharma* in Daoism, see Livia Kohn, "Steal Holy Food and Come Back as a Viper: Conceptions of Karma and Rebirth in Medieval Daoism," *Early Medieval China* 4 (1998): 14.
93 This portion of the inscription is discussed in further detail in Chapter Three.
94 Yoshie Akiko, "Tenjukoku Shūchō mei keifu no ikkosatsu," *Nihon shi kenkyū* 325 (1989): 1–18; also published in Yoshie Akiko, *Nihon kodai keifu yōshiki ron* (Tokyo: Yoshikawa Kōbunkan, 2000). The latter publication includes Yoshie's response to her critics; see pages 85–86.
95 Yoshie, "Tenjukoku Shūchō," 5–6.
96 Ibid., 7–10. For a discussion of the role of the Soga kinship group, see McCallum, *Four Great Temples*, 23–29.
97 For a complete genealogical chart, see Ishida, ed., *Shōtoku Taishi jiten*, 269ff.
98 Yoshie, "Tenjukoku Shūchō," 12–13.
99 Ōhashi Katsuaki, "Tenjukoku Shūchō no seisaku nendai ni tsuite," *Nanto bukkyō* 70 (1994): 43.
100 Ōyama, "Shōtoku Taishi no seiritsu," 309–25. Yoshie does not agree with Ōyama's arguments. To further support her own position, she has explained that the format "A takes B as a wife, and C is born" developed later than the genealogies recorded in the *Imperial Biography* and *Kojiki*, but earlier than *Jōgūki*, another of the Remnant Texts, no longer extant, but partially quoted in the thirteenth-century *Shaku Nihongi* (an annotated version of *Nihon shoki*) by Urabe Kanekata. Yoshie, *Nihon kodai keifu*, 89.
101 NS entry for Kōgyoku 2/11: Aston, *Nihongi*, part 2, 183; *NKBT*, vol. 68, 252.
102 *Shōtoku Taishi denryaku*, in *STZ*, vol. 2, 116–17.
103 Yoshie Akiko, "Gender in Early Classical Japan: Marriage, Leadership, and Political Status in Village and Palace," *Monumenta Nipponica* 60, no. 4 (2005): 442–43.
104 Ibid., 467.
105 NS entry for Kōgyoku 4/6/12 and 13: Aston, *Nihongi*, part 2, 191–94; *NKBT*, vol. 68, 262–66.
106 A genealogical chart of the Soga clan may be found in Mayuzumi Hiromichi, "Kodai kokka to Soga-shi," in *Soga-shi to kodai kokka*, ed. Mayuzumi Hiromichi (Tokyo: Yoshikawa Kōbunkan, 1991), 6–7.
107 NS entry for Kōtoku, Taika 1/7/2: Aston, *Nihongi*, part 2, 198; *NKBT*, vol. 68, 270–71.
108 NS entries for Tenji 7/2/23 and Tenmu 2/2/27: Aston, *Nihongi*, part 2, 287–88, 321; *NKBT*, vol. 68, 367–68, 410.
109 Mayuzumi, "Kodai kokka to Soga-shi," 8–11.
110 Katō Kenkichi, *Hata-shi to sono tami: Torai shizoku no jitsuzō* (Tokyo: Hakusuisha, 1998), 8.
111 The people who came across the sea and settled in the islands are known as *toraijin*, translated as "immigrants." Immigrants from the Korean peninsula were called *kikajin* in the Japanese court. This is a politically charged term, as it denoted a person who became civilized by emigrating to the realm of a *tennō* and becoming a subject. Joan R. Piggott, ed., *Capital and Countryside in Japan, 300–1180: Japanese Historians in English* (Ithaca, NY: Cornell University, 2006), 428. The term "allochthons" is used by Ooms, *Imperial Politics*.
112 NS entries for Kōtoku 4/6 and Saimei 5/7/15: Aston, *Nihongi*, part 2, 244, 263; *NKBT*, vol. 68, 320, 341.
113 Michael Como discusses the role of the Hata in the Nara and Heian periods. See Michael Como, "Immigrant Gods and the Road to Shindō," in Como, *Weaving and Binding*, 1–24.
114 For a detailed discussion of the Aya kinship group, see Katō Kenkichi, *Yamato seiken to kodai shizoku* (Tokyo: Yoshikawa Kōbunkan, 1991), 196–204. For the Hata, see Hirano, "Hata-shi no kenkyū"; and Katō, *Hata-shi to sono tami*.
115 Katō, *Hata-shi to sono tami*, 216–17.

116 Seki Akira, *Kodai no kikajin*, Seki Akira chosakushū, vol. 3 (Tokyo: Yoshikawa Kōbunkan, 1996), 70–71. For an account in English about the Hata and their association with silk and weaving, see Como, *Weaving and Binding*, 139–45.

117 For the Hata and Aya in *Kogoshūi*, see the English translation by Bentley, *Historiographical Trends*, 84–85.

118 *NS* entry for Ōjin 14/2: Aston, *Nihongi*, part 1, 261; *NKBT*, vol. 67, 370. See also Seki, *Kodai no kikajin*, 67–70.

119 See Katō, *Hata-shi to sono tami*, 165–74.

120 *Kabane* are noble titles granted by the Yamato rulers. More than thirty *kabane* were used in premodern Japan. These titles, such as *omi*, *muraji*, *sukune*, *miyatsuko*, *kimi*, *atai*, and *obito*, generally are not translatable. The titles were inherited by the descendants of the original recipient. See Piggott, *Emergence of Japanese Kingship*, 314.

121 *NS* entries for Yūryaku 15, 16/7: Aston, *Nihongi*, part 1, 364–65; *NKBT*, vol. 67, 493–94.

122 Seki has argued that perhaps the Hata brought weaving technology to Japan, but over time, this technology became common knowledge, and their role as *miyatsuko* of weaving was no longer needed. Seki, *Kodai no kikajin*, 77.

123 Bentley, *Historiographical Trends*, 85.

124 Katō, *Hata-shi to sono tami*, 63–69. *Kura* can be written using the graphs 椋, 蔵, or 倉.

125 Tsude Hiroshi, "Goseki no Naniwa to Hōenzaka iseki," in *Kura to kodai ōken*, ed. Naoki Kōjirō and Ogasawara Yoshihiko (Kyoto: Mineruva Shobō, 1991), 47–64.

126 Katō, *Hata-shi to sono tami*, 63–69.

127 The Three Han, or Samhan, were loose confederacies of the Proto–Three Kingdoms period (1st–3rd centuries). See Ki-baik Lee, *A New History of Korea*, trans. Edward W. Wagner and Edward J. Shultz (Cambridge, MA: Harvard University Press, 1984), 24–26.

128 Bentley, *Historiographical Trends*, 85.

129 *NS* entry for Yūryaku 7/8: Aston, *Nihongi*, part 1, 350; *NKBT*, vol. 67, 472–74.

130 *NS* entry for Yūryaku 16/10: Aston, *Nihongi*, part 1, 365; *NKBT*, vol. 67, 494.

131 *NS* entry for Ōjin 14/2: Aston, *Nihongi*, part 1, 261; *NKBT*, vol. 67, 370.

132 For the arrival of Achi no Omi and Tsuka no Omi, see the *NS* entry for Ōjin 20/9: Aston, *Nihongi*, part 1, 264–65; *NKBT*, vol. 67, 374.

133 *NS* entries from Ōjin 37/2/1 to Ōjin 41/2/15: Aston, *Nihongi*, part 1, 269–71; *NKBT*, vol. 67, 378–81.

134 *NS* entries for Yūryaku 10/9/4, 12/4/4, 14/1/13: Aston, *Nihongi*, part 1, 358–63; *NKBT*, vol. 67, 486–92.

135 Barnes, "Role of the *Be*," 94.

136 *NS* entry for Suiko 16/9/11: Aston, *Nihongi*, part 2, 139; *NKBT*, vol. 68, 192. The Aya who returned from China are discussed in Chapter Three.

137 *NS* entry for Sushun 5/10/4: Aston, *Nihongi*, part 2, 119–20; *NKBT*, vol. 68, 170.

138 *NS* entry for Kōgyoku 3/11: Aston, *Nihongi*, part 2, 189–90; *NKBT*, vol. 68, 259–60.

139 *NS* entry for Kōgyoku 4: Aston, *Nihongi*, part 2, 191–93; *NKBT*, vol. 68, 264.

140 *NS* entry for Tenmu 6/6: Aston, *Nihongi*, part 2, 336–37; *NKBT*, vol. 68, 428–29.

141 *NS* entry for Kōtoku 2/1/1: Aston, *Nihongi*, part 2, 209; *NKBT*, vol. 68, 282.

142 *NS* entry for Sushun 1/3: Aston, *Nihongi*, part 2, 118; *NKBT*, vol. 68, 167–68.

143 Ienaga, *Jōgū Shōtoku hōō teisetsu*, and Ienaga et al., *Shōtoku Taishi shū*.

144 The dates proposed in Ienaga's earlier publication, *Jōgū Shōtoku hōō teisetsu*, are slightly different from those given in his later publication, *Shōtoku Taishi shū*. See Ienaga, *Jōgū Shōtoku hōō teisetsu*, 77, and Ienaga et al., *Shōtoku Taishi shū*, 549–50. The dates in the later publication seem more acceptable.

145 For a short description of the contents of the *Imperial Biography*, see Matsuo Hikaru, "Shōtoku Taishi no denki," in Mayuzumi and Makoto, *Shōtoku Taishi jiten*, 292.

146 For *Jōgū Shōtoku Taishi den hoketsuki*, see vol. 2 of *STZ*, 55–62. For the passage about Shōtoku's death, see page 59.

147 Ienaga, *Jōgū Shōtoku hōō teisetsu*, 97–109. Kenshin is discussed in Chapter Four.

148 For the two commentaries, see Okimori, *Jōgū Shōtoku*, 101–6. For an English translation, see Bentley, *Historiographical Trends*, 107–10.

149 The continental elements of the Shūchō's iconography are discussed in Chapter One.

3

1 *Shūbutsu* literally means "embroidered Buddha."

2 *NS* entry for Suiko 16/8/3: Aston, *Nihongi*, part 2, 138; *NKBT*, vol. 68, 192.

3 *NS* entry for Tenmu 10/4/2: Aston, *Nihongi*, part 2, 350; *NKBT*, vol. 68, 446.

4 For a detailed discussion of the meaning of colors in East Asia, see Mary Dusenbury, "Introduction" and "Color at the Japanese Court in the Asuka and Nara Periods," and Monica Bethe, "Color in the *Man'yōshū*, an Eighth-Century Anthology of Japanese Poetry," in *Color in Ancient and Medieval East Asia*, ed. Mary Dusenbury (Lawrence, KS: Spencer Museum of Art, 2015), 11–15, 123–33, 135–42.

5 *NS* entries for Taika 3/12, Taika 5/2, and Tenchi 3/2/9: Aston, *Nihongi*, part 2, 228–29, 231, 280–81; *NKBT*, vol. 68, 303–4, 306, 360. For a handy chart of the ranking systems recorded in *Nihon shoki*, see Piggott, *Emergence of Japanese Kingship*, 86. See also Dusenbury, "Color at the Japanese Court."

6 Buddhist images made with needlework are known as *shūbutsu*. For *shūbutsu*, see NKH, *Shūbutsu*; Morita Kimio, *Shishū*, Nihon no bijutsu, no. 59 (Tokyo: Shibundō, 1971); and Itō, *Shūbutsu*.

7 For a complete account of the Four Great Temples, see McCallum, *Four Great Temples*.

8 *NS* entry for Suiko 13/4/1: Aston, *Nihongi*, part 2, 133; *NKBT*, vol. 68, 186.

9 *NS* entry for Suiko 14/4/8: Aston, *Nihongi*, part 2, 134; *NKBT*, vol. 68, 186.

10 For a discussion of the Asukadera icons, see McCallum, *Four Great Temples*, 68–80.

11 *NS* entry for Taika 1/8/8: Aston, *Nihongi*, part 2, 202–3; *NKBT*, vol. 68, 276.

12 For Kudara Ōdera, see McCallum, *Four Great Temples*, 81–153.

13 *NS* entry for Hakuchi 1/10: Aston, *Nihongi*, part 2, 240; *NKBT*, vol. 68, 316. For the Eight Classes of Beings, see Sawa Ryūken, *Butsuzō zuten* (Tokyo: Yoshikawa Kōbunkan, 1962), 126.

14 The appointment of the Ten Monks is recorded in the *NS* entry for Taika 1/8/8: Aston, *Nihongi*, part 2, 203; *NKBT*, vol. 68, 276. Among them, the monk Emyō was appointed head of Kudara Ōdera. For the dedication of the embroidery, see the *NS* entry for Hakuchi 2/3/14: Aston, *Nihongi*, part 2, 240; *NKBT*, vol. 68, 316.

15 *Daianji engi narabi ni ruki shizaichō*, in *Daianji shi shiryō*, ed. Daianji Shi Henshū Iinkai (Nara: Daianji, 1984), 541–69.

16 Mizuno Ryūtarō, "Daianji engi narabi ni ruki shizaichō ni tsuite," in *Daianji shi shiryō*, ibid., 670. See also McCallum, *Four Great Temples*, 146–47.

17 Mizuno, ibid., 673. For the ceremony, see the *NS* entry for Shuchō 1/8/2: Aston, *Nihongi*, part 2, 379; *NKBT*, vol. 68, 480.

18 Mizuno, ibid., 674. For the sutra lectures, see the *NS* entry for Jitō 7/10: Aston, *Nihongi*, part 2, 413; *NKBT*, vol. 68, 522.

19 Mizuno, ibid.

20 The date of compilation of *Yakushiji engi* is unknown. *Kokushi daijiten*, s.v. "Yakushiji engi," http://japanknowledge.com/lib/display/?lid=30010zz478050 (last accessed December 26, 2014).

21 See *Yakushiji shiryō shū: Yakushiji engi*, in *Kokan bijutsu shiryō: Jiin hen*, ed. Fujita Tsuneyo, vol. 2 (Tokyo: Chūō Kōron, 1999), 138. Among the many versions of this *engi*, the one that contains this information is *Yakushiji shiryō shū*; see *NRT*, vol. 6, 8. See also McCallum, *Four Great Temples*, 232–34.

22 As cited by Morita, *Shishū*, 25.

23 *Shichidaiji nikki*, in *DNBZ*, vol. 83, 362a, b; Itō, *Shūbutsu*, 22.

24 Itō, ibid., 23–25. Itō only lists four references to Heian-period embroideries.

25 Ishida Mosaku, "Nihon bukkyō to shūbutsu," in NKH, *Shūbutsu*, 4–5.

26 Hida, "Kajūji shūbutsu saikō."

27 The sizes of the rulers preserved in the Shōsōin and Hōryūji collections range between 29.5 and 30.2 centimeters per *shaku*. Rulers are discussed further in Chapter Five.

28 Arai Hiroshi, *Maboroshi no kodaijaku: Komajaku wa nakatta* (Tokyo: Yoshikawa Kōbunkan, 1992). Arai's research is discussed in detail in Chapter Five.

29 *NS* entry for Taika 2/8/14: Aston, *Nihongi*, part 2, 224; *NKBT*, vol. 68, 298.

30 NBK and Asahi Shinbunsha, *Asuka Fujiwara-kyō ten: Kodai ritsuryō kokka no sōzō* (Osaka: Asahi Shinbunsha, 2002), 98–117.

31 The catalogue of this exhibition is NKH, *Shūbutsu*.

32 For an example of this viewpoint, see NKH, *Bukkyō kōgei no bi* (Nara: Nara Kokuritsu Hakubutsukan, 1982), 19.

33 The Tenjukoku Shūchō Mandara was included in the first art-historical account published in French by the Commission Impériale du Japon a l'Exposition Universelle de Paris. The assemblage was identified as *rideau brodé* (embroidered curtain). See Commission Impériale du Japon a l'Exposition Universelle de Paris, *Histoire de l'Art du Japon* (Paris: Maurice Brunoff, 1900), 47.

34 Ōhashi's theory that the Shūchō served as curtains was first published in his "Tenjukoku Shūchō no genkei," 70–75. See also Ōhashi, *Tenjukoku Shūchō no kenkyū*, 96–101.

35 *NS* entry for Richū 1: Aston, *Nihongi*, part 1, 301; *NKBT*, vol. 67, 418. Aston refers to the bed as a "jewel-couch."

36 *NS* entry for Kinmei 23/8: Aston, *Nihongi*, part 2, 86; *NKBT*, vol. 68, 126. Aston translates this item as "curtains of seven-fold woof."

37 An entry in *NS* refers to curtains among offerings of Buddhist paraphernalia. See the *NS* entry for Jitō 3/7/1: Aston, *Nihongi*, part 2, 393; *NKBT*, vol. 68, 498.

38 See the *NS* entries for Keitai 9/4/6 and Saimei 2/9: Aston, *Nihongi*, part 2, 14, 250; *NKBT*, vol. 68, 32, 328.

39 For the regulations, see the *NS* entry for Kōtoku 2/2/22: Aston, *Nihongi*, part 2, 217–20; *NKBT*, vol. 68, 292–94.

40 Chari Pradel, "The Tenjukoku Shūchō Mandara: Reconstruction of the Iconography and Ritual Context," in *Images in Asian Religions: Texts and Contexts*, ed. Phyllis Granoff and Koichi Shinohara (Vancouver and Toronto: University of British Columbia Press, 2004), 257–89. For a similar theory, see Kita Kasuhiro, "Tenjukoku Shūchō meibun saidoku: Tachibana Ōiratsume to mogari no miya no ichō," *Bunka shigaku* 62 (2006): 25–45.

41 In Japan, metal fittings have been found in tombs dated to the seventh century in Chiba and Gunma Prefectures. In Korea, nails have been found in the walls of Songsanri Tomb No. 1 from Baekje, located in Gongju, near the famous tomb of King Muryeong. Sugetani Fuminori, "Yokoanashiki sekishitsu no naibu: Tengai to suichō," *Kodaigaku kenkyū* 59 (1971): 23–29.

42 As mentioned in Chapter One, this tomb is dated to 168 BCE. For the Mawangdui tombs, see Hunan Provincial Museum and Institute of Archaeology, *The Han Tomb*

43 For a complete discussion of "spirit seats" and ancient Chinese afterlife beliefs, see Wu, *Art of the Yellow Springs*, 63–84.

44 For the tomb at Mancheng, see Institute of Archaeology, CASS, and the Hopei CPAM, *Mancheng Han mu fa jue bao gao* (Beijing: Wen wu chu ban she, 1980), 160–78. See also Wu Hung, *Monumentality in Early Chinese Art and Architecture* (Stanford, CA: Stanford University Press, 1995), 132–33.

45 Wu, *Art of the Yellow Springs*, 67.

46 Ibid., 68–84.

47 Ibid., 64.

48 Fan Ye, *Hou Han shu* (Beijing: Zhonghua shu ju, 1973), 3195. Other than the *Shūchō*'s inscription, this is the only reference to the compound "embroidered curtains" discovered thus far in an ancient document.

49 A Han *chi* ruler in the Museum of Fine Arts, Boston, measures 0.2345 m. See F.S.K., "A Han Foot-Rule," *Bulletin of the Museum of Fine Arts* 28, no. 165 (1930): 8–9.

50 Wu, *Art of the Yellow Springs*, 64.

51 William Farris has asserted that the planning of capitals in Japan was based on Chinese models, particularly those found in *Zhou li* (Rites of Zhou; ca. 3rd century BCE), but that these models were not followed closely. Among the components omitted were the shrines dedicated to the ancestors of the ruling family and to the gods of the earth. Farris, *Sacred Texts and Buried Treasures*, 133.

52 NS entry for Jomei 1/1/4: Aston, *Nihongi*, part 2, 164, 161; NKBT, vol. 68, 226.

53 NS entries for Keitai 1/2/4, 7/12/8, and 24/2/1: Aston, *Nihongi*, part 2, 3, 12, 21; NKBT, vol. 68, 20–21, 30, 42.

54 For a comprehensive study of this festival in China, see Stephen Teiser, *The Ghost Festival in Medieval China* (Princeton, NJ: Princeton University Press, 1988).

55 NS entries for Suiko 14/4/8 and Saimei 3/7/15: Aston, *Nihongi*, part 2, 134, 251; NKBT, vol. 68, 186, 330.

56 NS entry for Saimei 5/7/15: Aston, *Nihongi*, part 2, 263; NKBT, vol. 68, 350.

57 *Hōryūji garan engi*, 42–43.

58 *Ikaruga koji binran*, in DNBZ, vol. 85, 140b. Among modern scholars, the first to research this issue was Kameda Tsutomu; see his "Chūgūji Tenjukoku Shūchō," in *Nihon kaigakan*, ed. Tanaka Ichimatsu et al., vol. 1 (Tokyo: Kōdansha, 1970), 143.

59 *Shōtoku Taishi denki*, in STZ, vol. 2, 444.

60 For the departure of this first envoy to China, see the NS entry for Suiko 16/9/11: Aston, *Nihongi*, part 2, 139; NKBT, vol. 68, 192.

61 It is believed that the monk Nichimon is also the monk known as Min.

62 For the return of the monk Min, see the NS entry for Jomei 4/8: Aston, *Nihongi*, part 2, 166; NKBT, vol. 68, 229. For the return of Takamuku and Shōan, see the NS entry for Jomei 12/10/11: Aston, *Nihongi*, part 2, 170; NKBT, vol. 68, 234. For the promotions of Min and Takamuku, see the NS entries for Kōtoku 1 and Taika 5/2: Aston, *Nihongi*, part 2, 197, 232; NKBT, vol. 68, 270, 308.

63 NS entry for Suiko 30/7: Aston, *Nihongi*, part 2, 149–50; in NKBT, the date is given as Suiko 31/7: NKBT, vol. 68, 205–6. *Nihon shoki* does not record the day that Enichi initially left for China, but he returned there in 629 and 654. NS entries for Jomei 2/8/5 and Hakuchi 5/2: Aston, *Nihongi*, part 2, 165, 245–46; NKBT, vol. 68, 228, 321.

64 Ute Engelhart, "Longevity Techniques and Chinese Medicine," in *Daoism Handbook*, ed. Livia Kohn, vol. 1 (Boston and Leiden: Brill, 2004), 75–108.

65 NS entries for Jomei 9/2/23 and 11/1/25: Aston, *Nihongi*, part 2, 167, 169; NKBT, vol. 68, 231, 233.

66 NS entry for Hakuchi 1/2/9: Aston, *Nihongi*, part 2, 236–37; NKBT, vol. 68, 312–13.

67 NS entries for Hakuchi 4/5/5 and 4/6: Aston, *Nihongi*, part 2, 244; NKBT, vol. 68, 319–20.

68 NS entry for Suiko 10/10: Aston, *Nihongi*, part 2, 126; NKBT, vol. 68, 178.

69 For more on omens and portents, see Ooms, *Imperial Politics*, 88–90. No specific references to Kwalluk as an omen reader are recorded. He is only mentioned twice in *Nihon shoki*: the entry about his arrival, and another relating his appointment as *sōjō* (senior prelate) in 623. For the latter, see the NS entry for Suiko 32/4: Aston, *Nihongi*, part 2, 152–53; NKBT, vol. 68, 208–10.

70 For Eon, see the NS entries for Jomei 12/5/5 and Hakuchi 3/4/15: Aston, *Nihongi*, part 2, 170, 241–42; NKBT, vol. 68, 234, 318.

71 NS entries for Suiko 34/5/20 and 36/3/7: Aston, *Nihongi*, part 2, 154–55; NKBT, vol. 68, 212–13.

72 For details about Umako, see McCallum, *Four Great Temples*, 18–29.

73 For Asukadera, see ibid., 23–82.

74 For the appointment of Prince Tamura, see the introductory section of Jomei's chronicles in NS: Aston, *Nihongi*, part 2, 157–64; NKBT, vol. 68, 216–27.

75 NS, Jomei chronicles: Aston, *Nihongi*, part 2, 157–70; NKBT, vol. 68, 227–35.

76 NS entry for Kōgyoku 1/12/30: Aston, *Nihongi*, part 2, 178; NKBT, vol. 68, 244.

77 Ooms, *Imperial Politics*, 145.

78 NS entry for Kōgyoku 1/12/30: Aston, *Nihongi*, part 2, 178; NKBT, vol. 68, 244.

79 NS entry for Kōgyoku 2/10/12: Aston, *Nihongi*, part 2, 181; NKBT, vol. 68, 249.

80 NS entries for Kōgyoku 2: Aston, *Nihongi*, part 2, 181–83; NKBT, vol. 68, 249–53.

81 *NS* entry for Kōgyoku 4/6: Aston, *Nihongi*, part 2, 190–93; *NKBT*, vol. 68, 261–64.

82 Aston, *Nihongi*, part 2, 161. See also the *NS* entry in Jomei's chronicles in *NKBT*, vol. 68, 222. In the *Imperial Biography*, Hatsuse 泊瀬 is recorded as Hase 長谷. See *NKBT*, vol. 68, 223n15.

83 Aston, *Nihongi*, part 2, 178. See also the *NS* entry for Kōgyoku 1/12/31 in *NKBT*, vol. 68, 244.

84 For a short discussion of these afterlife destinations, see François Macé, "Japanese Conceptions of the Afterlife," in *Asian Mythologies*, comp. Yves Bonnefoy (Chicago: The University of Chicago Press, 1993), 270–75.

85 Ooms, *Imperial Politics*, 132–53.

86 Ebersole, *Ritual Poetry*, 80–86.

87 *NS* entry for Suiko 29/2/5: Aston, *Nihongi*, part 2, 148–49; *NKBT*, vol. 68, 204.

88 For seventh-century inscribed icons, see NBK and Asuka Shiryōkan, *Asuka Hakuhō no zaimei kondōbutsu* (Kyoto: Dōhōsha, 1979).

89 我大王所告世間虛假唯佛是真玩味其法謂我大王應生於天壽國之中而彼國之形眼所圖看悕因圖像欲覩大王往生之狀 (or 位生之狀 or 住生之狀).

90 See Chapter Two, note 33.

91 For an example of this categorization, see Joji Okazaki, *Pure Land Buddhist Painting*, trans. Elizabeth ten Grotenhuis (Tokyo and New York: Kodansha International, 1977), 31–32.

92 Iida, "Tenjukoku Shūchō mei no fukugen," 41.

93 In Mahāyāna Buddhism (the form prevalent in East Asia), certain Buddhas reside in specific pure lands, which are described in the sutras. In light of the complexity of these textual descriptions, diagrams and paintings were created to render visually these unknown lands.

94 Barbara Ruch, "Coping with Death: Paradigms of Heaven and Hell and the Six Realms in Early Literature and Painting," in *Flowing Traces: Buddhism in the Literary and Visual Arts of Japan*, ed. James H. Sanford et al. (Princeton, NJ: Princeton University Press, 1992), 106–8.

95 Wu, *Art of the Yellow Springs*, 34–37.

96 Ibid., 53–63.

97 For a complete discussion of these iconographical elements, see "The Celestial Realm" in the section "Analysis of the Motifs on the Shūchō Fragments" in Chapter One.

98 *Shoku Nihongi*, vol. 12, 63, 75.

99 Excavations at a site known as Chongjisan, near the tomb of King Muryeong and his wife in South Chungcheong Province, suggest that this might have been the place for the temporary interment. See Kwon Oh Young, "The Influence of Recent Archaeological Discoveries on the Research of Paekche History," in *Early Korea*, vol. 1, *Reconsidering Early Korean History through Archeology*, ed. Mark Byington (Cambridge, MA: Early Korea Project, Korea Institute, Harvard University, 2008), 82–89.

100 The Chinese *bin* ritual is discussed in Wada, "Mogari no kisoteki kōsatsu," 290.

101 Ibid., 309–22.

102 *NS* entry for Bidatsu 14/8/15: Aston, *Nihongi*, part 2, 104–5; *NKBT*, vol. 68, 152.

103 *NS* entry for Suiko 36/4/16: Aston, *Nihongi*, part 2, 155–56; *NKBT*, vol. 68, 214.

104 *NS* entries for Jomei 13/10/9 and Kōgyoku 1: Aston, *Nihongi*, part 2, 170–73; *NKBT*, vol. 68, 234–38.

105 *NS* entry for Kōgyoku 1/12/13: Aston, *Nihongi*, part 2, 177; *NKBT*, vol. 68, 244.

106 For Tenmu's *mogari*, see the *NS* entries for Shuchō 1/9/9 to Jitō 2/9/5: Aston, *Nihongi*, part 2, 380–89; *NKBT*, vol. 68, 480–93.

107 See Yoshii Hideo, "The Influence of Baekje on Ancient Japan," *The International Journal of Korean Art and Archaeology* 1 (2007): 57.

108 Wada, "Mogari no kisoteki kōsatsu," 304–7; and Robert Borgen, "The Origins of the Sugawara: A History of the Haji Family," *Monumenta Nipponica* 30, no. 4 (1975): 405–22.

109 Borgen, ibid., 406.

110 *NS* entry for Suiko 11/2/4: Aston, *Nihongi*, part 2, 126–27; *NKBT*, vol. 68, 178–79.

111 *NS* entries for Kōgyoku 2/8/17 and Hakuchi 5/10/10: Aston, *Nihongi*, part 2, 180, 247; *NKBT*, vol. 68, 248, 322.

112 Wada, "Mogari no kisoteki kōsatsu," 305.

113 For the Daoist heavens, see Isabelle Robinet, "Shangqing—Highest Clarity," chapter 8 of *Daoism Handbook*, ed. Kohn, vol. 1, 214–16; and Yamada Toshiaki, "The Lingbao School," chapter 9 of *Daoism Handbook*, ed. Kohn, vol. 1, 246–47.

114 Evidence of the interaction between Buddhism and Daoism is not limited to textual material. Stone steles with Daoist subjects were produced in northern China due to the influence of Buddhist art. The subjects represented are Daoist, while the style is similar to that of Northern Wei Buddhist images. The inscriptions contain prayers for the dead, wishing that they may avoid rebirth as animals, ghosts, or in hell, and instead come back to life in heaven. The inscriptions also include statements about happiness and prosperity for the living and the imperial family. Stanley K. Abe, "Northern Wei Daoist Sculpture from Shaanxi Province," and Stephen Bokenkamp, "The Yao Boduo Stele as Evidence for the 'Dao-Buddhism' of the Early Lingbao Scriptures," *Cahiers d'Extrême Asie* 9, no. 2 (1996–97): 69–130 and 55–68, respectively.

115 Erik Zürcher, "Buddhist Influence on Early Taoism: A Survey of Scriptural Evidence," *T'oung Pao* 66, nos. 1, 3 (1980): 84–147.

116 See Kohn, "Steal Holy Food."

117 Livia Kohn, "Northern Celestial Masters," chapter 10 of *Daoism Handbook*, ed. Kohn, vol. 1, 302–3.

118 For a translation and comprehensive study of the Amitābha sutras, see Gómez, *Land of Bliss*.

119 Fukunaga Mitsuji, "Muryōjukyō to Dōkyō," in Fukunaga Mitsuji, *Dōkyō to kodai Nihon* (Kyoto: Jinbun Shoin, 1987), 224–47. Unfortunately, this study does not contain any references.

120 Ibid., 232.

121 Further research is needed regarding the term *jōdo* (pure land). Fukunaga has argued that the term is derived from *seijō no kokudo* (land of purity), a term associated with immortality beliefs. Luis Gómez, who translated the sutra from Sanskrit to English, agrees that the term *jōdo* might not reflect Buddhist ideas, but Chinese concepts. He has pointed out that the Sanskrit term *parisuddhabuddhaksetra*, which is the equivalent of *jōdo*, does not appear in the Sanskrit version of the sutra. Gómez, *Land of Bliss*, 320.

122 The *Medium-Length Agama Sutra* (S. *Madhyamāgama sūtra*; C. *Zhong ahan jing*; J. *Chūagongyō*) was translated from 397 to 398 by Gautama Samghadeva, and the *Connected Discourses* (S. *Samyuktāgama sūtra*; C. *Za ahan jing*; J. *Zōagongyō*) was translated from 435 to 443 by Gunabhadra. See Robert E. Buswell, Jr. and Donald S. Lopez, Jr., *The Princeton Dictionary of Buddhism* (Princeton, NJ: Princeton University Press, 2014), s.v. "Madhyamāgama" and "Samyuktāgama." The Maitreya sutras also were translated around this time.

123 Fukui, "Tenjukoku Mandara," 134-141. A similar conclusion has been drawn by Shigematsu Akihisa; see his *Nihon Jōdokyō seiritsu katei no kenkyū*.

124 The question of what is Daoist, and what is not, comprises an ongoing discussion in studies about Daoism. In Isabelle Robinet's opinion, "a way to define [Daoism's] boundaries is by means of the Taoist canon (Daozang). We could take it as axiomatic that all the texts in the canon are Taoist texts and must be a part of any history of Taoism." Robinet, *Taoism: Growth of a Religion*, 2. If this is the case, then *tianshou* could be a Daoist concept.

125 Kristopher Schipper and Franciscus Verellen, *The Taoist Canon: A Historical Canon to the Daozang*, vol. 1 (London and Chicago: University of Chicago Press, 2004), 277–80. For a comprehensive history and translation of the *Taiping jing*, see Barbara Hendrischke, *The Scripture on Great Peace: The Taiping Jing and the Beginnings of Daoism* (Berkeley, Los Angeles, and London: University of California Press, 2006).

126 Max Kaltenmark, "The Ideology of the T'ai-p'ing ching," in *Facets of Taoism: Essays in Chinese Religion*, ed. Holms Welch and Anna Seidel (New Haven and London: Yale University Press, 1979), 41–44.

127 Based on the translation by Hendrischke, *Scripture on Great Peace*, 177. Hendrischke does not explain her translation of "the neighborhood group of five" for the Chinese term *wushou* 仵壽. For the text in Chinese, see *Tai ping jing he jiao*, ed. Wang Ming (Beijing: Zhonghua shu ju, 1960), 464–65.

128 Hendrischke, ibid., 173.

129 For the role of immigrants in the transmission of Daoism to Japan, see Kohn, "Taoism in Japan." See also Shimode, "Toraijin no shinkō to Dōkyō."

130 Christine Mollier, *Buddhism and Taoism Face to Face: Scripture, Ritual and Iconographic Exchange in Medieval China* (Honolulu: University of Hawai'i Press, 2008).

131 Ibid., 100–133.

4

1 Lori Meeks has stated that this Amida triad belief at Shinaga began at Chūgūji, where it was created by nuns. She bases her argument on Hosokawa Ryōichi's analysis of *Chūgūji engi* (1463 version) and other documents associated with Shinnyo. Two versions of *Chūgūji engi* exist. The version mentioned previously in this study, dated to 1274, is attributed to the monk Jōen and titled *Chūgūji engi: Chūgūji mandara ama Shinnyo kishō tō no koto*; it may be found in *Fushimi no Miya ke Kujō ke kyūzō shoji engi shū. Zushoryō sōkan* (Tokyo: Kunaicho Shoryōbu, 1970). This text does not include a reference to the Shinaga Amida triad belief. The *engi* used by Hosokawa and Meeks is the longer version of 1463 written by the monk Tōrin; see *Chūgūji engi*, in *YKT*, ed. Ōta, vol. 1, 86–87. Lori Meeks, "In Her Likeness: Female Divinity and Leadership at Medieval Chūgūji," *Japanese Journal of Religious Studies* 34, no. 2 (2007): 351–92, and *Hokkeji*, 184–90, 291–98.

2 The Japanese "Amida" and the Chinese "Amituo" are both transliterations of the Sanskrit "Amita," the Buddha Measureless, who is known as Amitābha (J. Muryōkō), the Buddha of Measureless Light, and as Amitāyus (J. Muryōju), the Buddha of Measureless Lifespan. See Gómez, *Land of Bliss*, 282–83.

3 In 1929, Aizu Yaichi compiled a handy series of quotes from documents that refer to the Tenjukoku Shūchō Mandara. See Aizu Yaichi, "Chūgūji Mandara ni kansuru bunken," *Tōyō bijutsu* 1 (1929): 90–104. Although this compilation is useful for listing the documents in which the embroidery is mentioned, the information is limited to quotes.

4 For the Shōtoku cult, see Hayashi, *Taishi shinkō: Sono hassei to hatten*, and *Taishi shinkō no kenkyū*. For a discussion in English, see Carr, *Plotting the Prince*, 23–103.

5 For the proselytizing techniques used by devotional cults in the Kamakura period, see James H. Foard, "In Search of a Lost Reformation," *Japanese Journal of Religious Studies* 7, no. 4 (1980): 261–91.

6 NS entries for Sujun 1/7 and Suiko 1: Aston, *Nihongi*, part 2, 113–17, 123; *NKBT*, vol. 68, 162–66, 174.

7 For a brief history of Shitennōji, see *Shitennōji* (2008).

8 For a study on the origins of this narrative, see Sakakibara Fumiko, "*Shitennōji engi no seiritsu*," in *Shōtoku Taishi no shinjitsu*, ed. Ōyama, 356–59. The full title of the *engi* also may be read as *Arahakadera goshu in engi*.

9 See Ishida, ed., *Shōtoku Taishi jiten*, s.v. "Taishi miraiki."

10 Ono Kazuyuki, "Shōtoku Taishi bō no tenkai to Eifukuji no seiritsu," *Nihon shi kenkyū*, no. 342 (1991): 8–9.

11 For a comprehensive study in English of Zenkōji and the cult of its Amida triad, see Donald McCallum, *Zenkōji and its Icon: A Study in Medieval Japanese Religious Art* (Honolulu: University of Hawai'i Press, 1994).

12 Scrolls at Kakurinji in Hyōgo Prefecture contain a pictorial representation of Shōtoku's hagiography, including his interaction with the Zenkōji Amida. See *Shōtoku Taishi ten* (Tokyo: NHK Puromōshon, 2001), 178–81.

13 For a detailed discussion of the *Zenkōji engi*, see McCallum, *Zenkōji and its Icon*, 38–54.

14 Ibid., 49.

15 Shimaguchi Yoshiaki, "Shōtoku Taishi shinkō to Zenkōji," in *Taishi shinkō*, ed. Gamaike Seishi (Tokyo: Yūzankaku Shuppan, 1999), 67–92. For the role of the Zenkōji *hijiri*, see McCallum, ibid., 79–86.

16 For a history of the development of the site as the tomb of Prince Shōtoku, see Ono Kazuyuki, "'Shōtoku Taishi bō' tanjō," in *Shōtoku Taishi no shinjitsu*, ed. Ōyama, 367–80; and Ono, "Shōtoku Taishi bō no tenkai." See also Fujita Kiyoshi, "Shōtoku Taishi byō no shinkō to Kamakura bukkyō," in *Kamakura bukkyō keisei no mondaiten*, ed. Nihon Bukkyō Gakkai (Kyoto: Heirakuji Shoten, 1969), 238–39.

17 NS entry for Suiko 29/2/5: Aston, *Nihongi*, part 2, 148; NKBT, vol. 68, 205.

18 See Okimori, *Jōgū Shōtoku*, 127–28; and *Shōtoku Taishi denryaku*, 112. In the latter text, Shōtoku and Princess Kashiwade both die on the same day, and thus are buried together.

19 *Engishiki*, NKZ, ed. Yosano et al., vol. 5, 169. The site of Shinaga might have been a royal cemetery, as the tombs assigned to Bidatsu, Yōmei, Suiko, Kōtoku, and the prince are located in this area. In addition, funerary mounds of people associated with the Soga clan are found there. For this reason, Fujita Kiyoshi has suggested that Shinaga was probably the Soga clan's cemetery. Fujita, "Shōtoku Taishi byō no shinkō to Kamakura bukkyō," 236–37.

20 Ono, "'Shōtoku Taishi bō' tanjō," 371.

21 Scholars such as Imao Fumiaki have argued that Shinaga is not the burial site of the prince. See Imao Fumiaki, "Shōtoku Taishi haka e no gimon," *Higashi Ajia no kodai bunka*, no. 88 (1996): 48–65; and Ono, ibid., 368. For the report of the archaeological study of the tomb in 1921, see Umehara Sueji, "Shōtoku Taishi Shinaga no gobyō," in *Shōtoku Taishi ronsan*, ed. Heian Kōkokai (Kyoto: Heian Kōkokai, 1921), 344–70. Umehara also had doubts that the tomb belonged to Prince Shōtoku. For an analysis of Umehara's report, see Tanaka Shigehisa, "Shōtoku Taishi Shinaga Yamamoto misasagi no koki," in *Shumatsuki kofun: Ronshū*, ed. Mori Kōichi (Tokyo: Hanawa Shobō, 1973), 80–81.

22 *Ōsaka-fu no chimei*, Nihon rekishi chimei taikei, vol. 28 (Tokyo: Heibonsha, 1986), s.v. "Eifukuji."

23 For the origins of Eifukuji, see Ono, "Shōtoku Taishi bō no tenkai," 19–24.

24 Minamoto Akikane, *Kojidan*, annot. Kobayashi Yasuharu (Tokyo: Gendai Shichōsha, 1981), 95–97. For a discussion of the inscription, see Ono, ibid., 2–3.

25 Ono, ibid., 4.

26 Ibid., 8–9.

27 For the Shōryōin, see Nara Rokudaiji Taikan Kankōkai, ed., *Hōryūji*, vol. 1 of NRT, 57–63. "Kenshin" may also be read "Kenjin."

28 For this Nyoirin Kannon image, see ibid., vol. 4 of NRT, 6–62, plates 59, 60, 209–11.

29 Eison's autobiography informs us that he went to Hōryūji three times, but does not mention Kenshin at all. On 1256 (Kōgen 1)/3/20, Eison administered the bodhisattva precepts to 202 people at the Eastern Compound of Hōryūji. He went again two years later (1258), and got involved in the repairs of "the Nyoirin Kannon icon that belonged to the father of Chōshimaru." Eison was again at Hōryūji on 1259 (Shōgen 1)/3/11 for the eye-opening ceremony of the "main icon of Chōshimaru," which was enshrined in the Shōryōin. Eison, *Kongō busshi Eison kanshin gakushōki*, in *Saidaiji Eison denki shūsei*, ed. Nara Kokuritsu Bunkazai Kenkyūjo (Kyoto: Hōzōkan, 1977), 26–27.

30 Kenshin, *Shōtoku Taishi den shiki*, in HSS, vol. 4, 136. The indexed version by Ogino Minahiko, *Shōtoku Taishi den kokon mokurokushō* (Nara: Hōryūji, 1937), has been used in this study.

31 Fujii Yukiko has argued that Chōshimaru was Kenshin's invention. For a detailed discussion, see Fujii, *Shōtoku Taishi no denshō*, 63–81.

32 Tanaka, "Shōtoku Taishi Shinaga Yamamoto," 85–92. Tanaka has analyzed all of the entries about the tomb at Shinaga in Kenshin's work. See also Ogino, *Shōtoku Taishi den*, 33–34.

33 Nishiguchi Junko, "Shinaga Taishi byō to sono shūhen," in *Taishi shinkō*, ed. Gamaike Seishi (Tokyo: Yūzankaku Shuppan, 1999), 49–66.

34 Ogino, *Shōtoku Taishi den*, 67–68.

35 Ibid., 47–48.

36 For a literal translation of the whole verse, see Meeks, "In Her Likeness," 376. Meeks translates the verse included in the 1463 version of *Chūgūji engi*, and states that a visit to Chūgūji provides a chance to be reborn in Amida's Pure Land. The content of the verse, however, refers to a visit to the tomb at Shinaga, not Chūgūji.

37 Fujii, *Shōtoku Taishi no denshō*, 132–34. The verse is also recorded in *Shōtoku Taishi denki*. As Fujii notes, the earliest example of the verse is that found in Kenshin's *Shōtoku Taishi den shiki*. Shimaguchi Yoshiaki has observed that the passage bears a connection to the cult of the Zenkōji Amida triad: the idea of three deities manifesting as a single body relates to the characteristic form of this triad, in which a single mandorla unites the three figures. Shimaguchi, "Shōtoku Taishi shinkō to Zenkōji."

38 Ogino, *Shōtoku Taishi den*, 85–86.

39 No information about when this relief was placed at the gate has been located.

40 For an annotated translation of Chōgen's memoirs, see John Rosenfield, *Portraits of Chōgen: The Transformation of Buddhist Art in Early Medieval Japan* (Leiden and Boston: Brill, 2011), 222.

41 Nishiguchi, "Shinaga Taishi byō," 53. Nishiguchi believes that these two monks were from Taimadera in Nara.

42 Ogino, *Shōtoku Taishi den*, 69.

43 Imao, "Shōtoku Taishi haka e no gimon," 55.

44 Tanaka Ichimatsu, ed., *Nihon emakimono zenshū*, vol. 10, *Ippen hijiri-e* (Tokyo: Kadokawa Shoten, 1960), plates 109–11.

45 Eison, *Kongō busshi Eison*, 20.

46 Ibid., 27.

47 Ono, "Shōtoku Taishi bō no tenkai," 22.

48 Nakanoin Masatada no Musume, *The Confessions of Lady Nijō*, trans. Karen Brazell (Garden City, NY: Anchor Books, 1973), 205–6.

49 No evidence that any form of veneration of the prince took place in this hall has been found. Since 1078, the main ceremony performed in the Golden Hall has been the Kichijō keka, repentance rites dedicated to Kichijōten, a female deity of good fortune. Chari Pradel, "A Female Deity as the Focus of a Buddhist Ritual: *Kichijō Keka* at Hōryūji," paper presented at the workshop "Women, Rites, and Objects in Pre-modern Japan," University of Pittsburgh Asian Studies, March 3–6, 2016.

50 For the halls in the Eastern Compound of Hōryūji, see Nara Rokudaiji Taikan Kankōkai, ed., *Hōryūji*, vol. 5 of *NRT*, 7–23. For the ritual cycle at the Eastern Compound, see Carr, *Plotting the Prince*, 127–69.

51 For the Shōtoku cult and ceremonies at Hōryūji, see Takada Ryōshin, "Shōtoku Taishi shinkō no tenkai: Toku ni Hōryūji o chūshin to shite," in *Shōtoku Taishi to Asuka bukkyō*, ed. Tamura Enchō (Tokyo: Yoshikawa Kōbunkan, 1986), 389–417.

52 The current Shōryōin is dated to 1284. For a detailed discussion of the Shōtoku cult at Hōryūji in the Kamakura period, see Fujii, *Shōtoku Taishi no denshō*, 36–91.

53 See the temple's ritual calendar, http://www.horyuji.or.jp/syoryoin.htm (last accessed January 18, 2016).

54 Nishiguchi, "Shinaga Taishi byō," 54. In addition to the well-known Western and Eastern Compounds at Hōryūji, many subtemples that serve as monks' residences are located on the grounds of the temple complex. In 1210, Konkōin was renamed Sōgenji. For a history of Hōryūji's subtemples, see Takada Ryōshin, *Hōryūji shiin no kenkyū* (Kyoto: Dōhōsha Shuppan, 1981); for Konkōin, see pages 74–78.

55 Ogino, *Shōtoku Taishi den*, 51, 79.

56 See TKH, *Kokuhō Hōryūji ten*, 160.

57 For the Amida icon, see Nara Rokudaiji Taikan Kankōkai, ed., *Hōryūji*, vol. 2 of *NRT*, 38–43. See also Naitō Toichirō, *Hōryūji kenkyū: Kondō hen* (Osaka: Kodai Bunka Kenkyūkai, 1933), 37–55.

58 The attendant bodhisattvas currently in the Golden Hall are replicas. The original Seishi has been housed in the Musée Guimet in Paris since the Meiji period (1868–1912), and the Kannon image may be found in Hōryūji's Daihōzōden (Great Treasure Hall). A photograph of the three original icons was taken in 1994. Takada Ryōshin, *Hōryūji sen-yonhyakunen* (Tokyo: Shinchōsha, 1994), 96–97.

59 *Kondō nikki*, in *HSS*, vol. 2, 14, 28.

60 Ogino, *Shōtoku Taishi den*, 14–15.

61 Ibid., 62.

62 Pradel, "*Shōkō Mandara*."

63 Two sources at Hōryūji recreate the circumstances of the making of the *Shōkō Mandara*: "Shōryōin Mandara no koto" (About the Mandara of Shōryōin), in *Hōryūji butsuzōki* (Records of the Buddhist Images at Hōryūji); and "Shōryōin engi no koto" (About the Origins of Shōryōin), in *Hōryūji engi shirabyōshi* (Script of the Legend of Hōryūji). See these texts in *HSS*, vol. 8, 81–107, 6–79.

64 Ogino, *Shōtoku Taishi den*, 40.

65 Fukuyama Toshio, "Chūgūji no garan haichi," in Fukuyama Toshio, *Nihon kenchikushi no kenkyū* (Kyoto: Kuwana Bunseidō), 1943. For the excavations, see Inagaki Yukinari, "Kyū Chūgūji ato no hakkutsu to genjō," *Nihon rekishi*, no. 299 (1973): 120–25.

66 For the history of Chūgūji, see Takada Ryōshin, *Chūgūji, Hōrinji, Hokkiji no rekishi to nenpyō* (Tokyo: Wakō Bijutsu Shuppan, 1984), 21–60. For a comprehensive discussion of the sources, see Ōhashi Katsuaki, "Chūgūji kō," in Ōhashi, *Tenjukoku Shūchō no kenkyū*, 191–99.

67 *Hōryūji garan engi*, 8. For an English translation of sections of *Hōryūji engi*, see J. Edward Kidder, *The Lucky Seventh: Early Hōryūji and Its Time* (Tokyo: International Christian University Hachirō Yuasa Memorial Museum, 1999), 209–74.

68 *Hōryūji garan engi*, 9–10.

69 Okimori, *Jōgū Shōtoku*, 86–88.

70 As the Shōtoku cult spread, the number of temples allegedly established by the prince increased.

71 *Shōtoku Taishi denryaku*, 96, 113. Meeks has pointed out that the association of Anahobe with Chūgūji coincides with changes in the Shōtoku cult, specifically with the prince's deification as Guze Kannon in *Shōtoku Taishi denryaku*. Meeks, "In Her Likeness," 368–69.

72 *Fusō ryakki*, in *Kokushi taikei*, vol. 6 (Tokyo: Keizai Zasshisha, 1897–1901), 500, 504.

73 Ōhashi, "Chūgūji kō," 192.

74 As discussed by Meeks, "In Her Likeness," 369.

75 *Hōryūji bettō shidai*, in *Zoku gunsho ruijū: Honinbu*, vol. 4 (Tokyo: Zoku Gunsho Ruijū Kanseikai, 1930), 794–95, 800. This document is also found in *HSS*, vol. 3.

76 Ogino, *Shōtoku Taishi den*, 28.

77 Ibid., 58.

78 Ibid., 30.

79 For Shinnyo's biography, see Ogino Minahiko, "Chūgūji sanjū no tō to ama Shinnyo," *Nihon rekishi*, no. 326 (1975): 88–92; and Hosokawa Ryōichi, "Kamakura jidai no ama to amadera," in Hosokawa Ryōichi, *Chūsei no Risshū jiin to minshū* (Tokyo: Yoshikawa Kōbunkan, 1987), 100–168. In English, Paul Groner and Lori Meeks have done extensive research on Shinnyo and her association with the Shingon Ritsu lineage. See Paul Groner, "Tradition and Innovation: Eison's Self-Ordinations and the Re-establishment of New Orders of Buddhist Practitioners," in *Going Forth: Visions of Buddhist Vinaya*, ed. William M. Bodiford (Honolulu: University of Hawai'i Press, 2005), 210–35; and Meeks, "In Her Likeness," 361–65.

80 Groner, "Tradition," 224–25. See also *Shōdai senzai denki*, in *DNBZ*, vol. 64, 268–69. Shinnyo's biography is very brief in this document, and she appears as the founder of Shōhōji or Shōbōji. This source also refers to the Tenjukoku Mandara's size.

81 For a detailed discussion of these sources, see Meeks, "In Her Likeness," 361–62.

82 For Jōkei, see James Foard, "Competing with Amida: A Study and Translation of Jōkei's *Miroku kōshiki*," *Monumenta Nipponica* 60, no. 1 (2005): 43–79.

83 For Shinnyo's encounter with Eison, see Eison, *Kongō busshi Eison*, 18.

84 For a detailed account of Shinnyo's ordination, see Hosokawa, "Kamakura jidai no ama," 103–12; Groner, "Tradition," 224–29; and Meeks, "In Her Likeness," 361–65. Meeks has stated that the story of Chūgūji and Shinnyo is also recorded in a manuscript without a title in the collection of Saidaiji, dated to the Daiei era (1521–28). Meeks, *Hokkeji*, 344–45.

85 *Shōyoshō*, in *DNBZ*, vol. 72, 21c. The dating of this document is controversial. *DNBZ* dates the text to 1275; *HSS*, to the Ōei era (1394–1428); and the current extant copy was transcribed in 1574. See also *Shōyoshō*, in *HSS*, vol. 10, 235–40. Based on an analysis of the contents, the Ōei-era date seems more accurate.

86 Meeks has discussed the contents of *Shōtoku Taishi denki*, which she dates to 1275. This document, however, is dated to 1317–19. Nonetheless, her assertions about the Ritsu agenda in this document are accurate. Meeks, *Hokkeji*, 291–98.

87 See Chari Pradel, "Portrait of Prince Shōtoku and Two Princes: From Devotional Painting to Imperial Object," *Artibus Asiae* 74, no. 1 (2014): 191–217.

88 *Hōryūji bettō shidai*, 808; and Ogino, "Chūgūji sanjū no tō," 91. For the activities of Keisei, see Fujii, *Shōtoku Taishi no denshō*, 36–60.

89 Ogino, *Shōtoku Taishi den*, 9. See also Pradel, "Portrait of Prince Shōtoku," 196–99.

90 *Ryōjusen'in nenjū gyōji*, in *YKT*, ed. Ōta, vol. 1, 81–82.

91 These events are recounted in the following section.

92 The *ganmon* is discussed by Hosokawa, "Kamakura jidai no ama," 119; and Groner, "Tradition," 229. For a translation, see Meeks, *Hokkeji*, 293–94.

93 Nakanoin Masatada no Musume, *Confessions of Lady Nijō*, 205. See also Hosokawa, ibid., 116; and Meeks, ibid., 189.

94 These later sources are discussed in Chapter Five.

95 As mentioned previously, *Chūgūji engi* exists in two versions, one from 1274 and the other from 1463 (see note 1 of this chapter). For a discussion of these two versions, see Hayashi Mikiya, "Ekisai no mita Chūgūji engi," *Nihon rekishi*, no. 61 (1953): 44–45. The translation of a portion of the 1274 version included here is the author's own.

96 The text gives the year as "last year"; as Bun'ei 11 (1274) is stated in the previous paragraph, "last year" would correspond to 1273. The Shaka *nenbutsu* is the common name for the *nehan-e* (Nirvana festival), which was first practiced in the Bun'ei era (1264–74). For details about this ritual, see Nakamura Hajime, *Bukkyōgo daijiten*, 7th ed. (Tokyo: Tōkyō Shoseki, 1975), s.v. "Shaka nenbutsu."

97 Genga served as the abbot of Hōryūji from 1266 to 1284.

98 *Hōryūji bettō shidai*, 819; and Ogino, "Chūgūji sanjū no tō," 89.

99 Using all of the documents, without taking into account their dates of compilation, Ōhashi has argued that other people were involved. Ōhashi, *Tenjukoku Shūchō no kenkyū*, 63–84.

100 *Uragaki*, in *Shōyoshō*, in *HSS*, vol. 10, and in *DNBZ*, vol. 72, 552; and in *Ikaruga koji binran*, in *HSS*, vol. 15, and in *DNBZ*, vol. 85, 718. According to Ōhashi, *Uragaki* is also recorded in *Hōryūji tōin engi* (Account of the Origins of Hōryūji's Eastern Compound; 1736), but a version of this manuscript that contains the text has not been found by the present author. For a discussion of *Hōryūji tōin engi*'s contents and dating, see *HSS*, vol. 1, 166–70. See also Ōhashi, ibid., 78. He includes a very helpful diagram that traces the various sources of the text. The translation of *Uragaki* included here is the author's own.

101 The first date given is 仲秋上旬庚子; according to Hayashi Mikiya, this corresponds to the second day of the eighth month. Hayashi has argued that the second date given, 中旬庚辰, should be 下旬庚辰, which corresponds to the twenty-second day. Hayashi Mikiya, "Onjōji gon daisōzu Jōen," *Nihon rekishi*, no. 146 (1960): 42.

102 NKH, *Josei to bukkyō: Inori to hohoemi* (Nara: Nara Kokuritsu Hakubutsukan, 2003), 181–207, 251–57.

103 Hayashi, "Onjōji gon daisōzu Jōen," 42.

104 Ibid., 45.

105 For Hokke Chōkō Amida Sanmaidō, see Takeuchi Rizō, ed., *Kadokawa Nihon chimei daijiten*, vol. 26 (Tokyo: Kadokawa Shoten, 1982), 948.

106 For the facsimile version, see *Shōyoshō* as reproduced in *HSS*, vol. 10, 203.

107 No information about Fujiwara no Sadamitsu has been found by the present author.

108 For the Taima Mandara, see three publications by Elizabeth ten Grotenhuis: "Rebirth of an Icon: The Taima Mandara in Medieval Japan," *Archives of Asian Art* 36 (1983): 59–87; *The Revival of the Taima Mandala in Medieval Japan* (New York and London: Garland Publishing, 1985); and *Japanese Mandalas: Representations of Sacred Geography* (Honolulu: University of Hawai'i Press, 1999), 122–44.

109 The temple existed as Ryōzenji until 1383, when it became a temple of the Jishū school and changed its name to Shōbōji. *Kyōto-shi no chimei*, Nihon rekishi chimei taikei, vol. 27 (Tokyo: Heibonsha 1979), s.v. "Ryōzenji ato."

110 The whole text of *Taishi mandara kōshiki* appears in *STZ*, vol. 4, 131–38. An abridged version is available in *YKT*, ed. Ōta, vol. 1, 88–89. The author thanks Professor William Bodiford of UCLA for his help in the translation of this document. Translations included here are the author's own.

111 For *kōshiki*, see James Foard, "Competing with Amida," and "Buddhist Ceremonials (*kōshiki*) and the Ideological Discourse of Established Buddhism in Early Medieval Japan," in *Discourse and Ideology in Medieval Japanese Buddhism*, ed. Richard K. Payne and Taigen Dan Leighton (London and New York: Routledge, 2006), 97–125.

112 This practice shows similarities to *etoki*, the oral or written explanation or narration of paintings. See Ikumi Kaminishi, *Explaining Pictures: Buddhist Propaganda and Etoki Storytelling in Japan* (Honolulu: University of Hawai'i Press, 2006). The author thanks Karen Gerhart for this insight.

113 This quote is taken from the "Verse of the Tomb Chamber."

114 For this land, see Hisao Inagaki, *A Dictionary of Japanese Buddhist Terms: Based on References in Japanese Literature*, in collaboration with P.G. O'Neill (Kyoto: Nagata Bunshodo, 1984), s.v. "Jōjakōdo."

115 The phrase is "startle the illusion of the *bundan-hen'yaku* cycles of transmigration." *Bundan-hen'yaku* refers to *bundan shōji* and *hen'yaku shōji*. For these terms, see Inagaki, *Dictionary of Japanese Buddhist Terms*, s.v. "Bundan shōji" and "Hen'yaku shōji."

116 *Hōryūji bettō shidai*, 819–20.

117 For an English translation of, and comments on, Shinnyo's *ganmon*, see Meeks, *Hokkeji*, 293–95.

118 Ibid., 189.

119 Nakanoin Masatada no Musume, *Confessions of Lady Nijō*, 205–6.

120 *Hōryūji bettō shidai*, 822–23.

121 These later texts are discussed in Chapter Five.

5

1 For a list in English of selected events found in *Shōtoku Taishi denryaku*, see Carr, *Plotting the Prince*, 179–88.

2 For the Ritsu school and the revival of female monasticism in general, see Meeks, *Hokkeji*, 1–26, 250–300. For an analysis of documents from Chūgūji, see the same source, 281–83, 291–98. Meeks' general interpretations must be reviewed with an eye to the accurate dating of the documents. Her points of view regarding the Ritsu agenda, however, are well supported.

3 See *Shōtoku Taishi denki*, in *STZ*, vol. 2, 279–454. For the section about the Tenjukoku Mandara, see 442–46. Meeks has dated the document to 1274, the year that Shinnyo began her activities for the revival of Chūgūji. Meeks, "In Her Likeness," 371. Because *Shōtoku Taishi denki* mentions Jōen's *Taishi mandara kōshiki*, which was written in 1275, the former must have been compiled later. Fujiwara Yūsetsu has dated the document to the Bunpō era based on a date recorded in the manuscript; see Fujiwara Yūsetsu, *Taishi den*, *STZ*, vol. 2, 76.

4 Issues regarding women's karmic obstacles are discussed by Meeks, ibid., 374.

5 *Shōtoku Taishi denki*, 443–44. The translations of this text included here are the author's own.

6 In *Shōtoku Taishi denki*, the title *tennō* (heavenly sovereign) is used for Suiko. This narrative about the making of the Tenjukoku Mandara shows some relationship to another popular story of the Kamakura period, the *Taima Mandara engi*. In *Shōtoku Taishi denki*, Anahobe (an incarnation of Amida) and Shōtoku (an incarnation of Kannon) play an active role in the creation of the Tenjukoku Mandara. In the *Taima Mandara engi*, Kannon weaves the mandara and Amida explains its meaning. For the *Taima Mandara engi*, see ten Grotenhuis, "Rebirth of an Icon," and "Chūjōhime: The Weaving of Her Legend," in *Flowing Traces: Buddhism in the Literary and Visual Arts of Japan*, ed. James H. Sanford, William R. LaFleur, and Masatoshi Nagatomi (Princeton, NJ: Princeton University Press, 1992), 183–88.

7 *Shōtoku Taishi denki*, 444.

8. For the monk Sōji, see Meeks, *Hokkeji*, 138–39.
9. For an English translation of this passage, see ibid., 293.
10. *Shōtoku Taishi denki*, 445. It is difficult to determine if this reference to the bells is an objective description of the artifact, or if this statement was derived from the listing of an embroidered curtain with bands and bells in *Hōryūji engi* (discussed in Chapter Three). Some scholars argue that the bells and bronze plaques attached to wide woven bands found in the Hōryūji collection of ancient textiles are the remains of the Shūchō. See Hōryūji, *Hōryūji to shiruku rōdo*, 175.
11. Regarding Kanesuke, Ōhashi Katsuaki has suggested that, when the mandara was in Kyoto, the priest must have requested imperial permission to examine it, and then compiled the inscription in a document entitled *Tenjukoku mandara meibun* (currently in the Nishio City Library, Aichi Prefecture). This document indeed bears Kanesuke's name, but the dating is problematic. Iida Mizuho, who has studied all of the available versions of the Shūchō's inscription, considers it to be a later copy. *Tenjukoku mandara meibun* certainly seems to be a later document, particularly because the three turtles sketched in the manuscript are those recorded in *Ikaruga koji binran*, an Edo-period document that also mentions Kanesuke. For more on this controversy, see Ōhashi, *Tenjukoku Shūchō no kenkyū*, 74; and Iida, "Tenjukoku Mandara Shūchō," 57. The document *Tenjukoku mandara meibun* is reproduced in the Ōhashi source, 83.
12. *Kokushi daijiten*, s.v. "Hokke sanjikkō" (last accessed January 29, 2016).
13. This sentence of the text is 新曼陀羅與本曼荼羅共奉返中宮寺. See *Shōtoku Taishi denki*, 446. Ōhashi has interpreted the passage to mean that "the replica and the original mandara were both taken to Chūgūji," to support his theory that, in 1275, a replica was made. Ōhashi, *Tenjukoku Shūchō no kenkyū*, 12–13.
14. For information about Shōyo, the person who copied the oldest extant version, the contents of this document, and the sources used by Shōyo, see *Shōyoshō*, in *HHS*, vol. 10, 236–40.
15. See the Chūgūji section of *Shōyoshō* in *DNBZ*, vol. 72, 20–23. In this source, the document is reproduced in three rows of text. For clarity here, the page number followed by "a" is used to indicate the upper row, "b" for the middle row, and "c" for the lower.
16. Ibid., 20c.
17. Ibid., 21a.
18. For Shinnyo's biography and ordination, see Meeks, *Hokkeji*, 292; and Hosokawa, *Chūsei no Risshū*, 107–8. See also *Shōyoshō*, 21a, b, c, 22a, b.
19. Owada Tetsuo, ed., *Nihon shi shoka keifu jinmei jiten* (Tokyo: Kōdansha, 2003), 212–13.
20. *Shōyoshō*, 23.
21. *Chūgūji engi* (1463 version), reproduced in *YKT*, ed. Ōta, vol. 1, 86–87.
22. Note that this is not the official account of the arrival of Buddhism as narrated in *Nihon shoki*.
23. *Chūgūji engi* (1463 version), 86a. The text is divided in two rows; the page number followed by "a" is used to indicate the top row, and "b" for the bottom.
24. Ibid.
25. Ibid., 86b.
26. In 1584, Chūgūji was moved to its current location at the northeast corner of Hōryūji's Eastern Compound. The modern Main Hall was built in 1967. See Nishikawa Kyōtarō, "Chūgūji no rekishi," in *YKT*, ed. Ōta, vol. 1, 57–58.
27. *Chūgūji engi* (1463 version), 86b.
28. Ibid., 87a.
29. Ibid.
30. Ibid., 87b. For an analysis of this section, see Meeks, *Hokkeji*, 296–97.
31. As cited by Mita, "Gihō," 68. Apparently, Senjuji keeps the fragments in its repository. For a brief history of the temple's abbots, see "Takadaha ryaku nenpyō," *Shinshu Takadaha Honzan Senjuji*, http://www.senjuji.or.jp/about/rekidai.php#8 (last accessed January 1, 2015). For a short biography of Jōjun, see Senjuji, *Senjuji shiyō* (Tsu-shi: Takadaha Senjuji Onki Hōmuin Bunshobu, 1912), 101; for an electronic version, see http://dl.ndl.go.jp/info:ndljp/pid/822002?__lang=en (last accessed December 27, 2015).
32. See David Freedberg, *The Power of Images: Studies in the History and Theory of Response* (Chicago and London: University of Chicago Press, 1989), 99–135.
33. See Yoshida Eri, "Kobutsu: Edo kara Meiji e no keishō," *Kindai gasetsu* 12 (2003): 13–30.
34. Hayashi Sōho, *Wushū kyūseki yūkō*, vol. 6 (1681), 440. See also http://www.katch.ne.jp/~heday/YAMATO.htm (last accessed December 20, 2015).
35. See Ishida, ed., *Shōtoku Taishi jiten*, s.v. "Ryōkin."
36. For Ryōkin's *Hōryūji Ryōkin homōshū*, see *Zokuzoku gunsho ruijū*, vol. 11, *Shūkyō-bu* (Tokyo: Kokusho Kankōkai, 1909), 541.
37. For more on this document, see Chapter Four, note 100.
38. The section on the Tenjukoku Mandara in *Ikaruga koji binran* is reproduced in *DNBZ*, vol. 85, 139–40.
39. Kariya Ekisai was a nativist scholar who specialized in the study of ancient documents (*kōshōgaku*). He researched the *Imperial Biography* and completed an annotated version, *Jōgū Shōtoku hōō teisetsu shōchū*, in 1821 (Bunsei 4). See *Kokushi daijiten*, s.v. "Kariya Ekisai" (last accessed December 25, 2014). A version of Ekisai's work with supplementary notes by Hirako Takurei was published in 1913. Kariya Ekisai and Hirako Takurei, *Hokō Jōgū Shōtoku hōō teisetsu shōchū* (Tokyo: Heigo Shuppansha, 1913).

40 *Kokushi daijiten*, s.v. "Hoida Tadatomo" (last accessed December 25, 2014).
41 Hoida Tadatomo, *Kanko zatsujō*, in *NKZ*, ed. Yosano et al., vol. 3. See also http://kindai.ndl.go.jp/info/ndljp/pid/1051975 (last accessed December 23, 2015).
42 Reproduced in ibid., 20.
43 For *Dai Nihon shi*, see John S. Brownlee, *Japanese Historians and the National Myths, 1600–1945: The Age of the Gods and Emperor Jinmu* (Vancouver: University of British Columbia Press, 1999), 29–41.
44 This turtle and the group of three seated monks were found together. Chūgūji Monzeki, *Chūgūji* (Tokyo: Benridō, 1999), 25.
45 These measurements were taken from a facsimile of a photo of the Tenjukoku Shūchō Mandara, not directly from the artifact.
46 Ishida Mosaku, "Tenjukoku Mandara no fukugen ni tsuite," *Gasetsu* 4, no. 5 (1940): 398.
47 Ōhashi, *Tenjukoku Shūchō no kenkyū*, 85–89.
48 Mita, "Gihō," 93.
49 As measured from the forehead to the base of the lotus flower.
50 Ōhashi has identified B-18 as a figure riding an animal. Ōhashi, *Tenjukoku Shūchō no kenkyū*, 33.
51 Ōhashi Katsuaki and Taniguchi Masakazu, *Kakusareta Shōtoku Taishi no sekai: Fukugen maboroshi no Tenjukoku* (Tokyo: Nihon Hōsō Shuppan Kyōkai, 2002), 69. For the tile, see Chang Yang-mo et al., *Arts of Korea* (New York: Metropolitan Museum of Art, 1998), 54–57.
52 Sugiyama Hiroshi, *Bonshō*, Nihon no bijutsu, no. 355 (Tokyo: Shibundō, 1995).
53 See Ryōkin, *Hōryūji Ryōkin homōshū*.
54 Hayashi Mikiya, "Tenjukoku Shūchō zakkō," *Bunka shigaku* 12 (1956): 50. Specifically, these iconographical attributes identify the figure as Ungyō, or Naraen Kongō (S. Vajravīra), the closed-mouthed member of the two Niō.
55 Ōhashi, *Tenjukoku Shūchō no kenkyū*, 50–51.
56 For a discussion of these three monuments, see James C.Y. Watt, "Art and History in China from the Third to the Eighth Century," in Watt et al., *China: Dawn of the Golden Age*, 18–22, 162. For the Guyuan coffin, see Luo, "Lacquer Painting"; Karetzky and Soper, "Northern Wei Painted Coffin"; and Juliano and Lerner, *Monks and Merchants*, 77–81.
57 See Juliano and Lerner, ibid., 80.
58 Reproduced in TKH, *Hōryūji kennō hōmotsu: Tokubetsu ten* (Tokyo: Tokyo Kokuritsu Hakubutsukan, 1996), 233.
59 Ōhashi, *Tenjukoku Shūchō no kenkyū*, 34–35.
60 Mita, "Gihō," 90–91.
61 Ōhashi, *Tenjukoku Shūchō no kenkyū*, 110–12. See Ōhashi's reconstruction of these pedestals with figures of Shōtoku and a Buddha in Ōhashi and Taniguchi, *Kakusareta Shōtoku Taishi*, 195.

62 Pradel, "Fragments," 173. See also Mita Kakuyuki, "Tenjukoku Shūchō no genkei to shudai ni tsuite," *Bijutsushi* 57, no. 2 (2008): 273, for partial reconstructions of the pedestals.
63 For a detailed study of Hōryūji's bronze banner, see TKH, *Kanjōban*.
64 Tōno has argued that the stick is a brush, and the unidentified object is a *mokkan*. Tōno Haruyuki, "Tenjukoku Shūchō no seisaku nendai: Meibun to zuzō kara mita," in *Kōkogaku no gakusaiteki kenkyū*, ed. Tōno Haruyuki (Kishida-shi: Kishiwada-shi Kyōiku Iinkai, 2001), 15–16.
65 Ōhashi, *Tenjukoku Shūchō no kenkyū*, 158–59.
66 For monks' portraits, see Kajitani Ryōji, *Sōryo no shōzō*, Nihon no bijutsu, no. 388 (Tokyo: Shibundō, 1998).
67 Mita, "Gihō," 82–83.
68 *Shōtoku Taishi denki*, 444.
69 See Akashi Somendo, "Gakkan Tenjukoku Shūchō shi," *Yumedono* 17 (1937): 101–4; Ishida, "Kokuhō Tenjukoku Mandara Shūchō," 9; Kameda, "Chūgūji Tenjukoku Shūchō," 146–47; Ōhashi, *Tenjukoku Shūchō no kenkyū*, 119–21; and Tōno, "Tenjukoku Shūchō," 13–16.
70 Ishida, ibid.
71 Gakka is mentioned in *Nihon shoki*. See the NS entry for Suiko 1 (593)/4/10: Aston, *Nihongi*, part 2, 122; NKBT, vol. 68, 173.
72 Ōhashi, *Tenjukoku Shūchō no kenkyū*, 55; Mita, "Tenjukoku Shūchō no genkei," 270–74.
73 *Shōtoku Taishi denki*, 443–44.
74 *Chūgūji engi* (1274 version), 203; *Shōtoku Taishi denki*, 445; *Shōyoshō*, 23; Hayashi, *Washū kyūseki yūkō*, vol. 6, 440.
75 *Shōtoku Taishi denki*, 445.
76 *Chūgūji engi*, in YKT, ed. Ōta, vol. 1, 87; Kakuken, *Ikaruga koji binran*, in DNBZ, vol. 85, 718.
77 *Shōdai senzai denki*, 268–69.
78 *Digital Daijisen*, s.v. "Jōroku," http://japanknowledge.com/lib/display/?lid=2001009232100 (last accessed January 30, 2016).
79 For more on these embroidered icons and their measurements, see the section "Embroidery as Pictorial Medium and Status Symbol" in Chapter Three.
80 Ōno Genmyō, as cited by Hori Yukio, "Tenjukoku Shūchō fukugen kō," *Bukkyō geijutsu* 110 (1976): 111.
81 Ishida, "Tenjukoku Mandara no fukugen."
82 Adachi Kō, "Tenjukoku Shūchō no genkei," *Kenchiku shi* 2, no. 5 (1940): 86–87.
83 Hayashi Mikiya, "Tenjukoku Shūchō no fukugen," *Nanto bukkyō* 8 (1960): 59–61.
84 Hori, "Tenjukoku Shūchō fukugen kō," 110–17.
85 Ōhashi, *Tenjukoku Shūchō no kenkyū*, 109–20, 124–25.
86 Ibid., 89.
87 Inagaki, "Kyū Chūgūji."

88 The Shōsōin collection houses a total of nineteen rulers. *Shōsōin ten: Dai gojūni-kai* (Nara: Nara Kokuritsu Hakubutsukan, 2000), 25.

89 Arai, *Maboroshi no kodaijaku*, 4–7.

90 Ibid., 203–5.

91 Kawabata Shun'ichirō has used a similar approach, focusing on the architectural elements of Hōryūji. He has arrived at a similar number (26.95 centimeters), but argues that this unit was not used for the *shaku*, but for the *zai*, the module utilized for carpentry and wooden construction. Kawabata Shun'ichirō, *Hōryūji no monosashi: Kakusareta ōchō kōtai no nazo* (Kyoto: Mineruva Shobō, 2004), 93.

92 Kashima Masaru, "Hōryūji kennō hōmotsu: Kanjōban no mozōhin seisaku ni tsuite," *Museum*, no. 567 (2000): 50.

93 For grids, see David Summers, *Real Spaces: World Art History and the Rise of Western Modernism* (New York: Phaidon, 2003), 410–14.

94 Dieter Kuhn, "Silk Weaving in Ancient China: From Geometric Figures to Patterns of Pictorial Likeness," *Chinese Science* 12 (1995): 77–114.

95 NS entry for Kōtoku 2 (646)/1/1: Aston, *Nihongi*, part 2, 208; *NKBT*, vol. 68, 228.

96 *Engishiki*, 211.

97 Mita, "Tenjukoku Shūchō no genkei," 276–77.

98 As mentioned previously, the first document to print the inscription divided into sets of four characters was Hoida Tadatomo's *Kanko zatsujō* of 1841.

99 Robin R. Wang, *Yinyang: The Way of Heaven and Earth in Chinese Thought and Culture* (Cambridge: Cambridge University Press, 2012), 210.

100 For the moon and sun in yin yang, see ibid., 27–28.

Epilogue

1 Dōshin Satō, "The Formation of the Academic Discipline of Art History and its Development," in Dōshin Satō, *Modern Japanese Art and the Meiji State: The Politics of Beauty* (Los Angeles: Getty Research Institute, 2011), 153–83.

2 Ibid., 154.

3 James Edward Ketelaar, *Of Heretics and Martyrs in Meiji Japan: Buddhism and its Persecution* (Princeton, NJ: Princeton University Press, 1990).

4 Takahashi Takahiro, "Meiji 8–9 nen no 'Nara Hakurankai' chinretsu mokuroku ni tsuite," *Shisen*, nos. 56, 57 (1982): 87–118, 47–82. The Tenjukoku Mandara appears in the catalogue for the second Hakurankai; see *Shisen*, no. 57, 74.

5 Satō, "Formation of the Academic Discipline," 169.

6 The activities of Fenollosa and Okakura have received extensive study. See, for example, Karatani Kōjin, "Japan as Art Museum: Okakura Tenshin and Fenollosa," in *A History of Modern Japanese Aesthetics*, ed. Michael F. Marra (Honolulu: University of Hawai'i Press, 2001), 43–52; Kinoshita Nagahiro, "Okakura Kakuzō as a Historian of Art," *Review of Japanese Culture and Society* 24 (2012): 26–38; and John Clark, "Okakura Tenshin and Aesthetic Nationalism," in *Since Meiji: Perspectives on the Japanese Visual Arts, 1868–2000*, ed. J. Thomas Rimer (Honolulu: University of Hawai'i Press, 2012), 212–56.

7 Shinkawa, *Shōtoku Taishi no rekishigaku*, 138–68.

8 Kakuzō Okakura, *The Ideals of the East, with Special Reference to the Art of Japan* (New York and Tokyo: ICG Muse, 2000), 105. For the Japanese-language version, see Okakura Tenshin, *Nihon bijutsushi* (Tokyo: Heibonsha, 2001), 62. For the "Suiko period," see Commission Impériale du Japon, *Histoire de l'Art du Japon*, 35–47.

9 Satō, "Formation of the Academic Discipline," 155.

10 Kurokawa Mayori, "Honpō kaiga enkaku setsu dai san," *Kokka*, no. 80 (1896): 611–16.

11 Kurokawa compiled *Kōgei shuryo* (Historical Documents on Craft) in 1877; he was involved in defining the different categories of art. See Dōshin Satō, "Art and Social Class: The Class System in Early Modern Japan and the Formation of 'Art,'" in Satō, *Modern Japanese Art and the Meiji State*, 68–69.

12 Kosugi Sugimura, "Tenjukoku no Mandara," *Kokka*, no. 83 (1896): 677–79. Kosugi published a similar article in 1901: "Suiko mikado jidai no bijutsu kōgei oyobi Tenjukoku Mandara to iu mono," *Shigaku zasshi* 12, no. 5 (1901): 67–77.

13 See TKH, *Hōryūji kennō hōmotsu*, 308.

14 Chūgūji Monzeki, *Chūgūji*, 24–25.

15 "Nishijin ori de Tenjukoku Shūchō," *Nara shinbun*, http://www.nara-np.co.jp/20100518103618.html (last accessed January 9, 2015). See also "Chūgūji de saikō no shishū saigen," *Shikoku shinbun*, http://www.shikoku-np.co.jp/national/culture_entertainment/20100520000126 (last accessed January 9, 2015).

Appendix

1 For a brief overview of archaeological textiles, see Sawada Mutsuyo, *Senshoku: Genshi, kodai hen*, Nihon no bijutsu, no. 263 (Tokyo: Shibundō, 1988), 17–21, and Matsumoto, *Jōdai-gire*. For a detailed report on a specific site, see Sawada Mutsuyo, "Fujinoki kofun no hisōsha ni mirareru ikotsu no maisō hōhō ni kansuru isshiken," in Sawada, *Jōdai-gire shūsei*, 13–23.

2 For fabrics in both collections, see Sawada, *Jōdai-gire shūsei*; and Matsumoto, ibid. For fabrics in the Hōryūji collection, see Hōryūji, *Hōryūji to shiruku rōdo*, 136–59.

3 For the latest and most detailed study of the remains of the Tenjukoku Shūchō Mandara, see Mita, "Gihō."

4 For important research, see Nakagawa, "Tenjukoku Mandara"; Ishida, "Kokuhō Tenjukoku Mandara Shūchō"; Ōta, "Tenjukoku Mandara no shūgi"; Mōri, "Tenjukoku Shūchō" and "Tenjukoku Shūchō ni tsuite";

Nishimura, "Zuhan kaisetsu"; Yamabe and Domyō, "Tenjukoku Shūchō"; Sawada, "Tenjukoku Shūchō"; and Mita, ibid.

5 For textile terminology and fabric structures, see Emery, *Primary Structures*.
6 Ibid., 76.
7 Nakagawa, "Tenjukoku Mandara," 336. This was an important discovery, as it elucidated the embroidery process.
8 For twill patterns, see Emery, *Primary Structures*, 92–107.
9 Ibid., 180–92.
10 For diagrams and explanations of complex gauzes in the Shōsōin collection, see Shōsōin Jimusho, *Shōsōin no ra* (Tokyo: Nihon Keizai Shinbunsha, 1971).
11 Sawada, "Tenjukoku Shūchō," 16. Mita has explained that the purple plain weave is damaged due to a lack of processing of the silk. Mita, "Gihō," 78.
12 Mōri Noboru was the first to have noticed this fabric, but he observed a light brown color, rather than white. Mōri, "Tenjukoku Shūchō ni tsuite," 33–34. This difference in color was used by Mōri and Ōhashi to argue that the seventh-century embroidered curtains were replicated (rather than repaired) in the thirteenth century. Ōhashi, *Tenjukoku Shūchō no kenkyū*, 118–21.
13 Ōta, "Tenjukoku Mandara no shūgi," 163–68.
14 Ibid., 167–68.
15 This discussion of embroidery stitches is based on Ōta, ibid.; Sawada, "Tenjukoku Shūchō," 12–15; and Mita, "Gihō," 88–89. For a handy glossary of embroidery stitches in Japanese, see NKH, *Shūbutsu*, 90–91. For thread twisting, see Emery, *Primary Structures*, 10–14.
16 For English-language explanations, diagrams, and photographs of embroidery stitches, see Jan Eaton, *Mary Thomas's Dictionary of Embroidery Stitches* (Dubai: Oriental Press, 2007); and Emery, ibid., 231–48. For outline and stem stitches, see the former source, 14–15; and the latter, 238–39.
17 Eaton, ibid., 100; Emery, ibid., 237.
18 Eaton, ibid., 114; Emery, ibid.
19 Eaton, ibid., 104.
20 Eaton, ibid., 23; Emery, *Primary Structures*, 247.
21 Eaton, ibid., 55; Emery, ibid.
22 For the undecorated fabrics, see Sawada, "Tenjukoku Shūchō," 16–18. For a definition of *chijimi*, see Matsumoto, *Jōdai-gire*, 204.
23 Sawada, ibid.
24 For a description of these fragments, see NKH, *Shūbutsu*, 31–34.
25 No studies of the white fabric appear to have been published.
26 NKH, *Shūbutsu*, 31–34. See also Ishida, "Tenjukoku Mandara no fukugen," 396–97; and Okumura Hideo, "Tōkyō Kokuritsu Hakubutsukan hokan jōdai-gire ni tsuite: Toku ni Hōryūji hōmotsu no kennō to sono ato ni kansuru shiryō," *Museum*, no. 390 (1983): 4–18.
27 Hōryūji, *Hōryūji to shiruku rōdo*, 154.
28 NKH, *Shūbutsu*, 33. For the *kanjōban*, see TKH, *Kanjōban*.
29 See Patricia Fister et al., *Ama monzeki: A Hidden Heritage: Treasures of the Japanese Imperial Convents* (Tokyo: Sankei Shinbunsha, 2009), 44.

List of Characters

Achi no Omi 阿智便主
Agongyō 阿含経
akagane 銅
ama 尼
Ama no nunahara oki no mahito 天渟中原瀛眞人
Amakashi 甘樫
Amaterasu 天照
Ame mikoto hirakasu wake 天命開別
Amekuni oshihiraki hironiha 天國排開廣庭
Amekuni oshihiraki hironiha no mikoto 阿米久爾斯波留支比里爾波乃弥己等
Amida 阿弥陀
An'ei 安永
Anahatori (or Ayahatori) 穴織
Anahobe Hashihito no hime miko 孔部間人公主
Anahobe no Hashihito 穴穂部間人
Ankoku 安國
Annyō 安養
Arahakadera gotein (or goshuin) engi 荒陵寺御手印縁起
Asa 阿佐
Ashuku 阿閦
Asuka 飛鳥
Asuka Kiyomihara 飛鳥浄御原
Asukadera 飛鳥寺
Asukaike 飛鳥池
atai 直
aya 綾
aya katabira 綾帷
Aya no Nukakori 漢奴加己利
Beishi 北史
bessho 別所
Bidatsu 敏達
bikuni 比丘尼
Boinreki (C: Wuyinli) 戊寅暦
bosatsukai bikuni 菩薩戒比丘尼
bu 分
Bun'ei 文永
Bunpō 文保
Byōkutsuge 廟堀偈
Chi no iratsume 乳娘
chijimi 縮
Chion'in 知恩院
Chōgen 重源
Chōkan 長寛
Chōkōdō 長講堂
chōrō 長老
Chōshimaru 調子丸
Chūagongyō 中阿含経
chūgū 中宮

Chūgūji 中宮寺
Chūgūji engi 中宮寺縁起
Chūgūji engi: Chūgūji mandara ama Shinnyo kishō tō no koto 中宮寺縁起—中宮寺曼荼羅尼信如祈請等事
Chūgūji Tenjukoku Mandara mei kikkō no zu 中宮寺天寿国曼荼羅銘亀甲図
Chūzen 忠禅
dai ichigi 第一義
Dai Nihon shi 大日本史
Daianji 大安寺
Daianji engi narabini ruki shizaichō 大安寺縁起并流記資材帳
Daihannyakyō 大般若経
Daikandaiji 大官大寺
daikanjō 大灌頂
Dajōkan 太政官
darani 陀羅尼
Dōgo 道後
Dōji 道慈
dōkyō 道教
Dōmyōji 道明寺
Dōshō 道昭
Edo 江戸
Ehime 兄媛
Eifukuji 叡福寺
Eikaku 栄範
Eison 叡尊
Eji (K. Hyeja) 慧慈
ekō 廻向
Enchi 遠智
engi 縁起
Engishiki 延喜式
Enichi 惠日
Enkyō 延慶
Enkyū 延久
Enpō 延宝
Eshi (C: Huisi) 慧思
Foshuo qiqian fo shenfu yisuan jing 佛説七千佛神符益算經
Fugen kangyō 普賢観経
Fuhon 冨本
Fujii Kuniyoshi 藤井國良
Fujinoki 藤の木
Fujiwara no Michinaga 藤原道長
Fujiwara no Sadamitsu 藤原定光
Fukūkenjaku Kannon 不空羂索観音
Fumibe 文部
Furuhito 古人
Fusō ryakki 扶桑略記
Gakka 学呵、覚呵
Gakkō 月光

239

gakumonji 学問寺
Gangōji 元興寺
Gangōji garan engi narabini ruki shizaichō 元興寺伽藍縁起 幷流記資財帳
ganmon 願文
Genga 玄雅
Genka (C: Yuanjia) 元嘉
Genkyū 元久
Genmei 元明
Genroku 元禄
Genshō 元正
Gihō (C: Yifeng) 儀鳳
go nyūmetsu 御入滅
Gofukakusa 後深草
gogyō (C: wu xing) 五行
Gokuraku jōdo 極楽浄土
Gokurakukai 極楽界
Gosaga 御嵯峨
Goshirakawa 後白河
Guze Kannon 救世観音
hachibushū 八部衆
Hachiokadera 蜂岡寺
haha no miko 母王
Haji 土師
Hakuchi 白雉
Hakuhō 白鳳
Hakurankai Jimukyoku 博覧会事務局
Han jiu yi 漢舊儀
haniwa 埴輪
Hata 秦
Hata no Kawakatsu 秦河勝
Hata no Sake 秦造酒
Hata no Yashiro no Sukune 羽田矢代宿禰
Hatsuse 泊瀬
Heian 平安
hengeshō 変化生
hensō (C: bianxiang) 変相
Hetu Luoshu (J: Kato rakusho) 河図落書
Higashiyama 東山
hijiri 聖、真人
Hinokuma no Hakatoko 檜隈博徳
hiraginu 平絹
Hirakasu wake 開別
hirami, hiraobi 褶
Hirano 平野
hiranui 平繡い
hiraori 平織
Hirohime 廣姫
Hitachi no iratsume 常陸娘
hōben 方便
Hōgen Ryōchi 法眼良知
hōin daikashōi gon daisōzu 法印大和尚位權大僧都
hōjū hōi 法住法位
Hokekyō 法華経

Hokikimi no iratsume 菩岐々美郎女
Hokke Chōkō Amida Sanmaidō 法華長講阿弥陀三昧堂
Hokke Sanjikkō 法華三十講
Hokke zanmai 法華三昧
Hokkeji 法華寺
Hokkiji 法起寺
hokkyō 法橋
Hōkōji 法興寺
hongan 本願
honji 本地
hontai 本体
hōō 法王
hōō (C: fenghuang) 鳳凰
Hōrinji 法輪寺
Hōryūji 法隆寺
Hōryūji bettō shidai 法隆寺別当次第
Hōryūji garan engi narabini ruki shizaichō 法隆寺伽藍縁起 幷流記資材帳
Hōryūji Ryōkin homōshū 法隆寺良訓補忘集
Hōryūji tōin engi 法隆寺東院縁起
Hosshin 發心
Hossō 法相
Hotete no Iratsume 法提郎女
Huainanzi 淮南子
Huangquan 黄泉
Hyakurenshō 百練抄
Iga 伊賀
Ikaruga 斑鳩
Ikaruga koji binran (benran) 斑鳩古事便覽
Ikarugadera 斑鳩寺
Ikebe 潰辺
Ikejiridera 池後寺
Imaki Ayahito Kōsai 新漢人廣濟
Imaki Ayahito Nichimon 新漢人日文
Imaki Ayahito Ōkuni 新漢人大圀
Imaki no Aya 新漢
Imbe no Hironari 斎部広成
Imi 斎
Inabe Tachibana 位奈部橘
Inariyama 稲荷山
inju 院主
Ippen 一遍
Ippen shōnin eden 一遍上人絵伝
irimoya 入母屋
Isonokami 石上
Iyo fudoki 伊予風土記
Jian 治安
Jien 慈円
Jingo keiun 神護景雲
Jinki 神亀
Jinmu 神武
Jinshin no ran 壬申の乱
Jiren 慈蓮
Jishōin 慈性院

Jishū 時宗
Jitō 持統
jitsumei 実名
jō (C: *zhang*) 丈
jōdo 浄土
Jōe 定恵
Jōei 貞永
Jōen 定圓
Jōgū Shōtoku hōō 上宮聖徳法王
Jōgū Shōtoku hōō teisetsu 上宮聖徳法王帝説
Jōgū Shōtoku Taishi den hoketsuki 上宮聖徳太子伝補闕記
Jōgū Taishi 上宮太子
Jōgū Taishi gyoki 上宮太子御記
Jōgū Taishi no kofun 上宮太子の古墳
Jōgūki 上宮記
Jōgūin 上宮王院
jōgyō sanmai 常行三昧
jōjakkōdo 常寂光土
Jōjun Shōnin 定順上人
Jōkai 浄戒
Jōkan 定觀
Jōkei 貞慶
Jomei 舒明
jōroku 丈六
Jōryaku 承暦
Jōtoku 承徳
Jūichimen Kannon 十一面観音
kabane 姓
kada 伽陀
kaeshinui 返し繍い
Kagen 嘉元
Kagu 香久
Kaikei 快慶
Kajūji 勧修寺
Kakujō 覚盛
Kakuken 覚賢
Kamakura 鎌倉
Kameyama 亀山
Kamitsumiya no miko 上宮皇子
kan 干
kanbun 漢文
kanejaku 曲尺
Kanesuke 兼輔
Kangen 寛元
Kangi 寛喜
kanjōban 灌頂幡
Kankō 寛弘
Kanko zatsujō 観古雑帖
Kanmuryōjukyō 観無量寿経
Kannon 観音
kanoto-mi 辛巳
Kanroku (K. Kwalluk) 觀勒
Kanshō 寛正
Kanshun 桓舜

Kashiwade no Hokikimi 膳部菩岐々美
Kashiwade no Katabuko 膳部加多夫古
Katei 嘉禎
katen 加点
Katsuragi 葛城
Katsuraki no Sotsuhiko 葛城襲津彦
Kawachi 河内
Kawachi Dōmyōji 河内道明寺
Kawakami no Iratsume 河上娘
Kawaradera 川原寺
Kawashima Orimono Kenkyūjo 川島織物研究所
Kazan'in Chūnagon Fujiwara Morotsugu 花山院中納言藤原諸継
Kazuraki 葛木
kechien 結縁
Kegonkyō 華厳経
kei 磬
Keisei 慶政
Keitai 継体
Kenji 健治
Kenkō 顕光
Kenkyū 建久
Kenpō jūshichijō 憲法十七条
Kenshin 顕真
kesa 袈裟
keshō 化生
ki (C: *qi*) 気
Kibi 吉備
Kii 紀伊
kikajin 帰化人
Kinmei 欽明
kinoe-inu 甲戌
kinunui 衣縫、縫工女
kinunuibe 衣縫部
kirin (C: *qilin*) 麒麟
kisaki 妃、后
Kitashi hime 堅鹽媛
Kitashi hime no mikoto 吉多斯比弥乃弥己等
Kōan 弘安
Kōchō 弘長
Kōfukuji 興福寺
Kofun 古墳
Kogoshūi 古語拾遺
Kōgyoku 皇極
Kojidan 古事談
Kojiki 古事記
kokan'on 古韓音
kokanjaku 古韓尺
Kokikyūbutsu hozon kata 古器旧物保存方
Kokka 国華
Kokki 国記
Koma no Ekaki no Komaro 高麗畫師子麻呂
Koma no Kasei 高麗加西溢
Komajaku 高麗尺

komanui 駒繡い
Kōmyō 光明
Kondō nikki 金堂日記
Kongō Rikishi 金剛力士
Kongōbuji 金剛峰寺
Kōnin 弘仁
Kōnin (monk) 康仁
Konkōin 金光院
konpon sonzō 根本尊像
Kōryūji 広隆寺
Kose no Mitsue 巨勢三杖
kōshiki 講式
Kōshō 康勝
Kōtoku 孝徳
Kōwa 康和
Kudara hongi 百済本紀
Kudara Ōdera 百済大寺
Kuji hongi 旧事本紀
Kujiki 旧事紀
Kūkai 空海
Kume 来目
Kunikami 國守
Kurahitobe Hata no Kuma 椋部秦久麻
Kurehatori 呉織
Kurohime 黒媛
Kuromaro Genri Takamuku no Ayahito 黒麻呂玄理高向漢人
Kyōgi 教義
Kyōhō 享保
ling zuo 靈座
Lingbao 靈寶
Makami no Hara 真神原
man'yōgana 万葉仮名
Man'yōshū 万葉集
mandara 曼荼羅
mappō 末法
matsuinui 纏繡い
meguri ni めぐりに
Mei no iratsume 姪娘
Meiji 明治
Min 旻
Minabuchi no Ayahito Shōan 南淵漢人請安
Minami Kawachi 南河内
Minamoto no Akikane 源顕兼
minori 法
Minori no nushi no mikoto 法主王
Miroku 弥勒
Miroku taisei bukkyō 弥勒大成仏経
Misasagi 陵
Miwa 三輪
miyatsuko 造
mizuno-tori 癸酉
mogari no miya 殯宮
mokkan 木簡
Momohara 桃原

Monmu 文武
Mononobe 物部
Mononobe no Moriya 物部守屋
Moto Gangōji 本元興寺
moya 喪屋
Mujū Ichien 無住一円
Munakata 胸形
muraji 連
Muromachi 室町
Muryōgikyō (C: *Wuling yi jing*) 無量義経
Muryōju Tenju 無量寿天寿
Muryōjukoku 無量寿国
Muryōjukyō (C: *Wuling shou jing*) 無量寿経
Muryōkō 無量光
Musa no Suguri no Ao 身狭村主青
mushiharai 虫払い
Myōkikoku 妙喜国
naga kaeshinui 長返し繡い
Naidaijin 内大臣
Naka no Ōe 中大兄
Nakatomi no Kamatari 中富鎌足
Nakatsu 仲
Namu Amidabutsu sazenshū 南無阿弥陀佛作善集
Naniwa 難波
Nanto 南都
Nara 奈良
Nara no Osa Emyō 奈羅譯語惠明
nenbutsu 念仏
Nichijō Shōnin 日浄上人
Nichira 日羅
Nihon shoki 日本書紀
niji 尼寺
Nijō 二条
Nikkō 日光
Ninnōe 仁王会
Ninnōkyō 仁王経
Nintoku 仁徳
Niō 仁王
Nishijin Bijutsuori Kōbō 西陣美術織工房
Nomi no Sukune 野見宿禰
Nukatabe 額田部
Nunakura no Futotama shiki 渟中倉太珠敷
Nunakura no Futotama shiki no mikoto 蕤名久羅乃布等多麻斯支乃弥己等
nyoi 如意
Nyoirin Kannon 如意輪観音
Ōama 大海人
Oane no mikoto 乎阿尼乃弥己等
obi nijūni jō 帯廿二条
obito 首
Ochi no Iratsume 遠智娘
Ōchō 応長
Ōe no Chikamichi 大江親通
Ōei 応永

Ohonu no iratsume 太蘾娘
Ōjin 応神
ōjō 往生
ōjō no mandara 往生曼荼羅
ōkimi 大王
ōkimi tennō 大王天皇
Okinaga 息長
ōkisaki 大后
okugaki 奥書
Ōkura 大蔵
okurina 諡
omi 臣
Ōmi 近江
Ōmi Ōtsu 近江大津
Ōmiwa 大三輪
Ōmiyain Fujiwara no Kitsushi 大宮院藤原姞子
omote hiranui 表平繡い
Onjōji 園城寺
Ono no Imoko 小野妹子
ōomi 大臣
Oribe 織部
Osada 乎沙多
Ōsazaki no mikoto 大鷦鷯尊
Oshisaka no Hikohito 押坂彦人
Otohime 弟媛
Ōtomo no Sadehiko no Muraji 大伴狹手彦連
Ōtoribe Aya no Matsuko 大鳥部文松子
Ōtsu 大津
Owari 尾治
ra 羅
raigō 来迎
Rakutō 洛東
ranshō 卵生
renge keshō 蓮華化生
Richū 履中
Ritsu 律
Ritsuon sōbōden 律苑僧寶傳
Ritsuryō 律令
ritsuryō kokka 律令国家
ro 絽
ro heiken 絽平絹
Ruiyingtu 符瑞図
Ryō no shūge 令集解
Ryōjusen'in nenjū gyōji 霊鷲山院年中行事
Ryōzenji 霊山寺
Saichō 最澄
Saidaiji 西大寺
Saihō jōdo 西方浄土
Saimei 斉明
Sairinji 西林寺
Sakaibe no Marise 境部摩理勢
sankotsu ichibyō no Amida sanzon 三骨一廟の阿弥陀三尊
sanmaidō 三昧堂
sashinui 刺し繡い

Seishi 勢至
seken wa munashi, tada hotoke nomi kore makoto nari 世間虚仮唯仏是真
sen (C: *xian*) 仙人
setsuwa 説話
Settsu 摂津
sha 紗
Shaka 釈迦
Shaka nenbutsu 釈迦念仏
Shakadō 釈迦堂
Shaku Nihongi 釈日本紀
shaku (C: *chi*) 尺
Shasekishū 沙石集
shen wei 神位
shi 支
shibi 鴟尾
Shichidaiji nikki 七大寺日記
Shien 思円
Shiga no Ayahito Eon 志賀漢人慧隠
Shikishima 斯帰斯麻
shikorobuki 錏葺
Shin Daibutsuji 新大佛寺
shinabe 品部
Shinaga 磯長
shinbutsu bunri 神仏分離
Shingon 真言
Shingon Ritsu 真言律
Shinnyo 信如
shinobigoto 誄
Shinran 親鸞
Shinsen shōjiroku 新撰姓氏録
shishin (C: *sixiang*) 四神
shisshō 湿生
Shitennō 四天王
Shitennōji 四天王寺
Shitennōji engi 四天王寺縁起
Shō 聖
Shō Kannon 聖観音
Shōbōji 正法寺
Shōdai senzai denki 招提千歳伝記
Shōen 璋圓
Shōka 正嘉
Shōkō Mandara 聖皇曼荼羅
Shoku Nihongi 続日本紀
Shōmangyō 勝鬘経
Shōmu 聖武
Shōryakuji 正暦寺
Shōryōe 聖霊会
Shōryōin 聖霊院
Shōshiden 松子伝
Shōsōin 正倉院
Shōtoku Taishi den hoketsuki 聖徳太子伝補闕記
Shōtoku Taishi den shiki 聖徳太子伝私記
Shōtoku Taishi denki 聖徳太子伝記

Shōtoku Taishi denryaku 聖徳太子伝暦
Shōtoku Taishi Heishi den zakkanmon 聖徳太子平氏伝雑勘文
Shōyo 聖誉
Shōyoshō 聖誉抄
shubi 麈尾
shūbutsu 繡仏
Shuchō 朱鳥
shūchō nichō 繡帳二張
Shūgyokushū 拾玉集
shujaku (C: *zhu niao*) 朱雀
shusuzashi 朱子刺し
shūzō 繡像
sōbyō 宗廟
Soga Iname no Sukune 蘇我稲目宿禰、巻奇伊奈米足尼
Soga no Akae 蘇我赤兄
Soga no Emishi 蘇我蝦夷
Soga no Iruka 蘇我入鹿
Soga no Kurayamada no Ishikawamaro 蘇我倉山田石川麻呂
Soga no Machi no Sukune 蘇我満智宿禰
Soga no Umako 蘇我馬子
Sōji 惣持
sōrei 惣禮
suguri 勝
suijaku 垂迹
Suiko 推古
Suikochō ibun 推古朝遺文
sumera no mikoto 天皇
sun 寸
Suō 周芳
suppon 鼈
Sushun 崇峻
tabanenui 束ね繡い
Tachibana no Ōiratsume 橘大女郎、多至波奈大女郎
Tachibana no Toyohi 橘豐日
Tachibana no Toyohi no mikoto 多至波奈等已比乃弥己等
Tachibanadera 橘寺
Taihō 大宝
Taika 大化
Taima Mandara 当麻曼荼羅
Taima Mandara engi 当麻曼荼羅縁起
Taimadera 当麻寺
Taiping jing 大平經
Taira no Kunimoto 平国本
Taishang Laojun shuo changsheng yisuan miaojing 太上老君説長生益算妙經
Taishi den kokon mokurokushō 太子伝古今目録抄
Taishi Mandara kōshiki 太子曼荼羅講式
Taishi no miraiki 太子未来記
Taishi shinkō 太子信仰
taishō 胎生
Taishō 大正
Taiyi 太一
Takada Honzan Senjūji 高田本山博修寺
Takahashi Ason 高橋朝臣

Takama no Hara 高天原
Takamatsuzuka 高松塚
Takamiya 高宮
Takara 財
Takechi Ōdera 高市大寺
Takeda 竹田
Tamamushi 玉虫
Tamitsukai 民使
Tamura 田村
Tanakami 田上
tasuki 襷
ten renge 天蓮華
Tenbun 天文
Tendai 天台
Tengi 天喜
Tenji 天智
tianshou (J: *tenju*) 天壽
Tenjukoku (shin) Mandara uragaki 天壽国[新]曼荼羅裏書
Tenjukoku Mandara Shūchō engi kantenbun 天壽国曼荼羅繡帳縁起観点文
Tenjukoku Shūchō Mandara 天壽国繡帳曼荼羅
tenka 天下
Tenmu 天武
Tennin 天仁
tennin (C: *tianren*) 天人
tennō 天皇
Tennō ki 天皇記
Tennōji hiketsu 天王寺秘訣
Tenpuku 天福
Tenpyō 天平
Tenpyō hōji 天平宝字
Tenpyō shōhō 天平勝宝
Tenri 天理
Tenshō 天承
Tōdaiji 東大寺
Tōdaiji yōroku 東大寺要録
Tōgū Jōgū Shōtoku Hōō 東宮上宮聖徳法王
Tōin 東院
Tojiko no Iratsume 刀自古郎女
Tokoyo no kuni 常世国
Tomimi 聡耳
tomo no miyatsuko 伴造
toraijin 渡来人
Tōrin 董麟
Tōshōdaiji 唐招提寺
Tosotsu tenju 兜率天寿
Tosotsuten 兜率天
Towazugatari とわずがたり
Toyomi kekashikiya hime 豐御食炊屋姫
Toyomi kekashikiya hime no mikoto 等已弥居加斯支移比弥乃弥己等
Toyomimito Shōtoku 豊耳聰聖徳
Toyotomimi Minori no Ōkimi 豊聰耳法大王
Toyotomimi no mikoto 等己刀弥弥乃弥己等

tsugi harinui 次針縫い
Tsuka no Omi 都加便主
Tsukishine 舂米
Tsukushi 筑紫
tsumadoikon 妻問い婚
tsūshō 通称
Uchikura 内倉
Ue no miya (or Kamitsumiya) 上宮
Uji 宇治
Uji no Kaidako 宛道貝鮹
Umayado 厩戸
Umayado Toyoto Yamimi 厩戸豊聰八耳
Umayado Toyotomimi 厩戸豊聰耳
uneme 釆女
ungenzashi 繧繝刺し
Unkei 運慶
unki (C: *yunqi*) 雲気
Uno 鸕野
Urabe Kanebumi 卜部兼文
Urabon (C: Yulanpen) 盂蘭盆
Uzumasa 太秦
wafū shigō 和風諡号
Wani 王仁
Washū kyūseki yūkō 和州旧跡幽考

Yakushi 薬師
Yakushiji engi 薬師寺縁起
Yamadadera 山田寺
Yamashiro 山背
Yamato meishoki 大和名所記
Yamato no Aya no Atai Fukuin 倭漢直副福因
Yamato no Aya no Makken 東漢末賢
Yamato no Aya no Tsuka 東漢直掬
Yisuan jing 益算經
Yōmei 用明
Yomi no kuni 黄泉国
Yugashijiron 瑜伽師地論
Yuima 維摩
Yuimakyō 維摩経
Yumedono 夢殿
Yumedono Kannon 夢殿観音
Yuzuki 弓月
zashiki 座敷
Ze-amidabutsu 是阿弥陀仏
Zenkōji 善光寺
Zenkōji engi 善光寺縁起
Zhoushu 周書
Zōagongyō 雑阿含経
zokusan ō 粟散

Bibliography

Key to abbreviations used in the notes

DNBZ *Dai Nihon Bukkyō zensho*
HSS *Hōryūji shiryō shūsei: Eiinbon*
NBK Nara Bunkazai Kenkyūjo
NKBT Nihon koten bungaku taikei
NKH Nara Kokuritsu Hakubutsukan
NKZ Nihon koten zenshū
NRT Nara rokudaiji taikan
NS Nihon shoki
STZ *Shōtoku Taishi zenshū*
TKH Tokyo Kokuritsu Hakubutsukan
YKT *Yamato koji taikan*

Primary Sources

Chūgūji engi. In *Yamato koji taikan*, edited by Ōta Hirotarō, vol. 1. Tokyo: Iwanami Shoten, 1977.

Chūgūji engi: Chūgūji mandara ama Shinnyo kishō tō no koto. In *Fushimi no Miya ke Kujō ke kyūzō shoji engi shū. Zushoryō sōkan*. Tokyo: Kunaicho Shoryōbu, 1970.

Daianji engi narabi ni ruki shizaichō. In *Daianji shi shiryō*, edited by Daianji Shi Henshū Iinkai. Nara: Daianji, 1984.

Eison. *Kongō busshi Eison kanshin gakushōki*. In *Saidaiji Eison denki shūsei*, edited by Nara Kokuritsu Bunkazai Kenkyūjo. Kyoto: Hōzōkan, 1977.

Engishiki. Nihon koten zenshū, edited by Yosano Hiroshi et al., vol. 5. Tokyo: Nihon Koten Zenshū Kankōkai, 1927–29.

Fan Ye. *Hou Han shu*. Beijing: Zhonghua shu ju, 1973.

Fudoki. Compiled by Yoshino Yutaka. Tōyō bunko, vol. 145. 1969. Reprint, Tokyo: Heibonsha, 1981.

Fusō ryakki. In *Kokushi taikei*, vol. 6. Tokyo: Keizai Zasshisha, 1897–1901.

Fusō ryakki. Shintei zōho kokushi taikei, vol. 12. Tokyo: Yoshikawa Kōbunkan, 1931.

Gangōji garan engi narabi ni ruki shizaichō. In *Jisha engi*, Nihon shisō taikei, edited by Sakurai Tokutarō et al., vol. 20. Tokyo: Iwanami Shoten, 1978.

Hayashi Sōho. *Washū kyūseki yūkō*. 1681.

Hoida Tadatomo. *Kanko zatsujō*. Nihon koten zenshū, edited by Yosano Hiroshi et al., vol. 3. Tokyo: Nihon Koten Zenshū Kankōkai, 1928.

Hōryūji bettō shidai. In *Zoku gunsho ruijū: Honinbu*, vol. 4. Tokyo: Zoku Gunsho Ruijū Kanseikai, 1930.

Hōryūji butsuzōki. In *Hōryūji shiryō shūsei: Eiinbon*, vol. 8. Tokyo: Wakō Shuppan, 1983–85.

Hōryūji engi shirabyōshi. In *Hōryūji shiryō shūsei: Eiinbon*, vol. 8. Tokyo: Wakō Shuppan, 1983–85.

Hōryūji garan engi narabi ni ruki shizaichō. In *Dai Nihon Bukkyō zensho*, vol. 85. Tokyo: Suzuki Gakujutsu Zaidan, 1970–73. Also published in *Hōryūji shiryō shūsei: Eiinbon*, vol. 1. Tokyo: Wakō Shuppan, 1985.

Hōryūji shiryō shūsei: Eiinbon. 15 vols. Tokyo: Wakō Shuppan, 1983–85.

Hōryūji tōin engi. In *Dai Nihon Bukkyō zensho*, vol. 85. Tokyo: Suzuki Gakujutsu Zaidan, 1970–73. Also published in *Hōryūji shiryō shūsei: Eiinbon*, vol. 1. Tokyo: Wakō Shuppan, 1985.

Jōen. *Taishi mandara kōshiki*. In *Shōtoku Taishi zenshū*, vol. 4. Kyoto: Rinsen Shoten, 1988.

Jōgū Shōtoku hōō teisetsu. In *Dai Nihon Bukkyō zensho*, vol. 71. Tokyo: Suzuki Gakujutsu Zaidan, 1972.

Jōgū Shōtoku Taishi den hoketsuki. In *Shōtoku Taishi zenshū*, vol. 2. Kyoto: Rinsen Shoten, 1988.

Kakuken. *Ikaruga koji binran*. In *Dai Nihon Bukkyō zensho*, vol. 85. Tokyo: Suzuki Gakujutsu Zaidan, 1970–73. Also published in *Hōryūji shiryō shūsei: Eiinbon*, vol. 15. Tokyo: Wakō Shuppan, 1984.

Kenshin. *Shōtoku Taishi den shiki*. In *Hōryūji shiryō shūsei: Eiinbon*, vol. 4. Tokyo: Wakō Shuppan, 1985.

Kondō nikki. In *Hōryūji shiryō shūsei: Eiinbon*, vol. 2. Tokyo: Wakō Shuppan, 1985.

Minamoto Akikane. *Kojidan*. Annotated by Kobayashi Yasuharu. Tokyo: Gendai Shichōsha, 1981.

Nakanoin Masatada no Musume. *The Confessions of Lady Nijō*. Translated by Karen Brazell. Garden City, NY: Anchor Books, 1973.

Nihon shoki. Nihon koten bungaku taikei, edited by Sakamoto Tarō, vols. 67, 68. Tokyo: Iwanami Shoten, 1965.

Ryōjusen'in nenjū gyōji. In *Yamato koji taikan*, edited by Ōta Hirotarō, vol. 1. Tokyo: Iwanami Shoten, 1977.

Ryōkin. *Hōryūji Ryōkin homōshū*. In *Zokuzoku gunsho ruijū*, vol. 11, *Shūkyō-bu*. Tokyo: Kokusho Kankōkai, 1909.

Shichidaiji nikki. In *Dai Nihon Bukkyō zensho*, vol. 83. Tokyo: Suzuki Gakujutsu Zaidan, 1970–73.

Shōdai senzai denki. In *Dai Nihon Bukkyō zensho*, vol. 64. Tokyo: Suzuki Gakujutsu Zaidan, 1970–73.

Shoku Nihongi. Shin Nihon koten bungaku taikei, annotated by Aoki Kazuo, vols. 12–16. Tokyo: Iwanami Shoten, 1990.

Shōtoku Taishi denki. In *Shōtoku Taishi zenshū*, vol. 2. Kyoto: Rinsen Shoten, 1988.

Shōtoku Taishi denryaku. In *Dai Nihon Bukkyō zensho*, vol. 71. Tokyo: Suzuki Gakujutsu Zaidan, 1972. Also published in *Shōtoku Taishi zenshū*, vol. 2. Kyoto: Rinsen Shoten, 1988.

Shōtoku Taishi kokon mokuroku sho. In *Dai Nihon Bukkyō zensho*, vol. 71. Tokyo: Suzuki Gakujutsu Zaidan, 1970–73.

Shōyo. *Shōyoshō*. In *Dai Nihon Bukkyō zensho*, vol. 72. Tokyo: Suzuki Gakujutsu Zaidan, 1970–73. Also published in *Hōryūji shiryō shūsei: Eiinbon*, vol. 10. Tokyo: Wakō Shuppan, 1985.

Tai ping jing he jiao. Edited by Wang Ming. Beijing: Zhonghua shu ju, 1960.

Yakushiji shiryō shū: Yakushiji engi. In *Kokan bijutsu shiryō: Jiin hen*, edited by Fujita Tsuneyo, vol. 2. Tokyo: Chūō Kōron, 1999.

Secondary Sources

Abe, Stanley K. "Northern Wei Daoist Sculpture from Shaanxi Province." *Cahiers d'Extrême Asie* 9, no. 2 (1996–97): 69–130.

———. *Ordinary Images*. Chicago and London: University of Chicago Press, 2002.

Aboshi Yoshinori. "Kankoku no hekiga kofun." *Bukkyō geijutsu*, no. 89 (1972): 3–15.

———. "Kofun hekiga, boshi nado ni miru shujaku, hōō no zuzō." In Aboshi Yoshinori, *Hekiga kofun no kenkyū*. Tokyo: Gakuseisha, 2006, 152–91. First published in *Kansei daigaku hakubutsukan kiyō* 8 (2002).

———. "Nihon Takamatsu, Kitora kofun no hekiga." *Higashi Ajia no kodai bunka*, no. 124 (2005): 2–10.

Adachi Kō. "Tenjukoku Shūchō no genkei." *Kenchiku shi* 2, no. 5 (1940): 85–87.

Aida Hanji. "Tenjukoku Mandara meibun kō." *Yumedono* 13 (1935): 66–79. Also published in *Chūgūji no shomondai*, edited by Saeki Keizō. Nara: Ikaruga Kokyōsha Shuppanbu, 1943, 104–14.

Aizu Yaichi. "Chūgūji Mandara ni kansuru bunken." *Tōyō bijutsu* 1 (1929): 90–104.

———. "Hōryūji Kondō Amidazō ni kansuru bunken." *Tōyō bijutsu* 2 (1929): 78–82.

Akashi Somendo. "Gakkan Tenjukoku Shucho shi." *Yumedono* 17 (1937): 86–109.

———. "Tenjukoku Shūchō no kōsatsu." *Tōyō bijutsu* 4 (1930): 105–8.

Amstutz, Galen, and Mark L. Blum. "Pure Lands in Japanese Religion." *Japanese Journal of Religious Studies* 33, no. 2 (2006): 217–21.

Aoki Mosaku. *Tenjukoku Mandara no kenkyū*. Nara: Ikaruga Kokyōsha Shuppanbu, 1946.

———. "Zoku Tenjukoku Shūchō no shin kenkyū." In *Chūgūji no shomondai*, edited by Saeki Keizō. Nara: Ikaruga Kokyōsha Shuppanbu, 1943, 74–103.

Arai Hiroshi. *Maboroshi no kodaijaku: Komajaku wa nakatta*. Tokyo: Yoshikawa Kōbunkan, 1992.

Ariga, Yoshitaka. "Korean Elements in Japanese Pictorial Representation in the Early Asuka Period." In Washizuka Hiromitsu et al., *Transmitting the Forms of Divinity: Early Buddhist Art from Korea and Japan*. New York: Japan Society, 2003, 96–105.

The Arts of Korea. 5 vols. Seoul: Dong Hwa Publishing Co., 1979.

Aston, W.G., trans. *Nihongi: Chronicles of Japan from the Earliest Times to A.D. 697*. Rutland, VT and Tokyo: Charles E. Tuttle Co., 1988.

Asukamura Kyōiku Iinkai. *Kamegata sekizōbutsu ikō*. Asuka: Asuka Kokyō Kenshōkai, 2000.

———. *Kitora kofun to hekiga*. Asuka: Asuka Kokyō Kenshōkai, 2001.

Azuma Ushio and Tanaka Toshiaki. *Kōkuri no rekishi to iseki*. Tokyo: Chūō Kōronsha, 1995.

Bagley, Robert. *Ancient Sichuan: Treasures from a Lost Civilization*. Princeton, NJ: Princeton University Press, 2001.

Bambling, Michele. "Kanshukushō Tensuishi hakken no Zuimatsu Tōsho no jitsugetsu byōbu ni tsuite." *Bukkyō geijutsu*, no. 222 (1995): 15–40.

Barnes, Gina L. *China, Korea and Japan: The Rise of Civilization in East Asia*. London: Thames and Hudson, 1993.

———. "The Role of the *Be* in the Formation of the Yamato State." In *Specialization, Exchange, and Complex Societies*, edited by Elizabeth M. Brumfiel and Timothy K. Earle. Cambridge and New York: Cambridge University Press, 1987, 86–101.

———. *Women in the* Nihon shoki: *Mates, Mothers, Mystics, Militarists, Maids, Manufacturers, Monarchs, Messengers and Managers*. Durham East Asian Papers, vol. 20. Durham, England: Department of East Asian Studies, Durham University, 2006.

Barret, Tim. "Shinto and Taoism in Early Japan." In *Shinto in History: Ways of the Kami*, edited by John Breen and Mark Teeuwen. Honolulu: University of Hawai'i Press, 2000, 13–31.

Bender, Ross. "Auspicious Omens in the Reign of the Last Empress of Nara Japan, 749–770." *Japanese Journal of Religious Studies* 40, no. 1 (2013): 45–76.

Bentley, John. *Historiographical Trends in Early Japan*. Lewiston, NY: Edwin Mellen Press, 2002.

———. "The Origin of Man'yōgana." *Bulletin of the School of Oriental and African Studies* 64, no. 1 (2001): 59–73.

Berling, Judith A. "Death and Afterlife in Chinese Religions." In *Death and Afterlife: Perspectives of World Religions*, edited by Hiroshi Obayashi. New York: Greenwood Press, 1992, 181–92.

Bethe, Monica. "Color in the *Man'yōshū*, an Eighth-Century Anthology of Japanese Poetry." In *Color in Ancient and Medieval East Asia*, edited by Mary Dusenbury. Lawrence, KS: Spencer Museum of Art, 2015, 135–42.

Bialock, David. *Eccentric Spaces, Hidden Histories: Narrative, Ritual and Royal Authority from* The Chronicles of Japan *to* The Tale of Genji. Stanford, CA: Stanford University Press, 2007.

Bock, Felicia. *Classical Learning and Taoist Practices in Early Japan with a Translation of Books XVI and XX of the Engi-shiki*. Tempe, AZ: Center for Asian Studies, Arizona State University, 1985.

Bokenkamp, Stephen. "Death and Ascent in Ling-pao Taoism." *Taoist Resources* 1, no. 2 (1989): 1–20.

———. *Early Daoist Scriptures*. With a contribution by Peter Nickerson. Berkeley, Los Angeles, and London: University of California Press, 1997.

———. "Stages of Trascendence: The *Bhūmi* Concept in Taoist Scripture." In *Chinese Buddhist Apocrypha*, edited by Robert E. Buswell. Honolulu: University of Hawai'i Press, 1990, 119–47.

———. "The Yao Boduo Stele as Evidence for the 'Dao-Buddhism' of the Early Lingbao Scriptures." *Cahiers d'Extrême Asie* 9, no. 2 (1996–97): 55–68.

Borgen, Robert. "The Origins of the Sugawara: A History of the Haji Family." *Monumenta Nipponica* 30, no. 4 (1975): 405–22.

Bowring, Richard. *The Religious Traditions of Japan*. Cambridge: Cambridge University Press, 2005.

Brownlee, John S. *Japanese Historians and the National Myths, 1600–1945: The Age of the Gods and Emperor Jinmu*. 1997. Reprint, Vancouver: University of British Columbia Press, 1999.

Bucher, Jo. *The Complete Guide to Embroidery Stitches and Crewel*. New York: Creative Home Library, 1971.

Bulling, A.G. "The Guide of the Souls Picture in the Western Han Tomb in Ma-wang-tui near Ch'ang-sha." *Oriental Art* 20, no. 2 (1974): 158–73.

Bunkachō, Tokyo Kokuritsu Hakubutsukan, and Nara Bunkazai Kenkyūjo. *Kitora kofun hekiga: Tokubetsuten*. Tokyo: Asahi Shinbunsha, 2014.

Bunkazai Hogo Iinkai. *Kokuhō*. 6 vols. Tokyo: Mainichi Shinbunsha, 1963–67.

Bunkazai Kyōkai. *Kokuhō zuroku*. Tokyo: Bunkazai Kyōkai, 1952.

Bush, Susan. "Floral Motifs and Vine Scrolls in Chinese Art of the Late Fifth to Early Sixth Centuries A.D." *Artibus Asiae* 38, no. 1 (1976): 49–83.

———. "Some Parallels between Chinese and Korean Ornamental Motifs of the Late Fifth and Early Sixth Centuries A.D." *Archives of Asian Art* 37 (1984): 60–78.

———. "Thunder Monsters and Wind Spirits in Early Sixth Century China and the Epitaph Table of Lady Yuan." *Boston Museum Bulletin* 72 (1975): 24–55.

———. "Thunder Monsters, Auspicious Animals, and Floral Ornament in Early Sixth-Century China." *Ars Orientalis* 10 (1975): 19–33.

Buswell, Robert E., Jr., and Donald S. Lopez, Jr. *The Princeton Dictionary of Buddhism*. Princeton, NJ: Princeton University Press, 2014.

Cahill, Suzanne. *Transcendence and Divine Passion: The Queen Mother of the West in Medieval China*. Stanford, CA: Stanford University Press, 1993.

Cammann, Schuyler. "Some Early Chinese Symbols of Duality." *History of Religions* 24, no. 3 (1985): 215–54.

Campany, Robert F. *Making Transcendents: Ascetics and Social Memory in Early Medieval China*. Honolulu: University of Hawai'i Press, 2009.

———. *To Live as Long as Heaven and Earth: A Translation and Study of Ge Hong's* Traditions of Divine Transcendence. Berkeley, CA: University of California Press, 2002.

Carter, William. "Aya family." *Kodansha Encyclopedia of Japan*, vol. 1. Tokyo and New York: Kodansha, 1983, 125.

———. "Hata family." *Kodansha Encyclopedia of Japan*, vol. 3. Tokyo and New York: Kodansha, 1983, 111.

Carr, Kevin Gray. *Plotting the Prince: Shōtoku Cults and the Mapping of Medieval Japanese Buddhism*. Honolulu: University of Hawai'i Press, 2012.

Chang Yang-mo et al. *Arts of Korea*. New York: Metropolitan Museum of Art, 1998.

Chaves, Jonathan. "A Han Painted Tomb at Loyang." *Artibus Asiae* 30, no. 1 (1968): 5–27.

Ch'en, Kenneth. *Buddhism in China*. Princeton, NJ: Princeton University Press, 1973.

Chŏn Ho-t'ae (Jeon Ho-Tae). "Artistic Creation, Borrowing, Adaptation, and Assimilation in Koguryo Tomb Murals of the Fourth to Seventh Century." *Archives of Asian Art* 56 (2006): 81–104.

———. *The Dreams of the Living and Hopes of the Dead: Goguryeo Tomb Murals*. Seoul: Seoul National University Press, 2007.

Chūgūji Monzeki. *Chūgūji*. Tokyo: Benridō, 1999.

Clark, John. "Okakura Tenshin and Aesthetic Nationalism." In *Since Meiji: Perspectives on the Japanese Visual Arts, 1868–2000*, edited by J. Thomas Rimer. Honolulu: University of Hawai'i Press, 2012, 212–56.

Commission Impériale du Japon a l'Exposition Universelle de Paris. *Histoire de l'Art du Japon*. Paris: Maurice Brunoff, 1900.

Como, Michael. "Ethnicity, Sagehood, and the Politics of Literacy in Asuka Japan." *Japanese Journal of Religious Studies* 30, no. 1 (2003): 61–84.

———. "Of Temples, Horses, and Tombs: Hōryūji and Chūgūji in Heian and Early Kamakura Japan." In *Hōryūji Reconsidered*, edited by Dorothy Wong and Eric M. Field. Cambridge: Cambridge Scholars Publishing, 2008, 263–88.

———. *Shōtoku: Ethnicity, Ritual and Violence in the Japanese Buddhist Tradition*. Oxford: Oxford University Press, 2008.

———. *Weaving and Binding: Immigrant Gods and Female Immortals in Ancient Japan*. Honolulu: University of Hawai'i Press, 2010.

Cranston, Edwin A. "Asuka and Nara Culture: Literacy, Literature and Music." In *The Cambridge History of Japan*, edited by John W. Hall et al., vol. 1, edited by Delmer Brown. Cambridge: Cambridge University Press, 1997, 453–86.

Cuevas, Bryan J., and Jacqueline I. Stone, eds. *The Buddhist Dead: Practices, Discourses, Representations*. Studies in East Asian Buddhism, vol. 20. Honolulu: Kuroda Institute and University of Hawai'i Press, 2007.

Date Muneyasu. "Kofun, tera, shizoku." In *Shumakki kofun: Ronshū*, edited by Mori Kōichi. Tokyo: Hanawa Shobō, 1973, 255–84.

Davis, Richard. *Lives of Indian Images*. Princeton, NJ: Princeton University Press, 1997.

Deal, William A. "Hagiography and History: The Image of Prince Shōtoku." In *Religions of Japan in Practice*, edited by George J. Tanabe. Princeton, NJ: Princeton University Press, 1999, 316–33.

Diény, Jean-Pierre. "Le fenghuang et le phénix." *Cahiers d'Extrême Asie* 5 (1989–90): 1–14.

Dobbins, James C. "Envisioning Kamakura Buddhism." In *Re-Visioning "Kamakura" Buddhism*, edited by Richard K. Payne. Honolulu: University of Hawai'i Press, 1998.

Donohashi Akio. "Kitora kofun no shijinzu: Shujaku no shutsugen." *Bukkyō geijutsu*, no. 258 (2001): 13–17.

Dunhuang Institute of Research on Cultural Relics. "The Recently Discovered Embroideries of the Northern Wei." *Wenwu* 2 (1972): 54–60. Also published in *Chinese Archaeological Abstracts 4, Post Han*, edited by Albert E. Dien, Jeffrey K. Riegel, and Nancy T. Price. Los Angeles: Institute of Archaeology, University of California, Los Angeles, 1985, 1549–54.

Dusenbury, Mary M., ed. *Color in Ancient and Medieval East Asia*. Lawrence, KS: Spencer Museum of Art, 2015.

Duthie, Torquil. *Man'yōshū and the Imperial Imagination in Early Japan*. Leiden: Brill, 2014.

Eaton, Jan. *Mary Thomas's Dictionary of Embroidery Stitches*. 1998. Reprint, Dubai: Oriental Press, 2007.

Ebersole, Gary L. *Ritual Poetry and the Politics of Death in Early Japan*. Princeton, NJ: Princeton University Press, 1989.

———. "Tama Belief and Practice in Ancient Japan." In *Religions of Japan in Practice*, edited by George J. Tanabe. Princeton, NJ: Princeton University Press, 1999, 141–52.

Eckfeld, Tonia. *Imperial Tombs in Tang China, 618–907: The Politics of Paradise*. London and New York: RoutledgeCurzon, 2005.

Edwards, Walter. "Contested Access: The Imperial Tombs in the Postwar Period." *Journal of Japanese Studies* 26, no. 2 (2000): 371–92.

Eliade, Mircea. "Mythologies of Death: An Introduction." In *Religious Encounters with Death: Insights from the History and Anthropology of Religions*, edited by Frank E. Reynolds and Earle H. Waugh. University Park and London: Pennsylvania State University Press, 1973.

———, ed. *Encyclopedia of Religion*. 16 vols. New York: Macmillan, 1987.

Emery, Irene. *The Primary Structures of Fabrics: An Illustrated Classification*. Washington, DC: The Textile Museum, 1966.

Engelhart, Ute. "Longevity Techniques and Chinese Medicine." In *Daoism Handbook*, edited by Livia Kohn, vol. 1. Boston and Leiden: Brill, 2004, 75–108.

Fairbank, Wilma. *Adventures in Retrieval: Han Murals and Shang Bronze Molds*. Harvard-Yenching Institute Studies, vol. 28. Cambridge, MA: Harvard University Press, 1972.

Fan Shuying. *Xincheng, fangling, Yontai gong zhu mu bi hua*. Beijing: Wen wu chu ban she, 2002.

Farris, William W. *Sacred Texts and Buried Treasures: Issues in the Historical Archaeology of Ancient Japan*. Honolulu: University of Hawai'i Press, 1998.

Fenollosa, Ernest. *Epochs of Chinese and Japanese Art: An Outline History of East Asiatic Design*. First published in 1912. New York and Tokyo: ICG Muse, 2000.

Fister, Patricia, et al. *Ama monzeki: A Hidden Heritage: Treasures of the Japanese Imperial Convents*. Tokyo: Sankei Shinbunsha, 2009.

Foard, James H. "Buddhist Ceremonials (*kōshiki*) and the Ideological Discourse of Established Buddhism in Early Medieval Japan." In *Discourse and Ideology in Medieval Japanese Buddhism*, edited by Richard K. Payne and Taigen Dan Leighton. London and New York: Routledge, 2006, 97–125.

———. "Competing with Amida: A Study and Translation of Jōkei's *Miroku kōshiki*." *Monumenta Nipponica* 60, no. 1 (2005): 43–79.

———. "In Search of a Lost Reformation." *Japanese Journal of Religious Studies* 7, no. 4 (1980): 261–91.

Fong, Mary. "Four Chinese Royal Tombs of the Early Eighth Century." *Artibus Asiae* 35, no. 4 (1973): 307–34.

Freedberg, David. *The Power of Images: Studies in the History and Theory of Response*. Chicago and London: University of Chicago Press, 1989.

F.S.K. "A Han Foot-Rule." *Bulletin of the Museum of Fine Arts* 28, no. 165 (1930): 8–9.

Fu Juyou and Chen Songchang. *A Comprehensive Introduction about the Cultural Relics Unearthed from the Han Tombs at Mawangdui*. Translated by Zhou Shiyi and Chen Kefeng. Changsha: Hunan Publishing House, 1992.

Fujii Yukiko. "Chūsei Hōryūji to Shōtoku Taishi kanren denshō no saisei." In *Nihon kodai chūsei no seiji to bunka*, edited by Saeki Arikiyo. Tokyo: Yoshikawa Kōbunkan, 1997, 302–53.

———. *Shōtoku Taishi no denshō: Imēji no saisei to shinkō*. Tokyo: Yoshikawa Kōbunkan, 1999.

Fujita Kiyoshi. "Shōtoku Taishi byō no shinkō to Kamakura bukkyō." In *Kamakura bukkyō keisei no mondaiten*, edited by Nihon Bukkyō Gakkai. Kyoto: Heirakuji Shoten, 1969, 235–48.

———. "Shōtoku Taishi byō no shinkō to Tenjukoku." In *Shōtoku Taishi ronshū*, edited by Shōtoku Taishi Kenkyūkai. Kyoto: Heirakuji Shoten, 1971, 623–44.

———. "Shōtoku Taishi no Tenjukoku ni tsuite." *Indogaku bukkyōgaku kenkyū* 18, no. 2 (1970): 663–66.

Fujita Tsuneyo, ed. *Kokan bijutsu shiryō: Jiin hen*. 2 vols. Tokyo: Chūō Kōron, 1999.

Fujiwara Yūsetsu. *Taishi den*. Shōtoku Taishi zenshū, vols. 2, 3, edited by Shōtoku Taishi Hōsankai. Kyoto: Rinsen Shoten, 1988.

Fukui, Fumimasa. "The History of Taoist Studies in Japan and Some Related Issues." *Acta Asiatica* 68 (1995): 1–18.

Fukui Kōjun. "Tenjukoku Mandara no shisōteki seikaku." In Fukui Kōjun, *Tōyō shisō no kenkyū*. Tokyo: Risōsha, 1955, 128–52. First published in *Indogaku bukkyōgaku kenkyū* 2, no. 2 (1953).

Fukunaga Mitsuji. *Dōkyō to kodai Nihon*. Kyoto: Jinbun Shoin, 1987.

———. *Dōkyō to Nihon bunka*. Kyoto: Jinbun Shoin, 1982.

———. *Dōkyō to Nihon shisō*. Tokyo: Tokuma Shoten, 1985.

———. "*Muryōjukyō* to Dōkyō." In Fukunaga Mitsuji, *Dōkyō to kodai Nihon*. Kyoto: Jinbun Shoin, 1987, 224–47. Originally published in *Ōtani Daigaku shūkyō shimpojiumu kōen*, November 1985.

———. "Tenjukoku Shūchō no Mandara." In Fukunaga Mitsuji, *Dōkyō to kodai Nihon*. Kyoto: Jinbun Shoin, 1987, 106–11. Originally published in *Kansai Daigaku tsūshin*, February 1987.

Fukushima Masao. "Taishi no goshinkō to Tenjukoku Mandara no meibun." In *Chūgūji no shomondai*, edited by Saeki Keizō. Nara: Ikaruga Kokyōsha Shuppanbu, 1943, 39–45.

Fukuyama Toshio. "Chūgūji no garan haichi." In Fukuyama Toshio, *Nihon kenchikushi no kenkyū*. Kyoto: Kuwana Bunseidō, 1943, 265–76.

———. "Hōryūji no kinsekibun ni kansuru ni, san no mondai." *Yumedono* 13 (1935): 48–64.

Gamaike Seishi, ed. *Taishi shinkō*. Tokyo: Yūzankaku Shuppan, 1999.

Gangōji Bunkazai Kenkyūjo. *Nihon jōdo mandara no kenkyū*. Tokyo: Chūō Kōron Bijutsu Shuppan, 1987.

Gerhart, Karen. *The Material Culture of Death in Medieval Japan*. Honolulu: University of Hawai'i Press, 2009.

Goepper, Roger, and Roderick Whitfield. *Treasures from Korea*. London: British Museum Publications, 1984.

Gómez, Luis O. *The Land of Bliss: The Paradise of the Buddha of Measureless Light*. Honolulu: University of Hawai'i Press, 1996.

Grapard, Allan G. "The Shinto of Yoshida Kanemoto." *Monumenta Nipponica* 47, no. 1 (1992): 27–58.

Groner, Paul. "Tradition and Innovation: Eison's Self-Ordinations and the Re-establishment of New Orders of Buddhist Practitioners." In *Going Forth: Visions of Buddhist Vinaya*, edited by William M. Bodiford. Honolulu: University of Hawai'i Press, 2005, 210–35.

Gülberg, Niels. *Buddhistische Zeremoniale (Koshiki) und ihre Bedeutung für die Literatur des japanischen Mittelalters*. Stuttgart: Steiner, 1999.

Haga Noboru. *Sōgi no rekishi*. Tokyo: Yūzankaku Shuppan, 1987.

Haguenauer, Charles. "Du Caractère de la Representation de la Mort dans le Japon Antique." *T'oung Pao* 33, no. 2 (1937): 158–83.

Hall, John W., et al., eds. *The Cambridge History of Japan*. Vol. 1. Edited by Delmer Brown. 1993. Reprint, Cambridge: Cambridge University Press, 1997.

Hamada Takashi, ed. *Kokuhō daijiten*. 5 vols. Tokyo: Kōdansha, 1985–86.

Harada Yoshito. *Kan Rikuchō no fukusoku*. 1937. Reprint, Tokyo: Tōyō Bunko, 1967.

Hashimoto Gyōin. "Tenjukoku Mandara kō." *Yumedono* 4 (1931): 36–46.

Hayashi Makoto and Matthias Hayek. "Onmyōdō in Japanese History." *Japanese Journal of Religious Studies* 40, no. 1 (2013): 1–18.

Hayashi Mikiya. "Ekisai no mita Chūgūji engi." *Nihon rekishi*, no. 61 (1953): 44–45.

———. "Jōdai no tennō no yobina." *Shikan* 45 (1955): 32–44.

———. "Onjōji gon daisōzu Jōen." *Nihon rekishi*, no. 146 (1960): 41–45.

———. "Taishi shinkō." In Ishida Mizumaro and Miya Tsugio, *Shitennōji to Ōsaka, Hyōgo no koji*. Zenshū Nihon no koji, vol. 15. Tokyo: Shūeisha, 1985, 105–18.

———. *Taishi shinkō no kenkyū*. Tokyo: Yoshikawa Kōbunkan, 1980.

———. *Taishi shinkō: Sono hassei to hatten*. Tokyo: Hyōronsha, 1972.

———. "Tenjukoku Shūchō ni kansuru ichi, ni no mondai." *Shigaku zasshi* 66, no. 9 (1957): 44–54.

———. "Tenjukoku Shūchō no fukugen." *Nanto bukkyō* 8 (1960): 48–61.

———. "Tenjukoku Shūchō zakkō." *Bunka shigaku* 12 (1956): 46–50.

Hayashi On. *Hiten to shinsen*. Nihon no bijutsu, no. 330. Tokyo: Shibundō, 1993.

Hayashi Ryōichi. "Parumetto." *Bukkyō geijutsu*, nos. 108, 114 (1976, 1977): 83–107, 66–94.

———. *Tōyō bijutsu no sōshoku mon'yō*. Kyoto: Dōhōsha, 1992.

He Jiejun. *Mawangdui Han mu*. Beijing: Wen wu chu ban she, 2004.

Henan Sheng wen hua ju wen wu gong zuo dui. *Deng Xian cai se hua xiang zhuan mu*. Beijing: Wen wu chu ban she, 1958.

Henan Sheng wen wu yan jiu suo. *Gong Xian shi ku si*. Beijing: Wen wu chu ban she, Fa xing Xin hua shu dian, 1989.

———. *Mixian Dahuting Han mu* (in Chinese with an English abstract). Beijing: Wen wu chu ban she, 1993.

Hendrischke, Barbara. *The Scripture on Great Peace: The Taiping Jing and the Beginnings of Daoism*. Berkeley, Los Angeles, and London: University of California Press, 2006.

Hida Romi. "Kajūji shūbutsu saikō." *Bukkyō geijutsu*, no. 212 (1944): 62–88.

Higashi Ajia no kodai bunka, nos. 102, 104 (2000).

Hino Akira. "Tenjukoku no kōsatsu." *Ryūkoku daigaku ronshū*, no. 423 (1984): 36–63.

Hirano Kunio. "Hata-shi no kenkyū." *Shigaku zasshi* 70, nos. 3, 4 (1961): 25–46, 42–74.

Ho, Peng Yoke. *Chinese Mathematical Astrology: Reaching Out for the Stars*. London and New York: Routledge Curzon, 2003.

Hong, Wontack. *Paekche of Korea and the Origins of Yamato Japan*. Seoul: Kudara International, 1994.

———. *Relationship between Korea and Japan in Early Period: Paekche and Yamato Wa*. Seoul: ILSIMSA, 1988.

Hongō Masatsugu. *Wakakoku no kyōshu: Shōtoku Taishi*. Tokyo: Yoshikawa Kōbunkan, 2004.

Hori Yukio. "Tenjukoku Shūchō fukugen kō." *Bukkyō geijutsu*, no. 110 (1976): 100–124.

Hōryūji. *Hōryūji to shiruku rōdo bukkyō bunka*. Nara: Hōryūji, 1989.

Hōryūji ten: Shōtoku Taishi 1380 nen goonki kinen. Tokyo: Nihon Keizai Shinbunsha, 2001.

Hosokawa Ryōichi. *Chūsei no Risshū jiin to minshū*. Tokyo: Yoshikawa Kōbunkan, 1987.

———. *Onna no chūsei: Ono no Komachi, Tomoe, sonota*. Tokyo: Nihon Editā Sukūru Shuppanbu, 1989.

Hunan Provincial Museum and Institute of Archaeology. *The Han Tomb No. 1 at Mawangtui, Changsha* (in Chinese with an English abstract). Peking: Wenwu Press, 1973.

Hurvitz, Leon, trans. *Scripture of the Lotus Blossom of the Fine Dharma*. New York: Columbia University Press, 1976.

Ienaga Saburō. *Jōgū Shōtoku hōō teisetsu no kenkyū*. 1951. Reprint, Tokyo: Sanseidō, 1972.

———. "Shōtoku Taishi no jōdo." In Ienaga Saburō, *Jōdai bukkyō shisōshi kenkyū*. 1942. Reprint, Kyoto: Hōzōkan, 1966, 10–37. First published in *Rekishi chiri* 312, nos. 3, 4 (1934–35).

——— et al. *Shōtoku Taishi shū*. Tokyo: Iwanami Shoten, 1975.

Iida Mizuho. *Shōtoku Taishi den no kenkyū. Iida Mizuho chosakushū*, vol. 1. Tokyo: Yoshikawa Kōbunkan, 2000.

———. "'Tenjukoku Mandara Shūchō engi kantenbun' ni tsuite." *Shoryōbu kiyō* 16 (1964): 41–59.

———. "Tenjukoku Shūchō mei no fukugen ni tsuite." *Chūō daigaku bungakubu kiyō shigakuka* 11 (1966): 23–43.

———. "Tenjukoku Shūchō mei o megutte." *Kobijutsu* 11 (1965): 39–49.

———. "Tenjukoku Shūchō to Asuka bukkyō." In *Ronshō Nihon bukkyō shi*, edited by Kawagishi Kokyō. Tokyo: Yūzankaku Shuppan, 1989, 177–97.

Imao Fumiaki. "Shōtoku Taishi haka e no gimon." *Higashi Ajia no kodai bunka*, no. 88 (1996): 48–65.

Inagaki, Hisao. *A Dictionary of Japanese Buddhist Terms: Based on References in Japanese Literature*. In collaboration with P.G. O'Neill. Kyoto: Nagata Bunshodo, 1984.

———. *Three Pure Land Sutras: A Study and Translation from Chinese*. Berkeley, CA: Numata Center for Buddhist Translation and Research, 1995.

Inagaki Yukinari. "Kyū Chūgūji ato no hakkutsu to genjō." *Nihon rekishi*, no. 299 (1973): 120–25.

Inokuchi Shōji, ed. *Sōsō girei. Sōsō bosei kenkyū shūsei*, vol. 2. Tokyo: Meichō Shuppankai, 1979.

Inokuma Kanekatsu. *Asuka no kofun o kataru*. Tokyo: Yoshikawa Kōbunkan, 1994.

Inoue Kazutoshi. "Hōryūji Kondō Shaka sanzonzō kōhai mei o yomu." *Bunka shigaku* 62 (2006): 1–24.

Inoue Mitsusada et al., eds. *Higashi Ajia ni okeru girei to kokka. Higashi Ajia sekai ni okeru Nihon kodaishi kōza*, vol. 9. Tokyo: Gakuseisha, 1982.

Inoue Tadashi. "Rengemon: Sōzō to keshō no sekai." In Uehara Mahito, *Rengemon*, Nihon no bijutsu, no. 359. Tokyo: Shibundō, 1996, 87–98.

Institute of Archaeology, CASS, and the Hopei CPAM. *Mancheng Han mu fa jue bao gao* (in Chinese with an English abstract). Beijing: Wen wu chu ban she, 1980.

Ishida Hisatoyo, ed. *Shōtoku Taishi jiten*. Tokyo: Kashiwa Shobō, 1997.

Ishida Mosaku. "Kokuhō Tenjukoku Mandara Shūchō." In *Chūgūji ōkagami, Hokkiji ōkagami*, edited by Ishida Mosaku. Tokyo: Ōtsuka Kōgeisha, 1940, 6–10.

———. "Nihon bukkyō to shūbutsu." In Nara Kokuritsu Hakubutsukan, *Shūbutsu*. Tokyo: Kadokawa Shoten, 1964, 2–9.

———. "Shōtoku Taishi zō no kusagusa sō." In *Shōtoku Taishi zenshū*, vol. 4, edited by Shōtoku Taishi Hōsankai Kanshū. Kyoto: Rinsen Shoten, 1988, 8–25.

———. "Tenjukoku Mandara no fukugen ni tsuite." *Gasetsu* 4, no. 5 (1940): 391–406.

Ishino Hironobu. "Rites and Rituals of the Kofun Period." *Japanese Journal of Religious Studies* 19, nos. 2, 3 (1992): 191–216.

——— et al., eds. *Kofun jidai no kenkyū*. 13 vols. Tokyo: Yūzankaku Shuppan, 1990–93.

Itō Shinji. *Shūbutsu*. Nihon no bijutsu, no. 470. Tokyo: Shibundō, 2005.

Itō Zuiei. "Shōtoku Taishi no bukkyō shisō—Sono ichi, koto ni Tenjukoku o megutte." *Hokke bunka kenkyū* 4 (1978): 15–29.

Izutsu Gafū. *Nihon josei fukushoku shi*. Kyoto: Kōrinsha Shuppan, 1986.

Juliano, Annette. *Teng-hsien: An Important Six Dynasties Tomb*. Artibus Asiae Supplementum, vol. 37. Ascona: Artibus Asiae Publishers, 1980.

Juliano, Annette, and Judith Lerner. *Monks and Merchants: Silk Road Treasures of Northwest China*. New York: Harry N. Abrams with The Asia Society, 2001.

Jung Jae-seo. "Daoism in Korea." In *Daoism Handbook*, edited by Livia Kohn. Boston and Leiden: Brill, 2004, 792–820.

Kajitani Ryōji. *Sōryo no shōzō*. Nihon no bijutsu, no. 388. Tokyo: Shibundō, 1998.

Kaltenmark, Max. "The Ideology of the T'ai-p'ing ching." In *Facets of Taoism: Essays in Chinese Religion*, edited by Holms Welch and Anna Seidel. New Haven and London: Yale University Press, 1979, 19–45.

Kameda Tsutomu. "Chūgūji Tenjukoku Shūchō." In *Nihon kaigakan*, edited by Tanaka Ichimatsu et al., vol. 1. Tokyo: Kōdansha, 1970, 143–47.

———. "Shōkō Mandara zusetsu." In Kameda Tsutomu, *Nihon bukkyō bijutsushi josetsu*. Tokyo: Gakugei Shorin, 1945, 212–27.

Kaminishi, Ikumi. *Explaining Pictures: Buddhist Propaganda and Etoki Storytelling in Japan*. Honolulu: University of Hawai'i Press, 2006.

Kamstra, Jacques H. *Encounter or Syncretism: The Initial Growth of Japanese Buddhism*. Leiden: E.J. Brill, 1967.

Kanaji Isamu. *Shōtoku Taishi kyōgaku no kenkyū*. Osaka: Shōtoku Taishi Kai, 1962.

———. "Waga kuni jomin no jōdokan." *Indogaku bukkyōgaku kenkyū* 24, no. 1 (1975): 43–46.

Kananshō Bunbutsu Kenkyūjo, ed. *Kyōken sekkutsuji*. Tokyo: Heibonsha, 1983.

Kanazawa Hideyuki. "Tenjukoku Shūchō mei no seiritsu nendai ni tsuite: Gihōreki ni yoru keisan kekka kara." *Kokugo to kokubungaku* 78, no. 11 (2001): 33–42.

Kanda Kiichirō. "Shina no shūbutsu ni tsuite." *Bukkyō bijutsu* 3 (1925): 27–32.

Kang Woobang. "Shitennōji shutsudo saiyu shitennō ukiborizō no fukugenteki kōsatsu." Translated by Kim Chonggyo. *Bukkyō geijutsu*, no. 171 (1987): 11–58.

Karatani Kōjin. "Japan as Art Museum: Okakura Tenshin and Fenollosa." In *A History of Modern Japanese Aesthetics*, edited by Michael F. Marra. Honolulu: University of Hawai'i Press, 2001, 43–52.

Karetzky, Patricia Eichenbaum. "The Engraved Designs on the Late Sixth Century Sarcophagus of Li Ho." *Artibus Asiae* 47, no. 2 (1986): 81–108.

———. "A Scene of the Taoist Afterlife on a Sixth Century Sarcophagus Discovered in Loyang." *Artibus Asiae* 44, no. 1 (1983): 5–20.

Karetzky, Patricia Eichenbaum, and Alexander Soper. "A Northern Wei Painted Coffin." *Artibus Asiae* 51, nos. 1, 2 (1991): 5–28.

Kariya Ekisai and Hirako Takurei. *Hokō Jōgū Shōtoku hōō teisetsu shōchū*. Tokyo: Heigo Shuppansha, 1913.

Kasai Masaaki. "Hōryūji kondō Shaka sanzonzō kōhai narabi ni kōhai mei ni tsuite—Ōhashi Katsuaki shi ni kotaete." *Bukkyō geijutsu*, no. 189 (1990): 87–105.

Kashihara Kōkogaku Kenkyūjo. *Shōtoku Taishi no iseki*. Nara: Nara Kenritsu Kashihara Kōkogaku Kenkyūjo Fuzoku Hakubutsukan, 2001.

Kashima Masaru. "Hōryūji kennō hōmotsu: Kanjōban no mozōhin seisaku ni tsuite." *Museum*, no. 567 (2000): 25–54.

Katō Kenkichi. *Hata-shi to sono tami: Torai shizoku no jitsuzō*. Tokyo: Hakusuisha, 1998.

———. *Yamato seiken to kodai shizoku*. Tokyo: Yoshikawa Kōbunkan, 1991.

Katsuki Gen'ichirō. "Chūgoku ni okeru Amida sanzon gojū bosatsu zu no zuzō ni tsuite." *Bukkyō geijutsu*, no. 214 (1994): 61–74.

———. "Shōnankai sekkutsu chūkutsu no sanbutsu zōzō to kuhon ōjōzu ukibori ni kansuru ikkosatsu." *Bijutsushi* 45, no. 1 (1996): 68–86.

———. "Tonkō Mogao kutsu dai 220 kutsu Amida jōdo hensōzu kō." *Bukkyō geijutsu*, no. 202 (1992): 67–86.

Kawabata Shun'ichirō. *Hōryūji no monosashi: Kakusareta ōchō kōtai no nazo*. Kyoto: Mineruva Shobō, 2004.

Kawahara Yoshio. *Jōdozu*. Nihon no bijutsu, no. 272. Tokyo: Shibundō, 1989.

Ketelaar, James Edward. *Of Heretics and Martyrs in Meiji Japan: Buddhism and its Persecution*. Princeton, NJ: Princeton University Press, 1990.

Kidder, J. Edward. "*Busshari* and *Fukuzō*: Buddhist Relics and Hidden Repositories of Hōryūji." *Japanese Journal of Religious Studies* 19, nos. 2, 3 (1992): 217–44.

———. *The Lucky Seventh: Early Hōryūji and Its Time*. Tokyo: International Christian University Hachirō Yuasa Memorial Museum, 1999.

———. "The Newly Discovered Takamatsuzuka Tomb." *Monumenta Nipponica* 27 (1972): 245–51.

———. "Reviving the Burning Question: Hōryūji Fires and Its Reconstruction." In *Hōryūji Reconsidered*, edited by Dorothy Wong and Eric M. Field. Cambridge: Cambridge Scholars Publishing, 2008, 5–26.

———. "Yakushi, Shaka, the 747 Inventory, and the Cult of Prince Shōtoku." In *Hōryūji Reconsidered*, edited by Dorothy Wong and Eric M. Field. Cambridge: Cambridge Scholars Publishing, 2008, 99–130.

Kiley, Cornelius J. "A Note on the Surnames of Immigrant Officials in Nara Japan." *Harvard Journal of Asiatic Studies* 29 (1969): 177–89.

———. "Uji and Kabane in Ancient Japan." Review of Richard J. Miller, *Ancient Japanese Nobility: The Kabane Ranking System. Monumenta Nipponica* 32, no. 3 (1977): 365–76.

Kim Ki-ung. *Kudara no kofun*. Kyoto: Gakuseisha, 1976.
———. *Shiragi no kofun*. Kyoto: Gakuseisha, 1976.
Kim, Lena. "Goguryo People Wearing Jougwan in Tang Chinese Art." *The International Journal of Korean Art and Archaeology* 2 (2008): 92–111.
———, ed. *World Cultural Heritage: Koguryo Tomb Murals*. Seoul: ICOMOS-Korea and Cultural Properties Administration, 2004.
Kinoshita Nagahiro. "Okakura Kakuzō as a Historian of Art." *Review of Japanese Culture and Society* 24 (2012): 26–38.
Kirihata Ken. "Nishimiyayama kofun shutsudohin chōsa o shuppatsu to shite: Tenjukoku Shūchō no saku kisetsu kansō." *Ōtemae daigaku shigaku kenkyūjō kiyō* 5 (2005): 19–22.
Kita Kasuhiro. "Tenjukoku Shūchō meibun saidoku: Tachibana Ōiratsume to mogari no miya no ichō." *Bunka shigaku* 62 (2006): 25–45.
Kitamura Tetsurō. "Shoku ni tsuite." *Museum*, no. 13 (1952): 6–10.
Kodai Nihon no dōkyō, shinsen shisō. Special issue, *Higashi Ajia no kodai bunka*, no. 116 (2003).
Kodansha Encyclopedia of Japan. 9 vols. Tokyo and New York: Kodansha, 1983.
Koguryŏ kobun pyŏkhwa. Seoul: Yŏnhap Nyusŭ, 2006.
Kohn, Livia. "Steal Holy Food and Come Back as a Viper: Conceptions of Karma and Rebirth in Medieval Daoism." *Early Medieval China* 4 (1998): 1–47.
———. "Taoism in Japan: Positions and Evaluations." *Cahiers d'Extrême Asie* 8, no. 1 (1995): 389–413.
———, ed. *Daoism Handbook*. 2 vols. Boston and Leiden: Brill, 2004.
———, trans. *Laughing at the Tao: Debates among Buddhists and Taoists in Medieval China*. Princeton, NJ: Princeton University Press, 1995.
Kohn, Livia, and Harold D. Roth, eds. *Daoist Identity: History, Lineage, and Ritual*. Honolulu: University of Hawai'i Press, 2002.
Kōkuri kofun hekiga. Tokyo: Chōsen Gahōsha, 1985.
Kokushi daijiten. Tokyo: Yoshikawa Kōbunkan, 1979–97. http://japanknowledge.com/contents/kokushi/index.html
Kondō Ariyoshi. "Tenjukoku Shūchō no seisaku jiki ni tsuite: Shūchō meibun ni yoru kentō." *Bijutsushi kenkyū* 47 (2009): 131–48.
Kopytoff, Igor. "The Cultural Biography of Things: Commodization as Process." In *The Social Life of Things: Commodities in Cultural Perspective*, edited by Arjun Appadurai. Cambridge: Cambridge University Press, 1986, 64–94.
Kosugi Kazuo. "Kaku hazama ni tsuite." *Bijutsushi kenkyū* 7 (1969): 1–15.
———. "Zōkei ni mirareru kame to moji to no kankei." In *Fukui hakushi shōju kinen tōyō shisō ronshū*. Tokyo: Fukui Hakushi Shōju Kinen Ronbunshū Kankōkai, 1960, 236–42.
Kosugi Sugimura. "Suiko mikado jidai no bijutsu kōgeihin: Tenjukoku no mandara to iu mono." *Shigaku zasshi* 12, no. 1 (1901): 69–74.
———. "Suiko mikado jidai no bijutsu kōgei oyobi Tenjukoku Mandara to iu mono." *Shigaku zasshi* 12, no. 5 (1901): 67–77.
Kubo Noritada. *Dōkyō no sekai*. Tokyo: Gakuseisha, 1987.
Kuhn, Dieter. "Silk Weaving in Ancient China: From Geometric Figures to Patterns of Pictorial Likeness." *Chinese Science* 12 (1995): 77–114.
Kumagai Kimio. "Tennō no shutsugen." In Kumagai Kimio, *Ōkimi kara tennō e*. Tokyo: Kōdansha, 2001, 333–47.
Kuno Takeshi. "Asuka-Hakuhō shōkondōbutsu no hatsugansha, seisakusha (jo-ge)." *Bijutsu kenkyu*, nos. 309, 310 (1979): 18–32, 1–10.
Kurokawa Mayori. "Honpō kaiga enkaku setsu dai san." *Kokka*, no. 80 (1896): 611–14.
Kwon Oh Young. "The Influence of Recent Archaeological Discoveries on the Research of Paekche History." In *Early Korea*, vol. 1, *Reconsidering Early Korean History through Archaeology*, edited by Mark Byington. Cambridge, MA: Early Korea Project, Korea Institute, Harvard University, 2008, 65–112.
Kyōto-shi no chimei. Nihon rekishi chimei taikei, vol. 27. Tokyo: Heibonsha, 1979.
Lam, Susan, ed. *Ancient Taoist Art from Shanxi Province*. Hong Kong: University Museum and Art Gallery, The University of Hong Kong, 2003.
Ledyard, Gary. "Galloping Along with the Horse Riders: Looking for the Founders of Japan." *Journal of Japanese Studies* 1 (1974): 217–54.
Lee, Junghee. "Sixth Century Buddhist Art." *Korean Culture* 2, no. 2 (1981): 28–35.
Lee, Kenneth D. *The Prince and the Monk: Shōtoku Worship in Shinran's Buddhism*. New York: State University of New York Press, 2007.
Lee, Ki-baik. *A New History of Korea*. Translated by Edward W. Wagner and Edward J. Shultz. Cambridge, MA: Harvard University Press, 1984.
Levy, Ian Hideo, trans. *The Ten Thousand Leaves: A Translation of the Man'yōshū, Japan's Premier Anthology of Classical Poetry*. Princeton, NJ: Princeton University Press, 1981.
Liebenthal, Walter. "The Immortality of the Soul in Chinese Thought." *Monumenta Nipponica* 8, nos. 1, 2 (1952): 327–97.
Little, Stephen, with Shawn Eichman. *Taoism and the Arts of China*. Chicago and Berkeley, CA: Art Institute of Chicago and University of California Press, 2000.

Liu Hongshi. "Futo wa kyūsō, unshō ni sobieru—Kaiseiji to tō sono shutsudo bunbutsu." Translated by Machida Akira et al. *Bukkyō geijutsu*, no. 221 (1995): 42–54.

Loewe, Michael. *Ways to Paradise: The Chinese Quest for Immortality*. London and Boston: George Allen and Unwin, 1979.

Loewe, Michael, and Carmen Blacker, eds. *Oracles and Divination*. Boulder: Shambhala, 1981.

Longmen wen wu bao guan suo, Beijing da xue kao gu xi bian, *Longmen shi ku*. Beijing: Wen wu chu ban she, 1991.

Luo Feng. "Lacquer Painting on a Northern Wei Coffin." *Orientations* 21, no. 7 (1990): 18–29.

Lurie, David B. "The Origins of Writing in Early Japan: From the 1st to the 8th Century C.E." Ph.D. dissertation, Columbia University, 2001.

———. *Realms of Literacy: Early Japan and the History of Writing*. Cambridge, MA: Harvard University Press, 2011.

———. "The Subterranean Archives of Early Japan: Recently Discovered Sources for the Study of Writing and Literacy." In *Books in Numbers*, edited by Wilt L. Idema. Cambridge, MA: Harvard-Yenching Library and Harvard University, 2007, 91–112.

Macé, François. "Japanese Conceptions of the Afterlife." In *Asian Mythologies*, compiled by Yves Bonnefoy. Chicago: The University of Chicago Press, 1993, 270–75.

———. *La Mort et les Funérailles dans le Japon Ancien*. Paris: Publications Orientalistes de France, 1986.

———. "Les Funérailles des Souverains Japonais." *Cahiers d'Extreme Asie* 4 (1988): 157–66.

———. "Mogari to Yomi no kuni." *Hikaku bunka* 28, no. 1 (1981): 4.

Machida Kōichi. "Hokkiji no rekishi." In *Yamato koji taikan*, edited by Ōta Hirotarō, vol. 1. Tokyo: Iwanami Shoten, 1977, 7–14.

Maeda Eun. "Tosotsu ōjō shisō hassei jidai kō." *Shigaku zasshi* 13, no. 1 (1902): 21–26.

Maeda Haruto. "Kashiwade uji." In *Shōtoku Taishi jiten*, edited by Mayuzumi Hiromichi and Takemitsu Makoto. Tokyo: Shin Jinbutsu Ōraisha, 1991, 214–17.

Maekawa Akihisa. "Haji-shi to kikajin." *Nihon no rekishi* 255 (1969): 18–31.

———. "Shōtoku Taishi kisaki jūdai no shiteki haikei." In Maekawa Akihisa, *Nihon kodai seiji no tenkai*. Tokyo: Hōsei Daigaku Shuppankyoku, 1991, 3–16.

Mair, Victor H. "Record of Transformation Tableaux (Pien-hsiang)." *T'oung Pao* 72 (1986): 3–43.

———. *T'ang Transformation Texts*. Cambridge, MA: Council on East Asian Studies, Harvard University, 1989.

Major, John S. *Heaven and Earth in Early Han Thought: Chapters Three, Four and Five of the Huainanzi*. Albany, NY: State University of New York Press, 1993.

Masuo Shin'ichirō. "Chinese Religion and the Formation of Onmyōdō." *Japanese Journal of Religious Studies* 40, no. 1 (2013): 19–43.

———. "Tennō gō no seiritsu to Higashi Ajia." In *Shōtoku Taishi no shinjitsu*, edited by Ōyama Seiichi. 2003. Reprint, Tokyo: Heibonsha, 2004, 45–70.

Matsudaira Narimitsu. "The Concept of Tamashii in Japan." In *Studies in Japanese Folklore*, edited by Richard M. Dorson. Bloomington: Indiana University Press, 1963, 181–97.

Matsumoto Bunzaburō. *Miroku jōdo ron: Gokuraku jōdo ron*. Tokyo: Heibonsha, 2006.

Matsumoto Eiichi. "Tonkō hon zuiō zukan." *Bijutsu kenkyū*, no. 184 (1956): 241–58.

Matsumoto Kaneo. *Jōdai-gire: Shōsōin-gire to Asuka Tenpyō no senshoku*. Kyoto: Shikisha, 1984.

Mayuzumi Hiromichi. "Kodai kokka to Soga-shi." In *Soga-shi to kodai kokka*, edited by Mayuzumi Hiromichi. Tokyo: Yoshikawa Kōbunkan, 1991, 1–11.

Mayuzumi Hiromichi and Takemitsu Makoto, eds. *Shōtoku Taishi jiten*. Tokyo: Shin Jinbutsu Ōraisha, 1991.

McCallum, Donald. "The Buddhist Triad in Three Kingdoms Sculpture." *Korean Culture* 16, no. 4 (1995): 18–35.

———. "The Earliest Buddhist Statues in Japan." *Artibus Asiae* 62, no. 2 (2001): 149–88.

———. *The Four Great Temples: Buddhist Archaeology, Architecture, and Icons of Seventh-Century Japan*. Honolulu: University of Hawai'i Press, 2009.

———. "Korean Influence on Early Japanese Buddhist Sculpture." *Korean Culture* 3, no. 1 (1982): 22–29.

———. "The Shaka Triad in the Hōryūji Golden Hall: Old Theories and New Perspectives." Paper presented at the Symposium "New Research in Chinese and Japanese Art in Honor of Alexander Soper." Institute for Asian Studies, New York, November 13, 1993.

———. "'Tori-busshi' and the Production of Buddhist Icons in Asuka-Period Japan." In *The Artist as Professional in Japan*, edited by Melinda Takeuchi. Stanford, CA: Stanford University Press, 2004, 17–37.

———. "The 'Yamada Den' Amida Triad in the Tokyo National Museum: Aspects of Soga Patronage in Seventh Century Japan." Unpublished manuscript.

———. *Zenkōji and its Icon: A Study in Medieval Japanese Religious Art*. Honolulu: University of Hawai'i Press, 1994.

McNair, Amy. *Donors of Longmen: Faith, Politics, and Patronage in Medieval Chinese Buddhist Sculpture*. Honolulu: University of Hawai'i Press, 2007.

Meeks, Lori R. "Chūgūji and Female Monasticism in the Age of Shōtoku." In *Hōryūji Reconsidered*, edited by Dorothy Wong and Eric M. Field. Cambridge: Cambridge Scholars Publishing, 2008, 237–62.

———. *Hokkeji and the Reemergence of Female Monastic Orders in Premodern Japan*. Studies in East Asian Buddhism, vol. 23. Honolulu: University of Hawai'i Press, 2010.

———. "In Her Likeness: Female Divinity and Leadership at Medieval Chūgūji." *Japanese Journal of Religious Studies* 34, no. 2 (2007): 351–92.

Miki, Fumio. *Haniwa*. Translated by Gina Lee Barnes. New York: Weatherhill, 1974.

Minamoto Toyomune. "Tenjukoku Shūchō." *Bukkyō bijutsu* 13 (1929): 59–68.

Miner, Earl Roy, et al. *The Princeton Companion to Classical Japanese Literature*. Princeton, NJ: Princeton University Press, 1985.

Mita Kakuyuki. "Gihō kara mita Tenjukoku Shūchō." *Fuirokaria* 25 (2008): 67–98.

———. "Hōryūji denrai: Shūbutsu retsu no bunrui to kisoteki kōsatsu." *Museum*, no. 637 (2012): 7–29.

———. "Tenjukoku Shūchō no genkei to shudai ni tsuite." *Bijutsushi* 57, no. 2 (2008): 265–82.

Miyai Giyū. "Sangyō gishō to Tenjukoku Shūchō no kankei." *Nihon bukkyō* 26 (1967): 15–29.

Miyata Toshihiko. "Tenjukoku Shūchō jō-ge." *Rekishi kyōiku* 6, nos. 5, 6 (1958): 77–84, 90–95.

———. "Tenjukoku Shūchō mei seiritsu shikō." *Shigaku zasshi* 47, no. 7 (1936): 910–27.

Mizuno Ryūtarō. "Daianji engi narabi ni ruki shizaichō ni tsuite." In *Daianji shi shiryō*, edited by Daianji Shi Henshū Iinkai. Nara: Daianji, 1984, 661–83.

Mizuno, Seiichi. *Asuka Buddhist Art: Hōryūji*. Translated by Richard L. Gage. New York and Tokyo: Weatherhill/Heibonsha, 1974.

Mizuno Yū. *Kōkuri hekiga kofun to kikajin*. Tokyo: Yūzankaku Shuppan, 1972.

Mochizuki Shinjō. "Tenjukoku Shūchō no saikō." In *Nihon jōdai bunka no kenkyū*, edited by Yoshida Kakuin. Nara: Hōsōshu Kangakuin Dōsōkai, 1941, 393–408.

Mogami Takayoshi. "The Double-Grave System." In *Studies in Japanese Folklore*, edited by Richard M. Dorson. Bloomington: Indiana University Press, 1963, 167–80.

Mollier, Christine. *Buddhism and Taoism Face to Face: Scripture, Ritual and Iconographic Exchange in Medieval China*. Honolulu: University of Hawai'i Press, 2008.

Mōri Hisashi. "Sangoku chōkoku to Asuka chōkoku." In *Kudara bunka to Asuka bunka*, edited by Tamura Enchō. Tokyo: Yoshikawa Kōbunkan, 1978, 1–82.

Mori Kōichi. *Tennōryō kofun*. Tokyo: Taikōsha, 1996.

Mōri Noboru. "Tenjukoku Shūchō." *Museum*, no. 13 (1952): 22–24.

———. "Tenjukoku Shūchō ni tsuite—Shūchō no genpon to Kenji saikō no Shūchō ni tsuite." *Kobijutsu* 11 (1965): 27–38.

Morimoto Rokuji. "Shōtoku Taishi Shinaga gobyō no yōshiki ni kansuru ikkōsatsu." *Yumedono* 9 (1933): 15–24.

Morishita Wakiko. "Chūgūji Tenjukoku Shūchō no genkei." In *Ronsō Nara bijutsu*, edited by Ōhashi Katsuaki. Tokyo: Heibonsha, 1994, 68–96.

Morita Kimio. *Shishū*. Nihon no bijutsu, no. 59. Tokyo: Shibundō, 1971.

Nagahiro Toshio. *Tennin no fu*. Kyoto: Tankō Shinsha, 1967.

Nagatomi Hisae. "Urabe no seiritsu ni tsuite." In *Shintō shi ronsō*, edited by Takigawa Masajirō Sensei Beiju Kinen Ronbunshū Kankōkai. Tokyo: Kokusho Kankōkai, 1984, 88–115.

Naitō Toichirō. *Hōryūji kenkyū: Kondō hen*. Osaka: Kodai Bunka Kenkyūkai, 1933.

———. *Nihon bukkyō kaigashi*. Tokyo: Seikei Shoin, 1935.

Nakagawa Tadayori. "Tenjukoku Mandara ni tsuite." *Shisō* 20 (1923): 333–41.

Nakagawa Zenkyō. "Kōbo Daishi no honji to zenshin oyobi sono goshin." In *Kōbō Daishi shinkō*, edited by Hinonishi Shinjō. Tokyo: Yūzankaku Shuppan, 1988, 115–35.

Nakamura Hajime. *Bukkyōgo daijiten*. Tokyo: Tōkyō Shoseki, 1975.

———. *Shōtoku Taishi*. Tokyo: Tōkyō Shoseki, 1992.

———, ed. *Shōtoku Taishi*. Nihon no meicho, vol. 2. Tokyo: Chūō Kōronsha, 1970.

Nanjing Museum. "A Large Tomb of the Southern Dynasties Period with Decorated Bricks at Huqiao, Danyang, Jiangsu." *Wenwu* 2 (1974): 44–52. Also published in Albert E. Dien, Jeffrey K. Riegel, and Nancy T. Price, eds., *Chinese Archaeological Abstracts 4, Post Han*. Los Angeles: Institute of Archaeology, University of California, Los Angeles, 1985, 1484–93.

———. "Two Tombs of the Southern Dynasties at Huqiao and Jianshan in Danyang County, Jiangsu Province." Translated by Barry Till and Paula Swart. *Chinese Studies in Archaeology* 1, no. 3 (1979–80): 74–124. Originally published in *Wenwu* 2 (1980): 1–17.

Naoki Kōjirō. *Kura to kodai ōken*. Kyoto: Mineruva Shobō, 1991.

———. *Nihon kodai no shizoku to tennō*. Tokyo: Hanawa Shōbo, 1964.

Nara Bunkazai Kenkyūjo. *Takamatsuzuka kofun hekiga foto mappu shiryō*. Nara: Nara Bunkazai Kenkyūjō, 2009.

Nara Bunkazai Kenkyūjo and Asahi Shinbunsha. *Asuka Fujiwara-kyō ten: Kodai ritsuryō kokka no sōzō*. Osaka: Asahi Shinbunsha, 2002.

Nara Bunkazai Kenkyūjo and Asuka Shiryōkan. *Asuka Hakuhō no zaimei kondōbutsu*. Kyoto: Dōhōsha, 1979.

Nara Hiromoto. "Shōtoku Taishi no jōdokan ni tsuite." *Indogaku bukkyōgaku kenkyū* 17, no. 1 (1968): 228–31.

Nara Kokuritsu Bunkazai Kenkyūjō. *Shōtoku Taishi no sekai*. Nara: Asuka Shiryōkan, 1988.

Nara Kokuritsu Hakubutsukan. *Bukkyō kōgei no bi*. Nara: Nara Kokuritsu Hakubutsukan, 1982.

———. *Josei to bukkyō: Inori to hohoemi*. Nara: Nara Kokuritsu Hakubutsukan, 2003.

———. *Nihon bukkyō bijutsu meihō ten*. Nara: Nara Kokuritsu Hakubutsukan, 1995.

———. *Shōsōin ten mokuroku*. Nara: Nara Kokuritsu Hakubutsukan, 1998–99.

———. *Shūbutsu*. Tokyo: Kadokawa Shoten, 1964.

———. *Yamato Ikaruga Chūgūji no bi*. Nara: Chūgūji Monzeki, 1988.

Nara Kokuritsu Hakubutsukan, Hōryūji, and Asahi Shinbunsha. *Kokuhō Hōryūji Kondō ten*. Tokyo: Asahi Shinbunsha, 2008.

Nara Rokudaiji Taikan Kankōkai, ed. *Nara rokudaiji taikan*. 14 vols. Revised edition. Tokyo: Iwanami Shoten, 1999–2001. Vols. 1–5, *Hōryūji*; vol. 6, *Yakushiji*; vols. 7, 8, *Kōfukuji*; vols. 9–11, *Tōdaiji*; vols. 12, 13, *Tōshōdaiji*; vol. 14, *Saidaiji*.

Nishigori Ryōsuke. *Tenbu no butsuzō jiten*. Tokyo: Tōkyō Bijutsu, 1983.

Nishiguchi Junko. "Shinaga Taishi byō to sono shūhen." In *Taishi shinkō*, edited by Gamaike Seishi. Tokyo: Yūzankaku Shuppan, 1999, 49–66.

Nishikawa Kyōtarō. "Chūgūji no rekishi." In *Yamato koji taikan*, edited by Ōta Hirotarō, vol. 1. Tokyo: Iwanami Shoten, 1977, 55–59.

——— et al., eds. *Kokuhō*. 16 vols. Tokyo: Mainichi Shinbunsha, 1984.

Nishimura Hyōbu. "Zuhan kaisetsu—Tenjukoku Shūchō." In Nara Kokuritsu Hakubutsukan, *Shūbutsu*. Tokyo: Kadokawa Shoten, 1964, 12–18.

Nishizaki Tooru. "Shoryōbu zō 'Tenjukoku Mandara Shūchō engi kantenbun' shakubun narabi ni kenkyū." *Mukogawa kokubun* 67 (2006): 46–56.

Noguchi Tetsurō et al. *Dōkyō jiten*. Tokyo: Hirakawa, 1994.

Nomiyama Yuka. "Tenjukoku Shūchō ni tsuite ikkōsatsu." *Hōsei shigaku* 66 (2006): 17–33.

———. "Tenjukoku Shūchō no seiritsu nendai ni tsuite." *Arena* 5 (2008): 250–58.

Obayashi, Hiroshi, ed. *Death and Afterlife: Perspectives of World Religions*. New York: Greenwood Press, 1992.

Ogawa Yasurō. *Man'yōshū no fukushoku bunka*. Tokyo: Rokkō, 1986.

Ogino Minahiko. "Chūgūji sanjū no tō to ama Shinnyo." *Nihon rekishi*, no. 326 (1975): 88–92.

———. "Hōō teisetsu shosha nendai ni kansuru shin shiryō." In Ogino Minahiko, *Nihon komonjogaku to chūsei bunkashi*. Tokyo: Yoshikawa Kōbunkan, 1995, 412–16.

———. "Hōryūji no Shōkō Mandara." *Bijutsushi* 59 (1936): 459–73.

———. *Shōtoku Taishi den kokon mokurokushō*. Nara: Hōryūji, 1937.

Ōhashi Katsuaki. "Bunei jūichinen no Tenjukoku Shūchō shutsugen o megutte." *Waseda daigaku daigakuin bungaku kenkyūkai* 4 (1977): 95–112.

———. "Chūgūji kō." In Ōhashi Katsuaki, *Tenjukoku Shūchō no kenkyū*. Tokyo: Yoshikawa Kōbunkan, 1995, 191–99.

———. "Hōryūji kondō Shaka sanzonzō no kōhai meibun ni tsuite—Kasai Masaaki shi ni kotaeru." *Bukkyō geijutsu*, no. 198 (1991): 11–29.

———. "Hōryūji kondō Shaka sanzonzō no seisaku nendai ni tsuite." *Bukkyō geijutsu*, no. 204 (1992): 15–37.

———. *Ronsō Nara bijutsu*. Tokyo: Heibonsha, 1994.

———. "Saikon Hōryūji to Shaka sanzonzō: Taishi shinkō no seiritsu." *Bukkyō geijutsu*, no. 224 (1996): 15–32.

———. *Saikon Hōryūji to Taishi shinkō*. Tokyo: Waseda Daigaku Sōchōshitsu, 2007.

———. "Shin hakken no sekizō kamegata suiban ni tsuite." *Bukkyō geijutsu*, no. 250 (2000): 122–32.

———. *Shōtoku Taishi e no chinkon—Tenjukoku Shūchō zanshō*. Tokyo: Gurafu sha, 1987.

———. "Tenjukoku Shūchō fukugen shiron." In *Higashi Ajia to Nihon*, edited by Tamura Enchō Sensei Koki Kinenkai, vol. 3. Tokyo: Yoshikawa Kōbunkan, 1987, 156–81.

———. "Tenjukoku Shūchō no genkei." *Bukkyō geijutsu*, no. 117 (1978): 49–79.

———. *Tenjukoku Shūchō no kenkyū*. Tokyo: Yoshikawa Kōbunkan, 1995.

———. "Tenjukoku Shūchō no seisaku nendai ni tsuite." *Nanto bukkyō* 70 (1994): 31–63.

Ōhashi Katsuaki, and Taniguchi Masakazu. *Kakusareta Shōtoku Taishi no sekai: Fukugen maboroshi no Tenjukoku*. Tokyo: Nihon Hōsō Shuppan Kyōkai, 2002.

Okabe Chōshō. "Mitsui-kezō *Kegon kyō* okusho no soku butsuteki kōsatsu." *Nihon rekishi* 120 (1958): 76–80.

Okakura, Kakuzō. *The Ideals of the East, with Special Reference to the Art of Japan*. New York and Tokyo: ICG Muse, 2000.

Okakura Tenshin. *Nihon bijutsushi*. Tokyo: Heibonsha, 2001.

Okazaki, Joji. *Pure Land Buddhist Painting*. Translated by Elizabeth ten Grotenhuis. Tokyo and New York: Kodansha International, 1977.

Okimori Takuya. *Jōgū Shōtoku hōō teisetsu: Chūshaku to kenkyū*. Tokyo: Yoshikawa Kōbunkan, 2005.

Okuda Jirō. "Shōtoku Taishi no shinkō to Tenjukoku Mandara." *Nihon bukkyō gakkai nenpō* 32 (1966): 103–18.

Okumura Hideo. "Tōkyō Kokuritsu Hakubutsukan hokan jōdai gire ni tsuite: Toku ni Hōryūji hōmotsu no kennō to sono ato ni kansuru shiryō." *Museum*, no. 390 (1983): 4–18.

Ono Kazuyuki. "Shōtoku Taishi bō no tenkai to Eifukuji no seiritsu." *Nihon shi kenkyū*, no. 342 (1991): 1–27.

———. "'Shōtoku Taishi bō' tanjō." In *Shōtoku Taishi no shinjitsu*, edited by Ōyama Seiichi. 2003. Reprint, Tokyo: Heibonsha, 2004, 367–89.

Ōno Tatsunosuke. *Jōdai no jōdokyō*. Tokyo: Yoshikawa Kōbunkan, 1972.

———. "Tenjukoku jōdo no shinkō." In Ōno Tatsunosuke, *Shōtoku Taishi no kenkyū; sono bukkyō to seiji shisō*. 1970. Reprint, Tokyo: Yoshikawa Kōbunkan, 1996, 45–89.

———. "Tenjukoku no gengi ni tsuite." *Nihon rekishi* 101 (1956): 56–60.

Ooms, Herman. *Imperial Politics and Symbolics in Ancient Japan: The Tenmu Dynasty, 650–800*. Honolulu: University of Hawai'i Press, 2009.

Ōsaka-fu no chimei. Nihon rekishi chimei taikei, vol. 28. Tokyo: Heibonsha, 1986.

Ōta Hidezō. "Tenjukoku Mandara no shūgi to Kenji shūri ni tsuite." *Shiseki to bijutsu* 188 (1948): 161–76.

Ōta Hirotarō, ed. *Yamato koji taikan*. 7 vols. Tokyo: Iwanami Shoten, 1976–78.

Overmyer, Daniel L., et al. "Chinese Religions—The State of the Field. Part I: Early Religious Traditions: The Neolithic Period through the Han Dynasty (ca. 4000 B.C.E. to 220 C.E.)." *Journal of Asian Studies* 54, no. 1 (1995): 124–60.

———. "Chinese Religions—The State of the Field. Part II: Living Religious Traditions: Taoism, Confucianism, Buddhism, Islam and Popular Religion." *Journal of Asian Studies* 54, no. 2 (1995): 314–95.

Ōwa Iwao. *Hata-shi no kenkyū: Nihon no bunka to shinkō ni fukaku kanyoshita torai shūdan no kenkyū*. Tokyo: Yamato Shōbō, 1993.

Owada Tetsuo, ed. *Nihon shi shoka keizu jinmei jiten*. Tokyo: Kōdansha, 2003.

Ōya Tokujō. "Jōdai no zōzō ni okeru kosei no mondai: Tenjukoku Shūchō hō." In Ōya Tokujō, *Nihon bukkyō shi no kenkyū*. 1927. Reprint, Kyoto: Hōzōkan, 1951–53, 75–100.

———. "Saikin no Tenjukoku mondai ni tsuite." *Mikkyō kenkyū* 70 (1939): 37–51.

———. "Tenjukoku Shūchō kō." *Shūkyō kenkyū* 5, nos. 4, 5 (1928): 55–70, 73–85.

———. "Tenjukoku to wa nanzoya." *Yumedono* 4 (1931): 20–34.

Ōya Toru. *Kana genryu ko*. Tokyo: Kokutei Kyokasho Kyōdo Hanbaijo, 1911.

Ōyama Seiichi. "Shōtoku Taishi kankei shiryō no saikentō." *Higashi Ajia no kodai bunka*, no. 104 (2000): 124–49.

———. "Shōtoku Taishi no seiritsu to Ritsuryō kokka." In Ōyama Seiichi, *Nagayaōke mokkan to kinsekibun*. Tokyo: Yoshikawa Kōbunkan, 1998, 196–339.

———. *Shōtoku Taishi no "tanjō."* Tokyo: Yoshikawa Kōbunkan, 1999.

———. "Umayado ō no jitsuzō." *Higashi Ajia no kodai bunka*, no. 103 (2000): 121–35.

———, ed. *Shōtoku Taishi no shinjitsu*. 2003. Reprint, Tokyo: Heibonsha, 2004.

Paine, Robert, and Alexander Soper. *The Art and Architecture of Japan*. Third edition. Harmondsworth, UK: Penguin Books, 1987.

Park, Ah-Rim. "Tomb of the Dancers: Koguryo Tombs in East Asian Funerary Art." Ph.D. dissertation, University of Pennsylvania, 2002.

Payne, Richard, ed. *Re-Visioning "Kamakura" Buddhism*. Honolulu: University of Hawai'i Press, 1998.

Piggott, Joan R. *The Emergence of Japanese Kingship*. Stanford, CA: Stanford University Press, 1997.

———, ed. *Capital and Countryside in Japan, 300–1180: Japanese Historians in English*. Ithaca, NY: Cornell University, 2006.

Pradel, Chari. "Portrait of Prince Shōtoku and Two Princes: From Devotional Painting to Imperial Object." *Artibus Asiae* 74, no. 1 (2014): 191–217.

———. "*Shōkō Mandara* and the Cult of Prince Shōtoku in the Kamakura Period." *Artibus Asiae* 68, no. 2 (2008): 215–46.

———. "The Tenjukoku Shūchō Mandara: Reconstruction of the Iconography and Ritual Context." In *Images in Asian Religions: Texts and Contexts*, edited by Phyllis Granoff and Koichi Shinohara. Vancouver and Toronto: University of British Columbia Press, 2004, 257–89.

———. "Winged Immortals and Heavenly Beings Across the East Asian Skies." In *Spirits in Transcultural Skies—Essays on the Interactions and Iconography of Protective Winged Beings in Art and Architecture*, edited by Niels Gustchow and Katharina Weiler. Heidelberg: Springer Transcultural Research Books Series, 2015, 99–124.

Pradel, Maria del Rosario. "The Fragments of the Tenjukoku Shūchō Mandara: Reconstruction of the Iconography and the Historical Contexts." Ph.D. dissertation, University of California, Los Angeles, 1997.

Rawson, Jessica. *Chinese Ornament: The Lotus and the Dragon*. 1984. Reprint, London: British Museum Publications, 1990.

Robinet, Isabelle. "Metamorphosis and Deliverance of the Corpse in Taoism." *History of Religions* 19, no. 1 (1979): 37–70.

———. "Shangqing—Highest Clarity." Chapter 8 of *Daoism Handbook*, edited by Livia Kohn, vol. 1. Boston and Leiden: Brill, 2004, 196–224.

———. *Taoism: Growth of a Religion*. Translated by Phyllis Brooks. Stanford, CA: Stanford University Press, 1997.

Rosenfield, John. *Portraits of Chōgen: The Transformation of Buddhist Art in Early Medieval Japan*. Japanese Visual Culture, vol. 1. Leiden and Boston: Brill, 2011.

Rotermund, Hartmut O. "The Vital Spirit and the Soul in Japan." In *Asian Mythologies*, compiled by Yves Bonnefoy. Chicago: The University of Chicago Press, 1993, 267–70.

Ruch, Barbara. "Coping with Death: Paradigms of Heaven and Hell and the Six Realms in Early Literature and Painting." In *Flowing Traces: Buddhism in the Literary and Visual Arts of Japan*, edited by James H. Sanford, William R. LaFleur, and Masatoshi Nagatomi. Princeton, NJ: Princeton University Press, 1992, 93–130.

Ryūmon Bunbutsu Hokanjo and Pekin Daigaku Kōkokei, eds. *Ryūmon sekkutsu*. 2 vols. Tokyo: Heibonsha, 1987–88.

Saeki Arikiyo, ed. *Nihon kodai shizoku jiten*. Tokyo: Yūzankaku, 1994.

Saeki Keizō, ed. *Chūgūji no shomondai*. Nara: Ikaruga Kokyōsha Shuppanbu, 1943.

Saitō Rieko. "Tonkō dai 249 kutsu tenjō ni okeru Chūgokuteki zuzō no juyō keitai." *Bukkyō geijutsu*, no. 218 (1995): 39–56.

Saitō Tadashi. *Hekiga kofun no keifu*. Tokyo: Gakuseisha, 1989.

———. *Higashi Ajia sō, bosei no kenkyū*. Tokyo: Daiichi Shobō, 1987.

———. "Kokuri kofun hekiga ni arawareta sōsō girei ni tsuite." *Chosen gakuhō* 91 (1979): 1–14.

Sakai Atsuko. "Chūgoku Nanbokuchō jidai ni okeru shokubutsu unki mon ni tsuite." *Bijutsushi* 49, no. 1 (1999): 66–81.

Sakai, Tadao, and Tetsurō Noguchi. "Taoist Studies in Japan." In *Facets of Taoism: Essays in Chinese Religion*, edited by Holms Welch and Anna Seidel. New Haven and London: Yale University Press, 1979, 269–87.

Sakakibara Fumiko. "*Shitennōji engi* no seiritsu." In *Shōtoku Taishi no shinjitsu*, edited by Ōyama Seiichi. 2003. Reprint, Tokyo: Heibonsha, 2004, 355–66.

Sakamoto Tarō. *Shōtoku Taishi*. Tokyo: Yoshikawa Kōbunkan, 2000.

Saso, Michael. "What Is the 'Ho-T'u'?" *History of Religions* 17, nos. 3, 4 (1978): 399–416.

Satō, Dōshin. "Art and Social Class: The Class System in Early Modern Japan and the Formation of 'Art.'" In Dōshin Satō, *Modern Japanese Art and the Meiji State: The Politics of Beauty*. Los Angeles: Getty Research Institute, 2011, 66–96.

———. "The Formation of the Academic Discipline of Art History and its Development." In Dōshin Satō, *Modern Japanese Art and the Meiji State: The Politics of Beauty*. Los Angeles: Getty Research Institute, 2011, 153–83.

Sawa Ryūken. *Butsuzō zuten*. Tokyo: Yoshikawa Kōbunkan, 1962.

Sawada Mutsuyo. *Jōdai-gire shūsei: Kofun shutsudo no sen'i kara Hōryūji Shōsōin-gire made*. 2 vols. Tokyo: Chūō Kōron Bijutsu Shuppan, 2001.

———. *Senshoku: Genshi, kodai hen*. Nihon no bijutsu, no. 263. Tokyo: Shibundō, 1988.

———. "Tenjukoku Shūchō no genjō." *Museum*, no. 495 (1992): 4–25. Also published in Sawada Mutsuyo, *Jōdai-gire shūsei: Kofun shutsudo no sen'i kara Hōryūji Shōsōin-gire made*. 2 vols. Tokyo: Chūō Kōron Bijutsu Shuppan, 2001.

Schipper, Kristopher, and Franciscus Verellen. *The Taoist Canon: A Historical Canon to the Daozang*. 3 vols. London and Chicago: University of Chicago Press, 2004.

Seeley, Christopher. *A History of Writing in Japan*. Leiden: E.J. Brill, 1991.

Seidel, Ana. "Chronicle of Taoist Studies in the West 1950–1990." *Cahiers d'Extreme Asie* 5 (1989–90): 223–348.

———. "Post-mortem Immortality or the Taoist Resurrection of the Body." In *Gilgul: Essays on Transformation, Revolution, and Permanence in the History of Religions*, edited by S. Shaked, D. Shulman, and G.G. Stroumsa. Leiden, New York, Kobenhavn, and Koln: E.J. Brill, 1987, 223–35.

———. "Taoisme: Religion non-officielle de la Chine." *Cahiers d'Extreme Asie* 8, no. 1 (1995): 1–40.

———. "Traces of Han Religion in Funeral Texts Found in Tombs." In *Dōkyō to shūkyō bunka*, edited by Akizuki Kan'ei. Tokyo: Hirakawa Shuppansha, 1987.

Seki Akira. *Kodai no kikajin*. Seki Akira chosakushū, vol. 3. Tokyo: Yoshikawa Kōbunkan, 1996.

Sekine Shinryū. *Nara-chō fukushoku no kenkyū*. Tokyo: Yoshikawa Kōbunkan, 1974.

Sekino Tadashi. "Sen yori mitaru Kudara to Shina Nanchō toku ni Ryō to no bunka kankei." *Hōun* 10 (1934): 23–33.

Sema Masayuki. "Suiko chō ibun no saikentō." In *Shōtoku Taishi no shinjitsu*, edited by Ōyama Seiichi. 2003. Reprint, Tokyo: Heibonsha, 2004, 71–90.

Senda Minoru. "'Tennō' gō seiritsu Suiko chō setsu no keifu: Mō hitotsu no Yamataikoku ronsōteki jōkyō." *Nihon kenkyū* 35 (2007): 405–20.

——— et al., eds. *Dōkyō to Higashi Ajia: Chūgoku, Kankoku, Nihon*. Tokyo: Jinbun Shoin, 1989.

Senda Minoru and Uno Takao. *Kame no kodaigaku*. Osaka: Tohō Shuppan, 2001.

Senjuji. *Senjuji shiyō*. Tsu-shi: Takadaha Senjuji Onki Hōmuin Bunshobu, 1912.

Shanxi sheng Datong shi bowuguan and Shanxi sheng wenwu gongzuo weiyuanhui. "Shanxi Datong shijiazhai Beiwei Sima Jinlong mu." *Wenwu* 3 (1972): 20–34.

Shigematsu Akihisa. *Nihon Jōdokyō seiritsu katei no kenkyū*. Kyoto: Heirakuji Shoten, 1964.

———. "Sakabune ishi no zuzōteki kosatsu." In Shigematsu Akihisa, *Kodai kokka to Dōkyō*. Tokyo: Yoshikawa Kōbunkan, 1985, 163–202.

Shimaguchi Yoshiaki. "Shōtoku Taishi shinkō to Zenkōji." In *Taishi shinkō*, edited by Gamaike Seishi. Tokyo: Yūzankaku Shuppan, 1999, 67–92.

Shimaji Daitō. *Nihon bukkyō kyōgakushi*. 1933. Reprint, Tokyo: Nakayama Shobō, 1976.

Shimode Sekiyo. "Toraijin no shinkō to Dōkyō." *Rekishi kōron* 6 (1976): 88–101.

Shimomise Shizuichi. "Tenjukoku Mandara ni tsuite." In Shimomise Shizuichi, *Yamatoe shi kenkyū*. Tokyo: Fuzanbō, 1956, 97–130.

Shinkawa Tokio. *Dōkyō o meguru kōbō*. Tokyo: Taishūkan Shoten, 1999.

———. *Shōtoku Taishi no rekishigaku: Kioku to sōzō no senyonhyakunen*. Tokyo: Kōdansha, 2007.

Shitennōji. Osaka: Sōhonzan Shitennōji, 2005.

Shitennōji. Koji o meguru: Oshie, bi, rekishi, vol. 25. Tokyo: Shōgakkan, 2008.

Shitennōji no Hōmotsu to Shōtoku Taishi Shinkōten Jikkō Iinkai. *Shitennōji no hōmotsu to Shōtoku Taishi shinkō: Kaisō sen-yonhyakunen kinen.* Osaka: Shitennōji no Hōmotsu to Shōtoku Taishi Shinkōten Jikkō Iinkai, 1992.

Shōsōin Jimusho. *Shōsōin no ra.* Tokyo: Nihon Keizai Shinbunsha, 1971.

Shōsōin ten: Dai gojūni-kai. Nara: Nara Kokuritsu Hakubutsukan, 2000.

Shōtoku Taishi ten. Tokyo: NHK Puromōshon, 2001.

Sickman, Laurence, and Alexander Soper. *The Art and Architecture of China.* Third edition. Baltimore: Penguin, 1968.

Sobukawa Naoko. "Tenjukoku Shūchō ni tsuite." *Bigaku ronkyū* 19 (2004): 1–20.

Song, Hang-Nyong. "A Short History of Taoism in Korea." *Korea Journal* 26, no. 5 (1986): 13–18.

Soper, Alexander. *Literary Evidence for Early Buddhist Art in China.* Ascona: Artibus Asiae, 1959.

———. "A New Chinese Tomb Discovery: the Earliest Representation of a Famous Literary Theme." *Artibus Asiae* 24 (1961): 79–86.

———. "Notes on Hōryūji and the Sculpture of the 'Suiko Period.'" *Art Bulletin* 33 (1951): 77–94.

———. "A Pictorial Biography of Prince Shōtoku." *The Metropolitan Museum of Art Bulletin* 1 (1977): 197–251.

———. "South Chinese Influence on the Buddhist Art of the Six Dynasties Period." *Museum of Far Eastern Antiquities Bulletin* 32 (1960): 47–107.

Spiro, Audrey. *Contemplating the Ancients: Aesthetics and Social Issues in Early Chinese Portraiture.* Berkeley, Los Angeles, and Oxford: University of California Press, 1990.

———. "How Light and Airy: Upward Mobility in the Realm of Immortals." *Taoist Resources* 2, no. 2 (1990): 43–69.

———. "Shaping the Wind: Taste and Tradition in Fifth-Century South China." *Ars Orientalis* 21 (1991): 95–117. http://www.jstor.org/stable/4629415

Stanley-Baker, Joan. *Japanese Art.* London: Thames and Hudson, 1986.

Stein, Rolf. "Religious Taoism and Popular Religion from the Second to Seventh Centuries." In *Facets of Taoism: Essays in Chinese Religion,* edited by Holms Welch and Anna Seidel. New Haven and London: Yale University Press, 1979, 53–81.

Steinhardt, Nancy. "Changchuan Tomb No. 1 and Its North Asian Context." *Journal of East Asian Archaeology* 4, nos. 1, 2 (2003): 225–92.

———. "Seeing Hōryūji through China." In *Hōryūji Reconsidered,* edited by Dorothy Wong and Eric M. Field. Cambridge: Cambridge Scholars Publishing, 2008, 49–98.

Stevenson, Miwa. "The Founding of the Monastery Gangōji and a List of Its Treasures." In *Religions of Japan in Practice,* edited by George J. Tanabe. Princeton, NJ: Princeton University Press, 1999, 299–316.

———. "Webs of Signification: Representation as Social Transformation in Muraled Tombs of Koguryo." Ph.D. dissertation, Columbia University, 1999.

Sugaya Fuminori. "Kitora kofun hekiga no shujakuzō." *Higashi Ajia no kodai bunka,* no. 108 (2002): 95–107.

Sugetani Fuminori. "Yokoanashiki sekishitsu no naibu: Tengai to suichō." *Kodaigaku kenkyū* 59 (1971): 23–29.

Sugiyama Hiroshi. *Bonshō.* Nihon no bijutsu, no. 355. Tokyo: Shibundō, 1995.

Summers, David. *Real Spaces: World Art History and the Rise of Western Modernism.* New York: Phaidon, 2003.

Sun Zuoyun. "An Analysis of the Western Han Murals in the Luoyang Tomb of Bo Qianqiu." Translated by Suzanne Cahill. *Chinese Studies in Archaeology* 1, no. 2 (1979): 44–78. Originally published in *Wenwu* 6 (1977): 17–22.

Suzuki, Yui. *Medicine Master Buddha: The Iconic Worship of Yakushi in Heian Japan.* Leiden and Boston: Brill, 2012.

Swann, Peter C. *A Concise History of Japanese Art.* Tokyo, New York, and San Francisco: Kodansha International, Ltd., 1983.

Takada Ryōshin. *Chūgūji, Hōrinji, Hokkiji no rekishi to nenpyō.* Tokyo: Wakō Bijutsu Shuppan, 1984.

———. *Hōryūji sen-yonhyakunen.* Tokyo: Shinchōsha, 1994.

———. *Hōryūji shiin no kenkyū.* Kyoto: Dōhōsha Shuppan, 1981.

———. "Shōtoku Taishi shinkō no tenkai: Toku ni Hōryūji o chūshin to shite." In *Shōtoku Taishi to Asuka bukkyō,* edited by Tamura Enchō. Tokyo: Yoshikawa Kōbunkan, 1986, 389–417.

Takahashi Shunjō. "Tenjukoku Mandara to Shōtoku Taishi no kyōiku shisō." In *Chūgūji no shomondai,* edited by Saeki Keizō. Nara: Ikaruga Kokyōsha Shuppanbu, 1943, 46–51.

Takahashi Takahiro. "Meiji 8–9 nen no 'Nara Hakurankai' chinretsu mokuroku ni tsuite." *Shisen,* nos. 56, 57 (1982): 87–118, 47–82.

"Takamatsuzuka hekiga kofun tokushō." *Bukkyō geijutsu,* no. 87 (1972).

Takamatsuzuka Kofun Sōgō Gakujutsu Chōsakai. *Takamatsuzuka kofun hekiga chōsa hōkokusho.* Kyoto: Benridō, 1974.

Takase Tamon. "Mitsui Bunko hon *Kegon kyō* bun ni mieru 'Tenjukoku' ni tsuite: Shinshiryō no shōkai to 'ten' ji no sai kentō." *Sagami joshi daigaku kiyō* 64A (2000): 13–22.

———. "Tenjukoku Shūchō shōkō." In *Sei to shi no zuzōgaku: Ajia ni okeru sei to shi no kosumorojī,* edited by Hayashi Masahiko. Tokyo: Shibundō, 2003, 155–88.

Takeda Sachiko. *Shinkō no ōken: Shōtoku Taishi.* Tokyo: Chūkō Shinsho, 1993.

Takeuchi Rizō, ed. *Kadokawa Nihon chimei daijiten.* 47 vols. Tokyo: Kadokawa Shoten, 1978–90.

———. *Nara ibun*. 2 vols. Tokyo: Yagi Shoten, 1943–44.

Takioto Yoshiyuki. "Shōtoku Taishi no tsumatachi." In *Shōtoku Taishi jiten*, edited by Mayuzumi Hiromichi and Takemitsu Makoto. Tokyo: Shin Jinbutsu Ōraisha, 1991, 80–84.

Tamura Enchō. *Kodai Chōsen bukkyō to Nihon bukkyō*. Tokyo: Yoshikawa Kōbunkan, 1980.

———. "Kudarakei bukkyō to Shiragikei bukkyō." *Rekishi kōron* 6 (1976): 73–84.

———. "Shōtoku Taishi to bukkyō." *Higashi Ajia no kodai bunka*, no. 54 (1988): 2–14.

Tanaka Fumio. *Wakoku to toraijin: Kōsakusuru "uchi" to "soto."* Tokyo: Yoshikawa Kōbunkan, 2005.

Tanaka Ichimatsu, ed. *Nihon emakimono zenshū*. Vol. 10, *Ippen hijiri-e*. Tokyo: Kadokawa Shoten, 1960.

Tanaka Shigehisa. "Shōtoku Taishi Shinaga Yamamoto misasagi no koki." In *Shumatsuki kofun: Ronshū*, edited by Mori Kōichi. Tokyo: Hanawa Shobō, 1973, 79–106.

———. "Shōtoku Taishi to Soga shi." *Higashi Ajia no kodai bunka*, no. 88 (1996): 24–31.

Tanaka Toyozō. "Tenjukoku Shūchō engi bun ihon no danpen." *Gasetsu* 4, no. 7 (1940): 583–92.

Tanaka Tsuguhito. *Shōtoku Taishi shinkō no seiritsu*. Tokyo: Yoshikawa Kōbunkan, 1983.

Tatematsu Wahei. *Shōtoku Taishi: Kono kuni no mahoroba*. Tokyo: Nihon Hōsō Shuppan Kyōkai, 2002.

Tatsumi Kazuhiro et al. "Seikatsu." In *Seikatsu to saishi*, vol. 3 of *Kofun jidai no kenkyū*, edited by Ishino Hironobu et al. Tokyo: Yūzankaku Shuppan, 1990–93, 27–80.

Teiser, Stephen. *The Ghost Festival in Medieval China*. Princeton, NJ: Princeton University Press, 1988.

ten Grotenhuis, Elizabeth. "Chūjōhime: The Weaving of Her Legend." In *Flowing Traces: Buddhism in the Literary and Visual Arts of Japan*, edited by James H. Sanford, William R. LaFleur, and Masatoshi Nagatomi. Princeton, NJ: Princeton University Press, 1992, 180–201.

———. *Japanese Mandalas: Representations of Sacred Geography*. Honolulu: University of Hawai'i Press, 1999.

———. "Rebirth of an Icon: The Taima Mandara in Medieval Japan." *Archives of Asian Art* 36 (1983): 59–87.

———. *The Revival of the Taima Mandala in Medieval Japan*. New York and London: Garland Publishing, 1985.

Thorpe, Robert L. "The Mortuary Art and Architecture of Early Imperial China." Ph.D. dissertation, University of Kansas, 1980.

Tokiwa Daijō. "Tenjukoku ni tsuite." In *Shina bukkyō no kenkyū*, vol. 1. Tokyo: Shunjūsha, 1939, 37–51.

Tokyo Kokuritsu Hakubutsukan. *Hōryūji kennō hōmotsu*. Tokyo: Tokyo Kokuritsu Hakubutsukan, 1975.

———. *Hōryūji kennō hōmotsu: Tokubetsu ten*. Tokyo: Tokyo Kokuritsu Hakubutsukan, 1996.

———. *Kanjōban. Hōryūji kennō hōmotsu tokubetsu chōsa gaihō* 11. Tokyo: Tokyo Kokuritsu Hakubutsukan, 1991.

———. *Kokuhō Hōryūji ten: Hōryūji Shōwa shizaishō chōsa kansei kinen*. Tokyo: Shogakkan, 1994.

———. *Nihon no fukushoku bijutsu*. Tokyo: Tōkyō Bijutsu, 1965.

———. *Shiruku rōdo dai bijutsuten*. Tokyo: Yomiuri Shinbunsha, 1996.

Tonkō Bunbutsu Kenkyūjo, ed. *Tonkō bakukōkutsu*. Vol. 1. Tokyo: Heibonsha, 1980–82.

Tōno Haruyuki. "Ōkimi gō no seiritsu to tennō gō." In Tōno Haruyuki, *Nihon kodai kinsekibun no kenkyū*. Tokyo: Iwanami Shoten, 2004, 347–59.

———. "Tenjukoku Shūchō no seisaku nendai: Meibun to zuzō kara mita." In *Kōkogaku no gakusaiteki kenkyū*, edited by Tōno Haruyuki. Kishiwada-shi: Kishiwada-shi Kyōiku Iinkai, 2001, 1–28.

———. "Tennō gō no seiritsu nendai ni tsuite." In Tōno Haruyuki, *Shōsōin monjo to mokkan no kenkyū*. Tokyo: Hanawa Shobō, 1977, 397–420.

Tseng, Lillian Lan-ying. *Picturing Heaven in Early China*. Cambridge, MA: Harvard University Asia Center, 2011.

Tsubota Itsuo. *Nihon josei no rekishi*. Vol. 3, *Kodai ōchō no josei*. Tokyo: Akatsuki Kyōiku Tosho, 1982.

Tsuda Sōkichi. "Tennō kō." In Tsuda Sōkichi, *Nihon jōdaishi no kenkyū*. Tokyo: Iwanami Shoten, 1949, 474–91.

Tsude Hiroshi. "Goseki no Naniwa to Hōenzaka iseki." In *Kura to kodai ōken*, edited by Naoki Kōjirō and Ogasawara Yoshihiko. Kyoto: Mineruva Shobō, 1991, 47–64.

Tsuji Zennosuke. "Shōtoku Taishi no shinkō to Tenjukoku Mandara." In *Shōtoku Taishi ronsan*, edited by Heian Kōkokai. Kyoto: Heian Kōkokai, 1921, 81–88.

———. "Wakayama-ken oyobi Kyōto-fu e kenkyū ryokō ho (shōzen)." *Shigaku zasshi* 12, no. 2 (1901): 98–116.

Ueda Masaaki. "Kameishi to shūchō." *Asuka kaze* 75 (2000): 5–9.

———. *Kodai no Dōkyō to Chōsen bunka*. Kyoto: Jinbun Shoin, 1989.

Uehara Kazu. "Fujinoki kofun shutsudo no fukusōhin ni tsuite—monyō isho kara mita Chōsen Sangoku to no kankei." *Bukkyō geijutsu*, no. 184 (1989): 80–93.

———. "Kōkuri kaiga no Nihon e oyoboshita eikyō." *Bukkyō geijutsu*, no. 215 (1994): 75–103.

———. *Shōtoku Taishi*. Tokyo: Sansaisha, 1969.

———. *Tamamushi zushi no kenkyū: Asuka, Hakuhō bijutsu yōshiki shiron*. Tokyo: Yoshikawa Kōbunkan, 1991.

Uehara Mahito. *Rengemon*. Nihon no bijutsu, no. 359. Tokyo: Shibundō, 1996.

Uesugi Yoshimaro. "Taishi shinkō." In *Hōryūji bijutsu: Ronsō no shiten*, edited by Ōhashi Katsuaki. Tokyo: Gurafusha, 1998, 355–79.

Umehara Sueji. "Shōtoku Taishi Shinaga no gobyō." In *Shōtoku Taishi ronsan*, edited by Heian Kōkokai. Kyoto: Heian Kōkokai, 1921, 344–70. Also published in *Nihon kōkogaku ronkō*. Tokyo: Kōbundō Shobō, 1940.

Umehara, Suyeji [sic]. "The Newly Discovered Tombs with Wall Paintings of the Kao-kou-li Dynasty." *Archives of the Chinese Society of America* 6 (1952): 5–17.

Umehara, Takeshi. "Prince Shōtoku: Ancient Internationalist." *Japan Quarterly* 26, no. 3 (1979): 318–29.

Uwai Hisayoshi, ed. *Haka no rekishi*. Sōsō bosei kenkyū shūsei, vol. 5. Tokyo: Meichō Shuppankai, 1979.

Wada Atsumu. "Bukkyō to sōsō girei no henka." *Rekishi kōron* 6 (1976): 102–13.

———. "Mogari no kisoteki kōsatsu." In *Shumatsuki kofun: Ronshū*, edited by Mori Kōichi. Tokyo: Hanawa Shobō, 1973, 285–386.

———. *Nihon kodai no girei to saishi, shinkō*. 3 vols. Tokyo: Hanawa Shobō, 1995.

———. "Wafū shigō no seiritsu to kōtōfu." In *Zeminaru Nihon kodai shi ge*, edited by Ueda Masaaki et al. Tokyo: Kōbunsha, 1980, 327–34.

Walley, Akiko. *Constructing the Dharma King: The Hōryūji Shaka Triad and the Birth of the Prince Shōtoku Cult*. Leiden and Boston: Brill, 2015.

Wang, Eugene Y. "Coffins and Confucianism: The Northern Wei Sarcophagus in the Minneapolis Institute of Arts." *Orientations* 30, no. 6 (1999): 56–64.

Wang, Robin R. *Yinyang: The Way of Heaven and Earth in Chinese Thought and Culture*. Cambridge: Cambridge University Press, 2012.

Washizuka Hiromitsu, Park Youngbok, and Kang Woobang. *Transmitting the Forms of Divinity: Early Buddhist Art from Korea and Japan*. New York: Japan Society, 2003.

Watsuji, Tetsurō. "The Reception of Buddhism in the Suiko period." Translated by Hirano Umeyo. *The Eastern Buddhist* 5, no. 1 (1972): 47–54.

Watt, James C.Y., et al. *China: Dawn of the Golden Age, 200–750 AD*. New York, New Haven, and London: The Metropolitan Museum of Art and Yale University Press, 2004.

Weinstein, Lucie. "The Yumedono Kannon: Problems in Seventh-Century Sculpture." *Archives of Asian Art* 42 (1989): 25–48.

Whitfield, Roderick. *The Art of Central Asia: The Stein Collection in the British Museum*. Vol. 3. Tokyo: Kodansha, 1982–85.

Wong, Dorothy. *Chinese Steles: Pre-Buddhist and Buddhist Use of a Symbolic Form*. Honolulu: University of Hawai'i Press, 2003.

———. "Reassesing the Wall Paintings of Hōryūji." In *Hōryūji Reconsidered*, edited by Dorothy Wong and Eric M. Field. Cambridge: Cambridge Scholars Publishing, 2008, 131–90.

Wong, Dorothy, and Eric M. Field, eds. *Hōryūji Reconsidered*. Cambridge: Cambridge Scholars Publishing, 2008.

Wu Hung. "Art in a Ritual Context: Rethinking Mawangdui." *Early China* 17 (1992): 111–44.

———. *The Art of the Yellow Springs: Understanding Chinese Tombs*. Honolulu: University of Hawai'i Press, 2010.

———. "Buddhist Elements in Early Chinese Art (2nd and 3rd Centuries A.D.)." *Artibus Asiae* 47, nos. 2, 3 (1986): 263–316.

———. "From Temple to Tomb: Ancient Art and Religion in Transition." *Early China* 13 (1988): 78–115.

———. "Mapping Early Taoist Art: The Visual Culture of the Wudoumi Dao." In *Taoism and the Arts of China*, edited by Stephen Little with Shawn Eichman. Chicago and Berkeley: The Art Institute of Chicago and University of California Press, 2000, 77–94.

———. *Monumentality in Early Chinese Art and Architecture*. Stanford, CA: Stanford University Press, 1995.

———. "The Origins of Chinese Painting: Paleolithic Period to Tang Dynasty." In *Three Thousand Years of Chinese Painting*, edited by Yang Xin et al. New Haven and London: Yale University Press, 1997, 15–86.

———. "A Sanpan Shan Chariot Ornament and the Xiangrui Design in Western Han Art." *Archives of Asian Art* 37 (1984): 38–59.

———. *The Wu Liang Shrine: The Ideology of Early Chinese Pictorial Art*. Stanford, CA: Stanford University Press, 1989.

Yamabe Tomoyuki. "Shishū ni tsuite." *Museum*, no. 13 (1952): 11–15.

Yamabe Tomoyuki and Domyō Mihoko. "Tenjukoku Shūchō." In *Yamato koji taikan*, edited by Ōta Hirotarō, vol. 1. Tokyo: Iwanami Shoten, 1977, 70–77.

Yamada Hideo. "Kodai tennō no okurina ni tsuite." In Yamada Hideo, *Nihon kodaishi kō*. Tokyo: Iwanami Shoten, 1987, 102–34.

Yamada Shōzen. "Kōshiki: Sono seiritsu to tenkai." In *Bukkyō bungaku kōza*, edited by Itō Hiroyuki et al., vol. 8, *Shōdō no bungaku*. Tokyo: Benseisha, 1995, 11–53.

Yamada Toshiaki. "The Lingbao School." Chapter 9 of *Daoism Handbook*, edited by Livia Kohn, vol. 1. Boston and Leiden: Brill, 2004, 225–55.

Yamamoto Tadanao. *Karakusamon*. Nihon no bijutsu, no. 358. Tokyo: Shibundō, 1996.

Yokokura Nagatsune. "Sōka kara banka e no kakehashi: Tenjukoku Shūchō kihaibun no kataru mono." In Yokokura Nagatsune, *Kodai bungaku shiron*. Tokyo: Musashino Shoin, 1992, 19–72.

Yoshida Eri. "Kobutsu: Edo kara Meiji e no keishō." *Kindai gasetsu* 12 (2003): 13–30.

Yoshida Kazuhiko. "'Gangōji garan engi narabi ni ruki shizaichō' no shinyōsei." In *Shōtoku Taishi no shinjitsu*, edited by Ōyama Seiichi. Tokyo: Heibonsha, 2004, 91–122.

———. "Kindai rekishigaku to Shōtoku Taishi kenkyū." In *Shōtoku Taishi no shinjitsu*, edited by Ōyama Seiichi. Tokyo: Heibonsha, 2004, 19–44.

———. "Revisioning Religion in Ancient Japan." *Japanese Journal of Religious Studies* 30, nos. 1, 2 (2003): 1–26.

———. "Tenjukoku Mandara Shūchō meibun no jinmei hyōki." *Arena* 5 (2008): 236–46.

———. "The Thesis That Prince Shōtoku Did Not Exist." *Acta Asiatica* 91 (2006): 1–20.

———, ed. *Henbōsuru Shōtoku Taishi: Nihonjin wa Shōtoku Taishi o donoyō ni shinkō shite kita ka*. Tokyo: Heibonsha, 2011.

Yoshie Akiko. "Gender in Early Classical Japan: Marriage, Leadership, and Political Status in Village and Palace." *Monumenta Nipponica* 60, no. 4 (2005): 437–79.

———. *Nihon kodai keifu yōshiki ron*. Tokyo: Yoshikawa Kōbunkan, 2000.

———. "Tenjukoku Shūchō mei keifu no ikkosatsu." *Nihon shi kenkyū*, no. 325 (1989): 1–18.

Yoshii Hideo. "The Influence of Baekje on Ancient Japan." *The International Journal of Korean Art and Archaeology* 1 (2007): 48–61.

Yoshimura Rei. "Asuka Hakuhō chōkokushi shiron—ichijidai ichiyōshikiteki riron e no gimon." *Bukkyō geijutsu*, no. 227 (1996): 15–40. Also published in Yoshimura Rei, *Tennin tanjōzu no kenkyū: Higashi Ajia bukkyō bijutsu ronshū*. Tokyo: Tōhō Shoten, 1999, 309–34.

———. *Chūgoku bukkyō zuzō no kenkyū*. Tokyo: Tōhō Shoten, 1983.

———. "Kudara Mutei ōhi ki makura ni egakareta tennin tanjō zu." In Yoshimura Rei, *Chūgoku bukkyō zuzō no kenkyū*. Tokyo: Tōhō Shoten, 1983, 117–35. First published in *Bijutsushi kenkyū* 14 (1977). Also published in Yoshimura Rei, *Tennin tanjōzu no kenkyū: Higashi Ajia bukkyō bijutsu ronshū*. Tokyo: Tōhō Shoten, 1999, 91–107.

———. "Kyōken sekkutsu ni okeru keshō no zuzō ni tsuite." *Waseda daigaku daigakuin bungaku kenkyūka kiyo* 21 (1976): 115–26. Also published in Yoshimura Rei, *Tennin tanjōzu no kenkyū: Higashi Ajia bukkyō bijutsu ronshū*. Tokyo: Tōhō Shoten, 1999, 73–90.

———. "Mogao sekkutsu ni okeru tennin zō no keifu." *Kokka*, no. 1177 (1993): 3–17. Also published in Yoshimura Rei, *Tennin tanjōzu no kenkyū: Higashi Ajia bukkyō bijutsu ronshū*. Tokyo: Tōhō Shoten, 1999, 137–61.

———. "Nanchōteki tennin no Nihon e no denba." In *Hōryūji kara Yakushiji e: Asuka Nara no kenchiku, chōkoku*, edited by Mizuno Keizaburō et al. Tokyo: Kōdansha, 1990, 171–77.

———. "Nanchō tennin zuzō no Hokuchō oyobi shūhen shokoku e no denba." *Bukkyō geijutsu*, no. 159 (1985): 11–29. Also published in Yoshimura Rei, *Tennin tanjōzu no kenkyū: Higashi Ajia bukkyō bijutsu ronshū*. Tokyo: Tōhō Shoten, 1999, 163–80.

———. "Nihon no bukkyō bijutsu to shiruku rōdo: Renge keshōzō no keifu." *Rekishi kōron* 12, no. 4 (1978): 130–37.

———. "Ryūmon Hoku Gi kutsu ni okeru tennin tanjō no hyōgen." *Bijutsushi* 69 (1968): 1–12. Also published in Yoshimura Rei, *Tennin tanjōzu no kenkyū: Higashi Ajia bukkyō bijutsu ronshū*. Tokyo: Tōhō Shoten, 1999, 55–72.

———. "Sennin no zukei o ronzu." *Bukkyō geijutsu*, no. 184 (1989): 29–48. Also published in Yoshimura Rei, *Tennin tanjōzu no kenkyū: Higashi Ajia bukkyō bijutsu ronshū*. Tokyo: Tōhō Shoten, 1999, 341–63.

———. "Tenjukoku Shūchō to Kondō Kanjōban ni mirareru tennin tanjō no zuzō." *Museum*, no. 354 (1979): 4–17. Also published in Yoshimura Rei, *Tennin tanjōzu no kenkyū: Higashi Ajia bukkyō bijutsu ronshū*. Tokyo: Tōhō Shoten, 1999, 107–20.

———. "Tennin no gogi to Chūgoku no sōki tennin zō." *Bukkyō geijutsu*, no. 193 (1990): 73–93. Also published in Yoshimura Rei, *Tennin tanjōzu no kenkyū: Higashi Ajia bukkyō bijutsu ronshū*. Tokyo: Tōhō Shoten, 1999, 365–83.

———. *Tennin tanjōzu no kenkyū: Higashi Ajia bukkyō bijutsu ronshū*. Tokyo: Tōhō Shoten, 1999.

———. "Unkō ni okeru renge keshō no hyōgen." In Yoshimura Rei, *Chūgoku bukkyō zuzō no kenkyū*. Tokyo: Tōhō Shoten, 1983, 35–53. First published in *Bijutsushi* 37 (1960). Also published in Yoshimura Rei, *Tennin tanjōzu no kenkyū: Higashi Ajia bukkyō bijutsu ronshū*. Tokyo: Tōhō Shoten, 1999, 23–37.

———. "Unkō ni okeru renge sōshoku no igi." In Yoshimura Rei, *Chūgoku bukkyō zuzō no kenkyū*. Tokyo: Tōhō Shoten, 1983, 55–73. First published in *Bijutsushi kenkyū* 3 (1964). Also published in Yoshimura Rei, *Tennin tanjōzu no kenkyū: Higashi Ajia bukkyō bijutsu ronshū*. Tokyo: Tōhō Shoten, 1999, 39–54.

Yu Ying-shih. "Life and Immortality in the Mind of Han China." *Harvard Journal of Asiatic Studies* 25 (1964–65): 162–86.

———. "O Soul, Come Back: A Study of the Changing Perception of the Soul and Afterlife in Pre-Buddhist China." *Harvard Journal of Asiatic Studies* 47 (1987): 363–95.

Zürcher, Erik. *The Buddhist Conquest of China: The Spread and Adaptation of Buddhism in Early Medieval China*. 1959. Reprint, Leiden: E.J. Brill, 1972.

———. "Buddhist Influence on Early Taoism: A Survey of Scriptural Evidence." *T'oung Pao* 66, nos. 1, 3 (1980): 84–147.

Illustration Credits

Permission to reproduce photographs has been granted by the temples, museums, and institutions that own or supervise the objects; the names of these institutions are given in the figure captions. In most cases, photography requests were handled by image archives operated by museums or private institutions, listed below. In some cases, permission was received to use a previously published photograph; the applicable publications also are listed below, with full reference information provided in the Bibliography.

Photographs
Agency for Cultural Affairs Collection, Museum of the Kashihara Archaeological Research Institute. fig. 60
Asuka Village Board of Education: figs. 45, 47, 48
Benridō, Kyoto: fig. 4
©DNP Art Communications: figs. 5, 6, 8, 34, 34a, 92, 93
Gongju National Museum: figs. 54, 59
Ikarugadera: fig. 95
The Mainichi Newspapers/AFLO: fig. 102
©Minneapolis Institute of Art: fig. 52
Mita Kakuyuki: figs. 103–20, and frontispiece to Appendix
Nara National Museum: figs. 1, 3, 10, 10a, 11, 13, 15, 17, 19, 20, 26, 27, 33, 33a, 35, 44, 62, 80, 82–86, 88, 90, 94, 101, 121, and frontispieces to Prologue, Chapters One through Five, and Epilogue

Nara National Research Institute for Cultural Property: figs. 23, 24, 24a, 36, 37
National Museum of Korea: fig. 91
Chari Pradel: figs. 77, 78
©RMN-Grand Palais/Art Resources, NY. Photo by Thierry Ollivier: fig. 81
Office of the Shōsōin Treasure House, Nara Prefecture: figs. 2, 9, 9a, 21, 46, 99
Audrey Spiro: fig. 29

Publications
Fan Shuying, *Xincheng, fangling, Yongtai gong zhu mu bi hua*: fig. 25
He Jiejun, *Mawangdui Han mu*: fig. 28
Henan Sheng wen wu yan jiu suo, *Gong Xian shi ku si*: figs. 49, 63, 63a, 64
Lena Kim, ed., *World Cultural Heritage: Koguryo Tomb Murals*: figs. 22, 22a, 30–32, 38, 39, 39a, 40, 41, 41a, 42, 43, 53, 61, 67, 68, 75
Longmen wen wu bao guan suo, Beijing da xue kao gu xi bian, *Longmen shi ku*: fig. 50
Shanxi sheng Datong shi bowuguan and Shanxi sheng wenwu gongzuo weiyuanhui, "Shanxi Datong shijiazhai Beiwei Sima Jinlong mu": fig. 58
Shitennōji (2005): fig. 76

Index

Amida's Western Pure Land
    belief in, 159
    ceremonies performed at Shitennōji, 219n80
    Tenjukoku identified as, 7, 79, 133, 156–158, 215n21
"Amida triad in one tomb with three remains" (*sankotsu ichibyō no Amida sanzon*) devotion at Shinaga, 133, 159–160
Amida triads
    in the Tachibana Shrine at Hōryūji, 221n134
    Zenkōji Amida triad
        and the Pure Land form of the Shōtoku cult, 146
        and Shitennōji, 135–136, 146
    See also Hōryūji Golden Hall, Amida triad in; Shinaga Amida triad
Anahobe. *See* Empress Anahobe Hashihito
Anak tombs. *See under* Goguryeo tombs
ancestral shrines
    erected by Emishi in Takamiya, 122–123
    safeguarding by rulers, 118
    See also Wu Liang Shrine
animal symbolism
    crow in the sun and hare in the moon
        from a tomb at Jianjia, 40, 40f29
        on the bronze banner from Hōryūji, 42, 45, 45ff34–34a
        Han period examples, 39–40
        moon with hare (A-1 motif) from the Shūchō, 23f12, 36, 38f27, 39, 45–46, 79
        on the Tamamushi Shrine, 42, 44f33a, 45
    twelve animals of the Chinese zodiac, 47
    See also birds; dragons; Four Divinities; tigers; turtles
Arai Hiroshi, 115, 190
ashlar stone wall at Asuka, 56–57, 57f48
Asukadera. *See under* Gangōji
Azure Dragon, 34f23, 46, 47

Baekje
    administrative system, 102, 224n49
    fragment of a tile, 177, 179f91
    King Seongmyeong of, 86
    kinunui (dressmakers) origins in, 103
    monk Kwalluk (J. Kanroku) from, 228n69
    monk Nichira from, 155, 167
    writing introduced to the Yamato court by, 85–86
Baekje tombs
    iconography
        and Chinese funerary iconography, 126
        Four Divinities, 47
        sun and moon imagery, 42
    King Muryeong's tomb, 63–64, 65ff54–55, 69, 69f59, 70, 227n41, 229n99
    Songsanri tombs, 42, 47, 227n41
birds
    crow in the sun and hare in the moon
        from a tomb at Jianjia, 40, 40f29
        Han period examples, 39–40
    red bird
        destroyed in Takamatsuzuka tomb, 47
        from Gangseo daemyo tomb, 49–50, 70, 71f61
        in Kitora tomb, 47, 49f37
        as an omen, 46, 47, 49, 50, 58
        Shūchō A-3 motif of, 37f26, 38, 46, 46f35
    three legged bird at Kitora, 42
Bo Qianqiu tomb (Luoyang), 39–40
brocade. *See under* fabric types
Buddha Preaching. *See* Kajūji embroidered icon *Buddha Preaching*
Buddhism
    and bells, 177, 179
    and Daoism, 127–128, 229n114
    See also Pure Land school; Shingon Ritsu school
Buddhist sutras
    "birth by transformation in a lotus flower" (*renge keshō*) derived from, 72
    subjects of embroidered fabrics derived from, 114
Buddhist sutras and *śāstras*—individual titles
    Benevolent Kings Sutra (*Ninnōkyō*), 114
    Buddha of Measureless Life Sutra (S. *Sukhāvativyūha Sūtra*; C. *Wulingshou jing* J. *Muryōjukyō*), 72, 121
        Chinese rendering of the title as the "Sutra of Measureless Lifespan," 128
    Flower Garland Sutra (S. *Avataṃsaka sūtra*; J. *Kegonkyō*), 7, 114
    Greater Perfection of Wisdom Sutra (S. *Mahāprajñāpāramitā*; J.*Daihannyakyō*), 114
    Lion's Roar Sutra (S. *Śrīmālā-devīsiṃhanāda-sutra*; J. *Shōmangyō*), Prince Shōtoku's lecturing on, 6, 84, 158, 184–185, 184f95
    Lotus Sutra (S. *Saddharmapuṇḍarīka Sūtra*; J. *Hokkekyō*)
        chanting of, 142
        and the dedication as the Tenjukoku Mandara, 158, 165
        Devadatta Chapter of, 72
        in Hokke Sanjikkō ceremony, 165
        Prince Shōtoku's lecturing on, 84, 148
    Sutra of Immeasurable Meanings (S. *Ananta nirdeśa Sūtra*; C. *Wuliang yi jing*; J. *Muryōgikyō*), 165
    Sutra of Maitreya's Great Buddhist Accomplishments (*Miroku taisei bukkyō*), 185
    Yisuan jing (Sutra to Increase the Account), 129
    Yugashijiron (S. *Yogācara-bhūmi śāstra*, Discourse on the Stages of Concentration Practice), 150

Bush, Susan, 67, 69
Byōkutsuge (Verse of the Tomb Chamber), 139, 155

Campany, Robert F., 58
cartouche-shaped stone receptacle at Asuka, 55–56, 57f48
celestial beings (C. *tianren*; J. *tennin*). *See* transcendents or immortals
celestial imagery
    "clouds of energy" (C. *yunqi*; J. *unki*) motif, 62–63
    sun and moon iconography
        in Goguryeo tombs, 40, 41–42ff30–32
        on Hōryūji's bronze banner, 42, 45, 45ff34–34a
        in Kitora tomb, 42
        in Southern Qi-period brick tombs, 40, 40f29
        in Takamatsuzuka tomb, 34ff23–24, 42
        in tombs from Baekje, 42
    on the Tamamushi Shrine, 42, 44f33a, 45, 184, 221n127
    See also transcendents
Chōgen (1121–1206), and the tomb at Shinaga, 136, 139, 140
Chōshimaru
    and Kenshin's claims regarding, 138, 231n31
    and the Nyoirin Kannon at Hōryūji, 231n29
Chūgūji
    Anahobe's founding of, 1, 148–149, 150
    fragments of the Tenjukoku Shūchō Mandara in, turtles with graphs, 1, 3f4, 172, 181
    Golden Hall
        plan of, 148, 158, 188f98
        repair work on, 149
        Tenjukoku Mandara displayed in, 188, 191–193
    Hōryūji's protection of, 148, 149
    multiple names of, 149
    as "the palace of Empress Hashihito Anahobe," 148–149
    and Shinnyo, 149–150, 233n84
        restoration work of, 1, 10, 152–153, 156, 159, 165
        selection as abbess of, 165
    and the Tenjukoku Shūchō Mandara embroidery, ownership of, 1
Chūgūji engi
    Hōryūji portrayed negatively in the 1463 version, 168
    Jōen's writing of, 152, 159, 230n1
    measurements of the mandara in the 1463 version, 186
    one hundred turtles mentioned in 1274 version, 87, 151
        placement of described in, 185, 192
    on the search for the mandara
        determining the date of Anahobe's death as a motivation for, 151, 158, 164
        restoration of Chūgūji as a motivation for, 164, 165
        Shinnyo's discovery of, 151, 154, 156, 167
    and the *Shōtoku Taishi denki*, 165
    two versions compared, 167–168, 233n95
clothing
    cultural commonalities between Japan and the Korean peninsula, 21, 33
    similarities of garments worn by the seventh-century and thirteenth-century figures, 174–176
    sumptuary laws, 33, 112
    See also kinunui (dressmakers); skirts
color. *See* fabric color
Como, Michael, 8, 215n30, 224n56, 225n113
craftspeople
    Aya brocade weavers from Baekje, 103
    involved in the production of the Shūchō, 5, 9–10, 83, 153
    involved in the production of the Tenjukoku Mandara, 153
    kinunui (dressmakers)
        embroidered icons for Asukadera and Kudara Ōdera possibly made by, 104, 115
        migration from Baekje or China to Japan, 103
    shinabe (skilled craftspeople) within the centralized-state system (*ritsuryō kokka*), 115
cult of Prince Shōtoku (*Taishi shinkō*). *See under* Prince Shōtoku (Umayado Toyotomimi)
curtains
    on a tent frame from Liu Sheng's tomb, 117–118, 117f74, 188
    for Buddhist icons, 116, 227n37
    embroidered curtains in the Eastern Han royal temple in Luoyang, 118
    embroidered curtains ordered by Suiko, 5, 89
    Shūchō possibly used for, 117, 119–120, 123–124, 130

Daianji engi narabini ruki shizaichō (Account of the Establishment of Daianji and List of Accumulated Treasures), 113–114
Daoism
    and Buddhism, 127–128, 229n114
    defined by Isabelle Robinet, 230n124
    iconographical program of a painted coffin from Guyuan (Northern Wei), 40
    iconographical program of Goguryeo tombs
        Deokhungri tomb (408), 50
        Ohoebun Tomb No. 4, 78
    Taiping jing (Scripture of the Great Peace), 129, 130, 230n127
    Taishang Laojun shuo changsheng yisuan miaojing (Marvelous Scripture for Prolonging Life and for Increasing the Account, Revealed by the Most High Lord Lao), 129
Dark Warrior (snake intertwined with a turtle), 46, 47, 48f36
Davis, Richard, 8
Dengxian tombs, 62, 67, 76, 77f66
Deokhungri (Tokhungri) tombs. *See under* Goguryeo tombs
design elements
    "clouds of energy" (C. *yunqi*; J. *unki*) motif, 62–63
    figure emerging from a lotus, term
    See also animal symbolism; celestial imagery; clothing; leaf-shaped elements; palmette design; rhythmic

arrangement of motifs; Shūchō (seventh-
        century embroidery) motifs; skirts; Tenjukoku
        Mandara motifs
dragons
    Azure Dragon, *34f23*, 46, 47
    a dragon described as part of the composition of the
        Shūcho, 47, 185, 218n63
    images in tombs and sarcophagi, 58, 60, 68, 126
    as omens, 50
    and the *Yellow River Chart* (*Hetu*), 55
Dunhuang
    Cave No. 150 motifs of repeated circles, 69
    Cave No. 285
        figures of monks, 184
        Southern-style floral motifs, 69
    inscription on silk fabric from, 190, *191table6*
    ninth-century copy of an omen index, 49
    procession in the Buddhist cave temples at, 217n32
    Śakyamuni Preaching on Vulture Peak, 16–17

Eifukuji
    appearance of the name of, 136
    tomb of Prince Shōtoku at Shinaga at, 136, *137f77*
        Amida triad relief at, 139, *140f78*
    See also Shinaga
Eison (1201–1290)
    as the abbot of Saidaiji, 150, 165, 169
    and the repairs of the Nyoirin Kannon at Hōryūji, 138,
        231n29
    Shingon Ritsu school founded by, 138
    and Shinnyo, 134, 150, 165
    and the tomb at Shinaga, 136, 139
embroidered fabric
    on a quiver found at Nishimiyayama funerary mound,
        216n10
    Daianji engi listing of, 113
    fragments found at Tōshōdaiji, 216n11
    fragments of an embroidered banner with celestial
        beings at Hōryūji, 15–16, *16f8*, 17, 104, 198, 213, *213f121*
    Kajūji embroidered icon, 16, *18f10*, 115, 216n12
    Nihon shoki on, 112–113
    paucity of examples dated to the seventh century, 15
    and politico-administrative ranks, 112
    shūbutsu (embroidered fabrics with Buddhist subjects)
        Kajūji embroidered icon *Buddha Preaching*, 16, *18f10*,
            115, 216n12
        Śakyamuni Preaching on Vulture Peak found in Dun-
            huang, 16–17
        Tenjukoku Mandara fragments categorized as, 15,
            112, 198–199
    sizes of embroideries for Buddhist icons, 113, 114–115,
        114table3, 216n12
    Uragaki on craftsmen involved in the production of
        embroidered textiles, 153

and the work of *kinunui* (dressmakers), 104, 115
See also Shūchō (seventh-century embroidery);
    Tenjukoku Mandara; Tenjukoku Shūchō Mandara
embroidery stitches
    antiquity of technique of, 216nn10–11
    chain stitch, 17, *19f10a*
    couching (*komanui*), 15, 211, *211f118*
    fancy couching (*tabanenui*), 15, 211, *211f119*
    and the identification and evaluation of motifs, 9, 13,
        15–17
    long-and-short stitch (*sashinui* or *shusuzashi*), *210f116*, 211
    long stem stitch (*naga kaeshinui*), *210f117*, 211
    outline stitch (*matsuinui*), 15, *210f112*, 211
    running stitch (*tsugi hiranui*), 16, 104
    satin stitch (*hiranui*), *210f114*, 211
        used in Shōsōin embroideries, 16–17, *17ff9–9a*
    stem stitch (*kaeshinui*), *210f113*
        used on Shūchō all fragments, 15, 104, *210f113*, 211
    surface satin stitch (*omote hiranui*), *210f115*, 211
Emishi. *See* Soga no Emishi
Empress Anahobe Hashihito
    and Chūgūji, 1, 148–149, 150
    date of death of, 88–89, 97–98, 107, 151, 166
    as an incarnation of Amida, 133, 139, 142, 146, 148, 149
    phonograms and logographs for her name in the
        Shūchō inscription, 96–97
Engishiki of 927, on fabric measurements, 190–191, *191table6*
etoki, 234n112

fabric color
    contrasting colors of undecorated fabrics, 15
        white painted heads, 212, *212f120*, 215n3
    purple associated with high rank, 112
    on the Shūchō
        of ground fabrics of fragments of, *14f7*, 15, 172, 208–
            209, 238n12
        purple gauze over purple plain weave of, 15, *209f111*
        vibrancy of, 15, 160, 209
    and the 681 sumptuary law, 112
    on the Tenjukoku Mandara, purple twill and white plain
        weave of, *14f7*, 15, *207ff104–106*, *208f108*
    white fabric on walls of the northern chamber of Tomb
        No. 1 at Mawangdui, 117
    white fabric used for curtains on biers, 117
fabric measurements
    of Chinese curtains
        on a tent frame from Liu Sheng's tomb, 117–118,
            117f74, 188
        in the Eastern Han royal temple in Luoyang, 118
    Engishiki of 927 on, 190–191, *191table6*
    of gauze fabrics from the late seventh and early eighth
        centuries, 191
    inscription on silk fabric from Dunhuang, 190, *191table6*
    Nihon shoki on, 190, *191table6*

INDEX

and the size of the Tenjukoku Mandara, 11
    and the layout of the one hundred turtles on, 191–193
    span between bays of Chūgūji, 191
    sizes of embroidered Buddhist icons, 113, 114–115, 114table3
    See also measurements
fabric types
    brocade
        Aya brocade weavers from Baekje, 103
        clothing worn by the elite, 112
        curtain stolen by Ōtomo no Sadehiko no Muraji, 116
        found in seventh-century tombs, 205
        Shūchō discovered in bag made of, 165
        Tenjukoku Shūchō Mandara framing with, 199
        Tenjukoku Shūchō Mandara replica made of, 199, 201f102
        Zenkōji Amida's letter to Prince Shōtoku covered in brocade fabric, 142
    crepe (*chijimi*), 15, 212, 238n22
    gauze (*ro*), 208
        complex gauze (*ra*), 207, 208, 208ff109–110
        and plain weave, 207, 207f104
        "plain-woven gauze" (*ro heiken*), 212
    plain weave (*hiraori*), 207, 207f104
        and gauze, 208, 209f111
        three fragments of white plain-weave silk, 184
        white paper with black outlines under, 207, 207f105
    twill (*aya*), 207, 208f107
        found in seventh-century tombs, 205
        panels of twill (*aya katabira*), 165
        purple twill ground of the Tenjukoku Mandara, 15, 184
        purple twill on thirteenth-century fragments with designs copied from the seventh-century, 171ff84–85, 172
        purple twill on thirteenth-century fragments with designs of indeterminate origin, 181–184
        purple twill on thirteenth-century fragments with designs probably copied from the seventh-century, 174–178
        and the 681 sumptuary law, 112
        Tenjukoku Mandara's use of, 207–208, 207f106, 208f108
        used for thirteenth-century reparations, 171
    undecorated fabrics
        diagram of the Tenjukoku Shūchō Mandara, 206f103
        different types of, 212
        pasted on, 15, 199, 205
    See also embroidered fabric
Farris, William W., 228
Fenollosa, Ernest, 197–198, 237n6
Foard, James H., 154
Four Divinities (C. *sixiang*; J. *shishin*)

Dark Warrior (snake intertwined with a turtle), 46, 47, 48f36
    in Goguryeo tombs, 47
    introduced, 46–47
    in the Takamatsuzuka and Kitora tombs, 19, 47
Fujii Yukiko, 231n31
Fujinoki tomb, leaf-shaped horse trapping, 70, 70f60
Fujita Kiyoshi, 231nn16,19
Fujiwara no Michinaga (966–1028), 135
Fukui Kōjun, 128
Fukunaga Mitsuji, 128, 230n121
Fukuyama Toshio, 6, 94–95, 96

Gakjeochong (Tomb of the Wrestlers). *See under* Goguryeo tombs
Gangōji (Asukadera)
    building of, 105
    finial inscription of the pagoda of, 85table2, 96, 104, 107, 224n72
Gangōji garan engi narabi ni ruki shizaichō (Account of the Establishment of the Monastery Gangōji and List of Accumulated Treasures)
    inscriptions in, 224n72
    on the pagoda finial at Gangōji, 85table2, 96, 104, 107, 224n72
    on Prince Shōtoku's writing abilities, 747
    problems associated with inscriptions in, 222n12
Gangseo daemyo (Kangso Great Tomb). *See under* Goguryeo tombs
Gangseo gungmyo (Kangso Middle Tomb). *See under* Goguryeo tombs
Gerhart, Karen, 234n112
Goguryeo tombs
    cultural commonalities between Japan and the Korean peninsula, 21, 33
    general overview of, 19–20, 20table1, 216n18
    imagery
        and Chinese funerary iconography, 19–20, 40, 42, 49–50, 126, 216n18, 219n69
        half-palmette motif, 69–70
        omens on the ceilings of, 49–50
        personal choices of occupants reflected in, 78
        processions, 32f22, 33
        symmetrical and rhythmic design of motifs, 50, 53f43, 72
Goguryeo tombs—individual groups of
    Anak Tomb No. 2, 20table1
    Anak Tomb No. 3, 20table1, 118, 119f75
    Deokhungri (Tokhungri), 20table1, 40, 49–50, 50f38, 51f39a, 52ff40–41
    Deokhwari (Tokhwari), Nos. 1 and 2, 20table1, 40–41, 41ff30–31, 47
    Gakjeochong (Tomb of the Wrestlers), 20table1
    Gangseo daemyo tomb (Kangso Great Tomb), 20table1, 50, 53ff42–43, 63, 64f53, 71f61, 72, 78, 81

Gangseo gungmyo tomb (Kangso Middle Tomb), 20*table1*, 42*f32*, 69–70
Jangcheon (Changchuan) No. 1, 20*table1*, 77–79, 78*f67*, 81
Jinpari tombs
    No. 1, 20*table1*, 42, 47, 70
    No. 2, 20*table1*, 42, 47
    No. 4, 79, 80*f69*, 81
Muyongchong (Tomb of the Dancers), 20*table1*, 49
Ohoebun tombs
    No. 4, 20*table1*, 47, 78, 78, 79*f68*
    No. 5, 20*table1*, 47
Samsilchong (Tomb of the Three Chambers), 20*table1*, 76–77
Sasinchong (Tomb of the Four Divinities), 20*table1*, 47
Ssangyeongchong (Twin Pillar Tomb), 20*table1*, 40
Susanri, 20*table1*, 21, 32*f22–22a*, 33, 36
Taeanri, 21
Yakusuri, 47
Gómez, Luis O., 230n121
Gongxian caves
    Cave No. 3 stupa-pillar, 49*f59*, 58, 74
    Cave No. 4 ceiling, 74, 74*f63*, 74–75*ff63–63a*, 76, 76*f64*
    figure emerging from a lotus, 74, 74–75*ff63–63a*, 76, 76*f64*, 79
    procession scenes, 33, 217n32
    rhythmic arrangement of motifs, 74, 76
    Southern style of floral motifs in, 69
Great Kings (*ōkimi*)
    as a title for Japanese rulers who reigned prior to the late seventh century, xi, 214n4
    names of, 90
Great King Bidatsu (r. 572–85), 231n19
    mogari of, 126
    sutras sent by King Seongmyeong during the reign of, 86
Great King Jomei (r. 629–41)
    Emishi and Iruka's support of reign of, 122, 123
    Kudara Ōdera established by, 113, 122
    mogari of, 126, 127
    posthumous name of, 95
    relationship to Princess Tachibana, 100, 123
    on safeguarding ancestral shrines (as Prince Tamura), 118
    son Furuhito, 123
Great King Keitai (r. 507–31), on safeguarding of ancestral shrines, 118
Great King Kinmei (r. 539–71)
    genealogy on the Shūchō inscription, 5, 88
    posthumous name of, 95
Great King Kōgyoku, 122
Great King Kōtoku (r. 645–72), 100, 113, 120, 231n19
    return of Japanese students during reign of, 120–121, 120*table4*
Great King Richū (r. 400–405), 102, 116
Great King Suiko (r. 593–628), 231n19
    embroidered curtains ordered by, 5, 156, 165

    and Prince Shōtoku, 6, 92
    referred to as *tennō* (heavenly sovereign), 88, 98, 156, 234n6
    seven temples founded by, 148
Great King Sushun (r. 588–93), 104
Great King Tenji (r. 661–72), 90, 100, 104, 126
Great King Yōmei (r. 585–87), 5, 88, 94, 231n19
    Yakushi as the *honji* of, 167
Guze Kannon (World-Saving Avalokiteśvara), Prince Shōtoku as an incarnation of, 133, 134, 139, 155, 214n10, 233n71

Han dynasty, Emperor Gaozu (r. 202–195 BCE), 101, 118
Han jiu yi (Old Ceremonies of the Han), by Wei Hong, 118, 188
Heavenly Sovereigns (*sumera no mikoto* or *tennō*)
    as a term, 94–95
    and *mokkan* excavated from the Asuka pond site, 86, 95, 107
    embroideries in the Kudara Ōdera offered to, 113–114
    Genmei (r. 707–15), 90, 100
    Genshō (r. 715–24), 90
    Jitō (r. 686–97), 100
        construction of the Fujiwara palace of, 57
        embroidered icon dedicated by, 114–115, 119
    Monmu (r. 697–707), 90, 95
    Record of the Heavenly Sovereigns (*Tennō ki*) attributed to Prince Shōtoku, 84
    Suiko
        referred to as, 88, 98, 156, 234n6
        See also Great King Suiko
    Tenmu (r. 673–86)
        clemency to the Aya, 104
        as the first ruler to be called *tennō*, 95
        and the Hata, 101
        names of, 90
Hendrischke, Barbara, 129, 230n127
hijiri (itinerant monks), 134, 135–136, 138
Hirako Takurei, 235n39
Hirano Kunio, 224n56
Histoire de l'art du Japon, 198, 227n33
Hoida Tadatomo, *Kanko zatsujō* (Booklet about Miscellaneous Antiquities), 169
Hori Yukio, 187
Hōryūji
    Abbot Genga, 151, 152, 158, 168, 233n97
    bronze banner
        crow in the sun and hare in the moon on, 42, 45, 45*ff34–34a*
        double-roofed pavilions on, 182, 182*f93*
    Chūgūji under the protection of, 148, 149
    fragments of an embroidered banner with celestial beings, 15–16, 16*f8*, 17, 104, 198, 213, 213*f21*
    inscription on halo of Yakushi image, 85*table2*, 94, 105, 106, 201

INDEX

inscription on mandorla of Shaka triad, 85table2, 93, 97, 105, 106, 201
   plan of, *141f79*
   Shūchō located at, 105, 106, 201
   subtemples, 232n54
   Yumedono Kannon at, 70, 141
Hōryūji bettō shidai (Record of Hōryūji's Abbots)
   on Chūgūji
      burning down of living quarters, 149
      pagoda rebuilt at, 149
      restoration work at, 158–159
   on the robbery of Hōryūji's repository, 152
   Shinnyo mentioned in, 150
Hōryūji Golden Hall
   Amida triad in, 159
      Kōshō's Buddha Amida, 142, *143f80*, 146
      Kōshō's Kannon, 142, *145f82*, 146
      Kōshō's Seishi, 142, *144f81*, 146
   design on wooden canopies of, 221n136
   motifs found in the murals of, 17
   Shaka triad
      mandorla inscription, 85table2, 201
         date of Anahobe's death, 107, 166
      mandorla pearl motifs, 181
   veneration of the prince not found in, 232n49
   See also Yakushi (S. Bhaiṣajyaguru), image in Hōryūji's Golden Hall
Huqiao tomb (Danyang, Jiangsu Province)
   birth by transformation portrayed in, 60, *61f51*, *66f56*
   "clouds of energy" motif, 62
Hyakurenshō (One Hundred Selected Refinements), 139–140

Ienaga Saburō, 105–106, 226n144
Iida Mizuho, 125
   on the Shūchō inscription in the *Imperial Biography*, 83, 87, 125
Imao Fumiaki, 140, 231n21
Imperial Biography (*Jōgū Shōtoku hōō teisetsu*)
   Ienaga Saburō's analysis of, 105–106, 226n144
   inscriptions from three works added to, 10, 105
   Kariya Ekisai's annotated version of, 170, 235n39
   Shūchō inscription in, 5, 83–84, 88–89, *88f70*, 104–108, 201
      as a faithful rendition
         Iida Mizuho's research on, 83, 87
         Okimori Takuya on, 87, 96
      commentaries on, 225n77, 226n148
      and the cult of Prince Shōtoku, 83
      tennō used as a term in, 94–95
Inabe, 93, 224n56
Inoue Tadashi, 63
Inukai Takashi, 96
Ippen (1239–1289), 136, 139, 140
Ishida Mosaku, 172, 184–185, 187

Jangcheon (Changchuan) tombs. *See under* Goguryeo tombs
Jinmu (r. 660–585 BCE, in traditional reckoning), 90
Jinpari tombs. *See under* Goguryeo tombs
Jōen
   Chūgūji engi written by, 159, 230n1
   and the dedication of the Tenjukoku Mandara, 1, 10, 152, 153, 201–202
      Taishi mandara kōshiki liturgical text composed for, 8–9, 10–11, 133, 154–159, 165, 201
   Hokke Sanjikkō ceremony performed at Ryōzenji, 165
   reading of the Tenjukoku Mandara's inscription by, 166, 170
   See also Taishi mandara kōshiki
Jōgūki, 85table2, 225n100
Jōgū Shōtoku hōō teisetsu. See Imperial Biography
Jōgū Shōtoku Taishi den hoketsuki (Supplemental Record of the Biography of Prince Shōtoku from the Upper Palace; ca. 9th century)
   names of Shōtoku's siblings, children, and grandchildren, 100
   and the Old Version of the *Imperial Biography*, 106–107, 136
Jōgū Taishi gyoki (Record of the Prince of the Upper Palace) of Shinran, 139
Jōgū Taishi no kofun ("funerary mound of the Prince of the Upper Palace"), 137
Jomei. *See* Great King Jomei

Kajūji embroidered icon *Buddha Preaching*, 16, *18f10*, 115, 216n12
Kakuken, *Ikaruga koji binran*, 119, 152, 169, 186
Kaltenmark, Max, 129
Kaminishi, Ikumi, 234n112
Kanazawa Hideyuki, 98
Kannon
   Kōshō's Kannon in Hōryūji Golden Hall, 142, *145f82*
   Yumedono Kannon at Hōryūji, 70, 141
   See also Guze Kannon (World-Saving Avalokiteśvara); Nyoirin Kannon
Kariya Ekisai, 170, 198, 225n83, 235n39
Katō Kenkichi, 102
Kenshin
   and the Amida triad in Hōryūji Golden Hall, 142, 146
   on Chūgūji, 149
   on events associated with the tomb at Shinaga, 138–140, 231n32
   family claims regarding Chōshimaru, 138, 231n31
   Shōkō mandara designed by, 146, 148
King Muryeong. *See under* Baekje tombs
kinunui (dressmakers)
   embroidered icons for Asukadera and Kudara Ōdera possibly made by, 104, 115
   migration from Baekje to Japan, 103

Kirihata Ken, 216n10
Kitashi hime no mikoto, 88
Kitora tomb
    and Chinese funerary iconography, 19, 126
        Red Bird on south wall of, 47, *49f37*
    discovery of, 218n52
    sun and moon iconography, 42
Kojidan (Talks about Ancient Matters; 1212–15) of Minamoto no Akikane, 136–137
Kondō nikki (Diary of the Golden Hall), 142
Kopytoff, Igor, 8
Kōryūji, 121, 148
Kose no Mitsue, 105, 107
kōshiki liturgical texts, 154
Kosugi Kazuo, 219n74
Kosugi Sugimura, 198, 214n19, 237n12
Kudara Ōdera (known subsequently as Takechi Ōdera, Daikandaiji, and Daianji), established by Great King Jomei, 113, 122
Kūkai (774–835)
    experience in the Shinaga tomb chamber, 139, 155
    pictured in the *Shōkō mandara* of Kenshin, 146
    tomb of, 135
Kurokawa Mayori, 198, 237n11

Lady Nijō (ca. 1304–7), 141, 150, 159
leaf-shaped elements
    A-5 sprouting-bud design, 58–62
    elongated leaf motif, 212
    Fujinoki tomb, leaf-shaped horse trapping, 70, *70f60*
    karakusamon (plant-derived scrolling design), 67, 220n115
    lotus leaf motifs
        A-13 and A-14 motifs on fragments, *22–23ff11–12*
        D-8 fragment of a zigzag motif, lotus leaf, and lotus flower, *28–29ff17–18*, 79, *80f69*, 172
        D-9 lotus leaf, *28–29ff17–18*, 79, *80f69*
    See also palmette design
Liu Sheng's tomb, 117–118, *117f74*, 188
    "spirit seats" from tomb of, 117–118
Longmen grottoes
    birth by transformation portrayed in Guyang Cave at, 59–60, *61f50*, 72
    Lotus Cave at, 60, 67, 70
Luo Feng, 40
Luoyang tombs
    Bo Qianqiu's tomb, 39–40
    engraved sarcophagus of Yuan Mi (or Prince Zhenjing), 62, *62f52*, 68, 219n65
    Tomb 61, 39–40
Lurie, David B., 85–86

McCallum, Donald, 135–136
mandorla of Buddha from Gangōji, *85table2*, 96, 104

Man'yōshū (Collection of Ten Thousand Leaves)
    phonograms used in, 96–97
    poem on the construction of Fujiwara palace in, 57, 219n84
    poems on afterlife options in, 124
Matsumoto Bunzaburō, 7
Mawangdui
    Tomb No. 1
        banner, 39, *39f28*, 217n42
        white silk fabrics, 117
    Tomb No. 2 seal with turtle-shaped grips, 55
measurements
    and embroidery as a pictorial medium, 112, 205
    length of a *shaku*
        Arai Hiroshi's theory of, 115, 190
        kanejaku (modern *shaku*), 188
        in the Taihō Code, 188–189, *190table5*
    regulation of sizes permitted for funerary mounds, 116–117
    sizes of rulers, 188, 227n27
    of *sun* and *bu* derived from ancient China, 58, 219n85
    See also fabric measurements
Meeks, Lori R., 150, 166, 218n63, 230n1, 231n36, 233n71, 233n79, 233n84, 233n86, 234nn2–3
Minamoto no Akikane (1160–1215), *Kojidan* (Talks about Ancient Matters; 1212–15), 136–137
Mita Kakuyuki, 17, 172, 181, 184, 185, 191, 205, 217n25, 238n11
Mochizuki Shinjō, 7–8
mogari (funeral rites)
    and the Chinese *bin* ritual in the *Liji* (Book of Rites), 126
    and the custom of giving rulers posthumous names, 95
    mogari no miya constructions, 95, 117, 126
    of Prince Shōtoku (Toyotomimi), 117
mokkan (wooden tablets used as surfaces for writing)
    and the management of *shinabe* (skilled craftspeople) within the centralized-state system (*ritsuryō kokka*), 115
    monk pictured holding a stick-like item, 182, 236n64
    and the term *tennō* (heavenly sovereign), 94, 107
Mollier, Christine, 129
Mōri Noboru, 217n25, 238n12

Nakagawa Tadayori, 205, 207
Nihon shoki
    on ancestral shrines (*sōbyō*), 118
    death of Anahobe not recorded in, 97
    death of Prince Shōtoku recorded in, 97
    on the end of the Kinmei–Soga line, 122–123
    on fabric measurements, 190, *191table6*
    on the *kinunui* (dressmakers), 103, 104
    record of a turtle with the character *shin* 申 (monkey) on its shell, 57
    records of funerary rites in, 126–127
    on the return of Japanese students during Kōtoku's reign, 120–121, *120table4*
    Richū narrative in, 116

INDEX

sumptuary laws
    605 regulations, 33
    681 regulations, 112
Nyoirin Kannon
    darani (S. *dhāraṇi*) performed by Eison at Shinaga, 140
    in the Golden Hall of Chūgūji as *honji* of Shōtoku, 167
    at Hōryūji, 138, 231n29
    inscription on a wooden image at Hōryūji of, 138

Ōhashi Katsuaki, 235n11
    on the Shūchō
        as curtains around Tachibana's bed, 116, 227n34
        reading of characters on a turtle in the inscription, 3f2, 172
        theory that a 1275 replica was made of, 172, 235n13
        women aligned in a procession identified on, 33
    Tenjukoku identified with Amida's Pure Land by, 7, 79
    on the term *tennō* in the *Imperial Biography*'s inscription, 95
    on *Uragaki* sources, 233n100
Ohoebun tombs. *See under* Goguryeo tombs
Ōkabe Chōshō, 215n21
Okakura Tenshin, 197–198, 237n6
Okimori Takuya, 87, 96
Old Ceremonies of the Han (*Han jiu yi*), 118, 188
omens
    on the ceilings of Goguryeo tombs, 49–50, 51f39a, 52f41a
    ninth-century copy of an omen index at Dunhuang, 49
    political significance of, 49–50
        portents for Kōtoku read by monk Min, 121
        Soga portents read by monk Kwalluk (J. Kanroku), 121, 228n69
    red bird as, 47, 49, 50
    turtles linked to in ancient Japan, 57–58
Ono Kazuyuki, 135, 136
Ooms, Herman, 12
Ōta Hidezo, 205, 209
Ōyama Seiichi, 6
Ōya Tokujō, 215n21
Ōya Tōru, 7, 84–85

palmette design
    full and half-palmette motifs, in Goguryeo decorations, 42f32, 69–70
    half-palmette motif
        in Baekje tomb artifacts, 69, 69f59
        on Liang dynasty Xiao Hong stele, 55, 68, 220n100
        in Northern Chinese Buddhist artifacts, 67
        on Northern Wei coffin from Guyuan, 67
        on Northern Wei stand from tomb of Sima Jinlong, 67
        on Northern Wei Yuan Mi stone sarcophagus from Luoyang, 62, 62f52, 68, 219n65
        in the Shūchō's iconographical program, 37f26, 38, 66, 70

Mediterranean palmette motif, 67
Portrait of Prince Shōtoku and Two Attendants, 150
Prince Shōtoku (Umayado Toyotomimi), 106, 107, 223n44
    communication with Zenkōji Amida, 142
    cult of (*Taishi shinkō*), 6
        and monks Keisei and Kenshin, 150
        and the *Shōkō mandara*, 146, 148, 159
        and the *Taishi mandara kōshiki*, 154–155, 158
        and the Tenjukoku Mandara, 133–134, 150, 163, 164, 167, 168, 194, 201–202
    death of
        in commentaries following the inscription in the *Imperial Biography*, 106–107
        in the inscription on the Shaka triad, 106
        Kose no Mitsue's poems on, 93, 107
        in the *Shōyoshō*, 166
    genealogy of, 5–6, 88–89, 89f71, 123–124
    as Guze Kannon, 133, 134, 139, 155, 214n10, 233n71
    marriage to Princess Kashiwade, 91, 92–93, 100, 123
    marriage to Princess Tachibana, 88, 93
    marriage to Princess Tojiko no Iratsume, 91, 93, 100
    marriage to Uji no Kaidako, 91–92, 223n44
    mogari of, 117
    names of, 90–91, 223n44
    as Nyoirin Kannon, 167
    seven temples founded by, 148
    textual sources associated with him, 84–86
    See also Shinaga (Shinaga Misasagi)
Princess Kashiwade (Jōe)
    death of, 93, 106–107, 141, 231n18
    deification as Seishi, 133, 139, 142, 146, 148, 150, 154, 159
    embroidered banner fragments from Hōryūji attributed to, 198
    and the establishment of Ikaruga, 92
    marriage to Prince Shōtoku (Umayado Toyotomimi), 91, 92–93, 100, 123
    residence at the Palace of Akunami, 100
Princess Tachibana
    and the genealogy on the Shūchō inscription, 5, 123–124
    as Inabe Tachibana, 93, 224n56
    and the making of the Shūchō embroidery, 100, 123
    marriage to Shōtoku, 88, 93
    relationship to Jomei (r. 629–41), 100, 123
procession scenes
    in Goguryeo tomb murals, 32f22, 33, 36
    in Gongxian Caves, 33
    on Shūchō fragments, 33, 36
    in the Takamatsuzuka tomb, 33, 34–35ff23–24a
    in tombs of the Southern Qi, 217n32
    of women in Princess Yongtai's tomb, 33, 36f25
provenance. *See* Tenjukoku Shūchō Mandara provenance
pure land
    and the term *jōdo*, 230n121
    See also Amida's Western Pure Land

Pure Land school
    "Amida triad in one tomb with three remains" devotion of, 133
    Eastern Gate to the Pure Land at Shitennōji, 135, 155

Queen Mother of the West, 40, 67, 126

Rawson, Jessica, 67
replication
    of the Taima Mandara, 154
    of the Tenjukoku Shūchō Mandara at Chūgūji (1982), 199, 200f101
    of the Tenjukoku Shūchō Mandara by Nishijin Bijutsuori Kobo (2010), 199, 201f102
    See also Shūchō (seventh-century embroidery) replication
rhythmic arrangement of motifs
    in the Deokhungri and Gangseo daemyo tombs at Goguryeo, 42f43, 50, 72
    in Gongxian caves, 74, 74–75ff63–63a, 76, 76f64
    on the Shūchō, 70–71, 172
    and the term karakusamon (plant-derived scrolling design), 67, 220n115
Robinet, Isabelle, 60, 230n124
Ruch, Barbara, 125
Ruiyingtu (Diagram of Auspicious Omens) of Sun Rouzhi, 58
Ryōkin
    Hōryūji Ryōkin homōshū (Collection of Notes by Ryōkin of Hōryūji), 169, 170, 198, 235n36
    "demon-like figure" identified in, 170
    Hōryūji tōin engi (Account of the Origins of Hōryūji's Eastern Compound), 169, 170
    "The Turtle Designs of the Tenjukoku Mandara's Inscription at Chūgūji" (Chūgūji Tenjukoku Mandara mei kikkō no zu), 169

Saidaiji
    Eison as abbot of, 150, 169
    and Shinnyo, 149–150
Sakai Atsuko
    on the "clouds of energy" motif at the Huqiao tomb, 62, 63
    on the sprouting-bud motif (A-5), 58–62
Samsilchong (Tomb of the Three Chambers). See under Goguryeo tombs
Sasinchong (Tomb of the Four Divinities). See under Goguryeo tombs
Sawada Mutsuyo, 16, 205, 208, 212
Seishi (S. Mahāsthāmaprāpta)
    Kōshō's Seishi in the Amida triad at Hōryūji, 142, 144f81
    Princess Kashiwade (Jōe; Prince Shōtoku's wife) as an incarnation of, 133, 139, 146, 148
Sema Masayuki, 96
Senda Minoru, 94
Senjuji. See Takada Honzan Senjuji

Shaanxi Province tombs
    Jiaoda tomb, 39
    Princess Yongtai (Li Xianhui), 33, 36f25
    sarcophagus for Li Ho, 219–220n95
Shigematsu Akihisa, 7
Shimomise Shizuichi, 7–8
Shinaga (Shinaga Misasagi), 136–141, 137f77
    belief in associated with the Shūchō, 151, 158, 159
    Kenshin on, 138–140, 231n32
    as the Soga clan's cemetery, 231n19
    "Verse of the Tomb Chamber," 139, 155, 167–168, 231–232nn36–37
    See also Eifukuji; Shinaga Amida triad
Shinaga Amida triad
    and "Amida triad in one tomb with three remains" devotion at Shinaga, 133, 159–160
    Kenshin on, 142, 146
    Pure Land devotion, 139, 141
    relief at Eifukuji, 139, 140f78
    and the Shōkō mandara designed by Kenshin, 146, 148, 159
    Tenjukoku identified as an impure land where the three royals live as incarnations of Kannon, Amida, and Seishi, 154, 159–160
Shingon Ritsu school
    and Chūgūji's revival, 165–168
    Kakujō (1193–1249), 149–150
    revival of female monasticism, 234n2
    Shinnyo's association with, 149–150, 165, 166, 233n79, 233n84
    See also Eison; Kūkai; Saidaiji; Tōshōdaiji
Shinnyo
    ganmon (dedication prayer; dated 1281) of, 150, 158–159, 185, 233n92, 234n117
    and the Shūchō mandara
        dedication as the Tenjukoku Mandara, 1, 10, 152, 165, 201–202
        discovery of, 1, 134, 152–153, 159–160, 165–166, 170, 193, 201–202
        and the renovation of Chūgūji, 1, 10, 152–153, 159, 165
Shinran
    Jōgū Taishi gyoki (Record of the Prince of the Upper Palace) of, 139
    Senjuji established by, 168
Shitennōji, 121, 135f76
    Eastern Gate to the Pure Land at Shitennōji, 135, 155
    and Shōtoku
        cult of the prince at, 6, 135, 137
        founding by the prince of, 105, 134–136
        Shitennōji engi (Account of the Origins of Shitennōji) discovered at, 135, 160
Shōkō mandara (Mandala of the Eminent Prince), 133f83detail, 147f83
    Hōryūji as the source of belief in the Shinaga Amida

INDEX

triad, 146, 148, 159
    Kenshin's designing of, 146
Shoku Nihongi (Chronicles of Japan Continued), 58, 95
Shoshisen (Narratives of Matsuko) complied by Ōtoribe Aya no Matsuko, 139
Shōsōin collection (eighth-century imperial repository at Tōdaiji)
    container with turtle-shaped lid, 55, *56f46*
    embroidered banner with peacock design, *17ff9–9a*
    fragments of the Tenjukoku Shūchō Mandara in, 1, *3f2*, 47
    turtles with graphs, 1, *3f2*, 83, 172, 212
    skirts, 21, *31f21*, 216n24
Shōtoku Taishi denki (Biography of Prince Shōtoku; 1317-1319)
    and the *Chūgūji engi*, 165
    dating of, 233n86, 234n3
    Shōyo's reading of, 166–167
    Shūchō described in
        bells on, 165, 235n10
        "people gathering" described, 185
    on the Tenjukoku Mandara
        creation story in, 234n6
        thirteenth-century reparations of, 184
        three panels of twill described, 165, 184
    on the transcription of the Shūchō inscription, 165
Shōtoku Taishi denryaku (Hagiography of Prince Shōtoku; 10th century)
    Chūgūji identified as "the palace of Empress Hashihito Anahobe" in, 148–149, 233n71
    on the deaths of Shōtoku and Princess Kashiwade, 231n18
    and Kenshin, 138
    names of Shōtoku's siblings, children, and grand-children, 100
    and the Old Version of the *Imperial Biography*, 106–107, 136
Shōtoku Taishi den shiki (Private Record of the Biography of Prince Shōtoku), of Kenshin
    as a hagiographical account of the prince's life, 164
    communications between the Zenkōji Amida and Prince Shōtoku referred to, 142
    Shōkō mandara's planing discussed in, 146
    "Verse of the Tomb Chamber" in, 139, 155, 231–232nn36–37
Shōtoku Taishi Heishi den zakkanmon. See *Shōtoku Taishi denryaku*
Shōyoshō ([Monk] Shōyo's Notes)
    on the date of Anahobe's death, 166
    on Shinnyo's ordination, 150
    on the Tenjukoku Mandara, 164, 166–167, 168, 185, 187, 198
    Uragaki transcribed in, 152, 153, 166, 170
shūbutsu (embroidered fabrics with Buddhist subjects). *See under* embroidered fabric
shūchō (embroidered curtains). *See* curtains

Shūchō (seventh-century embroidery)
    bells possibly attached to, 165, 235n10
    creating of
        and the Kinmei-Soga kinship, 104, 106, 107–108, 111–112, 122, 130, 199
        and Princess Tachibana, 99–100, 107, 123–124, 130
    dating of, 16–17, 89–90, 124, 223n27
    located at Hōryūji, 201
    Shinnyo's discovery of, 1, 134, 159–160, 165, 165–166, 170, 193, 201–202
Shūchō (seventh-century embroidery) motifs
    identified in the Tenjukoku Shūchō Mandara, 23–28*ff12–19*, *37f26*
        A section, 22–23*ff11–12*, *37f26*, *82f11detail*
        A-1 moon, *xiif11detail*, *12f11detail*, 22–23*ff11–12*, 36, *38f27*, 39, 45–46, 79
        A-2 half-palmette, 22–23*ff11–12*, *37f26*, 38, 66, 70
        A-3 red bird, 22–23*ff11–12*, *37f26*, 38, 46, *46f35*
        A-4 auspicious cloud, 22–23*ff11–12*, 38
        A-5 sprouting-bud design, 22–23*ff11–12*, 38, 58–66, *66f56*, *80f69*, 220n110
        A-6 turtle (no. 26), 22–23*ff11–12*, 38, 54, *54f44*, *82f11detail*, 172, *173f84*
        A-7 fragments of ribbons, 22–23*ff11–12*, 38, 66, *66f57*
        A-8 fragment of torso from a figure emerging from a lotus, 22–23*ff11–12*, 72, *221f128*
        A-9 unidentified, 22–23*ff11–12*, 38, 221n142
        A-10 fragment of a sprouting-bud design, 22–23*ff11–12*, 66, 220n110
        A-11 unidentified, 22–23*ff11–12*, 221n142
        B-1 floral motif, 24–25*ff13–14*, 64, 220n110, 221n142
        B-2 *Hengeshō* or metamorphosis phase, 24–25*ff13–14*, 64, *66f56*
        B-3 unidentified, 24–25*ff13–14*, 221n142
        B-4 incomplete seated male figure, 21, 24–25*ff13–14*, 36, 176
        B-5 standing male figure, 21, 24–25*ff13–14*, *30f19*, 33, 175, *210f112*
        B-6 small lotus flower, 24–25*ff13–14*, 79, *80f69*, 172
        C-1 upper body of a celestial being, 26–27*ff15–16*, 64, 66, *66ff56–57*
        C-2 lower body of a celestial being, 26–27*ff15–16*, 64, 66, *66f57*
        C-3 standing female figure, 21, 26–27*ff15–16*
        C-4 standing female figure holding a stem, 21, 26–27*ff15–16*
        C-5 fragment of a lotus flower, 26–27*ff15–16*, 79, *80f69*, 221n141
        D-1 incomplete figure emerging from a lotus with hands in prayer, 28–29*ff17–18*, 67, *73f62*, *77f65*, 172, *173f85*
            identified as "birth by transformation in a lotus flower" (*renge keshō*), 72
            size of, 172

273

term "figure emerging from a lotus," 76–77, 79
D-2 half-palmette, 28–29ff17–18, 66, 80f69
D-3 female figure, 21, 28–29ff17–18, 30f20, 210f113, 212f120
D-4 fragment of a flaming flower, 28–29ff17–18, 77, 79
D-5 female figure, 21, 28–29ff17–18, 30f20
D-6 incomplete group of three seated male figures, 21, 28–29ff17–18, 36, 185, 208–209
D-7 fragment of a leaf design, 28–29ff17–18, 80f69
D-8 fragment of a zigzag motif, lotus leaf, and lotus flower, 28–29ff17–18, 79, 80f69, 172, 209f111
D-9 lotus leaf, 28–29ff17–18, 79, 80f69
D-10 female figure, 21, 28–29ff17–18
D-11 fragment of a female figure, 21, 28–29ff17–18
D-12 fragment of a flaming motif, 28–29ff17–18, 72, 77, 77f65, 78
incomplete seated figure, 3, 3f3, 213, 213f21
reconstruction of the iconographical program of, 19, 111
and funerary iconography from China and Korea, 79, 81, 111, 125
rhythmic arrangement of, 70–71, 172
Shūchō (seventh-century embroidery) replication
characters on a turtle in the inscription of, 172
Uragaki on an "embroidered copy (寫繍) made" in 1275, 153–154, 160, 235n13
Shūchō inscription
Anahobe's date of death mentioned in, 1, 10
called the "Tenjukoku Mandara inscription" in the Edo period, 171
in Kakuken's *Ikaruga koji binran*, 169–170
date, 85table2, 107
elements of the cult of the prince absent from, 108
genealogy of Prince Shōtoku on, 5, 88–89, 89f71
Imperial Biography transcription of, 88–89, 107–108, 201
in Ryōkin's *Hōryūji tōin engi* (Account of the Origins of Hōryūji's Eastern Compound), 169
and succession claims, 123–124
transcription of, 222n2
Sima Jinlong tomb, 68f58, 180
size. *See* fabric measurements; measurements
skirts
Indian dhotis, 58, 67
long pleated skirts
from the Shōsōin collection, 21, 31f21, 216n24
worn by female figures, 21, 174–175, 174f86
worn by female figures in Goguryeo murals, 21, 32ff22–22a, 33
worn by *haniwa* (clay tomb figurines), 21
pleated overskirt (*hirami* or *hiraobi*), 21, 33, 175
and sumptuary laws, 33
short skirts
of "demon-like figure" motif, 26–27, 179
of seated figures with naked torsos, 68f58, 179–180

trumpet-shaped, 172, 173f85
Soga no Emishi (587–645), 100
ancestral shrine erected in Takamiya, 122–123
and the Aya, 103
execution of, 123
support of a non-Soga for the throne, 122
support of Great King Jomei, 122, 123
Soga no Iname (d. 570), genealogy on the Shūchō inscription, 5, 99, 122
Songsanri tombs. *See* Baekje tombs
Soper, Alexander, 67
Southern Qi period brick tombs, 40
celestial imagery in a tomb at Jianjia, 40, 40f29
"spirit seats" (C. *ling zuo* or *shen wei*)
in the Eastern Han royal temple in Luoyang, 118
Shūchō embroidery as curtains hung around a, 117, 119–120, 123–124, 130
from Tomb No. 1 at Mawangdui, 117
from the tomb of Liu Sheng, 117–118
See also curtains
Ssangyeongchong (Twin Pillar Tomb). *See under* Goguryeo tombs
Stele from Dōgo Springs in Iyo (Ehime), date, 85table2
Stevenson, Miwa, 20, 50, 216n18, 219n69
stitches. *See under* embroidery stitches
Sugiyama Hiroshi, 177, 179
sumptuary laws
605 regulations, 33
681 regulations, 112
Susanri tombs. *See under* Goguryeo tombs
sutras. *See* Buddhist sutras
Suzuki, Yui, 218n62, 224n62

Tachibana. *See* Princess Tachibana
Tachibana Shrine at Hōryūji, 221nn134,136
Taima Mandara, 154
story of Kannon's weaving of, 234n6
Taishi mandara kōshiki (Liturgy for the Prince's Mandala; 1275), 151
Jōen's composition of, 8–9, 10–11, 133, 154, 154, 165
lack of a Buddha presiding over Tenjukoku, 182
"people gathering" represented on the Shūchō described by, 185
"Tenjukoku Mandara" is used for the first time in, 154, 159
text of, 154–158, 234n110
Takada Honzan Senjuji, 168, 235n31
Takamatsuzuka tombs, 19, 34–35, 42
and Chinese funerary iconography, 19, 126
images of the Four Divinities, 47
sun and moon iconography, 42
Takase Tamon, 215n21
Takioto Yoshiyuki, 92
Tamamushi Shrine, 19, 42, 43–44ff33–33a, 45, 70, 110f33a(detail), 176, 182, 183f94, 184, 221n127

274

Tanaka Shigehisa, 231n32
Tenjukoku (shin) mandara uragaki. See *Uragaki*
Tenjukoku identified
    as Amida's Western Pure Land, 7, 79, 133, 159, 215n21
        and the figure emerging from a lotus motif, 72, 74
    as a synonym for heaven, 88
    as heaven by monk at Hōryūji, 201
    as an afterlife destination, 130
    as an impure land
        where Buddha has yet to appear, 182
        where the three royals live as incarnations of Kannon, Amida, and Seishi, 159–160
    as India, 7
    as Tosotsuten (S. Tuṣita Heaven), 7, 129
    as Vulture Peak (S. Gṛdhrakūṭa; J. Ryōzen), 7
Tenjukoku Mandara
    as a historical artifact, 169
    as an Amida mandara representing Muryōju Tenju (Measureless Lifespan), 133
    fragments categorized as *shūbutsu* (embroidered fabrics with Buddhist subjects), 15, 112, 115
    reconstruction proposed by the author, 9, 11, 163, 192ff100a–b
        analysis of design motifs as key to, 13–14, 19, 125, 171, 199
        and the placement of turtles, 187, 187f97, 191–193
        and remaining fragments, 171
    restoration of, 159–160, 163
    and the Shōtoku cult, 133–134, 150, 163, 164, 167, 168, 194, 201–202
    and "Amida triad in one tomb with three remains" devotion at Shinaga, 133, 159–160
    Shūchō dedicated by Jōen and Shinnyo as, 1, 10, 152, 154–159, 201–202
    thirteenth-century repairs, 184
Tenjukoku Mandara inscription. See under Shūchō inscription
Tenjukoku Mandara motifs, 23–28ff12–19
    A-12 figure emerging from a lotus with hands in prayer, 22–23ff11–12, 172, 173f85, 210f116
    A-13 lotus leaf, 22–23ff11–12
    A-14 lotus leaf, 22–23ff11–12
    A-15 unidentified, 22–23ff11–12
    A-16 unidentified, 22–23ff11–12
    A-17 turtle (no. 69), 22–23ff11–12, 172, 173f84
    B-7 border with spade-shaped motifs, 24–25ff13–14, 181
    B-8 border with circles, 24–25ff13–14, 181
    B-9 figure holding an offering, 24–25ff13–14, 175
    B-10 fragment of zig-zag motif, 24–25ff13–14
    B-11 group of three seated male figures, 21, 24–25ff13–14, 184, 185, 207, 208
    B-12 figure emerging from a lotus, holding a tray, 24–25ff13–14, 172, 173f85
    B-13 fragments of a celestial being with an offering, 24–25ff13–14, 174
    B-14 seated figure, 24–25ff13–14, 174
    B-15 seated figure holding a lotus flower, 24–25ff13–14, 26–27ff15–16, 33, 174
    B-16 seated figure, 24–25ff13–14, 174
    B-17 seated figure, 24–25ff13–14, 174, 176
    B-18 seated figure holding a lotus flower, 24–25ff13–14, 174, 176, 236n50
    B-19 lotus flower, 24–25ff13–14
    C-6 three seated monks, 26–27ff15–16, 181, 182, 210f114
    C-7 incense burner, 26–27ff15–16, 182
    C-8 fragment of a seated figure holding a flower, 26–27ff15–16, 174
    C-9 seated male figure holding a flower, 26–27ff15–16, 33, 174, 176
    C-10 small lotus flower, 26–27ff15–16, 80f69, 172
    C-11 zig-zag design representing a pond, 26–27ff15–16, 79, 80f69, 172, 210f117, 211
    C-12 fragment of a lotus pedestal with reversed petals, 26–27ff15–16, 181
    C-13 seated figure with a bare torso, 26–27, 179
    C-14 fragment of a lotus pedestal, 26–27ff15–16, 181
    C-15 fragment of a turtle (no. 1), 26–27ff15–16, 172, 173f84
    D-13 turtle (no. 65), 28–29ff17–18, 172, 173f84
    D-14 figure emerging from a lotus with hands in prayer, 28–29ff17–18, 172, 173f85
    D-15 male figure, probably dancing, 28–29ff17–18, 175
    D-16 figure with hands in prayer, 28–29ff17–18, 175
    D-17 seated figure with a small lotus flower, 28–29ff17–18, 174
    D-18 unidentified, 28–29ff17–18
    D-19 unidentified, 28–29ff17–18
    E-1 upper border with circles, 175ff86–87
    E-2 lower border with circles, 175ff86–87, 181, 208f108, 211f119
    E-3 incomplete architectural setting with three standing and two kneeling monks, 175ff86–87
    E-4 tree, 175ff86–87, 184, 207f105
    E-5 incomplete architectural setting with two standing and two kneeling monks, 175, 175ff86–87, 184
    E-6 *Hengeshō* or metamorphosis phase, 175ff86–87, 184
    E-7 unidentified, perhaps canopies, 175ff86–87, 184
    F-1 border with spade-shaped motifs, 176–177ff88–89, 181
    F-2 belfry with monk striking bell, 162f88detail, 176, 176–178ff88–90, 211, 211f118
    F-3 three male figures, two holding walking sticks and wearing straw coats, 176–177ff88–89
    F-4 border with circles, 176–177ff88–89, 181
Tenjukoku Shūchō Mandara
    composite name of, 1, 6
    motifs. See Shūchō (seventh-century embroidery) motifs; Tenjukoku Mandara motifs
    reconstruction of a lotus pond, 80f69
    reconstruction of the placement of turtles in, 186f96, 187, 187f97, 192–193ff100–100a

Tenjukoku Shūchō Mandara provenance
    at Chūgūji, 1, *2f1*, *3f4*, 212
    doubtful pieces at the Fujita Museum in Osaka, 213
    fragments of the Shūchō, at the Tokyo National Museum, *4f5*, 212–213
    fragments of the Tenjukoku Mandara, at the Tokyo National Museum, *5f6*, 212–213
    at Hōryūji, *3f3*, 15, 212–213
    at Kawashima Orimono Kenkyūjo, 213
    at Shōsōin, *3f2*, 212–213
Tenmu. *See* Heavenly Sovereigns (*sumera no mikoto* or *tennō*), Tenmu
tennō. *See* Heavenly Sovereigns (*sumera no mikoto* or *tennō*)
textual materials associated with the Tenjukoku Shūchō Mandara
    Buddhist interpretation of the artifact supported by, 112, 198–199
    changing and enduring significance of the embroidery revealed in, 199
    and the proposed reconstruction of the Tenjukoku Mandara, 163
    See also Imperial Biography
tigers
    in the Takamatsuzuka and Kitora tombs, 47
    on the wall of a tomb from the Southern Qi period, 60
    White Tiger (one of the Four Divinities), *34f24*, 46, 47, 126
Tōgū Jōgū Shōtoku Hōō. *See* Prince Shōtoku
Tokiwa Daijō, 215n21
Tokyo National Museum
    fragment of a tapestry border, *180–181f92*, 181
    Hōryūji embroidered banner with designs of celestial beings, 15–16, *16f8*, 17, 104, 198, 213, *213f21*
tombs. *See* Baekje tombs; Dengxian tomb; Goguryeo tombs; Huqiao tomb; Kitora tomb; Liu Sheng's tomb; Luoyang tombs; Mawangdui; Shaanxi Province tombs; Shinaga (Shinaga Misasagi); Southern Qi period brick tombs; Takamatsuzuka tomb
Tōno Haruyuki, 89–90, 95, 236n64
Tōshōdaiji
    embroidered fragments found at, 216n11
    and Shinnyo's ordination, 150
    Shōdai senzai denki (Tōshōdaiji Millenary Anniversary Hagiographies; 1701), 149, 186
Toyotomimi, as a name for Prince Shōtoku, 91
transcendents or immortals (C. *tianren*; J. *tennin*)
    and Chinese Daoist beliefs, 7–8
    ink sketch from wooden pedestal of the Yakushi image in the Golden Hall at Hōryūji, 220n111
    on the pillow from King Muryeong's tomb at Baekje, 63–64, *65f54–55*
    reconstructed from Shūchō fragments, 64, 66, *66f57*
    sprouting-bud motif associated with
        at Goguryeo, 63–64, *64f53*
        at Gongxian, 58, *59f49*
    xian ("immortals" or "wizards") distinguished from, 58
Tseng, Lillian Lan-ying, 38, 49
Tsuda Sōkichi, 6, 94
Tsude Hiroshi, 102
Tsuji Zennosuke, 7
turtles
    in ancient China
        and Daoists beliefs related to transcendents, 7–8, 50
        and the *Hetu* (Yellow River Chart) and *Luoshu* (Luo River Writing), 55
        meanings, 54
    in ancient Japan
        container with turtle-shaped lid in the Shōsōin collection, 55, *56f46*
        linked to omens, 57–58
        turtle-shaped stone receptacle at Asuka, *57f48*
    Dark Warrior (snake intertwined with a turtle), 46, 47, *48f36*
    placement on the Tenjukoku Shūchō Mandara, *186f96*, *187f97*, *192–193f100a*
    varying documentation of, 185–187
    on Tenjukoku Mandara fragments, Ryōkin's notes on, 169
    turtle-shaped receptacles from Shitennōji, 219n80
turtles with graphs
    carrying the name of Anahobe (Nos. 45–47), 50, 54, *54f44*, 191
    carrying the name of Shōtoku (Nos. 50–52), 191
    carrying the name of Tachibana (Nos. 54–55), 191
    in the Shōsōin collection, 1, *3f2*, 172
    Shūchō inscription mention of, 89
    Tenjukoku Shūchō Mandara motifs
        (A-6), *54f44*, *173f84*
        (A-17), 22–23ff11–12, 50, 54, 172, *173f84*
        (C-15), 26–27ff15–16, 172, *173f84*
        (D-13), 28–29ff17–18, 172, *173f84*
    at Chūgūji, 1, *3f4*, 172, 181, 212

Ullambana (C. Yulanpen; J. Urabon) festival, 118, 120
Umayado Toyotomimi. *See* Prince Shōtoku
Umehara Sueji, 231n21
Uragaki (*Tenjukoku* (*shin*) *mandara uragaki*)
    on an "embroidered copy (寫繡) made" in 1275 of the Shūchō, 153–154, 160, 235n13
    on craftsmen involved in the production of embroidered textiles, 153
    in Kakuken's *Ikaruga koji binran*, 169
    in Ryōkin's *Hōryūji tōin engi* (Account of the Origins of Hōryūji's Eastern Compound), 169
    on Shinnyo's discovery of the mandara, 152–153
    sources of, 233n100
    transcription in various documents at Hōryūji of, 152

INDEX

Vulture Peak (S. Gṛdhrakūṭa; J. Ryōzen)
    Śākyamuni Preaching on Vulture Peak embroidery from Dunhuang, 16–17
    Tenjukoku identified as, 7

Wada Atsumu, 90, 91, 95, 107, 127
Walley, Akiko, 214n17
Watt, James C.Y., 220n112
Wu Hung, 20, 78, 117, 125–126
Wu Liang Shrine, 49

Xiao Hong stele, 55, 68, 220n100

Yakushi (S. Bhaiṣajyaguru)
    image in Hōryūji's Golden Hall
        cult of, 94
        ink sketch of a celestial being from wooden pedestal of, 220n111
        as the *honji* of Yōmei, 167
        inscription on halo of, 7, 85table2, 94–95, 201
        pearl motifs, 181
    sculpture from Yakushiji in Nara, 47

Yoshida Kazuhiko, 96
Yoshimura Rei
    "birth by transformation in a lotus flower" (*renge keshō*) motif identified by, 72, 74
    on the bud motif on the stele of Xiao Hong, 220n100
    reconstruction, 220n110
    on the sprouting-bud motif (A-5), 58
Yuan Mi (or Prince Zhenjing) stone sarcophagus from Luoyang, 62, 62f52, 68, 219n65
Yungang
    "birth by transformation in a lotus flower" (*renge keshō*) motif in, 72–73, 76–77
    half-palmettes found in Cave No. 9, 67
    seated figures on lintel at an entrance to Yungang Cave No. 10, 180

Zenkōji Amida, communication with Prince Shōtoku (Toyotomimi), 142
Zenkōji engi (Account of the Origins of Zenkōji), on the Amida legend, 135–136
Zenkōji temple, and the popularization of Pure Land beliefs, *hijiri* (itinerant monks), 135–136
Zürcher, Erik, 128